WHO'S WHO OF CHELSEA

WHO'S WHO OF
CHELSEA

Tony Matthews

MAINSTREAM
PUBLISHING
EDINBURGH AND LONDON

First published in Great Britain in 2005 by
MAINSTREAM PUBLISHING COMPANY
(EDINBURGH) LTD
7 Albany Street
Edinburgh EH1 3UG

ISBN 1 84596 010 6

A catalogue record for this book is available
from the British Library

Typeset in Caslon and Gill Condensed
Printed and bound in Great Britain by
William Clowes Ltd, Beccles, Suffolk

CONTENTS

ACKNOWLEDGEMENTS

First and foremost I must say a special big 'thank you' to Bill Campbell, Graeme Blaikie and Claire Rose of Mainstream Publishing, and to my copy-editor, Ronnie Hanna.

Thanks also to David Barber (FA) and Zoe Ward (Premier League) for information on certain players, past and present, to Geoff Allman, Jim Brown, John Farrelly, Carole Salmon, Graham Hughes, Charlie Poultney, John Russell and Reg Thacker for loaning photographs and also providing the odd snippet of information, and even a bigger thank you to my forgiving wife Margaret who once again has had to sit and watch TV on her own or slave away in the garden while I've been seated in front of the computer, tapping away happily for hours on end . . . love you.

IMPORTANT NOTICE

The majority of pictures in this book have come via scrapbooks, albums and certain programmes/magazines owned by ex-players, Chelsea fans and collectors of soccer memorabilia. I have been unable to establish clear copyright on some of these pictures and therefore both the publishers and I would be pleased to hear from anyone whose copyright has been unintentionally infringed.

ABBREVIATIONS

app. = appearance
apps = appearances
CL = Champions League
CS = Charity Shield
cs = close season
ECWC = European Cup-Winners' Cup
FAC = FA Cup
FAI = Football Association of Ireland
FC = Football Club
FL = Football League
FLC = Football League Cup
FMC = Full Members' Cup
FRT = Freight Rover Trophy
FWA = Football Writers' Association
ICFC = Inter-Cities Fairs Cup
(N) = (North)
NASL = North American Soccer League
nc = non-contract
og = own goal
PFA = Professional Footballers' Association
PL = Premier League
(S) = (South)
SC = Simod Cup
sub = substitute
WW1 = First World War
WW2 = Second World War

INTRODUCTION

Details of every player who has appeared for Chelsea at senior level (in a major League and/or Cup game) over a period of 100 years are featured in this book.

The seasons covered are 1905–06 to 1914–15; 1919–20 to 1939–40 (just three League games were fulfilled before the declaration of WW2), 1945–46 (FA Cup only) and 1946–47 to 2004–05 inclusive.

Details of both wartime periods (1915–19 and 1939–46) are covered in the players' personal biographies. And in fact, there is a separate section listing certain players who served the club as guests during the two wars.

In respect of an individual player's fact-file, date and place of birth and death (if known) have been included. In most cases where a transfer fee has been given, this is an estimated figure, taken either from the Chelsea matchday programme or from local and national newspapers, and these can be subject to some variation.

Players' appearance and goal-scoring records are for all senior competitions. Wartime fixtures are not included, although FA Cup games for 1945–46 have been added. The number following the plus sign indicates appearances made as a substitute.

The position usually occupied by a player is stated under the name but over the years, certainly since 1970, the term to describe a chosen outfield position has varied considerably . . . forward/striker; centre-half/defender; inside-forward/midfield; wing-half/midfield; full-back/defender or wing-back; winger/midfield or forward.

Also listed are the men who have managed Chelsea FC down the years, along with many other interesting snippets of information.

If you spot any discrepancies, errors or omissions, I would appreciate it very much if you would contact me (via the publishers) so that all can be rectified in future editions. Also, if you have anything to add, this too would be greatly appreciated; people tend to reveal little-known facts from various sources when football is the topic of conversation.

WHO'S WHO OF
CHELSEA
1905—2005

ABRAMS, ROBERT LAURENCE
Wing-half: 49 apps, 7 goals
Born: Banks, Southport, 14 May 1889 – *Died:* 1966
Career: Southport Central, Colne Town, Stockport County (August 1907), Heart of Midlothian (December 1910), CHELSEA (June 1914); guested for Southport, Stockport and Hearts during WW1; Cardiff City (free transfer, June 1920), Southport (seasons 1921–23)
A strong-tackling powerfully built left-half, who could also occupy the outside-left position, Laurie Abrams had played very well in his first season at Stamford Bridge and was certainly unlucky not to gain a place in Chelsea's 1915 FA Cup final side. He appeared in 158 Football League games during his career.

ALEKSIDZE, RATI
Striker: 0+3 apps
Born: Tbilisi, Georgia, 3 August 1978
Career: Dinamo Tbilisi/Georgia (junior; professional, August 1996), CHELSEA (trialist during 1996–97), Dinamo Tbilisi, CHELSEA (£120,000, February 2000; released May 2001)
A Georgian international at both Under-21 and senior levels, left-sided striker Rati Aleksidze, 6 ft tall, was his country's Player of the Year in 2000. He never quite fitted into Chelsea's style of play although he did add four senior caps to his earlier tally of six during his time at the Bridge. Not retained after playing in the Blues' youth and reserve teams in 1996–97, his progress was monitored thereafter by the club.

ALEXANDER, DAVID BERTRAM
Right-half: 1 app.
Born: Glasgow, *circa* 1915 – Deceased by 2000
Career: Clyde (May 1935), CHELSEA (March 1939; released May 1945)
After making his League debut in the London derby against Charlton in April

11

1939, David Alexander became a regular in the Chelsea side during the 1939–40 season. However, his career came to a premature end when he was involved in a serious motorcycle accident whilst serving in the Army and was subsequently invalided out of the forces.

ALLEN, CLIVE DARREN

Striker: 13 apps

Born: Stepney, London, 20 May 1961

Career: Havering Schools, Essex Schools, London Schools, England Schools, Queens Park Rangers (apprentice, June 1976; professional, September 1978), Arsenal (£1.25 million, June 1980), Crystal Palace (£1.25 million, August 1980), Queens Park Rangers (£700,000, June 1981), Tottenham Hotspur (£700,000, August 1984), Bordeaux/France (£1 million, March 1988), Manchester City (£1.1 million, July 1989), CHELSEA (£250,000, December 1991), West Ham United (£250,000, March 1992; retired May 1992); later played American football for London Monarchs and also worked for the media, covering football

Striker Clive Allen had a fine career, averaging a goal every two games, including 230 in 467 domestic League and Cup appearances. He netted a record 49 goals for Spurs in 1986–87 when he also gained an FA Cup runner's-up medal and was voted PFA Footballer of the Year. He spent only two months at Highbury, having just three friendly outings with the Gunners. Ex-Chelsea star Terry Venables (q.v.) signed him for Spurs and Ian Porterfield recruited him to the Bridge to partner Kerry Dixon following an injury to Kevin Wilson. He was relegated from the top flight with the Hammers.

Allen gained five full caps for England, three at Under-21 level and also played for his country's youth team and for the Football League representative side. His father, Leslie William Allen (q.v.) played for Chelsea in the 1950s.

ALLEN, LESLIE WILLIAM

Forward: 49 apps, 11 goals

Born: Dagenham, Essex, 4 September 1937

Career: West Ham United (trial, September 1952), Briggs Sports, CHELSEA (professional, September 1954), Tottenham Hotspur (£20,000 plus Johnny Brooks, December 1959), Queens Park Rangers (£21,000, July 1965; manager, December 1968–January 1971), Woodford Town (player–manager, April 1971), Swindon Town (manager, November 1972–February 1974); then manager of Greek team (1974–75) before working in the car industry at Dagenham; later lived in Hornchurch and became a professional model-maker

As a trialist with West Ham, Allen played only 45 minutes before being told to come back in two years' time. Meanwhile he went to work as a storeman in a car factory, played at weekends for Briggs Sports and at the age of 17 joined Chelsea, signed by Ted Drake. He found it difficult to hold down a regular place in Chelsea's side and moved to White Hart Lane. There he became a key figure in Spurs' Double-winning team of 1960–61, playing in every game and scoring 27 goals as partner to another ex-Chelsea man, Bobby Smith (q.v.). After losing his place to Jimmy Greaves (q.v.) he went on to win the League Cup and Third Division championship in 1967 taking over as manager at Loftus Road from Tommy Docherty (q.v.). Capped once by England at Under-23 level v. Wales in 1961, Allen also represented the Football League and scored 113 goals in a career total of 291 League appearances. Other footballing members of the Allen family include: Clive Darren Allen (q.v.) who also played for Chelsea; Martin who served with QPR and West Ham; Paul who assisted West Ham, Spurs, Southampton, Luton Town and Stoke City; and Bradley who was registered with QPR, Charlton Athletic, Colchester United, Grimsby Town, Peterborough United, Bristol Rovers and Hornchurch.

ALLISTER, JOHN GRANDISON
Wing-half: 4 apps, 1 goal
Born: Edinburgh, 30 June 1927
Career: Tranent Juniors (August 1945), CHELSEA (professional, July 1949), Aberdeen (October 1952), Chesterfield (June 1958)
A strong, hard-working right-half, highly competitive Jack Allister was basically a reserve during his three years with Chelsea. He could also perform as a centre-forward and after moving back to Scotland he netted 24 goals in 163 senior appearances for Aberdeen, helping the Dons win both the League title in 1955 and the Scottish League Cup the following season.

ALLON, JOSEPH BALL
Striker: 4+15 apps, 3 goals
Born: Washington, near Gateshead, 12 November 1966
Career: Newcastle United (apprentice, April 1983; professional, November 1984), Swansea City (free transfer, May 1987), Hartlepool United (loan, October 1988; signed for £12,500, November 1988), CHELSEA (£200,000, August 1991), Port Vale (loan, February–March 1992), Brentford (£275,000, November 1992), Southend United (loan, September–October 1993), Port Vale (March 1994), Lincoln City (£42,500, July 1995), Hartlepool United (£42,500, October 1995; retired February 1998)
Blond-haired Joe Allon scored almost 120 goals for Newcastle's second and third teams in fewer than 150 games when he overshadowed Paul Gascoigne. An FA Youth Cup winner at St James' Park in 1985, he also gained an England Youth cap that same year and in 1988 (with Swansea) and 1991 (with Hartlepool) twice won promotion from the Fourth Division. He joined Chelsea after finishing up as top-striker in the Fourth Division but never made his mark at the Bridge. The dressing-room joker, he retired in 1998 with 133 goals and 359 senior appearances under his belt. His brother Paul appeared for non-League Wickham in the 1981 FA Vase final.

ALLUM, LEONARD HECTOR
Right-half: 102 apps, 2 goals
Born: Reading, 8 July 1907 – *Died*: London, 1980
Career: Fulham (briefly, 1929), Reading (trialist, 1930), Maidenhead United (1931), CHELSEA (May 1932), Clapton Orient (May 1939–April 1946)
Len Allum proved to be a most reliable reserve for the majority of his seven years at the Bridge, having his best season (in terms of senior appearances) in 1934–35. Rewarded with England amateur international honours with Maidenhead, he went on to serve Orient throughout WW2, making 102 regional appearances.

AMBROSETTI, GABRIELE
Midfield: 11+12 apps, 1 goal
Born: Varese, Italy, 7 August 1973
Career: Varese/Italy (1990), Brescia/Italy (August 1993), Venezia/Italy (August 1994), Brescia (March 1995), Vicenza/Italy (July 1995), CHELSEA (£3.5 million, August 1999; released December 2002)
Talented left-sided midfielder Gabriele Ambrosetti produced an impressive display for Vicenza against Chelsea in the ECWC and was signed for a sizeable fee two weeks into the 1999–2000 season, Blues' boss Gianluca Vialli beating off challenges from Perugia and Lazio for his signature. Nicknamed 'Spidi Gabriele' in Serie 'A', he was, in Vialli's mind, the Italian version of Ryan Giggs but sadly he never performed at the Bridge and moved back 'home' after just 23 outings in English football. Ambrosetti, who made well over 250 appearances in Italian football before joining Chelsea, scored the winning goal for Brescia against Notts County in the 1994 Anglo-Italian Cup final at Wembley. His only goal for Chelsea came in that terrific 5–0 win over the Turkish side Galatasaray in the Champions League encounter in Istanbul in October 1999.

AMBROSIO, MARCO
Goalkeeper: 12 apps
Born: Brescia, Italy, 30 May 1973
Career: Lummezzane/Italy (June 1991), Atalanta/Italy (1992), Pisa/Italy (1993), Atalanta (1994), Prato/Italy (May 1995), Atalanta (late 1995), Revenna/Italy (early 1996), Prato/Italy (late 1996), Sampdoria/Italy (1997), Lucchese/Italy (2000), Chievo/Italy (August 2001), CHELSEA (free transfer, July 2003)
Experienced Italian goalkeeper Marco Ambrosio joined Chelsea along with Jurgen Macho as Ed De Goey and Rhys Evans left Stamford Bridge in the uncertain pre-Abramovich era. He had played mainly in the lower divisions of Italian football, amassing over 140 senior appearances in his home country before making his debut for the Blues against Notts County in a League Cup tie in October 2003. He lost his place late in the season to a fit-again Carlo Cudicini and was out in the cold after Petr Cech arrived in the summer of 2004.

ANDERSON, GEORGE RUSSELL

Centre-forward: 9 apps

Born: Saltcotes, Strathclyde, 29 October 1904 – *Died*: Cambridge, 9 November 1974

Career: Airdrieonians (1921; professional, 1922), Brentford (June 1925), CHELSEA (May 1927), Norwich City (May 1929), Carlisle United (August 1930), Gillingham (February 1931), Cowdenbeath (September 1931), Yeovil and Petters (1932), Bury (1933), Huddersfield Town (December 1934), Mansfield Town (January 1936–May 1937)

George Anderson deputised for Scottish international Hughie Gallacher at Airdrie. Never pretending to any footcraft, he found it difficult to adapt to the faster pace of football in the English First Division and flitted from League to non-League with celerity. He enjoyed his best scoring run at Mansfield (17 goals in 39 games).

ANDERTON, SYLVAN JAMES

Wing-half: 82 apps, 2 goals

Born: Reading, 23 November 1934

Career: Battle Athletic FC/Reading (1950), Reading (amateur, August 1951; professional, June 1952), CHELSEA (£10,000, March 1959), Queens Park Rangers (£5,000, January 1962); on quitting League football in May 1962, he moved to Bideford, Devon, where he writes poetry and is a part-time scout for Reading

A well-proportioned, strong-tackling but constructive wing-half, Sylvan Anderton made 197 senior appearances for Reading before spending almost three years at Stamford Bridge. One of the stars of former Chelsea manager Ted Drake's youth development scheme at Elm Park, he was a huge favourite with the discerning Chelsea crowd. The arrival of Andy Malcolm from West Ham was the signal for Anderton to leave the Bridge.

ARGUE, JAMES

Inside-forward: 125 apps, 35 goals

Born: Glasgow, 27 November 1911 – *Died*: August 1978

Career: Roch's Juniors/Glasgow, Birmingham (professional, August 1931), CHELSEA (free transfer, December 1933), Shrewsbury Town (July 1947)

Signed by his former boss at Birmingham, Leslie Knighton, red-haired Jimmy Argue was a well-built, aggressive, all-action inside-forward who enjoyed having a pop at goal, from any distance, with either foot. Although his career was interrupted frequently by injuries, he had at least four good seasons at Stamford Bridge, often producing awesome trickery. Nicknamed 'Ginger', he later captained the Blues' second XI (1946–47) before moving into the Birmingham and District League with Shrewsbury. His son played for St Johnstone.

ARMSTRONG, JAMES WILLIAM

Centre-/inside-forward: 31 apps, 10 goals
Born: Swalwell-on-Tyne, 6 September 1901 – *Died*: Gateshead, 12 August 1977
Career: Spen Black and White FC (from 1919), CHELSEA (professional, January 1922), Tottenham Hotspur (May 1927), Luton Town (June 1930), Bristol Rovers (March 1931–April 1932)

Jimmy Armstrong scored on his League debut for Chelsea as a frail but live-wire 21 year old against his future club Tottenham Hotspur in December 1922. Unfortunately he failed to establish himself at Stamford Bridge and moved to White Hart Lane where again he had to fight for first-team football, making only 28 League appearances in 3 years.

ARMSTRONG, KENNETH

Right-half: 402 apps, 30 goals
Born: Bradford, 3 June 1924 – *Died*: New Zealand, 15 June 1984
Career: Bradford Rovers, Army football, CHELSEA (professional, December 1946; retired May 1957); emigrated to New Zealand where he played, in turn, for Eastern Union FC, North Shore United and Gisborne as well as representing New Zealand at international level; later elected chief coach of the country's FA; as an England international (one full cap and three 'B' caps gained), Ken Armstrong also represented the Football League (1955) and was a First Division championship winner with Chelsea in 1954–55, missing only three games

A very consistent player, admired by the fans, he claimed a regular place in the side in 1947 and was virtually a first-choice selection for a decade. He was used as an emergency centre-forward (in place of Tommy Lawton) during the 1947–48 season and finished up as top scorer with 13 goals. His only senior game for England came at Wembley in 1955 when he helped thrash Scotland 7–2. He was Chelsea's all-time record appearance-maker until goalkeeper Peter Bonetti overtook his total in 1969 and now stands in fifth place in the club's all-time appearance list. After his death his ashes were returned to England and scattered over the pitch at Stamford Bridge.

ASHFORD, JAMES WILLIAM

Full-back: 8 apps
Born: Barlborough, Derbyshire, 24 May 1897 – *Died*: 1970
Career: Brodsworth Main Colliery, Ebbw Vale (March 1919), CHELSEA (March 1920), Doncaster Rovers (April 1925), Bristol Rovers (October 1926), Scunthorpe and Lindsey United (May 1927)

An adequate reserve to Walter Bettridge, Jack Harrow and George Smith during his five years at the Bridge, lightweight full-back Jimmy Ashford made his Football League debut in April 1921 in a 0–0 draw at Middlesbrough.

AYLOTT, TREVOR KEITH CHARLES

Striker: 27+3 apps, 2 goals
Born: Bermondsey, London, 26 November 1957
Career: Scott Lidgett School, Downside Boys' Club, Fisher Athletic (1973), CHELSEA (apprentice, November 1975; professional, July 1976), Barnsley (£60,000, November 1979), Millwall (£150,000, August 1982), Luton Town (£55,000 plus Vince Hilaire, March 1983), Crystal Palace (July 1984), Barnsley (loan, February–March 1986), AFC Bournemouth (£15,000, August 1986), Birmingham City (October 1990), Oxford United (loan, September 1991; signed permanently October 1991), Gillingham (1992), Wycombe Wanderers (loan, March–April 1993), Barnsley (July 1993)

A tall, heavily built target-man, Trevor Aylott was particularly adept at holding the ball up and then laying off to a colleague. Not a prolific scorer, he netted only 90 goals in a career total of 472 League games. He won the Third Division title with Bournemouth in 1987 – his only club honour. He lacked the finesse required at Chelsea but after leaving the Bridge he certainly gave a good account of himself in the lower divisions.

BABAYARO, CELESTINE

Left wing-back: 177+20 apps, 8 goals
Born: Kaduna, Nigeria, 29 August 1978
Career: Plateau University/Nigeria (September 1993), RSC Anderlecht/Belgium (amateur, August 1994; professional, September 1995), CHELSEA (£2.25 million, June 1997), Newcastle United (January 2005)

A quality Nigerian international, capped 6 times at Under-23 and on 40 occasions at senior level, Celestine Babayaro played in the 1993 World Youth tournament, in the 1996 Olympic Games when he won a soccer gold medal (with Geremi, q.v.) and in 3 African Nations Cup competitions. He made 75 League appearances for Anderlecht before his big-money transfer to Chelsea, signed by Ruud Gullit. He struggled with injuries during 2003–04, having previously been a regular performer in the side for five years. But with England's Wayne Bridge in such good form, his outings in the Premiership became more and more intermittent during the first half of the 2004–05 season and it was no surprise when he moved north to Newcastle when the transfer window opened in January. He made his debut for the Geordies against non-League side Yeading in a 3rd round FA Cup tie at Loftus Road a week after joining.

BAIN, JAMES ALISTAIR

Outside-left: 14 apps, 1 goal
Born: Blairgowrie, Perthshire, 14 December 1919 – Deceased by 2000
Career: Gillingham (professional, July 1939), CHELSEA (May 1945), Swindon Town (May 1947; retired May 1953)

Chelsea's first full-time professional after WW2, Jimmy Bain, slight in build, was unable to claim a first-team place at the Bridge but after leaving he starred in over 250 competitive games for Swindon.

BAKER, BENJAMIN HOWARD
Goalkeeper: 93 apps, 1 goal
Born: Aigburth, Liverpool, 12 February 1892 – *Died*: 10 September 1987
Career: Marlborough Old Boys (1909), Northern Nomads (1911), Blackburn Rovers reserves (1913), Corinthians (1914), Preston North End (1915), Lancashire County (1919), Liverpool (March 1920), Everton (November 1920), Northern Nomads (February 1921), CHELSEA (October 1921), Corinthians (March 1926) Everton (July 1926), Oldham Athletic (March 1929), Corinthians (September 1930; retired April 1931)

Initially a centre-half and an England amateur trialist in 1919, Howard Baker quickly became a goalkeeper and went on to win ten caps at that level between 1921 and 1929 and two for the senior side against Belgium in 1921 and Ireland four years later, as well as representing the Football League. One of the great all-round athletes of his day, he also starred for Great Britain in the high jump at the 1912 and 1920 Olympic Games, finishing sixth in the latter year while also winning six AAA titles in the same event. He was the British record holder at this event, clearing 6 ft 5 in. at an athletics meeting in Huddersfield on 5 June 1921.

Besides his footballing activities, Baker – who remained an amateur throughout his sporting career – was a fine batsman for Liverpool Cricket Club, scoring two centuries. He kept goal for a local water-polo team and was a useful lawn tennis player too. He made his debut for Everton in a 1–0 win at Chelsea in February 1921, played in 176 first-class games for the Corinthians and was a Welsh Cup winner with the Northern Nomads, also in 1921. The length of Baker's goal-kicks, his upfield sorties and his penalty-taking were all part of his remarkable repertoire. Registered with Chelsea for 5 years, his best seasons at the Bridge came in 1921–22 (24 outings) and 1924–25 (28). His solitary goal for the Blues (giving him the honour of being the only keeper to score for the club) came from the penalty spot and earned his side a 1–0 home League win over Bradford City in November 1921. He was 95 when he died.

BALDWIN, THOMAS
Striker: 227 apps, 92 goals
Born: Gateshead, 10 June 1945
Career: Wrekenton Juniors/Gateshead (1960), Arsenal (amateur, September 1962; professional December 1962), CHELSEA (£25,000, September 1966 in part-exchange for George Graham), Millwall (November 1974), Manchester United (loan, January–February 1975), Seattle Sounders/NASL (April–August 1975), Gravesend and Northfleet (August 1976), Brentford (player–coach, October 1977–March 1980)

Tommy Baldwin spent eight excellent years with Chelsea and played in four major Cup finals in the space of five seasons. He gained both FA Cup runner's-up and winner's medals in the 1967 (v. Spurs) and 1970 (v. Leeds United) finals respectively, was presented with a European Cup-Winners' Cup prize in 1971 (v. Real Madrid) and then received a runner's-up medal in the 1972 League Cup (v. Stoke City). Twice capped by England at Under-23 level, Baldwin netted 83 goals in a career total of 216 League appearances. Known as 'Sponge' at the Bridge (for his ability to keep hold of the ball under pressure) he lacked the flair of other players of similar style, but was nevertheless a vital member of Chelsea's front line for many years. Later resided in the Fulham district of London and is a keen golfer.

BAMBRICK, JAMES JOSEPH
Centre-forward: 66 apps, 37 goals
Born: Belfast, 1 November 1907 – *Died*: Belfast, 27 November 1983
Career: Ulster Rangers (1923), Glentoran (1924), Linfield (1925), CHELSEA (December 1934), Walsall (March 1938; retired September 1939); returning to Belfast, he purchased a house almost next door to Windsor Park; he also enjoyed a round of golf.

Joe Bambrick holds the international scoring record for the Home countries – netting six for Ireland against Wales at Belfast in February 1930. During his career he bagged over 200 goals, including 94 in season 1929–30 for Linfield. Although he had to work hard and long to compete earnestly in League football with Chelsea, he still averaged more than a goal every two games. Strong, hard to knock off the ball, he could shoot with both feet and was also powerful when using his head. He won a total of 11 caps.

BANNON, EAMONN JOHN
Midfield: 27 apps, 1 goal
Born: Edinburgh, 18 April 1958
Career: Links Boys Club/Edinburgh (1974), Heart of Midlothian (professional, April 1976), CHELSEA (£200,000, January 1979), Dundee United (£170,000, November 1979–May 1987)

Eamonn Bannon was manager Danny Blanchflower's first signing for relegation-threatened Chelsea. Unfortunately this talented, scheming midfielder was unable to adapt quickly enough, as required, to English conditions and left the Bridge after just nine months. After returning to his homeland (signed for a then record fee for Dundee United and indeed a Scottish club) he developed into one of Scotland's finest footballers. A schoolboy international at the age of 15, he subsequently won 11 full and 7 Under-21 caps and represented the Scottish League. During his time at Tannadice, he won a League championship medal (1983), two League Cup winner's medals in successive seasons (1980 and 1981), and also collected two Scottish Cup and two League Cup runner's-up medals between 1981 and 1985. Perhaps Chelsea regretted they didn't persevere with the cultured Bannon.

BARBER, GEORGE FREDERICK

Full-back: 294 apps, 1 goal

Born: West Ham, London, 1 August 1909 – *Died*: 1974

Career: Fairburn House (1924), Redhill (amateur, April 1925), Luton Town (professional, August 1927), CHELSEA (free transfer, May 1930; retired through injury, September 1941)

A real bargain signing by Chelsea, ever-reliable full-back George Barber, who could occupy both flanks, spent more than 11 seasons at the club and made almost 350 appearances, his last 54 coming during the first two years of WW2. Tutored by the former Scottish international Tommy Law (q.v.), he was a big man but light on his feet and covered the ground quickly. He was described as being a 'deadly tackler' and indeed was also renowned for his sliding tackles, which he timed to perfection, often knocking the wind out of opposing forwards, especially wingers, who came in contact with him.

Barber worked as a London railway porter for a number of years before turning pro with Luton.

BARKAS, EDWARD

Full-back: 28 apps

Born: Wardley, Northumberland, 21 January 1901 – *Died*: Little Bromwich, 21 April 1962

Career: St Hild's Old Boys, East Bordon, Hebburn Colliery, Bedlington United, South Shields (1918), Wardley Colliery (September 1919), Norwich City (amateur, October 1920), Bedlington United (November 1920), Huddersfield Town (professional, January 1921), Birmingham (£4,000, December 1928), CHELSEA (May 1937), Solihull Town (player–manager, May 1939), Willmott Breedon FC (1943–44), Nuffield Mechanics FC (1944–45); worked as a charge-hand on munitions during WW2

Ned Barkas, a former miner, skippered Birmingham in the 1931 FA Cup final. A tough-tackling defender, both authoritative and influential, he actually began his career as a centre-forward, playing for a variety of intermediate teams in the North-east of England and indeed he made his debut for Norwich City in that position. After signing as a professional for Huddersfield, he spent 7 years at Leeds Road, making 131 appearances and helping the Terriers win 3 successive First Division titles (1924–25–26). He then went on to score 9 goals in 288 outings for Birmingham before being reunited with his former manager Leslie Knighton at Chelsea. Although past his best and lacking in pace, Barkas played regularly during the second half of the 1937–38 campaign before age and fitness caught up with him. He toured Canada with the FA in 1926 – and represented the Football League on three occasions. Barkas was the eldest of five brothers, four of whom were professional footballers who collectively appeared in 1,125 League games between 1920 and 1949. Ned made the most, 404, Sam totalled 377, Tom amassed 279 and Harry 45.

BARNARD, DARREN SEAN

Left-back/midfield: 20+13 apps

Born: Rintein, Germany, 30 November 1971

Career: Wokingham Town (1987), CHELSEA (£50,000, July 1990), Reading (loan, November–December 1994), Bristol City (£175,000, October 1995), Barnsley (£750,000, August 1997), Grimsby Town (free transfer, August 2000)

Darren Barnard spent five years at Stamford Bridge, never really forcing his way into the Chelsea first XI on a regular basis. However, after leaving the club he developed into a fine lower division defender, making 94 appearances for Bristol City, 201 for Barnsley and almost 100 for Grimsby while also gaining 22 full caps for Wales, having represented England at schoolboy and youth-team levels as a teenager.

BARNESS, ANTHONY

Defender: 16+3 apps

Born: Lewisham, London, 25 March 1973

Career: Charlton Athletic (trainee, May 1989; professional, March 1991), CHELSEA (£350,000, September 1992), Middlesbrough (loan, August 1993), Southend United (loan, February–March 1996), Charlton Athletic (£165,000, August 1996), Bolton Wanderers (free transfer, July 2000)

A well-built, strong-tackling defender, able to occupy both full-back positions, Anthony Barness struggled to hold down a first-team place at Chelsea but after leaving the Bridge he did exceedingly well with his former club, Charlton, whom he helped win the First Division championship in 2000. He then played in the Premiership with Bolton and reached the milestone of 275 career appearances in 2004.

BARRACLOUGH, WILLIAM

Outside-left: 81 apps, 11 goals

Born: Hull, 3 January 1909 – *Died*: August 1969

Career: Bridlington Town (1924), Hull City (amateur, July 1927), Wolverhampton Wanderers (June 1928), CHELSEA (£1,500, October 1934), Colchester United (August 1937), Doncaster Rovers (August 1938; retired during WW2); later worked as a clerk in the Humberside docks and was also a fruit merchant; he enjoyed a round of golf as well as being a talented tennis player

A Second Division championship winner with Wolves in 1932, Bill Barraclough, who was only 5 ft 4 in. tall, realised his full potential at Molineux. A clever ball-player, he enjoyed taking on defenders but his directness somehow annoyed a section of the Stamford Bridge faithful. He made 263 League appearances during his career.

BARRETT, FREDERICK KYLE

Left-back: 70 apps, 6 goals
Born: Woodford, Essex, 12 April 1896 – *Died*: Ireland, *circa* 1970
Career: Belfast Celtic (August 1913), CHELSEA (May 1920), Dundalk
(August 1927)

Noted for his long, clean and precise kicking, Fred Barrett made over 150 appearances for Belfast Celtic and represented the Irish League before moving to Stamford Bridge where he spent a considerable amount of time in the reserves. He had his best season in the first team in 1925–26 (30 games) when he scored 2 of his 6 goals in the home League match against Darlington in February 1926 – both from powerful free kicks.

BARRON, JAMES

Goalkeeper: 1 app.
Born: Tantobie, County Durham, 19 October 1943
Career: Raby Street School, Byker and Newcastle Boys, Newcastle West End Boys Club (1959), Wolverhampton Wanderers (amateur, April 1960; professional, November 1961), CHELSEA (£5,000, April 1965), Oxford United (March 1966), Nottingham Forest (£35,000, July 1970), Swindon Town (August 1974), Connecticut Bi-centennials/NASL (May–July 1977), Peterborough United (August 1977; retired May 1981), Mansfield Town (briefly as assistant manager), Wolverhampton Wanderers (coach and assistant manager, September 1981–May 1983; later returned as coach and caretaker-manager, 1988–89), Cheltenham Town (manager, November 1989–October 1990, while also running a goalkeeping school in Gloucestershire), Everton (reserve team manager and goalkeeping coach under boss Howard Kendall, 1991–92), Aston Villa (assistant manager/coach, 1992–93), Sheffield United (coach, 1996–98), Birmingham City (coach, November 1998; then joint caretaker-manager, October 2001, until the appointment of Steve Bruce), Crystal Palace (assistant manager/coach, 2002–03)

One of the many keepers who understudied Peter Bonetti (q.v.), Jim Barron's only outing for Chelsea was in the 2–1 home defeat by Stoke City in September 1965. Safe and unspectacular, he amassed 416 League appearances (most of them for Oxford) in a fine career and was an FA Youth Cup winner with Wolves in 1962. His father kept goal for Blackburn Rovers and Darlington while his son occupied the same position for Cheltenham in the Vauxhall Conference. Between his appointments at Aston Villa and Sheffield United, Barron served a short prison sentence following a road traffic accident in which his wife was killed.

BASON, BRIAN
Midfield: 20+2 apps, 1 goal
Born: Epsom, Surrey, 3 September 1955
Career: CHELSEA (trainee September 1970; professional, September 1972), Plymouth Argyle (£30,000, September 1977), Crystal Palace (March 1981), Portsmouth (loan, January–March 1982), Reading (August 1982–May 1983); after retiring, ran a hotel in Truro, Cornwall

Converted from a striker into a midfielder, former England schoolboy international Brian Bason made his League debut for Chelsea against Sheffield United at Bramall Lane in September 1972 when still an apprentice. He suffered a double fracture of the shin during a League Cup tie with Arsenal in October 1976 at a time when he looked likely to establish himself in the first XI. He made 255 League appearances during his career, 129 for Plymouth.

BATHGATE, SIDNEY
Full-back: 147 apps
Born: Aberdeen, 20 December 1919 – *Died*: Scotland, 1962
Career: Parkvale Juniors/Aberdeen (April 1939), CHELSEA (September 1946), Hamilton Academical (1953)

Sid Bathgate was 26 when he joined Chelsea on his demob from the RAF – having lost 7 years of his footballing life due to WW2. He did, though, go on to give the Blues splendid service after battling with the likes of Billy Hughes and Danny Winter to earn his place in the side. Well built and a smart tackler, he lacked that extra yard of pace but nevertheless was a grand competitor.

BAXTER, THOMAS JAMES CHARLES
Right-half: 1 app.
Born: Wandsworth, London, 10 October 1893 – Deceased by 1985
Career: Army service (played football for the Salonika Expeditionary Force), CHELSEA (September 1919), Gillingham (free transfer, May 1920)

A regular in Chelsea's London Combination side, Tom Baxter spent just the one season at Stamford Bridge, his only League appearance coming against Burnley, three weeks after joining the club.

BEASANT, DAVID JOHN
Goalkeeper: 157 apps
Born: Willesden, London, 20 March 1959
Career: Old Uffintonians (1975), Legionnaires FC (1976), Edgware Town (1977), Wimbledon (£1,000, August 1979), Newcastle United (£800,000, June 1988), CHELSEA (£725,000, January 1989), Grimsby Town (loan, October–November 1992), Wolverhampton Wanderers (loan, January–February 1993), Southampton (£300,000, November 1993), Nottingham Forest (free transfer, August 1997), Portsmouth (free, August 2001), Tottenham Hotspur (free, November 2001), Portsmouth (free, January

2002), Bradford City (free, September 2002), Wigan Athletic (free, October 2002), Brighton and Hove Albion (free, January 2003; retired May 2003 to become a goalkeeping coach); Wycombe Wanderers (coach); Northern Ireland (assistant manager/coach, 2004–05); Fulham (coach)

At 6 ft 4 in. tall and weighing over 14st., Dave Beasant stood like a colossus between the posts in a total of 897 competitive matches, 773 of which came in the Football League/Premiership during a nomadic career that saw him serve with 12 different clubs. In fact, between August 1981 and October 1990, Beasant had a run of 394 consecutive League games, only Tranmere Rovers defender Harold Bell having a longer sequence (401). He was brilliant at times but was also likely to make a crucial error. Nonetheless, he was an inspiration to Wimbledon, helping the Dons leap up from non-League football to FA Cup winners in double-quick time. Indeed, he was the first goalkeeper to save a penalty in an FA Cup final at Wembley, denying John Aldridge of Liverpool in the 1988 showdown.

Initially a free-scoring centre-forward in non-League football, he had already accumulated over 400 senior appearances when he joined Chelsea and at the Bridge he performed superbly well on several occasions before moving on to pastures new. Capped twice by England at full international level and seven times by the Under-21s, he helped Wimbledon win the Fourth Division championship in 1983, Chelsea the Second Division title in 1989 and Forest the First Division crown in 1998. He also gained promotion with the Dons in 1984 (from Division Three) and 1986 (from Division Two) and won the Full Members' Cup with Chelsea in 1990. He was Newcastle's costliest player when signed in 1988 and when he retired from his last League club, Brighton, he was aged 44. Beasant ruined fellow goalkeeper Peter Shilton's 900th League appearance when he saved a last-minute penalty from Derby's Dean Saunders to earn Chelsea a 2–1 win in August 1990. He worked under former playing colleague Lawrie Sanchez at Wycombe and with Northern Ireland.

BELL, DR JOHN BARR

Outside-right: 44 apps, 10 goals
Born: Barrow-in-Furness, Cumbria, 5 April 1901 – *Died*: Scotland, *circa* 1980
Career: Queen's Park (amateur, 1918), CHELSEA (amateur, August 1920; professional, July 1921; released May 1923), Hamilton Academical (August 1923–April 1925)

Regarded as being the fastest winger in Scotland before joining Chelsea, Jack Bell was never the favourite son of the Stamford Bridge crowd and at times played well below par. He continued with his medical duties while still a professional footballer.

BELLETT, WALTER RONALD

Full-back: 35 apps, 1 goal
Born: Stratford, London, 14 November 1933
Career: Barking (from 1951), CHELSEA (September 1954), Plymouth Argyle (£12,000, plus Len Casey, December 1958), Chelmsford City (1960), Leyton Orient (January 1961), Chester (July 1961), Wrexham (July 1962), Tranmere Rovers (July 1963–April 1964)

A former England Youth international, Wally Bellett was a rock-solid defender, quick in the tackle, who had to fight for first-team football at Stamford Bridge with the Sillett brothers. His best season came in 1957–58 when he made 20 League appearances.

BENNETT, WALTER

Wing-half: 5 apps
Born: Sheffield, 17 April 1901 – *Died*: 1988
Career: Beighton FC/Sheffield (1918), Birmingham (professional, May 1921), CHELSEA (October 1922), Southend United (May 1924), Doncaster Rovers (August 1925), Portsmouth (March 1927), Gainsborough Trinity (August 1927), Bristol City (July 1928), Ballymena/Ireland (March 1930; retired May 1932)

Classed a reserve, Wally Bennett hardly got a look-in at the Bridge owing to the form of established half-backs Tom Meehan, Jack Priestley and Harold Wilding.

BENTLEY, ROY THOMAS FRANK

Centre-forward: 367 apps, 150 goals
Born: Bristol, 17 May 1923
Career: Portway School/Bristol, Bristol Rovers (amateur, August 1937), Bristol City (groundstaff, July 1938; professional, August 1941), Newcastle United (£8,500, June 1946), CHELSEA (£12,500, January 1948), Fulham (£8,600, September 1956), Queens Park Rangers (May 1961), Reading (manager, January 1963–February 1969), Bradford City (scout, March 1969), Swansea City (manager, August 1969–October 1972), Thatcham Town (manager, 1973–76), Reading (secretary, 1978–February 1984), Aldershot (secretary, January 1985–86)

Unorthodox in his ways, Roy Bentley was one of the first roving centre-forwards seen in the Football League. A fine header of the ball, he could use both feet and was also utilised as a right-winger and inside-forward. He later played at centre-half for Fulham and right-back at QPR. Captain of the Blues' League championship-winning side of 1954–55 when he netted 21 goals in 41 games, he became one of the greatest players in Chelsea's history, finishing up as leading scorer 8 times in 10 seasons. He once scored in eight consecutive League games from 10 September to 18 October 1952 – a club record. He shares second spot with Peter Osgood (q.v.) in the club's all-time scoring list. Capped 12 times by

England (1949–55) Bentley also appeared in 1 'B' international and represented the Football League on 3 occasions. Bentley appeared in seven FA Cup semi-final matches with three different clubs and was never on the winning side. He lost with Newcastle (v. Charlton) in 1947, Chelsea (v. Arsenal) in replays in 1950 and 1952, and with Fulham (also in a replay v. Manchester United) in 1958. He now resides in Reading.

BERRY, PAUL

Centre-half: 3 apps
Born: Chadwell St Mary, Essex, 15 November 1935
Career: CHELSEA (junior, May 1951; professional, April 1953), Tonbridge (June 1960)
Nurtured through the junior ranks at Stamford Bridge, Paul Berry spent most of his Chelsea days in the second and third teams. He made his League debut against Manchester City in March 1957.

BETTRIDGE, WALTER

Full-back: 255 apps
Born: Oakthorpe, Leicestershire, October 1886 – *Died*: 1931
Career: Measham (1905), Worksop Town (1907), Burton United (1908), CHELSEA (May 1909), Gillingham (June 1922; retired May 1924)
A grand servant to Chelsea, Wally Bettridge, an attacking full-back with strong limbs and a powerful kick, was a regular in the side for 11 seasons. He helped the team gain promotion to the First Division (as Jock Cameron's partner) in 1912 and collected an FA Cup runner's-up medal in 1915 when he had Jack Harrow as his full-back companion.

BIDEWELL, SIDNEY HENRY

Inside-/centre-forward: 4 apps, 2 goals
Born: Watford, 6 June 1918 – Deceased by 2000
Career: Watford schoolboy football, Wealdstone (August 1934), CHELSEA (May 1937), Army service (1939–46), Gravesend (May 1946; retired April 1947)
Scorer of two goals on his League debut for Chelsea against Huddersfield Town in December 1937, WW2 undoubtedly ruined Sid Bidewell's footballing career.

BILLINGTON, HUGH JOHN RICHARD

Inside-/centre-forward: 90 apps, 32 goals
Born: Ampthill, Bedfordshire, 24 February 1916 – *Died*: 1988
Career: Waterlows FC/Bedfordshire (1935), Luton Town (May 1938), CHELSEA (£8,000, March 1948), Worcester City (May 1951; retired April 1953)
Hugh Billington was a superb marksman who scored 63 goals in only 87 League games for Luton Town whom he helped win the Third Division (S) title in 1937–38. He then followed up by netting on average a goal every three games

for Chelsea. Strong and mobile, able to use both feet, he loved to shoot from distance and found the net more often than not with stunning drives from outside the penalty area. He was joint League scorer with Roy Bentley (q.v.) in 1949–50 with 17 goals.

BIRCHENALL, ALAN JOHN

Striker: 95+1 apps, 28 goals
Born: East Ham, London, 22 August 1945
Career: Thorneywood Thistle (1961), Sheffield United (June 1963), CHELSEA (£100,000, June 1967), Crystal Palace (£100,000 in same deal involving Bobby Tambling, valued at £40,000, June 1970), Leicester City (September 1971), Notts County (loan, March–April 1976), San Jose/NASL (April–July 1977), Notts County (September 1977), Memphis Rogues/NASL (April 1978), Blackburn Rovers (September 1978), Luton Town (March 1979), Hereford United (October 1979), Trowbridge Town (player–manager, July 1980), Leicester City (Public Relations Officer, 1983); also played in charity matches in the 1980s with the Geriatric Megastars (ex-Leicester City players); later ran a ladies' footwear import business
An extrovert blond striker who gained four England Under-23 caps, Alan Birchenall started out as a foil for Mick Jones at Sheffield United before becoming manager Dave Sexton's first signing for Chelsea. After losing his place to Ian Hutchinson (q.v.), he moved to Filbert Street before becoming a soccer nomad. He scored 74 goals in a career total of 458 League appearances, having his best years at Leicester (12 goals in 163 outings).

Birchenall was the first player sold by Chelsea for a six-figure fee (£100,000) having been signed for the same amount of money three years earlier. In fact, he was the first footballer to move to three clubs for the same price – £100,000.

BIRNIE, EDWARD LAWSON

Half-back/outside-left: 108 apps, 3 goals
Born: Sunderland, 25 August 1878 – *Died*: Southend, 21 December 1935
Career: Sunderland Seaburn FC (1896), Newcastle United (June 1898), Crystal Palace (May 1905), CHELSEA (£100, August 1906), Tottenham Hotspur (July 1910), Mulhiem/Germany (player–trainer, August 1911), Rochdale (July 1912), Leyton (player–manager, July 1914), Sunderland (assistant trainer and chief scout, August 1919), Rochdale (trainer, June 1921), Southend United (manager, January 1922–May 1924); in Germany (coaching); later Newcastle City (player–manager, 1926–27)
Star of Newcastle United's Northern League title-winning sides of 1903, 1904 and 1905, Ted Birnie made only 20 first-team appearances during his 7 years at St James' Park. Always looking leisurely on the ball, he was an intelligent player who hardly wasted a pass. He performed well with Chelsea, especially in 1907–08 having done a solid job when promotion was achieved the previous season. He represented Northumberland County as a Newcastle player.

BISHOP, SIDNEY MACDONALD

Wing-half: 109 apps, 6 goals
Born: Stepney, London, 10 February 1900 – *Died:* Chelsea, 4 May 1949
Career: Lexford School, Ilford (August 1915), RAF (1916–18), Crystal Palace
(trialist, 1919), West Ham United (May 1920), Leicester City (November
1926), CHELSEA (£3,800, June 1928; retired May 1933)

Capped four times by England (1927) and a Football League representative
(1928) as well an FA Cup runner-up with West Ham at Wembley's first final in
1923, the slender-looking Sid 'Sticks' Bishop possessed excellent ball control, had
an unflurried demeanour, was clever in the air and altogether a fine wing-half.
Injury prevented him from captaining his country against Scotland in 1928 and
he went on to gain promotion with Chelsea in his second season with the club.

BISWELL, GEORGE WILLIAM

Inside-forward/wing-half: 25 apps, 10 goals
Born: Southwark, Middlesex, 11 August 1907 – Deceased by 2000
Career: Villa Juniors (1921) Shaftesbury Athletic (August 1922), St Albans City
(September 1923), Watford (amateur, January 1924), Charlton Athletic
(amateur, May 1924; professional, July 1925), CHELSEA (£3,500, January
1928), Chester (loan, season 1929–30), Ards/Northern Ireland (briefly),
Charlton Athletic (free transfer, August 1931; retired May 1934)

A free-scoring forward when in the attack and a resolute competitor when
performing as a half-back, George Biswell scored 31 goals in 115 games in his
two spells with Charlton, serving under three different managers. His move to
Chelsea was for a club record fee but sadly it didn't prove to be a profitable move
for Biswell who struggled with his form at times and was subsequently loaned
out to Chester before returning to The Valley. He was a very competent golfer,
driving off the tee with a handicap of 12.

BLOCK, MICHAEL

Winger: 40 apps, 6 goals
Born: Ipswich, 28 January 1940
Career: CHELSEA (juniors, April 1955; professional, February 1957),
Brentford (£5,000, January 1962), Watford (October 1966–April 1967)

An England Youth international and product of Chelsea's flourishing nursery,
Micky Block, who had Peter Brabrook and Frank Blunstone to contend with,
failed to make headway in the first team, averaging just eight games a season
from 1957. He went on to appear in 146 League games for Brentford.

BLUNSTONE, FRANK

Outside-left: 347 apps, 55 goals
Born: Crewe, 17 October 1934
Career: Bedford Street School/Crewe, Cheshire FA, Crewe Alexandra (amateur,
August 1951; professional, January 1952), CHELSEA (£7,000, February

1953; retired through injury, June 1964; appointed youth-team coach); Brentford (manager, December 1969–June 1973), Manchester United (youth team manager, January 1973–June 1977), Derby County (assistant manager/coach, September 1977–May 1979), Ethnikos/Greece (coach, August 1979), Aris Salonika/Greece (coach, March–July 1980), Brentford (youth team manager, 1980–82), Sheffield Wednesday (youth team manager/coach 1982–84, then caretaker-manager, February 1984)

Frank Blunstone, who was once hailed as the new Cliff Bastin, broke his leg twice in seven months playing for Chelsea and missed the whole of the 1957–58 season. Earlier, he had gained five full England caps (1955–57), represented his country in five Under-23 internationals and in youth games (1951) and played for the Football League XI. A League championship winner with Chelsea in 1954–55, when he was a class act on the left-wing, he was still at the club when First Division status was reclaimed eight years later. With the ability to cross the ball at pace, his displays on the wing at times were superb. Precociously cool, clever and mature at the age of 22, it was a pity he suffered the injuries when he did, for he would have certainly been a regular in the England side. As a manager he worked on a shoestring budget at Brentford, did most of the jobs himself and bought and sold players wisely. He became a very respected coach after that. Blunstone came from a family of 13 children.

BODLEY, MICHAEL JOHN
Centre-half: 8 apps, 1 goal
Born: Hayes, Middlesex, 14 September 1967
Career: CHELSEA (apprentice June 1983; professional, September 1985), Northampton Town (£50,000, January 1989), Barnet (£15,000, October 1989), Southend United (free transfer, July 1993), Gillingham (loan, November–December 1994), Birmingham City (loan, January–February 1995), Peterborough United (July 1995), St Albans (May 1999), Dagenham and Redbridge (September 1999), Canvey Island (season 2001–02)

Mick Bodley played only 8 games for Chelsea and 22 for Northampton before dropping out of League football at the age of 22. He returned after helping Barnet win the Vauxhall Conference in 1991 and went on to appear in almost 300 competitive games before leaving Posh in 1999. A strong, competent defender, he made his Chelsea debut against Norwich City in September 1987 – four years, three months after joining the club.

BOGARDE, WINSTON
Defender: 4+8 apps
Born: Rotterdam, Holland, 22 October 1970
Career: SVV/Holland (April 1988), Excelsior/Holland (1990), SVV/Holland (late 1990), Sparta Rotterdam/Holland (1991), Ajax Amsterdam/Holland

(1994), AC Milan/Italy (1997), CF Barcelona/Spain (1998), CHELSEA (free transfer, September 2000; released May 2004)

At 6 ft 3 in. and weighing over 15 st., Dutch international Winston Bogarde was almost 30 years of age and had 20 full caps under his belt when he joined Chelsea. He trained hard and worked hard but failed to establish himself in the side. Indeed, he didn't make a Premiership appearance in his first three seasons and was released at the end of 2003–04. Earlier in his career he played in over 200 competitive games in Holland, Italy and Spain.

BOLLAND, GORDON EDWARD

Inside-forward: 2 apps

Born: Boston, Lincolnshire, 12 August 1943

Career: Boston United (amateur, 1958), CHELSEA (juniors, February 1959; professional, August 1960), Leyton Orient (£8,000, March 1962), Norwich City (£30,000, March 1964), Charlton Athletic (£20,000, November 1967), Millwall (October 1968), Boston United (April 1975; retired through injury, May 1977)

After having a cartilage operation at the age of 15, Gordon Bolland was unable to establish himself in Chelsea's first team. Nevertheless, he made a name for himself elsewhere, scoring over 100 goals in more than 450 first-class appearances for his 4 other senior clubs. He was a fine penalty-taker.

BONETTI, PETER PHILLIP

Goalkeeper: 729 apps

Born: Putney, London, 27 September 1941

Career: St Mary's School (Worthing), Worthing Roman Catholic Youth Club (1956), CHELSEA (amateur, May 1958; professional, April 1959; released May 1975; re-signed October 1975–May 1979); Dundee United (August–September 1979); retired and moved to the Isle of Mull; CHELSEA (coaching staff, late 1979 onwards); then employed as a goalkeeping coach by various clubs (including Birmingham City) and also assisted England in the same category; later lived in Birmingham

Nicknamed 'The Cat', Peter Bonetti made more appearances for Chelsea than any other goalkeeper, playing in 729 competitive games (600 in the League) during his 20-year association with the club. Outstanding at times, with amazing reflexes, he was spectacularly agile, brave, and his anticipation and shot-stopping at times were quite breathtaking. He did have his lapses – including costly mistakes in the 1970 World Cup quarter-final when playing against West Germany in Mexico – but these apart, he was one of England's finest goalkeepers during the late 1960s and early '70s. He gained seven full caps for his country (due to a certain Gordon Banks) and with Chelsea won the FA Youth Cup (1960), the Football League Cup (1965), the FA Cup (1970) and the European Cup-Winners' Cup (1971). He was also a runner-up in both the 1967 FA Cup and 1972 League Cup finals.

BOROTA, PETAR

Goalkeeper: 114 apps

Born: Belgrade, Yugoslavia, 5 March 1952

Career: Partizan Belgrade (1975), CHELSEA (£70,000, March 1979), Brentford (briefly, 1982), Benfica/Portugal (August 1982), FC Porto/Portugal (season 1984–85); then returned to Yugoslavia

Eccentric and unpredictable 6 ft-tall goalkeeper Petar Borota, signed to succeed Peter Bonetti, could be brilliant one minute and horrible the next. He would amble around his penalty area watching play at the other end of the field and often raced out of his box to the delight of the fans and opponents but not his Chelsea team-mates. Capped 14 times by Yugoslavia, he missed only one game in two seasons (1979–81), being voted the club's Player of the Year in the last two. He was replaced between the posts by Steve Francis.

After returning to Yugoslavia in 1985, Borota ran his own duty-free shop and was also implicated in a stolen picture racket, which resulted in a major court case.

BOSNICH, MARK JOHN

Goalkeeper: 7 apps

Born: Sydney, Australia, 13 January 1972

Career: Sydney Croatia (May 1988), Liverpool (trial, late 1988), Manchester United (non-contract, June 1989), Sydney Croatia (June 1991), Aston Villa (February 1992), Manchester United (free transfer, July 1999), CHELSEA (free, January 2001; released May 2003); worked for Sky TV; Grays Athletic (2005)

Mark Bosnich was brought up in the Croatian community of Sydney before getting the urge to move to the UK. After a trial at Anfield, he joined Manchester United and stayed at Old Trafford for two years during which time he was a student at Manchester Polytechnic. He made three first-team appearances for the Reds before returning to Australia. Bosnich moved back to England to replace Nigel Spink at Villa Park and after 228 outings was ironically re-signed by his former club Manchester United. Capped at youth and Under-23 levels by Australia, Bosnich has also played in 17 full internationals and starred in the semi-finals of the Olympic Games in Barcelona in 1992 but did not play for his 'host' country in the 2000 Games. He had a remarkable record of saving penalties, gained two League Cup winner's medals with Villa (1994 and 1996), and after helping United win the Premiership in 2000, suddenly found himself third-choice keeper at Old Trafford. He made only seven appearances for Chelsea (in two seasons) before he was banned from the game for alleged drug-taking. Bosnich was fined £1,000 and received a stern warning from the FA for his 'Hitler-style' impression ('Sieg Heil') at White Hart Lane in 1996.

BOWER, ALFRED GEORGE
Defender: 9 apps
Born: Bromley, Kent, 10 November 1895 – *Died*: 1970
Career: Corinthians (first registered in 1912), CHELSEA (August 1923–April 1925), Corinthians (retiring in 1934)

Nicknamed 'Baishe', Alf Bower was a fine, upright and self-confident defender who gained five amateur caps for England during a fine career. He was registered with Chelsea for two seasons (1923–25) but he also played for the famous amateur club the Corinthians when required.

BOWIE, JAMES DUNCAN
Inside-forward: 84 apps, 22 goals
Born: Aberdeen, 9 August 1924 – *Died*: Essex, August 2000
Career: Parkvale Juniors/Aberdeen; served in the Royal Navy during WW2; CHELSEA (£25, January 1944), Fulham (£20,000, January 1951), Brentford (March 1952), Watford (July 1952), Bedford Town (August 1956), Fulham (June 1957), March Town (July 1958), Wisbech Town (December 1959; retired April 1960)

A typical Scottish footballer, stockily built, fair hair with a sturdy frame, Jim Bowie was a live-wire bundle of energy. A clever little ball-player who could dribble brilliantly in a confined space, he played for Chelsea in the Wartime Cup final against Charlton Athletic at Wembley in April 1944, three months after signing for the club. After the hostilities he became a key member of the Blues' League side and went on to average a goal every four games before moving to Craven Cottage. Bowie scored 29 goals in 124 appearances for Watford. Knee problems affected his game late on.

BOWMAN, ANDREW
Wing-half: 1 app.
Born: Pittenweem, Fifeshire, 7 March 1934
Career: CHELSEA (juniors, May 1949; professional, June 1951), Heart of Midlothian (August 1955), Newport County (August 1961–May 1963)

Auburn-haired, former Scottish schoolboy international Andy Bowman was one of the early players to rise from Chelsea's nursery, but with Ken Armstrong and Derek Saunders bedded into the wing-half positions, he found if difficult to get a look-in. He later did well with Hearts.

BOYD, THOMAS
Left-back: 31+1 apps
Born: Glasgow, 24 November 1965
Career: Glasgow junior football, Motherwell (apprentice, May 1982; professional, November 1983), CHELSEA (June 1991), Celtic (player-exchange deal involving Tony Cascarino, February 1992; retired May 2002 to join the backroom staff)

Between 1991 and 2001, Tommy Boyd was rewarded with 71 full caps for Scotland to add to his collection of 3 at youth, 5 at Under-21 and 2 at 'B' team levels. He had a wonderful career during which time he amassed over 700 senior appearances for clubs and country, including 405 for Celtic, many as captain. With the Bhoys he gained two League championship, two Scottish Cup and two League Cup winner's medals as well as claiming several runner's-up prizes in all three competitions. He only spent eight months at the Bridge, during which time he hardly missed a game but when Celtic came in with an offer he couldn't refuse, he had no hesitation in moving back to Scotland where he became a permanent fixture at Parkhead for the next ten years.

BOYLE, JOHN

Defender/midfield: 253+13 apps, 12 goals
Born: Motherwell, 25 December 1946
Career: CHELSEA (apprentice, April 1962; professional, August 1964), Brighton and Hove Albion (£2,000, September 1973), Orient (£2,500, December 1973–May 1975); played in the NASL (season 1975–76)

John Boyle walked into Stamford Bridge, unannounced, as a shy, hesitant 15 year old asking for a trial. He got one, did well and was signed up – and spent over 11 years with Chelsea during which time he produced some gritty performances both in defence and midfield. A stern, tenacious tackler, he played in two cup-winning sides – the 1965 League Cup and the 1971 European Cup-Winners' Cup, wearing different numbered shirts each time: '6' and '8' in the former (over two legs v. Leicester City) and '2' in the latter (v. Real Madrid). He was also in Chelsea's 1967 FA Cup final side (beaten by Spurs) and the 1972 League Cup final team (defeated by Stoke City). He scored the winning goal on his senior debut for the Blues in the first leg of the 1965 League Cup semi-final clash with Aston Villa in 1965 (3–2).

BRABROOK, PETER

Outside-right/-left: 272 apps, 57 goals
Born: Greenwich, London, 8 November 1937
Career: Windsor and Napier Schools, East Ham, Middlesex FA, CHELSEA (junior, March 1953; professional, March 1955), West Ham United (£35,000, October 1962), Leyton Orient (July 1968), Romford (August 1971), Woodford Town (August 1972–May 1974); later ran a butcher's shop near Hornchurch, Essex, and also worked for the paper tycoon Neville Ovendon

An England Youth international who went on to win three full caps (1958–60), Peter Brabrook played on both wings, but preferred the right. Exceptionally quick over distances up to 30 yards, he possessed a strong right-foot shot though he could be somewhat uneven in performance, producing two or three brilliant displays followed by a mediocre one. He appeared in only three games when Chelsea won the First Division title in 1955, but after leaving Stamford Bridge he won the FA Cup with West Ham in 1964, played in the League Cup final two years later, beaten by West Brom, and helped Orient win the Third Division championship in 1970.

BRADBURY, TERENCE EUGENE

Wing-half: 29 apps, 1 goal
Born: Paddington, London, 15 November 1939
Career: CHELSEA (junior, April 1956; professional, July 1957), Southend United (£4,500, September 1962), Leyton Orient (June 1966), Wrexham (June 1967), Chester (June 1969–May 1971)

An England schoolboy international, Terry Bradbury, a well-built, forceful wing-half, was on the verge of first-team football at Stamford Bridge for two years before making his debut in August 1960. However, the emergence of Terry Venables and the arrival of Frank Upton effectively ended his chances of making progress at the Bridge. After leaving Chelsea, Bradbury played in 161 League games for Southend, 27 for Orient, 78 for Wrexham and 90 for Chester, ending his major career with well over 450 senior appearances under his belt.

BRADSHAW, JOSEPH JAMES

Inside-forward: 6 apps, 3 goals
Born: Burnley, April 1880 – *Died*: *circa* 1950
Career: Woolwich Polytechnic (1896), West Norwood (1898), Southampton (1900), Woolwich Arsenal (amateur, August 1901), Fulham (professional, March 1904), CHELSEA (May 1909), Queens Park Rangers (July 1910), Southend United (player–manager, season 1912–13); served abroad during WW1; Swansea Town (manager, June 1919–May 1926), Fulham (manager, May 1926–May 1929), Bristol City (manager, August 1929–February 1932); thereafter worked in insurance for 15 years

Joe Bradshaw was signed by his father as an amateur for Arsenal and as a professional for Fulham. An average sort of player, he failed to make the grade with the Gunners and made only six first-team appearances for the Cottagers. He struggled also with Chelsea but then made his name as a manager, first at Southend, whom he helped win promotion from the Southern League Division Two, then with Swansea, whom he guided to the Third Division (S) championship in 1925, and also with Fulham where he succeeded his father. Unfortunately he had a tough time with Bristol City. Joe's father, Harry Bradshaw, played for Burnley and was manager of Arsenal (1899–1904) and Fulham (1904–09) while his younger brother Will Bradshaw played for Arsenal, Fulham, Burton United, Burnley and Ton Pentre (1902–09). His cousin John served with Aberdare Athletic, Burnley, Southend United and Swansea Town between 1919 and 1924. Another member of the Bradshaw family, Dick, played for Blackpool (1908–11).

BRAWN, WILLIAM FREDERICK

Outside-right: 99 apps, 11 goals

Born: Wellingborough, Northamptonshire, 1 August 1878 – *Died*: London, 18 August 1932

Career: Rock Street School, Wellingborough White Star (1893), Wellingborough Principals (1894), Northampton Town (July 1895), Sheffield United (professional, January 1900), Aston Villa (December 1901), Middlesbrough (March 1906), CHELSEA (November 1907), Brentford (August 1911; retired May 1919 after guesting for Spurs, November 1918); later employed as advisory manager at Griffin Park; also ran a pub (the King's Arms) in Boston Road, Brentford

It was said that Billy Brawn was one of 'the most dangerous outside-rights in the kingdom' during the early 1900s. Renowned for his speed and shooting ability, he was unusually tall for a winger (6 ft 2 in.) and was also weighty at 13 st. 5 lb. Able to use both feet, he gained two England caps and collected an FA Cup winner's medal with Aston Villa in 1905. He later starred in Chelsea's first-ever season in Division One and retired with over 350 senior appearances to his name.

BREBNER, RONALD GILCHRIST

Goalkeeper: 19 apps

Born: Darlington, 23 September 1881 – *Died*: Darlington, 11 November 1914

Career: Edinburgh University (1897), Northern Nomads (1899), London Caledonians (August 1902), Sunderland (December 1905), Glasgow Rangers (February 1906), CHELSEA (October 1906), Darlington (November 1906), Elgin City (August 1907), Stockton (May 1909), Queen's Park (February 1910), Huddersfield Town (July 1911), Northern Nomads (June 1912), CHELSEA (September 1912) Leicester Fosse (May 1913–November 1914); a dentist by profession, he had a surgery in the north of England for over ten years (until his death)

An amateur throughout his career, goalkeeper Ron Brebner won 23 England caps at that level and also collected a gold medal with the United Kingdom soccer team at the 1912 Olympic Games, having followed Howard Baker (q.v.) into the UK side. He also played in one senior England trial (South v. North, November 1912) and represented the Amateurs v. the Professionals in the 1913 FA Charity Shield match. He deputised for Dick Whiting v. Grimsby Town when making his Chelsea debut in October 1906 and then played in 17 of the first 22 League games at the start of the 1912–13 season before being replaced by Jim Molyneux. Brebner's death, at the age of 33, came as a result of a head injury received while playing for Leicester in an away League game at Lincoln on Boxing Day 1913. He was carried off the pitch and never recovered.

BRIDGE, WAYNE MICHAEL
Left wing-back: 68+5 apps, 3 goals
Born: Southampton, 5 August 1980
Career: Southampton (trainee, August 1996; professional, January 1998), CHELSEA (£6.5 million, plus Graeme Le Saux, July 2003)

An England international with almost 20 senior caps to his credit plus three at youth and eight at Under-21 levels, Wayne Bridge arrived at Stamford Bridge in a £7 million deal that took Graeme Le Saux (q.v.) to Southampton (Le Saux being valued at £500,000). Bridge himself went straight into the left wing-back position at Stamford Bridge, although he has had to battle for his place with Celestine Babayaro (q.v.). One of the quickest and most attack-minded left-backs in the game, he formed a fine partnership down the left with Damien Duff during his first season at Stamford Bridge and followed up the good work in 2004–05 when he had a variety of assistants down the flank. He has over the years scored some cracking goals including a brilliant winner against Arsenal at Highbury that put Chelsea into the Champions League semi-final in 2004. Bridge made 174 appearances for Saints before his transfer to Chelsea. Unfortunately, he missed the last three months of the 2004–05 season with a broken leg.

BRIDGES, BARRY JOHN
Forward: 203+2 apps, 93 goals
Born: Horsford, near Norwich, 29 April 1941
Career: Norfolk Boys, CHELSEA (junior, July 1956; professional, May 1958), Birmingham City (£55,000, May 1966), Queens Park Rangers (August 1968), Millwall (September 1970), Brighton and Hove Albion (September 1972), Highlands Park/South Africa (1974), St Patrick's Athletic/Republic of Ireland (player–manager, 1976; retired as a player, 1977), Sligo Rovers/Republic of Ireland (manager, season 1978–79), Dereham Town (manager), King's Lynn (manager), Horsford FC (manager); later became a hotelier in Brighton and also worked as a milkman in Hove

A sprint champion at school, Barry Bridges had great acceleration and during his career gave defenders plenty to think about with his pace, goal-threat and presence inside the penalty area. One of the early products of Chelsea's youth set-up to play for England (he won six schoolboy, two youth and four full caps as well as representing the Football League), Bridges scored on his League debut as a 17 year old v. West Ham United in February 1959. He went on to net almost a goal every two games for the Blues with whom he won the League Cup (1965). He moved to Birmingham following the arrival of Peter Osgood and played in both the losing League Cup and FA Cup semi-finals for Birmingham in 1967 and 1968 respectively. He retired in 1977 with over 700 games under his belt, 567 in the Football League (215 goals).

BRIDGEMAN, WILLIAM WALTER

Inside-forward/winger: 160 apps, 22 goals
Born: Bromley-by-Bow, 12 December 1883 – *Died*: Essex, 1966
Career: Adam and Eve FC (1898), West Ham United (1903), CHELSEA
 (November 1906), Southend United (August 1919–May 1921)

Bill Bridgeman was a pacy left-winger who could also play as an inside-forward (his original position). A hard-worker, never afraid to battle it out with the tough defenders of his day, he was never considered a regular member of the side but still spent almost 13 years at Stamford Bridge, making over 30 appearances during WW1. He received a joint-benefit with George Hilsdon on Easter Monday, 1912, when the gate receipts amounted to £180.

BRITTAN, HAROLD PEMBERTON

Inside-/centre-forward: 24 apps, 7 goals
Born: Derby, 1894 – *Died*: USA, 1972
Career: Ilkeston United (1911), CHELSEA (December 1913–May 1920), later
 emigrated to USA and played for Bethlehem Steel, Philadelphia Field Club,
 Fall River Marksmen, New Bedford Wheelers and Fall River Marksmen
 again before retiring in 1931

Unfortunately Harry Brittan's career with Chelsea was marred initially by illness and then by WW1. He made his League debut in April 1914 against Sunderland (away) and then scored twice on his home debut v. Everton a week later. He was one of the first Englishmen to play in the USA.

BRITTON, IAN

Midfield: 279+10 apps, 34 goals
Born: Dundee, 19 May 1954
Career: CHELSEA (apprentice, June 1970; professional, July 1971), Dundee
 United (August 1982), Blackpool (December 1983), Burnley (August
 1986–May 1989), later with Kidderminster Harriers (initially as reserve and
 youth team manager, then manager, July 2002–October 2003)

Despite a lack of physical strength, Ian Britton was a real workhorse in midfield, featuring in Chelsea's first-team set-up for a decade. He had his best spell in the side between February 1975 and August 1978, missing only 12 League games out of a possible 140 when linking up with Ray Wilkins, Ray Lewington, Graham Stanley and others in the engine room. He made 106 League appearances for Blackpool and 108 for Burnley.

BROLLY, MICHAEL JOSEPH

Midfield: 8+1 apps, 1 goal
Born: Galston, near Kilmarnock, 6 October 1954
Career: Kilmarnock schoolboy football, CHELSEA (apprentice, April 1970;
 professional, November 1971), Bristol City (free transfer, June 1974),
 Grimsby Town (£60,000, September 1976), Derby County (free, August

1982), Scunthorpe United (£10,000, August 1983–May 1986), Scarborough (free, July 1986), Goole Town (loan, January 1987; signed, free, March 1987), Boston United (free, February 1988), Holbeach United (free, February 1989–May 1990)

A Scottish schoolboy international, Mick Brolly's opportunities at Stamford Bridge were limited owing to the presence and form of Charlie Cooke, John Hollins, Alan Hudson and Steve Kember. But after leaving Chelsea he did very well at both Grimsby (254 League games) and Scunthorpe (95), retiring from top-class football in 1986 with over 450 senior appearances to his credit. Able to occupy both wide positions as well as the middle of the park, he was a fine passer of the ball, possessed a powerful right-foot shot and helped the Mariners win the Third Division championship in 1980.

BROOKS, JOHN

Forward: 52 apps, 7 goals

Born: Reading, 23 December 1931

Career: Reading Schools, Berkshire Schools, Coley Old Boys, Mount Pleasant FC (1948), Reading (amateur, February 1949; professional, April 1949), Tottenham Hotspur (February 1953 in a deal that took Dennis Uphill and Harry Robshaw to Elm Park), CHELSEA (£20,000 plus Les Allen, December 1959), Brentford (September 1961), Crystal Palace (January 1964), Stevenage Town (October 1964), Cambridge City (1965), FC Toronto/Canada (1966), Knebworth Town (player–manager, 1967–68); after leaving football was employed in the City of London as a broker's messenger

A cogent inside-forward who zestfully plied his colleagues with scoring opportunities, Johnny Brooks had a good scoring record himself in a first-class career that covered some 15 years. Prior to joining Chelsea, he netted 5 times in 46 League games for Reading and then claimed 51 goals in 179 appearances for Spurs (plus 21 in 43 'other' games). He later struck 36 goals in 83 League outings for Brentford with whom he won a Fourth Division championship medal (1963). Well built, strong and mobile, he was capped three times in 1957 by England, lining up against Wales, Yugoslavia and Denmark and scoring against the first two. His son, Shaun, played for Crystal Palace and Leyton Orient.

BROWN, DENNIS JOHN

Inside-forward: 13 apps, 2 goals

Born: Reading, 8 February 1944

Career: CHELSEA (professional, June 1962), Swindon Town (£17,000, November 1964), Northampton Town (February 1967 in exchange for Bobby Jones), Aldershot (July 1969–May 1974); later assisted Margate, Barnet and Cheltenham Town; retired in 1980

Dennis 'Bullets' Brown packed a strong right-foot shot but he had to fight hard and long with Bobby Tambling and George Graham to get a game in the first team. After departing Stamford Bridge he went on to appear in over 400 League games and scored more than 100 goals for his three other clubs ... all this after losing a kneecap in a car accident in 1967. One who got away – maybe.

BROWN, JOHN ALEXANDER

Winger: 16 apps, 4 goals

Born: Dysart, near Kirkcaldy, Fife, May 1887 – *Died*: Scotland, 1943

Career: Heart o' Beath (1905), Alloa Athletic (1908), Falkirk (1910), Celtic (August 1911), CHELSEA (December 1912), Raith Rovers (August 1919), Dunfermline Athletic (1920), Falkirk (loan), Clackmannan (1922), Falkirk (1923), Clackmannan (1925), Lochgelly United (1926; retired 1927)

After doing well initially following his transfer from Scottish football into the English League, Jock Brown lost his form and spent much of his time in the reserves during the two pre-WW1 seasons. He returned to his homeland after the hostilities. During his career Brown appeared in over 200 competitive matches.

BROWN, WILLIAM

Inside-forward: 57 apps, 21 goals

Born: Fencehouses, near Chester-le-Street, County Durham, 22 August 1899 – *Died*: County Durham, 1985

Career: Hetton FC/County Durham, West Ham United, CHELSEA (February 1924), Fulham (June 1929), Stockport County (August 1930), Hartlepool United (1931), Annfield Plain, Blackhall Colliery Welfare; later worked as a baths superintendent at Easington Colliery, County Durham, and also stood as a cricket umpire for many years

Bill Brown, who would occupy any position to get a game of football, played for West Ham United in the first Wembley Cup final of 1923 and also helped the Hammers gain promotion from the Second Division that same season. An England reserve (v. France in 1923) he scored in his only senior international appearance against Belgium in Antwerp that same year. Skilful with an accurate shot, he netted a total of 20 goals in 71 games for West Ham before moving to Chelsea for whom he made a scoring debut against West Bromwich Albion a week after joining. Despite a fine strike-record, he failed to establish himself in the Blues' line-up and switched his allegiance to Craven Cottage after five years at the Bridge. He played in only 116 League games during his career.

BROWN, WILLIAM YOUNG

Inside-forward: 10 apps, 2 goals

Born: South Inch, Northamptonshire, April 1888 – *Died*: 1955

Career: South Inch Schools, Wellingborough (1906), Kettering Town (1908), Queens Park Rangers (August 1910), CHELSEA (July 1911), Bristol City (November 1913), Swansea Town (September 1920), Portsmouth (May 1922), Northampton Town (September 1922–May 1923)

Born of Scottish parents, Willie Brown scored at will for Chelsea's Football

Combination side but failed to hold down a place in the first XI and as time passed by, received a lot of barracking from the Stamford Bridge terraces. He was badly wounded during WW1 but recovered and continued to play competitive football until 1923.

BROWNING, JOHN

Outside-left: 6 apps, 2 goals
Born: Dumbarton, 29 November 1888 – *Died*: *circa* 1958
Career: Dumbarton White Rose, Vale of Leven (1907), Dumbarton Harp (June 1910), Celtic (August 1911), CHELSEA (June 1919), Vale of Leven (August 1920), Dumbarton (seasons 1921–23)

A sturdy player with neat control and an attack-minded approach, John Browning spent seven seasons with Celtic for whom he averaged a goal every three League games, having his best season in 1914–15 when he struck 15 times in 32 outings. He helped the Bhoys win four successive League titles (1914–17 inclusive) and the Scottish Cup, also in 1914 when he gained his only full cap v. Wales. He also represented the Scottish League on two occasions and played for Glasgow against Sheffield in 1914. He arrived at Stamford Bridge with a huge reputation but never settled in London and was soon replaced in the Chelsea line-up by Bobby McNeil (q.v.).

BUCHANAN, PETER SYMINGTON

Winger: 40 apps, 6 goals
Born: Glasgow, 13 October 1915 – *Died*: 1977
Career: St Mungo FC/Glasgow, Wishaw Juniors, CHELSEA (junior, April 1933), Wishaw Juniors (August 1934), CHELSEA (amateur, December 1935; professional, February 1936), Fulham (guest season 1945–46; signed permanently, September 1946), Brentford (August 1947), Headington United (June 1949; retired through injury, November 1950)

A player whose career was unfortunately interrupted by WW2, Peter Buchanan was homesick during his initial spell with Chelsea and returned to Scotland. Older and wiser, he was re-signed in 1935 and although vying with Dick Spence for a place in the side, he went on to give the club useful service until the outbreak of WW2. He drew up a sound record as a professional footballer, amassing 150 senior appearances for his three major League clubs while also gaining one full cap for Scotland v. Czechoslovakia in 1938. Tall and slim, good on the ball, he scored 14 goals in 42 wartime games for the Blues.

BUCHANAN, ROBERT

Full-back: 3 apps

Born: Bellshill, Lanark, 1888 – *Died*: 1970

Career: Bellshill, Leyton (1910), CHELSEA (May 1911), Southend United (June 1913); did not play after WW1

A reserve at Stamford Bridge for two seasons, Bob Buchanan deputised for Walter Bettridge in his three senior outings.

BUMSTEAD, JOHN

Midfield: 377+31 apps, 44 goals

Born: Rotherhithe, London, 27 November 1958

Career: CHELSEA (schoolboy forms, 1972; trainee, April 1975; professional, November 1976), Charlton Athletic (free transfer, July 1991–May 1993)

Twice a Second Division championship winner with Chelsea (1984 and 1988), John Bumstead also gained winner's medals in the Full Members' Cup of 1988 and the Zenith Data Systems Cup two years later before moving to Charlton after spending some 19 years at Stamford Bridge. Very competitive and hard-working, he could also fill in as a defender and an occasional attacker. He packed a powerful right-foot shot and played a major role in Chelsea's two promotion-winning sides. Bumstead was a free-kick specialist.

BURGESS, HENRY

Inside-/centre-forward: 155 apps, 37 goals

Born: Alderley Edge, Cheshire, 20 August 1904 – *Died*: 1968

Career: Alderley Edge FC (1919), Nantwich Ramblers (1922), Stockport County (May 1925), Sandbach Ramblers (loan, briefly in 1926), Sheffield Wednesday (1929), CHELSEA (March 1935); guest for Brentford, Fulham, Reading and Southampton (season 1939–40), Stockport County (1940–41); Brighton and Hove Albion (1941–42); retired in May 1942 through injury

A long-striding, stocky and forceful player, Harry Burgess scored with clockwork regularity. Clever in dribbling and possessing a strong shot in both feet, he joined Chelsea at the age of 30 having already drawn up a fine record of 156 goals in 363 first-class appearances for Stockport and Wednesday, whom he helped win the First Division championship and FA Charity Shield in 1930. He also gained four full caps for England as a Wednesday player (between October 1930 and May 1931) scoring four goals, two apiece against Ireland (on his debut) and Belgium. Recommended to Chelsea chief Leslie Knighton by Owls' manager Bob Brown, he was a vital cog in the Blues' forward-line for five seasons leading up to WW2. During the hostilities he continued to find the net and announced his retirement at the age of 36.

BURLEY, CRAIG WILLIAM

Midfield/right wing-back: 108+33 apps, 11 goals
Born: Irvine, Scotland, 24 September 1971
Career: CHELSEA (junior/trainee, April 1987; professional, September 1989), Celtic (£2.5 million, July 1997), Derby County (£3 million, December 1999), Dundee (September 2003), Preston North End (January 2004), Walsall (March 2004; retired May 2004)

During his Chelsea days, Craig Burley was a powerful, hard-working midfield player with a terrific engine and strong right-foot shot. He was a regular performer in the side for four seasons from 1993 and after leaving Stamford Bridge netted 25 goals in 93 outings for Celtic. He helped the Bhoys win the League Cup in 1997 and the Premier League title the following season when he was also voted Scotland's Player of the Year.

After a very good spell with Derby County, he underwent a cartilage operation and was then severely handicapped with an Achilles problem. He battled on bravely with Dundee, Preston (recruited by his former Scottish manager Craig Brown) and Walsall before retiring in 2004. The recipient of 45 senior and 7 Under-21 Scottish caps, Burley also represented his country as a schoolboy and youth team player.

BUSH, ROBERT JAMES

Wing-half: 4 apps, 1 goal
Born: West Ham, London, August 1879 – *Died*: London, 1950
Career: Britannia FC (East Ham), West Ham United (1904), CHELSEA (July 1906–May 1907)

A reserve team player during his one season at Stamford Bridge, all of Bob Bush's senior appearances were made in succession: November–December 1906.

BUTLER, DENNIS MICHAEL

Full-back: 18 apps
Born: Fulham, London, 7 March 1943
Career: Surrey Schools, CHELSEA (amateur, July 1958; professional, May 1960), Hull City (£10,000, June 1963), Reading (£8,000, December 1969; released, May 1974); Margate (part-time professional, 1974–76); later ran his own painting and decorating business in Tilehurst, Berkshire

A mobile, stocky, bow-legged defender, Dennis Butler had Ken Shellito and Eddie McCreadie to contend with for a place in Chelsea's first team. He battled on gamely, had his best season in 1961–62 (16 games) and then made a name for himself as Andy Davidson's partner at Hull. He appeared in 259 first-class matches for the Tigers and gained a Third Division championship medal in 1966. He then added another 195 senior appearances to his tally during his 5-year association with Reading. His son, Stephen, joined Reading as an apprentice, but his career was curtailed through injury.

BUTLER, GEOFFREY

Full-back: 8+1 apps

Born: Middlesbrough, 26 September 1946

Career: Middlesbrough (apprentice, June 1962; professional, May 1964), CHELSEA (£57,000, September 1967), Sunderland (£65,000, January 1968), Norwich City (October 1968), Baltimore Comets/NASL (loan, May–August 1974), Bournemouth (March 1976), Peterborough United (non-contract, August–October 1981), Salisbury City (team manager and also head of commercial department, 1981–88)

Geoff Butler's stay with Chelsea was restricted to just four months. He made a solid start but failed to settle at Stamford Bridge. After leaving he made almost 200 appearances for Norwich and over 125 for Bournemouth. He played in a total of 378 League games during his career. His first success as a manager came in 1985–86 when he guided Salisbury from the Beazer Homes League into the Southern League Premier Division.

BYRNE, MICHAEL PATRICK THOMAS GERALD

Goalkeeper: 5 apps

Born: Bristol, March 1880 – *Died*: Bristol, 1955

Career: Bristol Rovers (August 1902), Southampton (July 1903), CHELSEA (August 1905; contract cancelled, September 1906), Glossop (May 1907; retired May 1909); later worked for the Imperial Tobacco Company, Bristol

A popular Irishman, fearless and reliable, deputy to Billy Foulke, Mick Byrne began the 1905-06 season as Chelsea's first-choice goalkeeper. However, he dislocated his shoulder, lost his place and never played for the first team again. He was a soldier in the Irish Grenadier Guards for four years: 1898–1902.

CALDERHEAD, DAVID

Centre-half: 43 apps, 1 goal

Born: Dumfries, Scotland, 19 June 1886 – *Died*: 1958

Career: Dumfries Primrose, Maxwelltown Volunteers, Lincoln City (briefly, 1906–07), CHELSEA (September 1907), Motherwell (April 1914); guest for Leicester Fosse (WW1); Clapton Orient (August–November 1919), Lincoln City (secretary–manager, April 1921–May 1924)

The son of the former Chelsea manager of the same name, Dave Calderhead was not half as successful as his father but nevertheless at one time he looked all set to become the Blues' regular centre-half after impressing during the 1910–11 season. However, the arrival of Andy Ormston and Tom Logan restricted his outings to just 27 during the next three campaigns and he eventually moved to Motherwell. Like so many other footballers, his career was disrupted by WW1 and after the hostilities he played only one game for Orient.

CAMERON, DAVID FRANKLIN
Full-back/wing-half: 81 apps, 2 goals
Born: Partick, Scotland, 25 June 1902 – *Died*: Scotland, 1978
Career: Cameron Highlanders (from July 1917), Akeld FC (Scotland), Queen's Park (amateur, August 1918), CHELSEA (June 1920), Helensburgh (December 1926), Heart of Midlothian (August 1927), Dunfermline Athletic (briefly), Nottingham Forest (August 1928), Colwyn Bay (May 1930–April 1931)

A well-built, commanding defender and highly rated north of the border, David Cameron suffered early injury problems at Chelsea and made only 26 League appearances in his first two seasons. He recovered his fitness and had a decent 1922–23 campaign but thereafter found it difficult to hold down a place in the first team and eventually returned to Scotland. He was only 15 years of age when he went to war with the Highlanders. In 1919 a reporter had declared: 'There is no better defender in Scotland than the wily Cameron.'

CAMERON, JOHN
Full-back: 194 apps
Born: Kirkwoodin, Lanarkshire, 1880 – *Died*: 1945
Career: Kirkwood Thistle, St Mirren, Blackburn Rovers (April 1904), CHELSEA (October 1907), Port Vale (July 1913–May 1914); rejoined Port Vale (August 1916; appointed player–manager, August 1918; sacked as manager, January 1919; retired as player May 1919)

A Scottish international (capped v. Ireland), Jock Cameron also represented the Scottish League on three occasions before joining Blackburn. He added a second cap to his collection with Chelsea, lining up against England in 1909.

A well-proportioned, capable and confident defender, renowned for his fine positional play and fierce tackling, he had his critics at Ewood Park but silenced them with some solid and effective performances. One of the finest full-backs in Chelsea's history, he was a permanent fixture at Stamford Bridge for five seasons, partnering Walter Bettridge most of the time. Indeed, they were thought to be the best pairing in the Football League during that period.

CAMPBELL, ROBERT INGLIS
Outside-right: 213 apps, 40 goals
Born: Glasgow, 28 June 1922
Career: Glasgow Perthshire (1939), Falkirk (August 1941); guest for Queens Park Rangers (WW2); CHELSEA (£9,000, May 1947), Reading (August 1954; later player–coach at Elm Park; retired March 1961); Dumbarton (manager, April 1961), Bristol Rovers (coach, trainer and chief scout, May 1962; in office for 15 years; appointed manager November 1977; sacked December 1979; then chief scout again to September 1980), Gloucester City (manager, November 1980); later worked for Bristol City Council as a football coach to unemployed men

Bobby Campbell, an excellent footballer, fast and direct, could play anywhere in the front line but preferred the right-wing berth. He made plenty of goals for his colleagues and popped in a few himself, averaging one every five games for Chelsea. Capped five times by his country, the last three as a Chelsea player (1950), he certainly lost some of his best years to the war, but on his day was one of the best around, a typical Scottish winger, full of vim and vigour. He bought and sold well as a manager of Bristol Rovers before his surprise sacking.

CANOVILLE, PAUL KENNETH
Forward: 67+36 apps, 15 goals
Born: Hillingdon, 4 March 1962
Career: Hillingdon Borough (1979), CHELSEA (December 1981), Reading (£50,000, August 1986–May 1987), Northwood and Egam FC (1987–88), Erich FC (1988–89)

Paul Canoville was the first black player to appear at first-team level for Chelsea, making his League debut as a substitute against Crystal Palace in April 1982. Well built, he usually preferred to play down the flanks. He was quick over the ground, had good ball control and scored some spectacular goals for the Blues. However, he proved to be inconsistent and this limited his outings in the senior side. After a proposed move to Brentford had fallen through at the eleventh hour, he left Stamford Bridge for Reading but had only one season at Elm Park. Late in his career Canoville attracted media attention when he was involved in a court case for a drugs problem.

CARR, JOHN JAMES
Full-back: 1 app.
Born: Gateshead, June 1909 – Deceased by 2002
Career: Gateshead Council School, Crawcrook Albion (County Durham), CHELSEA (October 1928), Crawcrook Albion (March 1931), Chester (July 1931), Gateshead (May 1932–May 1934)

Lightweight defender Jack Carr, 5 ft 9 in. tall, was a regular performer in Chelsea's reserve side during his time at Stamford Bridge, deputising for Tommy Law against West Bromwich Albion in April 1929 for his only senior outing. He later played in 54 League games for his home-town club Gateshead.

CARTER, ROBERT
Centre-/wing-half: 18 apps
Born: Bolton, September 1911 – Deceased by 2000
Career: Army football (from 1925), CHELSEA (September 1929), Plymouth Argyle (April 1933), Watford (May 1934)

After an impressive debut against Leicester City in April 1931, Bob Carter played in 16 League games the following season before reverting back to reserve team football following the emergence of Allan Craig and the presence of Peter O'Dowd. He didn't make much of an impact with either Plymouth or Watford.

CARTWRIGHT, WILLIAM

Full-back: 46 apps

Born: Burton upon Trent, Staffordshire, 24 June 1884 – *Died*: Essex, 1956

Career: Gainsborough Trinity (July 1906), CHELSEA (May 1908), Tottenham Hotspur (June 1913), Swansea Town (May 1919), Southend United (coach, August 1920–30)

Except for one season (1909–10), full-back Bill Cartwright played most of his football in Chelsea's second XI during his five years at Stamford Bridge. He made only 15 first-class appearances for Spurs before WW1 intervened. He served Southend exceedingly well for a number of years and was rewarded with a testimonial.

CARVALHO, RICARDO

Defender: 36+3 apps, 1 goal

Born: Amarante, Portugal, 18 May 1978

Career: Amarante FC/Portugal, Leca/Portugal (1994), Vitoria Setubal/Portugal (professional, 1995), Alvera/Portugal (on loan, during season 1995–96), FC Porto/Portugal (professional, August 1996), CHELSEA (£19.85 million, July 2004)

Portuguese international Ricardo Carvalho, having helped his country reach the final of Euro 2004 and subsequently voted the competition's best defender, quickly adapted himself to English conditions and started his first Premiership match in the 1–0 win at Birmingham in Chelsea's second game. With William Gallas also vying to partner John Terry at the heart of the defence, he had to work hard to earn his place in the side. A solid performer, strong in all aspects of defensive play, he turned down Real Madrid in favour of Chelsea and is now an established member of the Portuguese national squad. Along with his current Chelsea colleague Paulo Ferreira, he was a Champions League winner with FC Porto (under José Mourinho) in 2004 and gained both League Cup and Premiership winner's medals with Chelsea in 2005.

CASCARINO, ANTHONY GUY

Striker: 43+2 apps, 8 goals

Born: St Paul's Cray, London, 1 September 1962

Career: Orpington Schools, Crockenhill FC (Kent), Gillingham (professional, January 1982), Millwall (June 1987), Aston Villa (£1.5m, March 1990), Celtic (July 1991), CHELSEA (£1.1m, February 1992), Olympique Marseilles/France (July 1993), FC Nancy/France (1996), Red Star/France (season 1999–2000); worked for TalkSport Radio, now a newspaper columnist

Tony Cascarino, a strong, aggressive striker, did very well with his first senior club, Gillingham, scoring 78 goals in 219 League appearances. He continued to find the net for Millwall, claiming almost 50 goals in 128 outings and in almost two years at Villa Park he averaged roughly a goal every four matches before moving to Celtic. He returned to England with Chelsea seven months later and played in 23 and 22 games respectively in his two seasons at the Bridge. Thereafter he spent seven years playing in France. He gained a then record 88 full caps for the Republic of Ireland (19 goals) . . . overtaking another ex-Aston Villa star, Paul McGrath, who won 83.

CASEY, LEONARD

Wing-half: 37 apps
Born: Hackney, London, 24 May 1931
Career: Leyton (amateur, from 1949), CHELSEA (professional, February 1954), Plymouth Argyle (£12,000 plus Wally Bellett, December 1958; retired May 1961)

An FA Amateur Cup winner with Leyton at Wembley in 1952, Len Casey was one of several quality amateur footballers recruited by Chelsea manager Ted Drake in the early to mid-1950s. He found it tough to adapt to the professional game and although he spent quite some time at the Bridge he was never classed as a first-team regular, having his best season in 1957–58 (24 games). He was appointed captain of Argyle on his arrival at Home Park and won a Third Division championship medal in his first season. He lost his place when Johnny Newman arrived in 1960 and retired a year later.

CASIRAGHI, PIERLUIGI

Striker: 10 apps, 3 goals
Born: Monza, Italy, 4 March 1969
Career: FC Monza/Italy (1987), Juventus/Italy (1990), SC Lazio/Italy (1993), CHELSEA (£5.4 million, July 1998; released May 2000), later with AS Roma/Italy (from 2001)

Almost immediately after helping Lazio win the European Super Cup, Italian international Pierluigi Casiraghi joined Chelsea for a club record fee, teaming up with his fellow countrymen Gianfranco Zola, Roberto Di Matteo and Gianluca Vialli (qq.v.). Strong and muscular, he replaced his own personal hero Mark Hughes in the Blues' front line, but unfortunately he suffered a nasty knee injury in his tenth Premiership game, at West Ham, and missed the rest of the season. Prior to his move to Chelsea, he was a national hero after scoring the winning goal for Italy against Russia that earned his country a place in the 1998 World Cup finals. However, he was surprisingly omitted from the final 22-man squad by boss Cesare Maldini, as was Chelsea's Zola. Prior to moving to Chelsea Casiraghi had found the net 89 times in 332 Serie 'A' and 'B' games, including 41 in 140 for Lazio with whom he won the Italian League title. He scored 12 goals in 44 full internationals for Italy. In November 1999, Casiraghi underwent his eighth knee operation and it was another six months before he started to play again.

CASTLE, SIDNEY ERNEST ROWLAND

Outside-right: 32 apps, 2 goals

Born: Basingstoke, Hampshire, 12 March 1892 – *Died*: Basingstoke, 21 January 1978

Career: Basingstoke Town, Thorneycrofts FC; guest for Crystal Palace and Reading during WW1; Guildford City (August 1919), Tottenham Hotspur (March 1920), Charlton Athletic (May 1921), CHELSEA (May 1923), Guildford United (June 1926; retired 1928); in the 1950s ran a works' canteen in his native Basingstoke

A winger who could operate on both flanks, Sid Castle never really made an impression with any of his clubs, having his best spell with Charlton for whom he scored 10 goals in 71 games. He was 28 years of age when he made his League debut for Spurs.

CECH, PETR

Goalkeeper: 48 apps

Born: Prague, Czechoslovakia, 20 May 1982

Career: Sparta Prague/Czech Republic (amateur, July 1999; professional, August 2001), Rennes/France (August 2002), CHELSEA (£7 million, July 2004)

Czech Republic international Petr Cech, 6 ft 5 in. tall, took over from the Italian Carlo Cudicini in the Chelsea goal and had a quite brilliant first season in the Premiership, conceding only 13 goals in 35 games and keeping 24 clean sheets. He also created footballing history by not conceding a Premiership goal for 1,024 minutes (from 12 December 2004 to 5 March 2005), having previously set a Czech record with Sparta Prague of remaining unbeaten for over 1,000 minutes, 913 (over 10 matches) in the League alone. A brilliant shot-stopper, safe in the air, he commands his area splendidly and has been capped by the Czech Republic at both Under-21 and senior levels. He played a major part in Sparta Prague's League championship triumph of 2001 when one of his team-mates was current Chelsea star Jiri Jarosik and was delighted to play his part in Chelsea's League Cup and Premiership-winning sides of 2004–05. One of the best goalkeepers anywhere in the world, Cech is currently on a five-year contract at Stamford Bridge.

CHARVET, LAURENT JEAN

Right wing-back: 7+6 apps, 2 goals

Born: Beziers, France, 8 May 1973

Career: Cannes/France (1992; League debut, 1994), CHELSEA (on loan, January–May 1998), Newcastle United (£750,000, July 1998), Manchester City (£1 million, October 2000), Sochaux/France (October 2002)

Also a competent centre-half, Laurent Charvet was certainly a useful asset to Chelsea's squad at the end of the 1997–98 season. Fast, aggressive and good in the air, he top-scored for Cannes before joining the Blues for whom he made his debut in the first leg of the League Cup semi-final against Arsenal at Highbury.

He later figured in Chelsea's European Cup-Winners' Cup semi-final against Vicenza and was an unused substitute in the final v. VfB Stuttgart – some sort of record for a loan signing. He scored 19 goals in 99 League games for Cannes, played in 53 senior games for Newcastle but struggled to hold down a first-team place at Maine Road.

CHEYNE, ALEXANDER GEORGE
Inside-forward: 69 apps, 13 goals
Born: Glasgow, 28 April 1907 – *Died*: Scotland, 5 August 1983
Career: Glasgow Churches League football, Shettleston Juniors/Glasgow (1923), Aberdeen (professional, December 1925), CHELSEA (£6,000, June 1930), Nîmes/France (May 1932), CHELSEA (March 1934), Chelmsford City (player–coach, 1936; retired as a player 1939); briefly associated with Colchester United; Arbroath (manager, May 1949–May 1955)
A versatile footballer, able to play in virtually every front-line position, Alex Cheyne was one of the first British players to join a French League club when he moved from Stamford Bridge to Nîmes in 1932. Good on the ball with a neat and tidy right foot, Cheyne possessed a cunning bodyswerve and was a master at the in-swinging corner delivered to perfection from the left. He scored the winning goal for Scotland against England at Hampden Park in 1929 direct from one of his measured flag-kicks. He won a total of five full caps for his country and also represented the Scottish League. He scored 55 goals in 138 appearances for Aberdeen.

CHITTY, WILFRED SIDNEY
Winger/full-back: 46 apps, 16 goals
Born: Walton-on-Thames, Surrey, 10 July 1912 – *Died*: Berkshire, 1997
Career: Woking (August 1928), CHELSEA (March 1930), Plymouth Argyle (December 1938), Reading (August 1939; retired May 1948)
A loyal servant to Chelsea, Wilf Chitty spent most of his 8 years at Stamford Bridge playing for the reserves, having his best spell in the first team in 1937–38 when he made 20 League and Cup appearances. A versatile footballer, able to play as an orthodox right-back or attacking winger, he played in 187 Regional League and Cup games for Reading during WW2.

CHIVERS, GARY PAUL STEPHEN
Defender: 143+5 apps, 4 goals
Born: Stockwell Green, London, 15 May 1960
Career: CHELSEA (schoolboy forms, 1975; apprentice, May 1976; professional, July 1978), Swansea City (August 1983), Queens Park Rangers (February 1984), Watford (September 1987), Brighton and Hove Albion (March 1988), Lyn Oslo/Norway (loan, July 1993), Bournemouth (non-contract, November 1993–May 1994)
During an excellent professional career that spanned 16 years, the hugely

talented Gary Chivers appeared in 465 League games in English football. He made his debut in the competition for Chelsea against Middlesbrough nine months after turning pro and was virtually a regular in the side (injuries permitting) for four seasons until his departure to Swansea.

CLARE, JAMES EDWARD
Midfield: 0+1 app.
Born: Islington, London, 6 November 1959
Career: CHELSEA (apprentice, May 1976; professional, November 1977), Charlton Athletic (August 1981–April 1982)
After graduating through the junior ranks at Stamford Bridge, lightweight midfielder Jim Clare was handed his senior debut as a substitute in a 3–2 win at Bolton in October 1980 – his only outing in League football.

CLARKE, STEPHEN
Defender: 407+14 apps, 10 goals
Born: Saltcoats, Strathclyde, 29 August 1963
Career: Beith Juniors (1978), St Mirren (professional, August 1980), CHELSEA (January 1987; retired October 1998; later assistant manager/coach)
A Scottish international at youth, Under-21 (eight caps), 'B' (three caps) and senior levels (six caps – four as a Chelsea player), Steve Clarke also represented the Football League against the Rest of the World in 1987. He served the Blues superbly well for 11 years, having appeared in over 150 League games for St Mirren. He played under seven different managers during his time at Stamford Bridge and skippered the side just prior to his retirement. At the time he was only the eighth player in the club's history to top 400 League appearances. He played in three winning Cup finals – FA Cup of 1997 and both the League Cup and European Cup-Winners' Cup of 1998. He also helped Chelsea win the Second Division championship in 1989. A model professional, Clarke had speed, recovered quickly, was strong and reliable in the tackle and was always there to assist and give assurance to the younger players in the side.

CLEMENT, NEIL
Left wing-back: 1+3 apps
Born: Reading, 3 October 1978
Career: Aston Villa (School of Excellence, July 1994), CHELSEA (apprentice, April 1995; professional, October 1995), Reading (on loan, November–December 1998), Preston North End (on loan, March–April 1999), Brentford (on loan, November–December 1999), West Bromwich Albion (on loan, March 2000; signed for £150,000, August 2000)
Neil Clement gained England schoolboy and youth recognition as a teenager while also making steady progress with Chelsea. After loan spells with Reading, Preston North End and Brentford he was signed on the same basis by West

Bromwich Albion manager Gary Megson who then signed him permanently five months later. With a superb left foot, Clement gained a huge reputation with his free kicks and penalties at The Hawthorns and has now made over 200 appearances for the Midlands club. Named in the PFA's Division One team for season 2001–02 when the Baggies gained promotion to the Premiership, he was also a key member of the side that returned to top-flight status two years later. Neil's father, Dave Clement, played for QPR, Bolton Wanderers, Fulham, Wimbledon and England (five caps).

CLISS, DAVID
Inside-forward: 24 apps, 1 goal
Born: Enfield, Middlesex, 15 November 1939
Career: Enfield Boys, CHELSEA (amateur, April 1955; professional, November 1956), Guildford City (July 1962–65)
A clever footballer with excellent ball skills, England Youth international David Cliss's career with Chelsea was cut short after he suffered a broken leg at the start of the 1960–61 campaign. He never regained his true form and moved into non-League football at the age of 22.

COADY, JOHN
Left-back/defender: 10+9 apps, 3 goals
Born: Dublin, 25 May 1960
Career: Shamrock Rovers (1980), CHELSEA (£25,000, December 1986; released May 1988)
An ex-postman, John Coady played in the European Cup with Shamrock Rovers before joining Chelsea for whom he scored on his debut in the London derby against Queens Park Rangers. Preferring the left-back position, he could also play at centre-half. Unfortunately he found it hard going to get into the first team at Stamford Bridge and was released by the club at the end of the 1987–88 season.

COCK, JOHN GILBERT
Centre-forward: 110 apps, 53 goals
Born: Hayle, Cornwall, 14 November 1893 – *Died*: Kensington, London, 19 April 1966
Career: West Kensington United (1908), Forest Gate (April 1910), Old Kingstonian, (December 1912), Brentford (amateur, March 1914), Huddersfield Town (April 1914); Army service (1915–18); CHELSEA (£2,500, October 1919), Everton (January 1923), Plymouth Argyle (March 1925), Millwall (November 1927), Folkestone (July 1931), Walton FC/Surrey (October 1932), Millwall (manager, November 1944–August 1948); then a licensee in New Cross, London
Perfectly proportioned, physical and dangerous, Jack Cock was a fine athlete, fast with good skills, able to shoot with both feet and a fine header of the ball.

He scored a goal every two games for Chelsea before joining Everton. Capped twice by England in 1919–20, he scored on his debut against Ireland and netted again in a 5–4 win over Scotland at Sheffield. He also played in one Victory international (1919) and represented the Football League (1920). A classy dresser, he was often seen walking the street clad in sophisticated attire – and in 1930, when registered with Millwall, he was signed up by a London company to star in a major film. Two years earlier he helped the Lions gain promotion as Third Division (S) champions and then in 1945, as manager, led them to runners-up in the Third Division (S) Cup. Cock – reported killed in action during WW1 – was later awarded the Military Medal. Born into a family of 10, one of his brothers, Don, played for Brentford, Fulham, Arsenal, Notts County, Wolves and Clapton Orient, and scored over 100 goals in almost 250 League games (1919–28). Another brother, Herbert, played for Brentford (1920).

COLE, CARLTON MICHAEL

Striker: 5+14 apps, 7 goals
Born: Croydon, Surrey, 12 November 1983
Career: CHELSEA (trainee, April 1999; professional, November 2000), Wolverhampton Wanderers (loan, November 2002–January 2003), Charlton Athletic (loan, August 2003–May 2004), Aston Villa (loan, August 2004–May 2005)

An England Youth and Under-21 international, Carlton Cole, 6 ft 3 in. tall and weighing 13 st. 4 lb, is decidedly quick for such a big man. He possesses strength and aggression and packs a powerful shot in his right foot. Unable to gain a regular place in Chelsea's first XI, he did well during his season at The Valley, scoring 5 goals in 22 games for Charlton, and followed up with 3 goals in 30 Premiership outings for Aston Villa.

COLE, JOSEPH JOHN

Midfield: 59+37 apps, 10 goals
Born: Islington, London, 8 November 1981
Career: West Ham United (trainee, April 1997; professional, December 1998), CHELSEA (£6.6 million, August 2003)

After representing England at schoolboy and youth team levels, Joe Cole went on to gain eight Under-21 caps before establishing himself in the senior squad under coach Sven-Goran Eriksson; he had over 20 full caps to his name in 2005. An FA Youth Cup winner with West Ham in 1999, he scored 13 goals in 150 appearances for the Hammers but when they were relegated from the Premiership, Cole stayed in the top flight by joining Chelsea. He has produced some excellent performances for the Blues, although during his first season at the Bridge he spent half of his time on the subs' bench. He gained both League Cup and Premiership winner's medals in 2005.

COLGAN, NICHOLAS

Goalkeeper: 1 app.

Born: Drogheda, Ireland, 19 September 1973

Career: CHELSEA (trainee, April 1990; professional, October 1992), Crewe Alexandra (loan, 1993), Grimsby Town (loan, 1994), Millwall (loan, 1995), Brentford (loan, October–November 1997), Reading (loan, February–March 1998), AFC Bournemouth (free transfer, July 1998), Hibernian (free, July 1999), Stockport County (loan, August–October 2003); he was out of contract at Hibernian in May 2004

Capped by the Republic of Ireland at schoolboy and youth team levels, Nick Colgan has since gained one 'B', nine Under-21 and eight senior caps for his country. He made his solitary Premiership appearance for Chelsea against West Ham United in March 1997 when Dmitri Kharine, Frode Grodas and Kevin Hitchcock were all out injured. He remained a registered player at Stamford Bridge for eight years before moving to Bournemouth. He later appeared in 147 senior games for Hibs.

COLLINS, RONALD MICHAEL

Goalkeeper: 1 app.

Born: Redcar, Yorkshire, 8 June 1933

Career: Redcar Albion (1949), CHELSEA (part-time professional, November 1951), Watford (July 1957–May 1959)

An efficient goalkeeper, good on his line, Mick Collins spent six years at Stamford Bridge during which time he acted as reserve to Harry Medhurst, Charlie Thomson and Bill Robertson. He made only one League appearance – deputising for the injured Thomson in the 3–3 draw at Middlesbrough in March 1954. He played in 50 senior games for Watford.

COMPTON, JOHN FREDERICK

Wing-half: 12 apps

Born: Poplar, London, 27 August 1937

Career: CHELSEA (professional, February 1955), Ipswich Town (July 1960), Bournemouth and Boscombe Athletic (June 1964–April 1965)

Unable to establish himself in Chelsea's first team owing to the form of Derek Saunders and Len Casey, John Compton moved on and was subsequently converted into a full-back by Alf Ramsey at Ipswich. He went on to appear in 131 League and Cup games for the Portman Road club, helping them win the Second Division title in his first season and then collecting a League championship medal in 1961–62 when he missed only three games as full-back partner to Larry Carberry.

COOKE, CHARLES
Midfield/winger: 360+13 apps, 30 goals
Born: St Monans, Fife, 14 October 1942
Career: Port Glasgow (1957), Renfrew Juniors (August 1958), Aberdeen (October 1959), Dundee (£44,000, December 1964), CHELSEA (£72,500, April 1966), Crystal Palace (£85,000, September 1972), CHELSEA (£17,000, January 1974), Los Angeles Aztecs/NASL (briefly, 1978), Memphis Rogues/NASL, (player–coach, 1979), California Surf/NASL (player–coach, 1980; retired as a player, 1981; continued coaching for two more years); now lives in Cincinatti, USA where he runs a successful soccer school

A wonderfully consistent and talented footballer with tremendous adhesive ball control and dribbling skills, Charlie Cooke played as a direct, old-fashioned winger and also as a hard-working, creative midfielder. He loved to run with the ball and would twist and wind his way past defenders with great aplomb. A wonderful entertainer wherever he played, he set up chances galore for his team-mates both north and south of the border and during a fine career amassed around 600 senior appearances at club and international levels. Capped 16 times by Scotland between 1966 and 1975 (14 as a Chelsea player), he also represented the Scottish League on 4 occasions and appeared in 4 Under-21 matches. A member of the Blues' beaten 1967 FA Cup final side, Cooke was a star performer when the silver pot was lifted at Leeds' expense three years later. He returned to Wembley for a third time with the Blues in 1972, but again finished up on the losing side as Stoke City carried off the League Cup. In between times, in 1971, Cooke helped Chelsea win the European Cup-Winners' Cup. His transfer from Aberdeen to Dundee in 1964 was, at that time, a record between two Scottish League clubs. He netted 30 goals in 165 appearances for the Dons.

COPELAND, DAVID CAMPBELL
Inside-/centre-forward: 26 apps, 9 goals
Born: Ayr, Scotland, 2 April 1875 – *Died*: Erdington, Birmingham, 16 November 1931
Career: Ayr Parkhouse (1892), Walsall (October 1893), Bedminster (June 1898), Tottenham Hotspur (May 1899), CHELSEA (May 1905), Glossop (September 1907–May 1908); later worked at the Rose and Crown Hotel in Erdington, Birmingham, and he was still in that employment when he collapsed and died of heart failure when chopping wood at his home nearby

An FA Cup winner with Spurs in 1901, David Copeland netted 110 goals in 303 first-team games for the White Hart Lane club before he and John Kirwan moved together to Stamford Bridge, being among Chelsea's first major signings. Initially a winger, Copeland, with a distinctive drooping moustache, developed into a classy goal-scoring forward and was always a handful for defenders. He played in Chelsea's first-ever League fixture against Stockport County in

September 1905 and was appointed captain at the start of the next campaign, but unfortunately he suffered a broken leg during the game at Burslem in November and never played for the Blues again. Surprisingly, Copeland never won a full cap for Scotland; the nearest he got was to appear in an international trial for the Anglo-Scots against the Home Scots in 1903. A Spurs supporter all his life, after retiring Copeland used to meet up with the travelling party whenever they were in and around the Birmingham area and regularly sat on the bench to assist the Spurs trainer.

COPELAND, JAMES LESLIE

Centre-forward: 2 apps, 1 goal
Born: Chorlton-cum-Hardy, Manchester, 1 October 1909 – Deceased by 2000
Career: Manchester United (March 1929), Park Royal (September 1931), CHELSEA (May 1932), Halifax Town (May 1937–May 1939)

Centre-forward Jackie Copeland (who was released by Manchester United without playing a first-team game), spent five years at Stamford Bridge. During that time he scored over 60 goals in reserve team football, finding it nigh on impossible to oust three of the game's finest strikers - Joe Bambrick, Hugh Gallacher and George Mills. His two League appearances for the Blues came in September 1933 when he scored on his debut in a 4–1 defeat at Sheffield United, and in December 1934 in a 2–0 reverse at Manchester City.

CORTHINE, PETER ALAN

Winger: 2 apps
Born: Highbury, London, 19 July 1937
Career: Leytonstone (amateur, August 1954), Army football, CHELSEA (professional, December 1957), Southend United (March 1960–May 1962), Chelmsford City (seasons 1962–64)

Signed as cover for Peter Brabrook, Peter Corthine never really got a chance at Chelsea but after leaving Stamford Bridge he scored 21 goals in 73 League games for Southend.

COURT, COLIN RAYMOND

Winger: 1 app.
Born: Ebbw Vale, 3 September 1937
Career: CHELSEA (juniors, April 1953; professional, September 1954), Torquay United (May 1959), Weymouth (August 1960)

A Welsh schoolboy international, Colin Court – a reserve at Stamford Bridge for five years – made only one senior appearance for Chelsea, lining up on the right-wing against the Copenhagen club, Frem, in the Fairs Cup in September 1958, when he deputised for Peter Brabrook in a 3–1 win.

CRAIG, ALLAN

Centre-half: 211 apps
Born: Paisley, Scotland, 7 February 1904 – Deceased by 1997
Career: Celtic Victoria (1919), Paisley Juniors (briefly, 1923), Motherwell (April 1924), CHELSEA (January 1933–May 1939); did not play after WW2

Described as being a 'tall, elegant, graceful and stylish defender, strong in the air', Allan Craig's ball distribution was also first class. A very consistent performer, he was the backbone of the Chelsea defence for seven years, skippering the side for several seasons and being utterly reliable throughout. He missed only 6 Scottish League games out of a possible 266 between 1925 and 1932. He was capped three times by his country – lining up against Holland and Norway in 1929 and England in 1932. He also made two appearances for the Scottish League and was a beaten Cup finalist and League championship winner with Motherwell in 1931 and 1932 respectively. Some reference books list this player's Christian name as Alan.

CRAIGIE, JAMES CHARLES MELBOURNE

Half-back: 2 apps
Born: Dundee, 1882 – *Died*: Scotland, 1950
Career: Dundee Harp (January 1903), CHELSEA (August 1905), Glossop (May 1910), Fulham (season 1911–12)

Reserve half-back Jim Craigie spent three seasons at Stamford Bridge during which time he starred in two FA Cup ties, the first against the First Grenadiers (won 6–1) and the second against Crystal Palace, in October and November 1905 respectively. He appeared in 32 League games for Glossop but failed to make the first team at Fulham. Some reference books state that this player served only with Glossop and Fulham.

CRAWFORD, JOHN FORSYTH

Winger: 308 apps, 27 goals
Born: Jarrow, Tyneside, 26 September 1896 – *Died*: Essex, 1975
Career: Palmer's Works (Jarrow), South Shields (trial), Jarrow Celtic; Naval Service (WW1); Hull City (March 1920), CHELSEA (£3,000, May 1923), Queens Park Rangers (May 1934; retired May 1937 to become QPR's first-team coach to 1939); later worked for the Ford motor company at Dagenham, Essex, where he remained until 1961; he was also part-time coach of Maldon Town for three seasons: 1945–48

An England international, capped against Scotland in March 1931, Jack Crawford spent over a decade in the first-class game. Initially a right-winger, he switched to the left to accommodate Alex Jackson and produced some brilliant displays for Chelsea in an all-international attack (the other three players being Hughie Gallacher, Alex Cheyne and Andy Wilson). A diminutive player, full of tricks, Crawford could centre the ball with great precision when racing down the flank at full speed, and he was also a specialist when it came to taking corner-kicks.

CRESPO, HERNAN JORGE
Striker: 21+10 apps, 12 goals
Born: Florida, Uruguay, 6 July 1975
Career: River Plate/Argentina (April 1993), Parma/Italy (August 1996), SC Lazio/Italy (for an Italian record fee of £37.5 million, July 2000), Inter Milan (£20 million, August 2002), CHELSEA (£16.8 million, August 2003), AC Milan/Italy, (season loan, August 2004–May 2005)

Top scorer in Serie 'A' in 2000–01 with 26 goals, Hernan Crespo was already an established and proven marksman with well over 150 club and international goals under his belt in fewer than 350 matches when he joined Chelsea for a huge fee in 2003. The Argentinian striker, with 46 caps to his credit, had featured in the Champions League with each of his three Italian clubs and he did likewise for the Blues. After starting his Stamford Bridge career off very well (scoring twice at Molineux and again at Highbury), calf and groin strains and illness ruined the second half of the season although he did play in the semi-final of the Champions League against Monaco. A threat inside and outside of the box, Crespo shoots with both feet, is good in the air and makes it difficult for defenders with his intelligent off-the-ball running. He was loaned out to AC Milan by new Chelsea boss José Mourinho for the 2004–05 season – thus having the distinction of playing for both Milan clubs in Serie 'A'. He helped River Plate win the Argentinian Professional League in 1994 and Parma lift the Italian Cup in 1999. He also gained two Serie 'A' runner's-up medals. He scored twice to no avail as Milan lost to Liverpool in the final of the 2005 Champions League. It is understood that Crespo earned £89,000 a week at Chelsea.

CRITTENDEN, NICHOLAS JOHN
Midfield: 1+2 apps
Born: Bracknell, Berkshire, 11 November 1978
Career: CHELSEA (trainee, April 1996; professional, July 1997), Plymouth Argyle (loan, October 1998), Yeovil Town (free transfer, August 2000), Aldershot (July 2004)

Perhaps out of his depth at Stamford Bridge (owing to the enormous midfield talent at the club), Nick Crittenden came good with Yeovil whom he helped win the GM Conference and gain entry to the Football League in 2003 when he scored 9 goals in 35 games. He also won the FA Trophy with the Glovers at Villa Park in 2002 and has one England semi-professional cap to his name.

CROAL, JAMES ANDERSON
Inside-forward: 130 apps, 26 goals
Born: Glasgow, 27 July 1885 – *Died*: South Petherton, Somerset, 16 September 1939
Career: Falkirk junior football, Glasgow Rangers (professional, April 1904); on loan to Ayr Parkhouse, Alloa Athletic and Dunfermline Athletic (between

1905 and 1909); Falkirk (November 1910), CHELSEA (£2,000, April 1914), Fulham (March 1922; retired May 1924)

Capped three times by Scotland (against Ireland 1913 and England and Wales 1914), Jimmy Croal also made three appearances for the Scottish League and won the Scottish Cup with Falkirk in 1913 before moving to Stamford Bridge. Two years later he played in the FA Cup final. A schoolmaster by profession and easily picked out on the field due to his bald head, he was a slightly built, bustling forward with an abundance of trickiness in both feet. A much-admired partnership with the Hamilton Academical star Bobby McNeil in a 1913–14 Inter-League game was successfully renewed at Chelsea where he became a huge favourite with the fans. A regular in the side before, during and after WW1, he appeared in almost 100 Regional games and scored over 30 goals for the Blues between 1915 and 1919.

CROWTHER, STANLEY

Wing-half: 58 apps

Born: Bilston, Staffordshire, 3 September 1935

Career: Stonefield Secondary Modern School, West Bromwich Albion (amateur, May 1950), Erdington Albion (briefly), Bilston Town (August 1952), Aston Villa (£750, August 1955), Manchester United (£18,000, February 1958), CHELSEA (£10,000, December 1958), Brighton and Hove Albion (March 1961), Solihull Town (October 1961), Rugby Town (December 1961), Hednesford Town (July 1963), Rushall Olympic (September 1965; retired May 1967); became a senior foreman for Armitage Shanks, Wolverhampton

Stan Crowther joined Manchester United in one of the most dramatic transfers in the game's history! One and a quarter hours after signing for the Reds he stepped out in front of almost 60,000 fans at Old Trafford for an FA Cup tie against Sheffield Wednesday in the aftermath of the Munich air crash . . . having earlier assisted Aston Villa against Stoke City in the same competition. He went to Wembley that year where United lost 2–0 to Bolton in the final. Twelve months earlier he had been an FA Cup winner with Villa, 2–1 over Manchester United. Crowther, who made over 60 appearances for Villa, was acquired as a stop-gap by United and after just 20 outings for the Reds moved to Chelsea where he had two useful seasons before ending his career with Brighton. Orphaned at the age of 15, Crowther gained three England Under-23 caps and represented the Football League as a Villa player.

CUDICINI, CARLO

Goalkeeper: 167+3 apps

Born: Milan, Italy, 6 September 1973

Career: In Italy with AC Milan (professional, September 1991), Como (September 1993), AC Milan (August 1994), Prato (August 1995), SC Lazio (July 1996), Castel di Sangro (August 1997); CHELSEA (£160,000, August 1999)

Prior to joining Chelsea, Carlo Cudicini had appeared in almost 100 League and Cup games in Italian football, having his best spells with Prato and Castel di Sangro. He made only one Premiership appearance in his first season at Stamford Bridge before eventually claiming the number one spot in 2001 from Ed De Goey. He became a class act and played superbly well for three years before losing his place in 2004 to new signing Petr Cech. He conceded only one goal in 14 hours and 24 minutes of top-class football during October and November 2003 and did not concede a goal at all in five volatile away Champions League matches in that same season, producing a quite brilliant display against his former club Lazio. Towards the end of the 2003–04 campaign he missed 11 matches with a broken finger and when he returned he saved a Ruud van Nistelrooy penalty to earn Chelsea a point at Old Trafford which secured the runner's-up spot in the Premiership. An FA Cup and Charity Shield winner with Chelsea in 2000, he was called into the Italy squad in 2003–04 at the age of 30.

CUNDY, JASON VICTOR

Defender: 56+1 apps, 1 goal
Born: Wimbledon, 12 November 1969
Career: CHELSEA (trainee, April 1986; professional, August 1988), Tottenham Hotspur (loan, March–May 1992; signed for £750,000, June 1992), Crystal Palace (loan, December 1995–January 1996), Bristol City (loan, August–September 1996), Ipswich Town (£200,000, October 1996), Portsmouth (free transfer, July 1999; retired, injured knee, December 2000); CHELSEA (academy coach); also media work

An England Under-21 international, capped three times, Jason Cundy bided his time at Stamford Bridge and although never a regular in the first team he gave the Blues useful service, having his best season in 1990–91 when he partnered Ken Monkou at the heart of the defence. He had made well over 170 appearances at senior level before announcing his retirement at the age of 31.

DALE, GEORGE HENRY

Inside-forward: 52 apps, 1 goal
Born: Nottingham, 2 May 1883 – *Died*: London, *circa* 1945
Career: Newark Town, Millwall Athletic, Notts County (May 1914), Queens Park Rangers (WW1 guest), CHELSEA (May 1919; retired May 1922)

A smart dribbler, able to go inside and outside his opponent, George Dale had an excellent first season at Stamford Bridge, making 39 appearances and scoring his only goal – alas to no avail – in a 5–2 defeat at Villa Park on Christmas Day. His finishing (lack of goal-scoring) undoubtedly went against him and after two seasons spent mainly in the reserves he quit the game and went into business in London.

DALLA BONA, SAMUELLE
Forward/midfield: 51+22 apps, 6 goals
Born: San Dona di Piave, Italy, 6 February 1981
Career: Atalanta/Italy (amateur, April 1996; professional, February 1998), CHELSEA (in a double deal with Gianluca Picassi, October 1998), AC Milan/Italy (July 2002), Lecce/Italy (August 2004)

Sam Dalla Bona was only 17 years of age when he joined Chelsea, having not played in a competitive game. His move (with Gianluca Picassi) to Stamford Bridge shook Italian football. He had to wait until April 2000 before making his Premiership debut at Sheffield Wednesday and he scored his first Chelsea goal in a 2–1 defeat at Everton seven months later. Unable to hold down a place in the first team, he returned to his homeland and immediately established himself in Milan's team that went on to win the Italian Cup in 2003.

D'ARCY, SEAMUS DONAL
Inside-forward: 31 apps, 14 goals
Born: Newry, County Down, Northern Ireland, 14 December 1921 – *Died*: Northwick Park Hospital, 22 February 1985
Career: Waterford (1938), Limerick (August 1943–May 1946), Ballymena (1947), Charlton Athletic (£5,000, February 1948), CHELSEA (£10,000, October 1951), Brentford (part-exchange for Ron Greenwood, October 1952; retired, injured, January 1954); later Charlton Athletic Development Association liaison officer (March–November 1955); worked as a quality control inspector in Sudbury until his death

Paddy D'Arcy made only 16 first-team appearances during his three and a half years at The Valley but he did score 80 goals in 112 reserve-team games. After moving to Chelsea he finished joint top scorer (12 goals) with Roy Bentley in his first season (1951–52). That was to prove his best campaign as a League player. Capped by Northern Ireland on five occasions, twice with Chelsea and three times with Brentford, he severely damaged his right ankle in a friendly game in Montreal while on tour with the Irish FA party to Canada and the USA in the summer of 1953. He never recovered full fitness and was forced to retire at the age of 32. Later he lived in Sudbury and worked as a machine operator for a glass manufacturing company.

DAVIDSON, ALEXANDER MORRISON
Winger: 2 apps
Born: Langholm, near Lockerbie, Dumfries, 6 June 1920
Career: Bankshill FC/Scotland, Hibernian (1938), CHELSEA (August 1946), Crystal Palace (August 1948–May 1949)

Fair-haired Alex Davidson spent virtually all of his time at Stamford Bridge playing in Chelsea's reserve side. He made just two League appearances, lining up at outside-left against Derby County in November 1946 and on the right-wing at Everton in April 1947. He played in ten first-class games for Palace.

DAVIES, GORDON JOHN

Forward: 13+2 apps, 6 goals

Born: Merthyr Tydfil, 3 August 1955

Career: Manchester City (apprentice, April 1972), Merthyr Tydfil (1974), Fulham (£5,000, March 1978), CHELSEA (£90,000, November 1984), Manchester City (£70,000, October 1985), Fulham (£50,000, November 1986), Wrexham (free transfer, August 1991–February 1992); later lived in Leighton Buzzard and worked as a pest control officer for Rentokil

Capped by Wales at schoolboy level, Gordon Davies went on to star in 16 full internationals for his country, the first 14 as a Fulham player (1980–85). Initially training to become a geography teacher, he was released by Manchester City as a teenager and went back home to develop his game in the Southern League with Merthyr while also working as a physical education instructor. He finally made his senior debut for Fulham at the age of 22 and went on to become one of the Cottagers' most prolific marksmen, scoring 126 goals in 289 games before transferring to Chelsea. Nicknamed 'Ivor the Engine' by his team-mates due to his non-stop efforts on the field of play, Davies spent less than a year at Stamford Bridge. He failed to oust Kerry Dixon or David Speedie from either of the two main striking positions . . . despite him netting a hat-trick against Everton in a League game at Goodison Park.

After a decent spell with his first club Manchester City (14 goals in 42 starts), he returned to Fulham and although plagued by injury, upped his tally of goals for the club to 136 and his appearance tally to 313. He is currently lying in fourth position in Fulham's all-time scoring charts behind Johnny Haynes' 157, Bedford Jezzard's 154 and Jim Hammond's 150. He ended his career with 160 goals to his credit in close on 400 League and Cup outings. A keen golfer and squash player, Davies was granted a well-deserved testimonial in 1991 when Fulham played a Welsh XI at the Cottage.

DE GOEY, EDUARD FRANCISCUS

Goalkeeper: 178+1 apps

Born: Gouda, Holland, 20 December 1966

Career: FC Gouda/Holland, Sparta Rotterdam/Holland (April 1984), Feyenoord/Holland (July 1990), CHELSEA (£2.25 million, July 1997), Stoke City (free transfer, August 2003)

Giant goalkeeper Ed De Goey – 6 ft 6 in. in height who once tipped the scales at 15 st. – represented Holland in 17 Under-21 and 31 full internationals, reaching the peak of his form in the late 1990s. He made 145 League appearances for Sparta and 201 for Feyenoord before embarking on a career in the Premiership. Commanding in the box and a fine shot-stopper, he was first choice at Stamford Bridge for virtually three seasons until losing his place to the Italian Carlo Cudicini in 2000, having made 179 outings for the Blues. He won the League Cup, European Cup-Winners' Cup and Super Cup (all in 1998) and was successful in the FA Cup and Charity Shield two years later. However, after almost two years of non-activity – and with new signing Petr Cech recruited by José Mourinho – he moved down the League ladder to Stoke at the age of 33.

DE LUCAS, ENRIQUE (QUIQUE)

Midfield: 21+10 apps, 1 goal

Born: Hospitalalet, Lobregat, Spain, 17 August 1978

Career: Espanyol/Spain (junior, April 1995; professional, August 1996), Paris St Germain/France (loan, April–May 2002), CHELSEA (July 2002), Deportivo Alaves (October 2003)

Owing to the financial meltdown of the European transfer market, Spanish Under-21 international midfielder Quique was Chelsea's only acquisition during the summer of 2002. An aggressive performer with a strong shot, he was highly rated in his home country and was signed initially on a four-year deal by manager Claudio Ranieri, having established himself as one of the hottest properties in Spain's La Liga. Although not a regular starter in the side, he was employed mainly on the right side of the park and had a decent enough first season at Stamford Bridge, scoring his only goal against Viking Stavanger in the UEFA Cup. Unfortunately he was not included at all at the start of the 2003–04 campaign and eventually moved back to Spain. Prior to joining Chelsea, De Lucas had scored 42 goals in 160 League games in Spain.

DEMPSEY, JOHN

Defender: 200+7 apps, 7 goals

Born: Hampstead, London, 15 March 1946

Career: Fulham (apprentice, October 1962; professional, March 1964), CHELSEA (£70,000 plus Barry Lloyd, January 1969), Philadelphia Fury/NASL (March 1976); later manager of Maidenhead United and then Edgware Town; after retiring from football he worked in a special school for handicapped children in north London

A strong, commanding centre-half, a pillar of strength at the heart of the Chelsea defence during the late 1960s and early '70s, John Dempsey – known as 'Mr Reliable' – was a strong header of the ball and possessed a timely tackle. He formed a fine partnership in the Blues' back division for many years with David Webb. He also scored a vital goal in the replay of the European Cup-Winners' Cup final against Real Madrid in Athens in 1971 when Chelsea claimed their first European prize, to go with the FA Cup they won the previous season when Dempsey again played a vital role. He also earned a League Cup runner's-up tankard in 1972. The recipient of 13 full caps for the Republic of Ireland (winning his first as a Fulham player), prior to joining Chelsea, Dempsey made 171 appearances for the Cottagers and in 1965–66 had a brief spell at centre-forward . . . not his favourite position!

DE OLIVEIRA, FELIPE VILACA

Midfield: 0+8 apps
Born: Braga, Portugal, 27 May 1984
Career: FC Porto/Portugal (amateur, June 2000; professional, May 2001), CHELSEA (£140,000, September 2001; released May 2003)

A creative right-sided midfielder, Felipe de Oliveira, a Portuguese youth international, had to work on his game during his first season at Stamford Bridge. He then did well on Chelsea's pre-season tour in 2002 and went on to appear in five senior games that season, all as a substitute. He looked to have a bright future ahead of him but failed to make the necessary headway required by manager Claudio Ranieri and was subsequently released.

DESAILLY, MARCEL

Defender: 209+3 apps, 7goals
Born: Accra, Ghana, 7 September 1968
Career: Nantes/France (professional, September 1986), Olympique Marseilles/France (August 1992), AC Milan/Italy (December 1993), CHELSEA (£4.6 million, July 1998–May 2004); played in Qatar (season 2004–05)

One of the star performers in France's World Cup and European Championship-winning sides of 1998 and 2000, Marcel Desailly went on to win 116 full caps for his country (3 goals scored) having earlier collected honours at Under-21 and 'B' team levels. He is now Chelsea's most-capped player (67). A magnificent defender with a commanding presence, he was widely recognised as one of the world's best in his position in 2000 and was aptly nicknamed 'The Rock'. With speed, aggression, enormous willpower, efficiency, stamina and total commitment, he even tried his luck in midfield and indeed would turn out in any position just to be part of the team. He had a spell as Chelsea's skipper and was certainly a great player in his prime. With well over 400 competitive appearances under his belt in France and Italy before joining Chelsea, in 2004 he reached the personal milestone of 500 appearances in top-flight League football (153 in the Premiership).

He was the first player to win the European Champions Cup with two different clubs – Marseilles (v. AC Milan) in 1993 and AC Milan (v. Barcelona) in 1994. He also won the European Super Cup with Milan in 1994 and collected two Serie 'A' championship medals with the same club in 1994 and 1996 and in between times was a Champions Cup runner-up (v. Ajax) in 1995. He had the misfortune to get sent off in the second-half of the 1998 World Cup final against Brazil, but two years later he made up for that with a double success as France won Euro 2000 and Chelsea lifted the FA Cup – and he also helped the Blues win the Charity Shield. His transfer to Italy was prompted by the financial collapse of Marseilles following revelations that the club had been deeply involved in match-fixing.

DESCHAMPS, DIDIER

Midfield: 44+3 apps, 1 goal

Born: Bayonne, France, 15 October 1968

Career: Bayonne FC/France (April 1983), Nantes/France (junior, October 1983; professional, October 1986), Olympique Marseilles/France (1989), Bordeaux/France (briefly, 1993), Olympique Marseilles (late 1993), Juventus/Italy (July 1994), CHELSEA (£3 million, July 1999); Valencia/Spain (July 2000; retired 2001); later manager of AS Monaco/France

French international central midfield player Didier Deschamps – who was described in derogatory terms by fellow countryman Eric Cantona as a 'water carrier' – joined Chelsea to boost the club's European Champions League prospects. The first Frenchman to win 100 caps for his country (finishing with 101 to his name), he helped his country win both the World Cup and European Championship in 1998 and 2000 respectively, captaining the side that beat Brazil 3–0 in Paris and Italy 2–1 in Rotterdam in those two finals, playing alongside Marcel Desailly.

Prior to moving to Stamford Bridge, he won two French League titles with Marseilles in 1990 and 1992, and then helped Juventus win Italy's Serie 'A' three times in five years: 1995, 1997 and 1998. He was twice a European Cup final winner, skippering Marseilles to victory in 1993 (with Desailly in the team) and starring for Juventus in 1998 when future Chelsea star Gianluca Vialli was captain. He was also an Italian Cup winner and UEFA Cup runner-up with Juventus in 1995. As manager, he guided Monaco to the 2004 Champions League final (beaten by FC Porto) after knocking out his former club Chelsea in the semi-final. Certainly a 'big match' player, Deschamps controlled the centre of the field superbly and during a wonderful playing career amassed well over 500 senior appearances in League, Cup and international competitions. He actually made his League debut for Nantes in August 1986, aged 17. As manager, he took Monaco to the Champions League final in 2004, where they were beaten by José Mourinho's FC Porto.

DI MATTEO, ROBERTO

Midfield: 155+20 apps, 26 goals

Born: Berne, Switzerland, 29 May 1970

Career: FC Schaffhausen/Switzerland (junior, 1986; professional, May 1988), FC Zurich/Switzerland (August 1991), FC Aarau/Switzerland (July 1992), SC Lazio/Italy (August 1993), CHELSEA (£4.9 million, July 1996; retired, injured, February 2002)

Born in Switzerland of Italian parents, Robbie (or Didi) Di Matteo was already an established Italian international and scorer of 9 goals in 116 Swiss League games and 7 in 88 Serie 'A' encounters before joining Chelsea for a club record fee of almost £5 million. A dynamic midfielder, he went on to give the Blues excellent service until a badly broken left leg, suffered in a first round, second leg UEFA Cup encounter against the Swiss side St Gallen in September 2000, eventually ended his career.

He had endured a roller-coaster ride during the year 2000, battling his way back into first-team contention after suffering a serious ankle injury and a broken arm. He then went on to score the winning goal in the last FA Cup final at Wembley (v. Aston Villa in 2000) and played brilliantly in the Charity Shield victory over Manchester United. Switzerland's Player of the Year in 1993 (when he helped FC Aarau win their first post-WW2 League championship), he created a record by scoring the fastest goal in a Wembley FA Cup final after just 43 seconds' play in Chelsea's 2–0 win over Middlesbrough in 1997 – a feat that also earned him the Man of the Match award. He also found the net for the Blues in the League Cup final, also v. Middlesbrough, a year later. Di Matteo went on to gain a total of 34 full caps for Italy. Chelsea won six major trophies during the time Di Matteo was at the club – the FA Cup twice, in 1997 and 2000, the League Cup, European Cup-Winners' Cup and Super Cup in 1998 and Charity Shield, also in 2000.

DICKENS, ALAN WILLIAM
Midfield: 46+9 apps, 4 goals
Born: Plaistow, London, 3 September 1964
Career: West Ham United (apprentice, April 1981; professional, August 1982), CHELSEA (£650,000, August 1989), West Bromwich Albion (loan, December 1992–January 1993), Brentford (February 1993), Colchester United (September 1993–May 1994), Chesham Town (August 1994), Hayes (briefly), Collier Row FC (1995), Billericay Town (August 1996), Purfleet FC (August 1997–May 1998); later employed as a London taxi driver
An England Youth and Under-21 international midfielder, Alan Dickens scored 30 goals in 234 appearances for West Ham during his 8 years at Upton Park. He struggled off and on at Stamford Bridge and after a loan spell at The Hawthorns, he wound down his senior career with moderate spells at Brentford and Colchester.

DICKIE, MURDOCK MCFARLANE
Outside-right: 1 app.
Born: Dumbarton, 28 December 1919 – Deceased by 2000
Career: Scottish junior football, Crewe Alexandra (professional, May 1937), Port Vale (May 1939; contract cancelled, December 1939), Walsall (guest, April 1943), Port Vale (October 1944), Guildford City (February 1945), CHELSEA (April 1945), Bournemouth (February 1947–May 1948)
WW2 affected Murdock Dickie's career considerably and he was 25 years of age when he joined Chelsea for whom he played in just one senior game – against Liverpool at Anfield in September 1946 when the Merseysiders won a thrilling First Division encounter 7–4 in front of almost 50,000 spectators. He also appeared in 3 League South games in 1945–46 and scored twice in 16 League outings for Bournemouth.

DICKIE, WILLIAM CUNNINGHAM

Half-back: 40 apps

Born: Kilmarnock, 2 May 1893 – *Died*: Sittingbourne, Kent, 15 January 1960

Career: Riccarton FC (1909), Kilbirnie Ladeside (1910), Kilmarnock (professional, May 1912); guest for CHELSEA (April 1917–April 1919), Everton, Southport and Wrexham during WW1; CHELSEA (signed for £500, June 1919), Stoke (£2,000, April 1921), Sittingbourne (May 1922), Sheppey United (season 1923–24), Sittingbourne (coach, seasons 1924–26)

A block cutter by trade, and a sergeant instructor during WW1, Bill Dickie was a tall, fair-haired, wholehearted Scottish defender whose best position was centre-half. As a guest player for Chelsea, he gained a London Victory Cup winner's medal in April 1919 when Fulham were defeated 3–0 in the final. Unfortunately he could not hold down a first-team place at any of his three major clubs.

DICKS, ALAN VICTOR

Wing-half: 38 apps, 1 goal

Born: Kensington, London, 29 August 1934

Career: Kensington Secondary School, London Schools, Dulwich Hamlet, Rainham Town (1949), Millwall (amateur, 1950), CHELSEA (amateur, April 1951; professional, September 1951), Southend United (£12,000, combined with Les Stubbs, November 1958), Coventry City (February; retired as a player May 1962; then assistant manager/coach/scout to May 1967), Bristol City (manager, October 1967–September 1980), Ethnikos/Greece (coach, season 1982–83), worked for the BBC (1983), Limassol/Cyprus (coach, 1984), then appointments in coaching in Qatar (for three years), Cyprus and USA (to February 1990); Fulham (assistant manager, April 1990; manager from June 1990 to November 1991)

An average wing-half at Stamford Bridge where he had to fight to get first-team action with the likes of Ken Armstrong, Stan Wicks and Derek Saunders, Alan Dicks nevertheless gave Chelsea seven years service before going on to make 85 League appearances for Southend. Having gained an FA coaching badge by the time he was 23, he was forced to retire early through injury after failing to make Coventry's first team. He did however, go on to serve the Sky Blues for five years, working alongside Jimmy Hill and seeing the Highfield Road club gain promotion to the First Division (1967). After that he bossed Bristol City for almost 13 years, a great achievement. At Ashton Gate, he introduced a youth policy, recruited some experienced international footballers, including Peter Cormack, Norman Hunter, Joe Royle and Terry Cooper, and in 1976 got the Robins into the First Division after an absence of 65 years. He survived a few scares of the 'sack', came through several relegation-threatened campaigns and took City to the 1971 League Cup semi-final (beaten by Spurs). When City were eventually relegated from the top flight (after four years) he found it tough to readjust to a lower level of football and was subsequently dismissed. He was engaged at Fulham by his former boss Jimmy Hill who at the time was chairman at Craven Cottage. His brother Ronnie Dicks, mainly a full-back, spent 12 years as a professional with Middlesbrough, for whom he made 334 senior appearances between 1947 and 1959.

DICKSON, WILLIAM

Half-back: 119 apps, 4 goals
Born: Lurgan, County Armagh, Northern Ireland, 15 April 1923
Career: Sunnyside FC (Lurgan), Glenavon (amateur, July 1939), Notts County (professional, November 1945), CHELSEA (part-exchange for Tommy Lawton, November 1947), Arsenal (£15,000, October 1953), Mansfield Town (July 1956); Arsenal (scout, late 1950s)

A Northern Ireland international, capped 12 times between 1951 and 1955, Bill Dickson was a powerfully built attacking wing-half who could also fill in adequately as a central defender. He turned out to be a tremendous acquisition by manager Ted Drake – after three seasons of problems during which time he suffered a dislocated shoulder, went down with appendicitis, had a knee operation and was laid up with a slipped disc. He finally made his mark in the senior side in 1950 and appeared in well over 100 games in his last three campaigns at Stamford Bridge. His career at Highbury was also affected by injury and his career ended when he again damaged his shoulder at Mansfield. Dickson, who worked as a joiner before joining Glenavon, later worked as Arsenal's scout in Northern Ireland before re-entering the joinery trade.

DIGWEED, PERRY MICHAEL

Goalkeeper: 3 apps
Born: Westminster, London, 26 October 1959
Career: Fulham (apprentice, April 1976; professional, August 1977), Brighton and Hove Albion (£150,000, January 1981), West Bromwich Albion (loan, October 1983), Charlton Athletic (loan, January 1985), Newcastle United (loan, December 1987), CHELSEA (loan, February–May 1988), Wimbledon (free transfer, August 1993), Watford (free, December 1993–May 1994)

During his 16-year career, 6-ft goalkeeper Perry Digweed amassed 227 League appearances (179 with Brighton) and was recruited by Chelsea manager John Hollins as deputy to Roger Freestone in 1988. His three First Division outings for the Blues all ended in draws, including 3–3 and 4–4 scorelines at Coventry City and Oxford United respectively.

DIXON, KERRY MICHAEL

Striker: 414+7 apps, 191 goals
Born: Luton, 24 July 1961
Career: Chesham United (1976), Tottenham Hotspur (apprentice, 1977; professional, July 1978), Dunstable Town (1979), Reading (£20,000 initially,

July 1980), CHELSEA (£150,000, August 1983, plus another £25,000 later in 1983), Southampton (£575,000, July 1992), Luton Town (free transfer, February 1993), Millwall (£25,000, March 1995), Watford (£25,000, January 1996), Doncaster Rovers (free, player–manager, August 1996–May 1997); Boreham Wood (seasons 1997–99), Letchworth Town (manager, seasons 2000–02)

After making his name and gaining a reputation as a prolific marksman with Reading (51 goals in 126 games, including a fourtimer in a losing League encounter at Doncaster in 1982), Kerry Dixon joined Chelsea in 1983 and immediately became a huge favourite with the Stamford Bridge supporters. A well-built, strong and forceful athlete, able to withstand the toughest of challenges, he seemed to set goal-scoring records wherever he played and in his first season at Chelsea netted a total of 34 – the highest for 21 years. Twelve months later he weighed in with 36 goals, won England Under-21 recognition and was selected by the senior side to tour Mexico, going on to claim four goals in his first three full internationals – which meant that his former club, Reading, collected a further payment of £25,000. He was later a member of England's 1986 World Cup squad and took his total number of caps to eight. He scored 276 goals in 711 club games (including 231 in 593 League matches) spread over 16 years (1980–96). Only Bobby Tambling (164 League and 202 in total) has scored more goals for the Blues. Twice a Second Division championship winner (in 1984 and 1989), he also helped Chelsea win the FMC in 1990. He had a fairly traumatic time during his season as manager at Belle Vue, Doncaster just avoiding relegation to the Conference. After leaving Rovers he ran a pub while still playing non-League football for Boreham Wood in the Rymans Isthmian League.

DOCHERTY, JAMES
Inside-forward: 2+1 apps
Born: Broxburn, Scotland, 8 November 1956
Career: East Stirling (1975; professional, January 1976), CHELSEA (£50,000, February 1979), Dundee United (£2,000, November 1979–May 1980)
After doing well with East Stirling for whom he struck 30 goals in 55 League and Cup games, Jim Docherty failed to adjust to life in the Football League and after just three outings for the Blues returned to his homeland.

DOCHERTY, THOMAS HENDERSON
Wing-half: 4 apps
Born: Pershaw, Glasgow, 24 August 1928
Career: Schoolboy football in the Gorbals district of Glasgow, Shettleston Juniors; served in the Highland Light Infantry (playing for his regiment in Palestine); Celtic (professional, July 1948), Preston North End (£4,000, November 1949), Arsenal (£28,000, August 1958), CHELSEA (player–coach, February 1961; retired as player four months later and then

succeeded Ted Drake as manager, September 1961–October 1967), Rotherham United (manager, November 1967 to early November 1968), Queens Park Rangers (manager, November 1968), Aston Villa (manager, December 1968–January 1970), FC Porto (manager, February 1970–June 1971), Hull City (assistant manager, July–September 1971), Scotland (national team manager September 1971–December 1972), Manchester United (manager, December 1972–July 1977), Derby County (manager, September 1977–May 1979), Queens Park Rangers (May 1979–October 1980), Preston North End (manager, June–December 1981), Sydney Olympic/Australia (manager, June 1982), South Melbourne (manager, July–December 1982), Sydney Olympic (manager, January–July 1983), Wolverhampton Wanderers (manager, June 1984–July 1985), Altrincham (manager, October 1987–February 1988); this was his last appointment in the game and now he is employed as an after-dinner speaker, travelling all over the world talking about football and his eventful career

Tommy Docherty certainly had a varied career in football. One could fill a dozen pages of this book talking about his soccer life. He was capped 25 times by Scotland, represented his country in one 'B' international and appeared in more than 450 League and Cup games north and south of the border. He gained Second Division championship and FA Cup runner's-up medals with Preston North End in 1951 and 1954 respectively, lining up behind Tom Finney each season.

With his playing days almost over he joined Chelsea and after just four outings he retired and was appointed team manager, duly guiding them back into the First Division in 1963, followed by victory in the 1965 League Cup final and runner's-up spot in the FA Cup of 1967 (beaten by London rivals Spurs) . . . this after failing in two previous semi-finals at the same venue (Villa Park). He broke Chelsea's transfer record four times during his time in charge at Stamford Bridge – signing Graham Moore (£35,000), Derek Kevan (£45,000), Charlie Cooke (£72,500) and Tony Hateley (£100,000) in that order. He also sold many quality players, among them Terry Venables and George Graham. He once shocked the soccer world by sending home eight senior Chelsea players from their training-base in Blackpool for staying out too late at night! He was also fined £100 for making ungentlemanly remarks to a referee, saying afterwards that it was worth every penny. He also rebelled against the Chelsea directors over the allocation of FA Cup final tickets to players and later threatened to abandon a tour of Bermuda after striker Hateley had been sent off. He was suspended for 28 days for his outburst. He left Stamford Bridge in controversial circumstances in 1967 (he couldn't work with the club's new chairman, Charles Pratt junior, following the death of former chairman Joe Mears).

He dropped 9 of Rotherham United's regular first-team members and fielded the youngest side in the League, while selling 14 players for a total of just £70,000 during his brief reign as manager at Millmoor. He then quit QPR after just 29 days in charge, resenting the influence of chairman Jim Gregory. After that he saved Aston Villa from relegation to the Third Division and doubled the crowds but was then dismissed with the club struggling again at the foot of the Second Division.

He was in charge of Manchester United when they were relegated to the Second Division in 1974 but brought them straight back up and in 1976 saw them lose to Southampton in the FA Cup final, only to win the star prize at Liverpool's expense a year later.

When boss of FC Porto he narrowly missed out on winning the Portuguese League title and he certainly restored Scotland's pride on the international front. The 'Doc' once said: 'The ideal board of directors should be made up of three men, two dead and one dying.' He also passed these comments about Ray Wilkins when he was at Old Trafford: 'He can't run, he can't tackle and he can't head a ball. The only time he goes forward is to toss the coin.'

DODD, GEORGE FREDERICK
Inside-forward: 31 apps, 9 goals
Born: Whitchurch, Shropshire, 7 February 1885 – *Died*: 1960
Career: Whitchurch Council School, Wallasey Town (1903), Stockport County (May 1905), Workington (June 1907), Notts County (December 1907), CHELSEA (October 1911), Millwall (February 1913), Brighton and Hove Albion (December 1913), Darlington (guest, 1915–16), West Ham United (guest, November 1917), Luton Town (October 1919); Treherbert FC (August 1920), Charlton Athletic (August 1921, retired May 1922), Catford Southend FC (secretary–manager, July 1924–26)

George Dodd was the first player to score a League goal against Chelsea – doing so for Stockport County at Edgeley Park on 2 September 1905. He was a regular in the Notts County side (20 goals in 91 League games) before his move to Stamford Bridge and duly held his place in the first team for most of the 1911–12 season before being succeeded in the front-line by the legendary Corinthian, Vivian Woodward. Dodd made his debut for Charlton at the age of 36 – not having played a League game for 8 years.

DODDS, WILLIAM
Striker: 0+4 apps
Born: New Cumnock, Ayrshire, 5 February 1969
Career: CHELSEA (trainee, April 1985; professional May 1986), Partick Thistle (loan, September 1987–May 1988); Dundee (August 1989), Aberdeen (July 1994), Dundee United (September 1998), Glasgow Rangers (December 1999), Dundee United (December 2002)

Nippy and alert, Scottish-born Billy Dodds found it tough going at senior level at Stamford Bridge and although he did very well at intermediate level, scoring plenty of goals (27 in 30 starts), he made only 4 substitute appearances for the first XI. After a successful loan spell with Partick, for whom he netted 12 times in 35 outings, he went on to become a full international, gaining 26 caps between 1996 and 2002. He scored more than 200 goals in over 500 games in Scottish football, including 174 in 468 League games, having his best spells with Dundee and Aberdeen. He helped Rangers complete the League and Cup Double in 2000 and then added a League Cup winner's medal to his collection with the Gers two years later. Certainly a player who escaped from the Stamford Bridge net!

DOLBY, HUGH ROWLAND
Winger: 2 apps
Born: Agra, India, *circa* 1885 – *Died*: *circa* 1960
Career: Nunhead FC, CHELSEA (June 1909), Brentford (May 1912); did not feature after WW1
A reserve at Stamford Bridge for three seasons, Hugh Dolby battled hard and long without success to get regular first-team football owing to the form of Billy Brawn and Angus Douglas.

DOLDING, DESMOND LEONARD
Winger: 27 apps, 2 goals
Born: Kolar Gold Fields, India, 13 December, 1922 – *Died*: Wembley, Middlesex, 23 November 1954
Career: Oordegem/Belgium (junior football), Wealdstone, Queens Park Rangers (guest, September 1943), CHELSEA (July 1945), Norwich City (July 1948), Margate (May 1951); also a member of the Lord's cricket groundstaff
Len Dolding joined Chelsea after serving in the RAF during WW2. His chances were limited at Stamford Bridge owing to the presence of many other fine wingers including Bobby Campbell and John McInnes. He played one game for Middlesex in 1951. Dolding was tragically killed in a car crash on the way from a match.

DONAGHY, CHARLES
Inside-/outside-left: 3 apps, 1 goal
Born: Meerut, India, 1883 – *Died*: London, 1949
Career: Glasgow Rangers (May 1904), CHELSEA (professional, September 1905; contract cancelled, September 1908)
A member of Chelsea's first senior squad, Charlie Donaghy played most of his football in the second team. He scored his only first-team goal on his League debut against Clapton Orient in March 1906 (won 6–1), having earlier played in his first senior game against Crystal Palace in the 3rd qualifying round of the FA Cup.

DONAGHY, MALACHY MARTIN

Defender: 45+1 apps, 2 goals
Born: Belfast, 13 September 1957
Career: Post Office SC (Belfast), Cromac Albion, Larne Town (April 1978), Luton Town (£20,000, June 1978), Manchester United (£650,000, October 1988), Luton Town (loan, December 1989–January 1990), CHELSEA (£100,000, August 1992; retired, injured, May 1994)

Defender Mal Donaghy made 483 first-class appearances for Luton Town and 119 for Manchester United before joining Chelsea a month before his 35th birthday. A steady, reliable defender with exceptional positional sense and awareness, he represented County Antrim at Gaelic football and played once for Northern Ireland at Under-21 level before going on to appear in 91 full internationals for his country, the last 15 with Chelsea. He starred in both the 1982 and 1986 World Cup finals and later skippered Northern Ireland at the age of 37. He helped Luton win the Second Division title in 1982 and the League Cup in 1988 and then partnered Steve Bruce at the heart of the United defence before the arrival of Gary Pallister. He gained a winner's medal (as a non-playing sub) when United won the European Cup-Winners' Cup in 1991 and also won runner's-up and winner's prizes in the Charity Shield and Super Cup respectively (1990–91). In his two seasons at Stamford Bridge, he was initially a solid partner alongside Paul Elliott and afterwards David Lee. He suffered an injury at his former home, Old Trafford, in April 1993 from which he never fully recovered.

DONALD, ALEXANDER

Full-back: 24 apps
Born: Kirkintilloch, Scotland, 25 September 1900 – *Died*: *circa* 1975
Career: Kirkintilloch Harp (1917), Partick Thistle (1919), Indiana Flooring FC (1921), Heart of Midlothian (1924), New York Nationals/USA (1927), CHELSEA (July 1930), Bristol Rovers (July 1932), Dunfermline Athletic (May 1936); did not play after WW2

Alex Donald deputised for Scottish international Tommy Law during his two seasons at Stamford Bridge, making 12 League appearances during each campaign. He made 136 senior appearances for Bristol Rovers.

DONNELLAN, LEO JOHN

Midfield: no apps
Born: Willesden, London, 19 January 1965
Career: Brent Schools, CHELSEA (apprentice, April 1981; professional, August 1982), Leyton Orient (loan, December 1984–January 1985), Fulham (August 1985–May 1989)

Although he never played a first-team game for Chelsea, busy midfielder Leo Donnellan was capped once by the Republic of Ireland at Under-21 level (v. England in 1985) whilst at Stamford Bridge. He scored 4 goals in 79 League appearances for Fulham.

DORIGO, ANTHONY ROBERT

Left-back: 180 apps, 12 goals

Born: Melbourne, Australia, 31 December 1965

Career: Birmingham junior football, Aston Villa (apprentice, 1981; professional January 1982), CHELSEA (£475,000, July 1987), Leeds United (£300,000, May 1991), Torino/Italy (free transfer, June 1997), Derby County (free, October 1998), Stoke City (free, July 2000; retired May 2002); entered media work with TV companies, covering football matches in the English Premiership and Italy's Serie 'A'; also involved with property development in Portugal

Tony Dorigo has three different passports – Australian, Italian and British. An efficient and steady defender who enjoyed his sorties upfield, he won seven England Under-21 caps whilst with Aston Villa who gave him a trial after he had pestered the club to answer his letters! He made his League debut as a 'sub' on the last day of 1983–84 against Ipswich Town and gained a regular place in the side the following season. After joining Chelsea for a record fee, he skippered the England Under-21s and added four more intermediate caps to his tally. He also played 7 times for England 'B', made the first of 15 full international appearances and helped the Blues win both the Second Division title (1989) and the Full Members' Cup (1990), partnering initially Steve Clarke and then Gareth Hall. In fact, he scored one of the finest goals ever seen at Wembley – Chelsea's winner in that FMC encounter against Middlesbrough. In his spell with Leeds, Dorigo (nicknamed 'Aussie') gained both First Division championship and FA Charity Shield medals in 1992 and retired in 2002 with well over 650 senior appearances under his belt, including 30 in Italy's Serie 'A'.

DOUGLAS, ANGUS

Outside-right: 103 apps, 11 goals

Born: Lochmaben, Dumfries, 1 January 1889 – *Died*: South Gosforth, Newcastle upon Tyne, 14 December 1918

Career: Castlemilk FC, Dumfries (briefly), Lochmaben Rangers (1907), Glasgow Rangers (trial), CHELSEA (May 1908), Newcastle United (£1,100, November 1913, taking half of the fee in lieu of lost benefit)

Angus Douglas chose Chelsea ahead of Everton when moving south into the Football League. A nicely built winger with good speed and a wee bit of skill but perhaps not direct enough, he took quite some time to settle down at Stamford Bridge. After establishing himself in the first team in 1910, he became a huge favourite with the fans and went on to serve the club for five and a half years until his transfer to Newcastle, whom he helped gain promotion from the Second Division in 1912. The previous year he won his only cap for Scotland v. Ireland. Douglas fell victim of the national influenza epidemic and died of pneumonia shortly after returning from service in WW1. He was only 29.

DOW, ANDREW JAMES
Left-back: 17+1 apps
Born: Dundee, 7 February 1973
Career: Sporting Club '85, Dundee (professional, November 1990), CHELSEA (£250,000, July 1993), Bradford City (loan, October–November 1994); Hibernian (£125,000, January 1996)
A Scottish Under-21 international, capped three times, Andy Dow could also play in midfield and always chose to come out of defence with the ball rather than clearing it hopefully downfield. He became surplus to requirements at Stamford Bridge (following the arrival of Dan Petrescu and Terry Phelan) and moved to Hibs early in 1996.

DOWNING, SAMUEL
Wing-half: 144 apps, 10 goals
Born: Willesden Green, London, 19 January 1885 – *Died*: North London, 12 March 1974
Career: West Hampstead, Park Royal (briefly), Willesden Town, Queens Park Rangers (April 1903), CHELSEA (April 1909), Croydon Common (April 1914); did not play after WW1
Sam Downing, a key member of the Chelsea side for more than four years, was an exceptionally fine footballer; a ball artiste who was both constructive and competitive yet hardly ever committed a serious foul. Powerfully built, although not the fastest over the ground, he loved to attack from centre-field and packed a powerful shot in his right foot. One of the most popular players at Stamford Bridge, he skippered the side on many occasions. He was rewarded with a benefit match to mark his retirement from first-class soccer. He scored 23 goals in 190 appearances for QPR.

DRIVER, PHILIP ANTHONY
Winger: 25+21 apps, 4 goals
Born: Huddersfield, 10 August 1959
Career: Bedford Town (1975), Luton Town (trainee, 1977), Wimbledon (professional, December 1978), CHELSEA (£20,000, September 1980), Wimbledon (free transfer, July 1983), St Albans City (May 1985)
Phil Driver had good speed, neat skills and could cross a ball exceedingly well from a wide position but his career was hampered by injuries and unfortunately he never realised his full potential. He made 20 League appearances in his two spells with Wimbledon.

DROGBA, DIDIER
Striker: 30+11 apps, 16 goals
Born: Ivory Coast, 11 March 1978
Career: Levallois-Perret/France (amateur, April 1994), Paris St Germain/France (trialist), Le Mans/France (professional, August 1996), FC Guingcamp/

France (£100,000, July 2001), Olympique Marseilles/France (July 2002), CHELSEA (£24 million, July 2004)

Ivory Coast international striker Didier Drogba was earning £500 a week at the age of 23 with Le Mans when first spotted by José Mourinho. Unfortunately his price rocketed and was way out of FC Porto's range and as a result he moved to Marseilles. But when Mourinho took over at Chelsea, the big man was one of his first signings, arriving at Stamford Bridge just three months after playing for Marseilles in the UEFA Cup final. Voted the French Footballer of the Year in 2004, he scored 50 goals in almost 100 League games in France, 35 coming in 69 outings in his last 2 seasons, and he also netted 6 times more in the Champions League. Brought to replace Jimmy-Floyd Hasselbaink for £24 million, making him Britain's second-costliest striker behind Wayne Rooney, he made his debut in the Premiership on the opening day of the 2004–05 season against Manchester United at Stamford Bridge, partnering Mateja Kezman in attack. Three games later he scored his first goal in a 2–0 win at Crystal Palace. Big and strong, a fine header of the ball with good control, a key factor in Drogba's armoury is his sprinting. He made a gentle-paced start to his footballing career and actually commenced playing as a right-back. He was nominated by FIFA for World Player of the Year in 2004 and helped Chelsea win both the League Cup and the Premiership in 2005.

DROY, MICHAEL ROBERT

Defender: 302+11 apps, 19 goals
Born: Highbury, London, 7 May 1951
Career: Slough Town, CHELSEA (October 1970), Luton Town (loan, November–December 1984), Crystal Palace (free transfer, March 1985), Brentford (free, November 1986–May 1987); served Kingstonian (as player, coach and briefly as manager between 1987 and 1994); now lives in south London

At 6 ft 4 in. tall and 15 st. 2 lb in weight, Mickey Droy was one of the sturdiest defenders in the game in the 1970s and he certainly put his immense frame to good measure when performing at the heart of Chelsea's back-four. Unfortunately Droy's time at Stamford Bridge coincided with the Blues performing modestly for long periods out on the pitch and, in fact, they twice suffered relegation from the First Division in 1975 and 1979. At the same time he also played under eight different managers but never let the side down when called into action. For such a big man, he was very strong in the air and often displayed some neat touches on the ground, and when clearing his lines, he regularly got great distance using his trusty left foot. Droy, who was 36 when he quit top-class football, made a total of 342 League appearances during his 17 years in the game.

DUBERRY, MICHAEL WAYNE
Defender: 106+9 apps, 3 goals
Born: Enfield, Middlesex, 14 October 1975
Career: CHELSEA (trainee, April 1992; professional, June 1993), Bournemouth (loan, September–October 1995), Leeds United (£4 million, July 1999), Stoke City (loan, October 2004–January 2005)

After producing some exquisite displays in Chelsea's second and third teams, defender Michael Duberry became a regular in the first XI at Stamford Bridge in 1997 and continued to perform splendidly, earning himself three England Under-21 caps, later adding two more to his collection. Standing 6 ft 1 in. tall and weighing 13 st. 6 lb, he played alongside Frenchman Frank Leboeuf and Steve Clarke in the back four and made over 100 senior appearances for the Blues, gaining winner's medals in the League Cup, European Cup-Winners' Cup and Super Cup, all in 1998. He did well initially at Elland Road but then suffered a series of injuries prior to Leeds being relegated from the Premiership in 2004.

DUBLIN, KEITH BARRY LENNOX
Full-back: 66+2 apps
Born: High Wycombe, Buckinghamshire, 29 January 1966
Career: Watford (trainee, April 1982), CHELSEA (trainee, July 1982; professional, January 1984), Brighton and Hove Albion (£3,500, August 1987), Watford (£275,000, July 1990), Southend United (free transfer, July 1994), Colchester United (loan, November 1998), Canvey Island (loan, March–May 1999), Farnborough Town (June 1999)

An England Youth international, Keith Dublin signed professional forms for Chelsea just as West Ham United and Crystal Palace had started to show interest in him. A well-built, efficient full-back, quick over the ground with a good technique, he celebrated Second Division promotion with the Blues when making his debut in the last home game of the 1983–84 season against Barnsley (won 3–1). He spent five years at Stamford Bridge before going on to make 151 appearances for Brighton, 190 for Watford and 198 for Southend.

DUDLEY, SAMUEL MORTON
Outside-left: 1 app.
Born: Tipton, Staffordshire, 7 September 1905 – *Died*: *circa* 1970
Career: Dudley Park Council School, Tipton Excelsior, Preston North End (professional, April 1927), Bournemouth and Boscombe Athletic (season 1928–29), Coleraine (August 1929), Clapton Orient (March 1931), CHELSEA (June 1932), Exeter City (1934; retired May 1935)

Signed as cover for George Pearson and Wilf Chitty, Sam Dudley's only League outing for Chelsea was on the left-wing against Newcastle United (away) in February 1933. He also played at left-half and inside-left during his nomadic career.

DUFF, DAMIEN ANTHONY

Wide-midfield: 68+17 apps, 16 goals
Born: Dublin, 2 March 1979
Career: Lourdes Celtic/Ireland (1994), Blackburn Rovers (professional, March 1996), CHELSEA (£17 million, July 2003)

Signed for a then club record fee from Blackburn Rovers, Damien Duff seemed precisely the right player to replace Gianfranco Zola in Chelsea's midfield. Straightaway, with full-back Wayne Bridge (who was signed on the same day from Southampton) he formed a wonderful partnership down the left flank, interchanging and overlapping like they had played together all their lives. With his brilliant dribbling skills, Duff teases and torments defenders at will but he has suffered his fair share of injury problems, especially in 2004, the worst being a damaged shoulder which resulted in him missing half of Chelsea's games in his first season at Stamford Bridge. He came back strongly, however, in 2004–05 and played his part in helping the Blues win the Premiership title and League Cup.

At his best, a mesmerising dribbler, ubiquitous inspiration and superb crosser of the ball, Duff scored 35 goals in 223 games for Blackburn whom he helped win the League Cup in 2002. Now the recipient of more than 50 full caps for the Republic of Ireland, he has played in both the finals of the World Cup and European Championship and has also represented his country at schoolboy, youth, Under-20 and 'B' team levels.

DUFFY, BERNARD

Wing-half: 3 apps
Born: Burnbank, Lanarkshire, April 1902 – *Died*: Glasgow, 1970
Career: Bellshill Athletic (Glasgow), CHELSEA (June 1923), Clapton Orient (March 1927), Shelbourne/Ireland (August 1929)

Despite being a dependable member of Chelsea's second XI, Bernard Duffy failed to establish himself in the first team and was released after four seasons at Stamford Bridge. He made 74 appearances for Orient.

DUNN, JOHN ALFRED

Goalkeeper: 16 apps
Born: Barking, 21 June 1944
Career: Barking and Essex Schools, CHELSEA (schoolboy forms, June 1959; apprentice, June 1960; professional, February 1962), Torquay United (October 1966), Aston Villa (£8,000, January 1968), Charlton Athletic (free transfer, July 1971), Ramsgate (loan, December 1974), Tooting and Mitchum (player–coach, February 1975), Woking, Grays Athletic, Craven FC (Essex Business Houses League); then refereed in the Essex Business Houses and Sunday Corinthian Leagues (1986–90); now lives in Hornchurch, Essex

Competent and courageous, goalkeeper John Dunn understudied Peter Bonetti at Chelsea and therefore his first-team outings were limited. After leaving

Stamford Bridge he made 49 appearances for Torquay and then went on to star in 118 games for Aston Villa, playing in the 1971 League Cup final at Wembley after taking over from future Chelsea keeper John Phillips. Unfortunately Dunn became the target of a group of fans during his last season at Villa Park. He then replaced Charlie Wright at The Valley and, like at Villa, he also played in 118 games for Charlton. During his professional career he amassed almost 300 appearances, 262 in the Football League, and after that had over 100 outings in non-League soccer.

DURIE, GORDON SCOTT
Striker: 152 apps, 62 goals
Born: Paisley, Scotland, 6 December 1965
Career: Hill o' Beath FC, East Fife (professional, December 1983), Hibernian (October 1984), CHELSEA (£380,000, April 1986), Tottenham Hotspur (£2.2 million, August 1991), Glasgow Rangers (£1.2 million, November 1993–May 2000)

A fast, well-built and brave striker, Gordon Durie operated mainly through the middle, causing defenders all sorts of problems with his direct approach. He was a folk hero at Hibs (22 goals scored) before joining Chelsea for whom he made his debut in a humiliating 5–1 defeat at Watford in May 1986. Early on it was tough going at Stamford Bridge as the Blues struggled on the field, avoiding relegation to the Second Division by one place in 1988. He and the team did far better after that and he ended up with an exceptionally fine scoring record. In February 1989, when competing against Walsall (Division Two) he became only the fourth Chelsea player to score five goals in a League game, following in the footsteps of George Hilsdon, Jimmy Greaves and Bobby Tambling.

After leaving the Blues, Durie had the honour of scoring Spurs' first goal in the Premiership – in the 2–2 home draw with Crystal Palace in August 1992. His final tally for the White Hart Lane club was 17 (in 78 competitive games). He then helped Rangers win five League titles, two Scottish Cup finals and three League Cup finals, and all told netted 59 goals in 179 first-class matches for the Ibrox Park club. Capped 4 times at Under-21 level as a Chelsea player, he went on to represent Scotland in 43 full internationals (7 goals scored).

DYKE, CHARLES HUGH
Outside-right: 25 apps, 2 goals
Born: Caerphilly, South Wales, 23 September 1926
Career: Troedyrhiw FC (1945), CHELSEA (November 1947), Barry Town (September 1951–May 1954)

A ginger-haired right-winger, slight of build with a good attitude and positive approach, Charlie Dyke had to battle it out with Bobby Campbell for a place in Chelsea's forward line. He spent four years at Stamford Bridge, playing mainly in the reserves, before returning home to continue his football in South Wales. He made his First Division debut in a 3–0 defeat at Villa Park in February 1948 and scored his first goal two months later to earn a 1–0 win over Sheffield United.

EDWARDS, ROBERT HENRY

Inside-forward: 13 apps, 2 goals

Born: Guildford, Surrey, 22 May 1931

Career: Woking (1947), CHELSEA (professional, November 1951), Swindon Town (£2,000, July 1955), Norwich City (£3,000, December 1959), Northampton Town (March 1961), King's Lynn (June 1962), Boston United (August 1965; retired May 1967, aged 36)

Bob Edwards signed as a professional for Chelsea on demob from the Army with whom he had served for two years. A finely tuned footballer, he understudied John McNichol for almost four years during which time he made only 13 senior appearances, his debut coming on Boxing Day 1952 when he played at inside-right in the 1–1 draw at Stoke City. He went on to appear in almost 200 games for Swindon. His elder brother Les played for Bristol Rovers.

ELLIOTT, PAUL MARCELLUS

Defender: 54 apps, 3 goals

Born: Lewisham, London, 18 March 1964.

Career: Woodhill Primary and Blackheath Bluecoat Secondary schools (London); trials with Luton Town, Millwall and West Ham United (1979–80); Charlton Athletic (apprentice, July 1980; professional, March 1981), Luton Town (£95,000, March 1983), Aston Villa (£400,000, December 1985), Pisa/Italy (£400,000, July 1987), Celtic (£600,000, June 1989), CHELSEA (July 1991; retired, injured, May 1993); later a summariser on Channel 4, covering Italy's Serie 'A'

Paul Elliott was a well-proportioned centre-half who gained England Youth honours (1982) and England Under-21 caps (1985 and 1986). In 1990 he gained Scottish Cup and Skol Cup runner's-up medals with Celtic. After the disappointment of being rejected by three major clubs, he made 70 appearances for Charlton and 73 for Luton before joining Aston Villa. After a spell in Italy, he had 54 League outings with Chelsea (as partner to Ken Monkou) before suffering a bad injury in September 1992 when challenged by the Liverpool striker Dean Saunders. In May 1994, a High Court case began (Elliott v. Saunders) when it was suggested that Saunders had supposedly put in a dangerous tackle that effectively ended Elliott's playing career. The hearing lasted almost four weeks before Saunders was cleared of all charges, leaving Elliott facing legal costs of £500,000.

Elliott made a total of 382 appearances at club level.

ELLIOTT, SIDNEY DUNCAN
Inside- or centre-forward: 30 apps, 9 goals
Born: Sunderland, 3 March 1908 – *Died*: *circa* 1980
Career: Arcade Mission, Durham City (August 1924; professional, April 1925), Fulham (June 1927), CHELSEA (£3,000, May 1928), Bristol City (July 1930), Notts County (March 1932), Bradford City (June 1934), Rochdale (September 1935), FB Minter Sports (August 1936–May 1938); did not play after WW2

As a teenager, Sid Elliott scored over 100 goals in a season for Arcade Mission before moving up the ladder with Durham City. Able to occupy all three central-forward positions, he went on to claim over 100 goals (93 in the Football League) during his senior career. He started off with a bang, scoring on his Chelsea debut in a 4–0 home win over Swansea Town in August 1928. He played in 11 games up to November of that year before losing his place to George Anderson. Regaining the centre-forward berth late in the season, he fought hard to retain it before slipping out of contention early in 1930 following the arrival of George Mills. And then when Hugh Gallacher was signed, Elliott left to join Bristol City, for whom he scored 24 goals in only 50 outings.

ELMES, TIMOTHY
Midfield: 2+2 apps
Born: Thornton Heath, Surrey, 28 September 1962
Career: Croydon schoolboy football, CHELSEA (apprentice, April 1979; professional, July 1980), Leyton Orient (May–November 1981); thereafter non-League football

A well-built, tough-tackling midfield player, Tim Elmes failed to reach the heights expected of him (after some very useful displays at intermediate level) and he quickly drifted out of League football.

EVANS, ROBERT
Defender: 37 apps, 1 goal
Born: Glasgow, 16 July 1927 – *Died*: Airdrie, Scotland, 1 September 2001
Career: Thornliebank Methodists FC, St Anthony FC (Glasgow); guest for Motherwell and Aberaman Athletic during WW2; Celtic (August 1944), CHELSEA (£12,500, May 1960), Newport County (free transfer, player–manager, May 1961), Morton (player, July 1962), Third Lanark (player–trainer/coach, June 1963; then player–manager, June 1964–June 1965), Raith Rovers (player, August 1965; retired May 1967)

Voted Scotland's Player of the Year in 1953, Bobby Evans appeared in 535 games (10 goals scored) for Celtic during his 16 years at Parkhead. He helped the Bhoys win the League title in 1954, the Scottish Cup in 1951 and 1954 and the League Cup in 1957 and 1958 while also collecting runner's-up medals in the Scottish Cup in 1955 and 1956. He gained 45 caps for Scotland (his first in 1949) and later added 3 more to his tally with Chelsea. He also represented the

Scottish League on 24 occasions, and his aggregate of international honours and medals created a new record at that time (since surpassed). A busy, hard-working redhead, one of the great stars of Scottish football in the 1950s, Evans, who could play as a right-half or centre-half, was skilful and brave, possessed a potent tackle, was strong in the air (despite his size – a fraction over 5 ft 8 in.) and was a marvellous tactician who read the game superbly. He was never outclassed or overawed by his opponent and although well past his best when he joined Chelsea (he was almost 33 years of age) he still gave the Blues excellent service for a season. Newport County finished bottom of the Third Division at the end of his first season as a manager and he did little better with Third Lanark who were relegated to the Scottish Second Division in 1965.

FAIRGRAY, NORMAN MURRAY

Outside-left: 84 apps, 6 goals

Born: Dumfries, Scotland, 28 October 1880 – *Died*: Dumfries, *circa* 1956

Career: Dumfries Primrose (1899), Maxwelltown Volunteers (1901), Kilmarnock (November 1903), Maxwelltown Volunteers (July 1904), Lincoln City (December 1903), CHELSEA (September 1907), Motherwell (May 1914), Queen of the South (August 1919–May 1921)

Norrie Fairgray made 3 appearances for Kilmarnock and 60 for Lincoln City (6 goals) before joining Chelsea at the start of the 1907–08 season. A clever dribbler with good pace over 25–30 yards, he was an orthodox winger, and very popular with the Stamford Bridge supporters. Unfortunately he tended to blow hot and cold – being quite brilliant one week, then hopeless the next. He followed David Calderhead to Chelsea and after some impressive displays for the Blues was selected for a Scottish international trial. After retiring from the game he settled in Dumfries where he took employment in a local motor works during the 1920s.

FALCO, MARK PETER

Striker: 3 apps

Born: Hackney, London, 22 October 1950

Career: Middlesex and London Schools, Tottenham Hotspur (apprentice, July 1977; professional, July 1978), CHELSEA (loan, November 1982), Watford (£350,000, October 1986), Glasgow Rangers (July 1987), Queens Park Rangers (December 1987), Millwall (August 1991), Worthing (August 1992; retired, injured, July 1993; then coach, later joint-manager, May–September 1996)

Six-foot striker Mark Falco had a wonderfully successful career as a goal-scorer, netting 166 times in 537 competitive matches at club level alone, including 90 in 236 senior encounters for Spurs. An England Youth international (four caps won), he scored on his League debut for Spurs against Bolton in May 1979 and also netted twice in the 1981 FA Charity Shield draw with Aston Villa. After a loan spell with Chelsea, he then established himself in the first XI at White

Hart Lane and collected a UEFA Cup winner's medal at the end of the 1983–84 campaign. However, he was subsequently transferred to Watford in 1986 (after David Pleat had taken over as manager) and following a decent spell with Rangers, he rounded off his career back in London, finally quitting competitive League football in 1992 after suffering a painful leg injury.

FASCIONE, JOSEPH VICTOR
Winger: 27+7 apps, 1 goal
Born: Coatbridge, near Glasgow, 5 February 1945
Career: Kirkintilloch Rob Roy (from 1960), CHELSEA (apprentice, September 1962; professional, October 1962), Durham City (July 1969); later with Romford and Barking
Basically a reserve-team player for the duration of his time at Stamford Bridge, Joe Fascione, for six seasons at least, was a useful stand-by player and gave some enterprising displays when called into action.

FEELY, PETER JOHN
Forward: 4+1 apps, 2 goals
Born: City of London, 3 January 1950
Career: Enfield (amateur, 1967), CHELSEA (professional, April 1970), Bournemouth (£1,000, February 1973), Fulham (July 1974), Gillingham (October 1974), Sheffield Wednesday (February 1976), Stockport County (loan, January–February 1976); released by Sheffield Wednesday (May 1977)
An England amateur and youth international before he was 20 years of age, Peter Feely scored on his League debut for Chelsea against Coventry City in April 1971. After that, however, he found it difficult to get a game in the first XI, owing to the form of Peter Osgood, Tommy Baldwin and Ian Hutchinson, among others. He played his best football for Gillingham, scoring 22 goals in 41 League games.

FERGUSON, CHRISTOPHER
Inside-forward: 1 app.
Born: Kirkconnel, near Cumnock, Ayrshire, February 1922
Career: Dalblair Boys, CHELSEA (professional, October 1927), Queens Park Rangers (August 1930), Wrexham (July 1931), Guildford City (season 1932–33)
Younger brother of William Ferguson (q.v.), Chris Ferguson spent three years at Stamford Bridge during which time he played mainly in the reserves. His only senior game was in a 2–1 League victory at Wolves in late April 1928.

FERGUSON, EDWARD
Full-back: 2 apps
Born: Seaton Burn, near Whitley Bay, Northumberland, 2 August 1895 – *Died*: Darwen, Lancashire, *circa* 1962
Career: Seaton Delaval FC, Ashington (professional, April 1915), Dunfermline

Athletic (briefly during WW1), CHELSEA (March 1920), Ashington (July 1923), Nelson (May 1928), Annfield Plain (season 1931–32)

Owing to the consistent form of Jack Harrow, and with other full-backs also available including Walter Bettridge and George Smith, Ted Ferguson was handed only two senior outings during his time at Stamford Bridge. He made his League debut against Blackburn Rovers at Stamford Bridge on the last day of the 1920–21 season and scored 5 goals in 121 League appearances during his second spell with Ashington.

FERGUSON, WILLIAM

Wing-half/inside-forward/winger: 294 apps, 11 goals
Born: Muirkirk, Strathclyde, 13 February 1901 – *Died*: Scotland, 1960
Career: Kelso Rovers (1915), Queen of the South Wanderers (1919), CHELSEA (October 1921), Queen of the South (June 1933; retired May 1937 when he was appointed manager)

Willie Ferguson gave Chelsea 12 years' loyal and dedicated service. Initially a wing-half north of the border, he played in the reserves at inside-left and made his League debut in that position against Aston Villa in March 1923. After a few outings on both wings and also in the right- and left-half berths, he finally settled down in the latter position where he performed admirably alongside George Rodger with Fred Barrett behind him. He helped Chelsea regain their First Division status in 1930, after six seasons out of the top flight, and was perhaps unlucky not to win international honours for his country. Only 5 ft 5 in. tall, he overcame the lack of height to play aggressively, maintaining a very high standard of consistency.

FERREIRA, PAULO

Right-back: 40+2 apps
Born: Lisbon, Portugal, 18 January 1979
Career: Vitoria Setubal/Portugal (professional, March 1996), FC Porto/Portugal (season 1998–99), CHELSEA (£13.2 million, July 2004)

Paulo Ferreira followed his manager José Mourinho to Stamford Bridge. The Portuguese international, who cost a record fee for a full-back, starred in Euro 2004 and made his debut in the Premiership against Manchester United at Stamford Bridge on the opening day of the 2004–05 season. A classy performer, cool under pressure, who enjoys venturing forward in support of his wide midfielders, he was certainly one of the best defenders in Europe in 2003–04 when he won the Champions League with FC Porto, playing alongside his current Chelsea colleague Ricardo Carvalho. He added League Cup and Premiership winner's medals to his collection of prizes in 2005.

FERRER, ALBERT LLOPES

Right-back: 105+8 apps, 1 goal

Born: Barcelona, Spain, 6 June 1970

Career: Tenerife/Spain (April 1988), CF Barcelona/Spain (July 1990), CHELSEA (£2.2 million, August 1998; retired, injured ankle, June 2003)

A composed footballer, alert, quick off the mark with a timely tackle, Albert Ferrer's first two seasons at Stamford Bridge were excellent. But then a niggling ankle injury began to interrupt his game. He battled on bravely, missed the 2000 FA Cup final and was eventually replaced by Mario Melchiot after making only 31 appearances in 3 years, 4 in 2002–03. A Spanish international, capped 36 times by his country at senior level, he also played for the Under-23 side and starred in the 1992 Olympic Games. He made 17 League appearances for Tenerife and 205 for Barcelona. Rated the best right-back in the Premiership after his first season, 'Chapi' scored his only goal for Chelsea in November 1999 against the German side Hertha Berlin in a Champions League Group 'H' clash. He retired from first-class football at the age of 33.

FERRIS, JAMES

Inside-forward: 39 apps, 9 goals

Born: Belfast, 28 November, 1894 – *Died*: Belfast, 1932

Career: Distillery (1910), Belfast Celtic (August 1913), CHELSEA (September 1920), Preston North End (March 1922), Pontypridd (August–September 1924), Belfast Distillery (October 1924; retired through poor health, May 1931)

Already an Irish international with two caps to his name, as well as being an Irish League representative, Jim Ferris added two more to his collection during his stay at Stamford Bridge and after returning to his native country he took his tally to six by 1928. He arrived at the club with a huge reputation, having played superbly well in his homeland for ten years. Unfortunately he failed to settle in London and after a brief spell at Deepdale and two games for Pontypridd he returned to his former club in Belfast.

FILLERY, MICHAEL CHRISTOPHER

Midfield: 176+5 apps, 41 goals

Born: Mitcham, Surrey, 17 September 1960

Career: Sutton United (1976), CHELSEA (apprentice, April 1977; professional, August 1978), Queens Park Rangers (£200,000, August 1983), Portsmouth (free transfer, July 1987), Oldham Athletic (£30,000, October 1990), Millwall (loan, March 1991), Torquay United (loan, September–October 1991); released by Oldham Athletic (April 1992)

Mike Fillery was a very talented midfield player whose appearances for Chelsea came mainly in the Second Division. At times he looked rather casual and uninterested, but suddenly he would burst into life and produce some brilliant skills and occasionally score a stunning goal. Capped by England at both schoolboy and youth-team levels, he was a regular in the side from 1979 until his departure to Loftus Road. He made over 100 appearances for QPR, ending his career with 332 League games under his belt (47 goals).

FINLAYSON, WILLIAM

Inside-left/centre-forward: 5 apps, 1 goal
Born: Thornliebank, Renfrewshire, 12 August 1897 – *Died*: USA, *circa* 1965
Career: Glasgow Ashfield FC (1913), Thornliebank FC (briefly 1919), CHELSEA (June 1920), Clapton Orient (October 1924), Brentford (July 1925–May 1926); emigrated to USA and played for Springfield Babes, Providence Clamdiggers and Bethlehem Steel between 1927 and 1931

Reserve to Jack Cock and Andy Wilson during his four years at Stamford Bridge, Billy Finlayson, tall and slim, scored his only goal for Chelsea in a 1–1 draw at Cardiff City in October 1923.

FINNIESTON, STEPHEN JAMES

Striker: 86+4 apps, 37 goals
Born: Edinburgh, 30 November 1954
Career: Weybridge Council School, CHELSEA (apprentice, April 1970; professional, December 1971), Cardiff City (loan, October–November 1974), Sheffield United (£90,000, June 1978); later with Addlestone FC (season 1981–82) and Hartney Whitney (August 1982; retired, injured, May 1983)

Scottish youth international Steve Finnieston was an enterprising player who scored more than a goal every two games for Chelsea whom he served for eight years. He replaced Teddy Maybank in attack and was leading marksman in 1976–77 with 26 goals in League and Cup. Injuries started to affect his game during his time at Bramall Lane.

FLECK, ROBERT WILLIAM

Striker: 43+5 apps, 4 goals
Born: Glasgow, 11 August 1965
Career: Possil Youth Club (Glasgow), Glasgow Rangers (July 1983), Partick Thistle (loan, November–December 1983), Norwich City (£580,000, December 1987), CHELSEA (£2.1 million, August 1992), Bolton Wanderers (loan, December 1993–January 1994), Bristol City (loan, January–March 1995), Norwich City (£650,000, August 1995), Reading (£60,000, March 1998; retired with back injury, November 1998), Gorleston Town (coach, December 1998)

A Scottish international at schoolboy and youth-team levels, Robert Fleck went on to gain 6 Under-21 and 4 senior caps for his country while also amassing a record of 126 goals in 479 club appearances spread over 15 years. On his day there wasn't a better goal-poacher around. He was sharp, alert and as quick as lightning in and around the penalty area, giving defenders no time whatsoever to think about their job! He played his best football at Norwich first time round when he netted 66 goals in 181 games.

A Scottish Premier Division winner (1987) and twice a League Cup winner (1987 and 1988) with Rangers, Fleck scored in Reading's first-ever League game at their new Madejski Stadium v. Luton Town in August 1998.

FLETCHER, JAMES
Full-back: 1 app.
Born: *circa* 1892 – Deceased by 1980
Career: CHELSEA (season 1905–06)
Unknown reserve full-back in Chelsea's first season, Jim Fletcher's only senior game was against Lincoln City at home in February 1906 when he deputised for Tommy Miller in a 4–2 win. It is believed he was not registered as a player with the Football League.

FLO, TORE ANDRÉ
Striker: 94+69 apps, 50 goals
Born: Strin, Norway, 15 June 1973
Career: Strin Juniors/Norway, Sogndal/Norway (professional, April 1994), Tromso/Norway (May 1995), Brann Bergen/Norway (May 1996), CHELSEA (£300,000, August 1997), Glasgow Rangers (£12 million, November 2000), Sunderland (£6.75 million, August 2002), Siena/Italy (£50,000, September 2004), FC Vaalerenga/Norway (July 2005)
Tore André Flo was a record sale by Chelsea when he moved from Stamford Bridge to Rangers and he was also Sunderland's record buy when he moved there from Ibrox Park. At 6 ft 4 in. tall, he made it difficult for opponents in the air and was awkward yet by no means underrated on the ground. He was quick to react, possessed a strong shot in both feet and could work down both flanks as well as through the middle. Recognised by Norway at Under-21 level, he went on to win 75 full caps (24 goals scored) and at club level helped Chelsea complete the 'Cup' Treble (League Cup, European Cup-Winners' Cup and Super Cup) in 1998 and lift both the FA Cup and Charity Shield in 2000. He was also a Double winner in 2002 with Rangers who triumphed in the finals of the Scottish Cup and League Cup. Flo, who scored 51 goals in 88 League games in Norway, held the record for most substitute appearances for Chelsea (69) before Eidur Gudjohnsen took on the mantle in 2005.

FORD, HENRY THOMAS
Inside-/outside-right: 248 apps, 46 goals
Born: Fulham, London, 1893 – *Died*: London, 1960
Career: Tunbridge Wells Rangers, CHELSEA (professional, April 1912; retired May 1924)
Spotted playing against Chelsea's second XI, Harry Ford was quickly snapped up and handed professional status at Stamford Bridge at the age of 19. He made

his League debut seven months later, away at Bolton Wanderers, and remained a permanent fixture in the first XI (injuries permitting) for the next nine years. He appeared in almost 250 senior games (46 goals) and in 62 WW1 Regional matches (22 goals) and in the immediate pre-WW1 seasons was regarded as one of the best wingers in the game. He was fast, clever with good control and could cross a ball inch-perfect, given the chance. Able and willing to turn out in any forward position, but preferring the right-wing, Ford even acted as an emergency goalkeeper on one occasion, such was his versatility. A huge favourite at Stamford Bridge, he played in the 1915 FA Cup final and gained a winner's medal when Chelsea beat Fulham in the Victory Cup final of 1919. He might well have set a new club appearance record had WW1 not arrived when it did.

FORSSELL, MIKAEL KAJ
Striker: 12+41 apps, 12 goals
Born: Steinfurt, Germany, 15 March 1981
Career: HJK Helsinki/Finland, CHELSEA (December 1998), Crystal Palace (loan, February 2000–May 2001); back at CHELSEA (briefly); Borussia Moenchengladbach/Germany (loan, season 2002–03); Birmingham; City (loan, August 2003–March 2005; signed for £3.2 million, June 2005)

A Finnish international, capped 29 times at senior level, 8 times by the Under-21 side as well as by the youth team, red-haired striker Mikael Forssell simply could not hold down a regular place in Chelsea's first team due to the goal-scoring form of Eidur Gudjohnsen and Jimmy-Floyd Hasselbaink. He did, however, net some excellent goals when called up for duty. After his lengthy loan spell at Selhurst Park (18 goals in 64 outings) he returned to Stamford Bridge and played for Chelsea in the Asia Cup campaign and in the Champions League qualifier against MSK Zilinia. He then helped Birmingham City consolidate themselves in the Premiership, notching 19 goals in 37 games in his first season at St Andrew's before a knee injury struck him down early in 2004–05 forcing him to miss six months of the campaign. He returned to Chelsea and came on as a late substitue in the home leg of the Champions League game with Bayern Munich in April 2005.

FOSS, SIDNEY LACY RICHARD
Wing-half/inside-right: 48 apps, 3 goals
Born: Barking, Essex, 28 November 1912 – *Died*: London, 1990
Career: Southall (1929), CHELSEA (May 1936; retired, injured, April 1952 to become manager of the youth scheme at Stamford Bridge, retaining that position for 14 years)

Sid Foss's career was severely hampered by WW2 – yet he still managed to appear in some 200 games for Chelsea during the hostilities, appearing in the 1944 and 1945 League Cup (South) finals against Charlton Athletic and Millwall respectively. In fact, he is one of only a handful of players to have served the club, before, during and after the war. He started out as an inside-forward but was successfully switched into the half-back line where he played with grim determination and no mean skill. As manager of Chelsea's youth scheme, he helped nurture several star players including Jimmy Greaves, Peter Brabrook, Barry Bridges, John Hollins, Bobby Tambling and Terry Venables, to name just six. One of the club's greatest-ever servants, Foss spent 30 years at Stamford Bridge.

FOULKE, WILLIAM HENRY

Goalkeeper: 35 apps
Born: Dawley, Shropshire, 12 April 1874 – *Died*: Blackpool, 1 May 1916
Career: Alfreton, Blackwell Colliery, Sheffield United (June 1894), CHELSEA
  (May 1905), Bradford City (April 1906; retired November 1907)
Bill 'Fatty' Foulke was a huge man whose weight during a wonderful career rose from 13 stone to a staggering 25 st. 2 lb, attained in his last season as a Bradford City player. He spent 11 years at Bramall Lane, making over 350 appearances for the Blades, before transferring to Chelsea, performing well during the club's first season of League football. He was certainly the colossus among goalkeepers; his clearances (by kicking) were quite exceptional and he could punch the ball as far as some players could kick it. As a Sheffield player, he won the League championship in 1898 and the FA Cup in 1899 and 1902, collecting a runner's-up medal in the latter competition in 1901. He gained one full England cap v. Wales in March 1897 (won 4–0) and twice represented the Football League, and he also scored two goals, both for Sheffield United against The Kaffirs (a Black African touring side) in a 7–2 friendly win in 1899. Besides being a fine keeper, Foulke was also a very useful cricketer who played 4 times for Derbyshire in the County Championship, scoring 65 runs and taking 2–92. Later in life he was the main attraction in a 'penny-a-shot' sideshow on the Blackpool promenade. Sadly he died of pneumonia, aged 42. Some reference books have Foulke's birthplace as Blackwell, Derbyshire.

FRANCIS, STEPHEN STUART

Goalkeeper: 88 apps
Born: Billericay, Essex, 29 May 1964
Career: CHELSEA (apprentice, July 1980; professional, May 1982), Reading
  (£15,000, February 1987), Huddersfield Town (£150,000, August 1993),
  Northampton (January 1999; retired May 1999)
Steve Francis gained England honours at youth-team level and was twice a winner at Wembley, with Chelsea in 1986 (FMC) and Reading in 1988 (Simod Cup). Confident on his line, he was first-choice keeper at Stamford Bridge for two seasons (1981–83) and eventually lost his place to Eddie Niedzwiecki, playing in only seven more first-class matches after that. He went on to appear in 259 senior games for Reading and 227 for Huddersfield.

FREEMAN, CHARLES REFEARN

Inside-forward: 105 apps, 22 goals

Born: Overseal, Derbyshire, 22 August 1887 – *Died*: London, March 1956

Career: Overseal Swifts, Burton United (May 1906), Fulham (briefly, early 1907), CHELSEA (trial, April 1907; professional, August 1907), Gillingham (May 1920), Maidstone United (August 1922); CHELSEA (backroom staff, June 1923, working as an odd-job man; appointed first-team trainer during WW2 and also acted as groundsman; retired in summer of 1953)

Charlie Freeman spent a total of 43 years at Stamford Bridge. Initially an amateur trialist, after being released by Fulham, he turned professional at the age of 20 but had to wait almost two years before making his debut for Chelsea against Sunderland in February 1909 when he deputised for George Hilsdon in a 2–1 win at Roker Park. He was never really a regular choice in the first XI, averaging only 14 appearances per season up to WW1 and not being selected for the 1915 FA Cup final. But when chosen he certainly gave a good account of himself, being utterly dependable, and he scored some important goals. During the hostilities Freeman played in 54 Regional matches (notching 20 goals) and made 3 appearances in 1919–20 before moving to Gillingham for whom he netted 21 times in 82 League games over two seasons.

FREESTONE, ROGER

Goalkeeper: 53 apps

Born: Newport, Gwent, 19 August 1968

Career: Newport County (trainee, April 1985; professional, April 1986), CHELSEA (£95,000, March 1987), Swansea City (loan, September–November 1989), Hereford United (loan, March–April 1990), Swansea City (£45,000, September 1991, released May 2004)

A tall, muscular goalkeeper with good reflexes and a safe pair of hands, Roger 'Dodger' Freestone, who was built like a man mountain, had appeared in only 14 competitive games before joining Chelsea. He remained a registered player at Stamford Bridge for four years, moving permanently to the Vetch Field in 1991 after Dave Beasant and Kevin Hitchcock had both staked their claim for first-team places. Freestone, who represented his country as a schoolboy and youth-team player and went on to gain one cap at both Under-21 and senior levels, passed the milestone of 750 club appearances in 2004. He helped Chelsea win the Second Division title in 1989 and Swansea win the Autoglass Trophy in 1994 and clinch promotion as Third Division champions in 2000.

FREW, JAMES
Centre-half: 43 apps
Born: Ballochmyle, near Inverness, 16 March 1900 – Deceased by 1990
Career: Campbeltown Juniors (1915), Kilmarnock (1917), Nithsdale Wanderers
(1919), CHELSEA (June 1922), Southend United (May 1927), Carlisle
United (July 1920–May 1930); returned to Scotland

Two of Jimmy Frew's four seasons at Stamford Bridge were spent in Chelsea's
reserve side, but in 1922–23 and in 1924–25 he gave valuable service to the first
XI when deputising at centre-half for David Cameron and then contesting the
position with Harry Wilding and George Rodger. A strong performer, he made
up for a lack of height with some timely tackles and intelligent positional play.

FRIDGE, LESLIE
Goalkeeper: 1 app.
Born: Inverness, 27 August 1968
Born: Inverness Thistle (July 1984), CHELSEA (trial, April 1985; junior, May
1985; professional, December 1985), St Mirren (£50,000, January 1987–May
1993)

Owing to the presence of Eddie Niedzwiecki and the arrival of Tony Godden,
curly-haired goalkeeper Les Fridge, a Scottish youth and Under-21
international, chose to return to his homeland after spending most of his time
playing junior football at Stamford Bridge. Unfortunately he let in five goals
when making his only League appearance for the Blues against Watford in May
1986. He played in more than 100 senior games for St Mirren.

FROST, JAMES LEWIS
Outside-right: 22 apps, 4 goals
Born: Wolverton, Buckinghamshire, April 1880 – *Died:* London, 1928
Career: Wolverton FC (1902), Northampton Town (August 1905), CHELSEA
(December 1906), West Ham United (briefly, season 1907–08), Croydon
Common (season 1908–09), Clapton Orient (briefly, season 1909–10)

Chelsea beat off challenges from several other League clubs to capture fast-
raiding right-winger Jimmy Frost from Northampton Town. But after
establishing himself in the first team at Stamford Bridge he suffered a leg injury
and failed to reclaim his spot from Billy Brawn after regaining full fitness.

FROST, LEE ADRIAN
Winger: 11+3 apps, 5 goals
Born: Woking, 4 December 1957
Career: CHELSEA (apprentice, April 1974, professional, July 1976), Brentford
(loan, October–November 1978; signed for £15,000, December 1980–May
1981)

After four promising years playing in Chelsea's youth and reserve sides, sprightly
winger Lee Frost made his League debut away to Aston Villa in April 1978.

The following season he made 3 senior appearances and was given 10 outings in 1979–80 when he scored a hat-trick in a 7–3 Second Division win over Leyton Orient at Stamford Bridge. He netted 3 goals in 21 League games for Brentford.

FURLONG, PAUL ANTHONY

Striker: 59+26 apps, 17 goals
Born: Wood Green, London, 1 October 1968
Career: Wood Green Boys, Enfield (from 1986), Coventry City (£130,000, July 1991), Watford (£250,000, July 1992), CHELSEA (£2.3 million, May 1994), Birmingham City (£1.5 million, July 1996), Queens Park Rangers (loan, August–September 2000), Sheffield United (loan, February–March 2002), Queens Park Rangers (signed, August 2002)

As an Enfield player, aggressive striker Paul Furlong was capped five times by England at semi-professional level and helped the non-League side win the FA Trophy in 1988. He then quickly adapted to the bread and butter of League football with Coventry City for whom he scored 5 goals in 43 outings before transferring to Watford. At Vicarage Road he continued to find the net regularly, securing 41 goals in 91 starts prior to his big-money transfer to Chelsea. He didn't slack and his two seasons at Stamford Bridge produced a useful return as the Blues hovered around mid-table in the Premiership. Signed by Birmingham City boss Trevor Francis, he netted the 100th goal of his career while playing for the St Andrew's club and after losing his place in the side, plus a couple of loan spells elsewhere, he was recruited by QPR boss Ian Holloway on a permanent basis. In 2004–05 Furlong reached two personal milestones, those of 500 senior appearances and 150 goals.

GALLACHER, HUGH KILPATRICK

Inside-/centre-forward: 144 apps, 81 goals
Born: Bellshill, Lanarkshire, 2 February 1903 – *Died*: Low Fell, near Gateshead, 11 June 1957
Career: Tannockside Athletic (March 1919), Hattonrigg Thistle (August 1919), Bellshill Academy (briefly, early 1920), Bellshill Athletic (May 1920), Queen of the South (December 1920), Airdrieonians (May 1921), Newcastle United (£6,500, December 1925), CHELSEA (£10,000, May 1930), Derby County (£3,000, November 1934), Notts County (£2,000, September 1936), Grimsby Town (£1,000, January 1938), Gateshead (£500, June 1938; retired September 1939)

Only 5 ft 5 in. tall, soccer immortal Hughie Gallacher, elusive yet brilliant at shielding the ball, was considered by many as the greatest centre-forward ever to grace a football pitch, certainly between the two world wars (even better than Dixie Dean). He had the knack of scoring 'impossible' goals and during a marvellous career notched 463 in 624 senior games including 387 in 543 League encounters – a wonderful set of statistics. Chelsea's first £10,000 signing, he had been playing League football for 9 years when he moved to Stamford Bridge, having netted 143 times in 174 appearances for Newcastle, whom he skippered to the First Division championship in 1927. Something of a 'playboy' on and off the field, he was certainly worshipped by the supporters. But he was also a very temperamental footballer, often in trouble with referees (he once received a two-month suspension) and occasionally with the police, which just added spice to the career of the player called the 'wizard of dribble'.

Newcastle fans were bitterly annoyed when he moved to Chelsea in 1930, so much so that protests took place for weeks after his departure. And when the Blues visited St James' Park for a League game in September 1930, a record crowd of 68,386 (with another 10,000 locked outside) turned up to welcome back their past idol. Gallacher made his mark wherever he played. He gave Chelsea excellent service for four and a half years. Capped 20 times by Scotland between 1924 and 1935, he also twice represented the Scottish League and was a Scottish Cup winner with Airdrie in 1924. He holds a Scottish record by scoring five goals in a full international against Ireland in 1929. Sadly, Gallacher took his own life, stepping in front of the York to Edinburgh express train at (ironically) a place called Dead Man's Crossing at Low Fell near his Gateshead home in 1957, while facing a charge of cruelty to his son. One headline in the *Newcastle Journal* read: 'Hughie of the Magic Feet is Dead'. His name will live as long as the game of football lasts. Two of Gallacher's sons, Hughie junior and Matty, had spells at Newcastle United without making the grade.

GALLAS, WILLIAM
Defender: 169+11 apps, 9 goals
Born: Asnieres, near Paris, France, 17 August 1977
Career: SM Caen/France (May 1996), Olympique Marseilles/France (August 1997), CHELSEA (£6.2 million, July 2001)
Able to play as an attacking right wing-back or central defender, William Gallas formed a tremendous partnership in Chelsea's back division with John Terry and also in the French national team with his Chelsea team-mate and colleague Marcel Desailly. Capped over 25 times by his country at senior level and on 4 occasions by the Under-21s, Gallas is fast, aggressive, positive and alert. He enjoys a battle, is totally committed and has already scored some vital goals. He appeared in 18 League games for Caen and 85 for Marseilles before moving into the English Premiership where he gained a championship winner's medal in 2005, as well as collecting a League Cup winner's prize.

GALLON, JAMES
Wing-half: 2 apps
Born: Burslem, Stoke-on-Trent, 1894 – *Died*: Stoke-on-Trent, *circa* 1965
Career: Hanley, CHELSEA (trial, May 1919; professional, August 1919; released May 1921); moved into non-League football
A reserve-team regular for two seasons, Jim Gallon's Football League debut for

Chelsea was against Bradford City in February 1920 when he deputised for Harold Halse.

GALLOWAY, JOHN ARTHUR
Inside-forward: 4 apps
Born: Grangemouth, Scotland, 29 October 1918 – Deceased by 2000
Career: Glasgow Rangers; Army football with the Wanderers (Middle East Select); CHELSEA (guest, season 1940–41; signed professional, August 1946; released May 1949); later a permit player with Leyton and Carshalton before retiring in 1951

A schoolteacher by profession, Jack Galloway was a captain in the Royal Signals Regiment, serving in the Middle East during WW2. He was badly wounded in the Italian campaign but after treatment, recovered and played football until he was over 30. Tall, well-built and useful in the air, he signed as a professional with Chelsea but on his release went back to playing at amateur level. He made his League debut in a 4–3 home win over Bolton Wanderers in August 1946.

GARLAND, CHRISTOPHER STEPHEN
Forward: 111+3 apps, 31 goals
Born: Bristol, 24 April 1949
Career: Bristol City (apprentice, June 1965; professional, May 1966), CHELSEA (£100,000, September 1971), Leicester City (£95,000, February 1975), Bristol City (£110,000, December 1976; contract cancelled, February 1982; re-signed as a non-contract player, August 1982; retired May 1983); suffers now from Parkinson's disease

A teenage local hero at Ashton Gate, well-built blond striker Chris Garland scored 38 goals in 170 appearances for Bristol City before transferring to Chelsea, initially as cover for Peter Osgood, Tommy Baldwin and Ian Hutchinson. Owing to injuries, illness and suspensions, he got his share of first-team football at Stamford Bridge and averaged a goal every four games for the Blues, playing in the 1972 League Cup final defeat by Stoke City, while also gaining an England Under-23 cap. Dangerous in and around the penalty area, he produced some enterprising performances before his departure to Leicester City in 1975, helping the Foxes retain their First Division status while his former club Chelsea were relegated! He returned for a second spell at Ashton Gate in 1979 and although he was released, with seven other players, he returned to the club on a non-contract for season 1982–83 and took his record with City to 54 goals in 252 games before a knee injury ended his career.

GARNER, WILLIAM DAVID
Striker: 105+14 apps, 37 goals
Born: Leicester, 14 December 1947
Career: Notts County (apprentice, May 1963; professional, July 1966), Bedford Town (July 1967), Southend United (November 1969), CHELSEA

(£80,000, September 1972), Cambridge United (free transfer, November 1978), Chelmsford City (May 1980), Brentford (August 1983), Whyteleafe FC (season 1984–85)

A well-built, strong and forceful striker, good in the air, useful on the ground, Bill Garner had a sound enough scoring record, but was an inconsistent performer and at times fell foul of the referee. He made only two senior appearances for Notts County before drifting into non-League football at the age of 19. After gaining experience with Bedford, he returned to Fourth Division action and scored 41 goals in 102 League games for Southend. He didn't do a great deal after leaving Stamford Bridge, netting 3 times in 24 outings for Cambridge and once in three for Brentford.

(GEREMI) N'JITAP FOTO GEREMI SORELE
Midfield: 40+19 apps, 1 goal
Born: Bafoussam, Cameroon, 20 December 1978
Career: Racing Bafoussam/Cameroon, Cerro Porteno/Paraguay (August 1997), Genclerbirligi/Turkey (October 1997), Real Madrid/Spain (July 1999), Middlesbrough (loan, July 2002–May 2003), CHELSEA (£7 million, August 2003)

An Olympic gold medalist with Cameroon in 1996, along with fellow countryman and Chelsea star Celestine Babayaro, Geremi made 45 appearances for Real Madrid in Primera Liga and then scored 7 goals in 34 games for Middlesbrough in his first season of English football – having done exceedingly well in Spain with Real Madrid. He was already an established international with over 50 caps to his tally when he arrived at the Riverside Stadium and after leaving Boro for Chelsea he continued to add to that tally which reached the 70 mark in 2004. Strong in all aspects of midfield play, Geremi has a terrific engine and has already had two fine campaigns at Stamford Bridge, working tirelessly in centre-field with Frank Lampard, Damien Duff, Claude Makelele, Joe Cole and others. He gained a Premiership championship medal in 2005.

GIBBS, DEREK WILLIAM
Inside-forward: 25 apps, 6 goals
Born: Fulham, London, 22 December 1934
Career: CHELSEA (juniors, April 1952; professional, April 1955), Leyton Orient (November 1960), Queens Park Rangers (August 1963–May 1964)

Derek Gibbs rose through the ranks at Stamford Bridge to make his Football League debut in January 1957. However, with the likes of Johnny Brooks, Jimmy Greaves and Tony Nicholas the mainstays in the first team, he found it increasingly hard going to claim a place in the senior side and subsequently moved across London to Leyton Orient for whom he scored 7 goals in 42 outings, later appearing in 29 competitive matches for QPR.

GIBSON, GEORGE BENNETT

Inside-left: 141 apps, 24 goals

Born: Hamilton, Lanarkshire, 29 September 1907 – *Died*: London, 1990

Career: Dundee (1924), Hamilton Academical (February 1925), Bolton Wanderers (£3,100, February 1927), CHELSEA (February 1933–May 1938); did not play after WW2

A clever forward of the accepted Scottish style, George Gibson loved to dribble with the ball and was one of the many 'big-name' signings made by Chelsea in the 1930s. At times similar in style to the great Hughie Gallacher, Gibson enjoyed running at and taking on defenders, charging straight down the middle of the pitch. A creator and scorer of goals, he was the complete footballer in many ways and did an excellent job during his eight years at Stamford Bridge. He scored 81 goals in 255 League and Cup games for Bolton, whom he helped win the FA Cup in 1929. He skippered the Trotters in 1931–32 and, ironically, his last game for Bolton was against Chelsea at Stamford Bridge.

GILKES, MICHAEL EARL GLENIS MCDONALD

Forward: 0+2 apps

Born: Hackney, London, 20 July 1965

Career: Waltham Borough Boys (London), Leicester City (apprentice, July 1982), Reading (professional, July 1984), CHELSEA (loan, January–February 1992), Southampton (loan, March 1992), Wolverhampton Wanderers (£155,000, March 1997), Millwall ('Bosman' free transfer, July 1999), Slough Town (July 2001)

A Barbadian international who played in the World Cup qualifying rounds in July–August 2000 at the age of 35, left-sided midfielder Michael Gilkes had just two substitute outings during his loan spell at Stamford Bridge. He went on to score 52 goals in 486 competitive games for Reading, whom he helped win the Third Division championship in 1986, the Full Members' Cup two years later (when he scored in the Wembley final) and the Second Division title in 1994. When he moved to Molineux in 1997, he was signed by his former manager Mark McGhee, who was also his boss at Millwall.

GODDARD, RAYMOND

Half-back: 15 apps, 1 goal

Born: Ecclesfield, Sheffield, 17 October 1920 – *Died*: Gornal, Dudley, 1 February 1974

Career: Red Rovers FC (Sheffield), Wolverhampton Wanderers (September 1928), Cardiff City (guest, WW2), CHELSEA (September 1946), Plymouth Argyle (July 1948), Exeter City (December 1949–May 1954), Bideford Town (player–manager, June 1954–April 1956); later lived and worked in the West Midlands (Dudley)

Ray Goddard played under manager Frank Buckley at Molineux before being engaged in military service in Burma, Ceylon and India as one of General

Wingate's soldiers. After the war had ended he signed for Chelsea for whom he made his League debut in a 7–4 defeat by Liverpool at Anfield. Useful in any of the three half-back positions, he possessed a solid tackle and was resilient to the last. He would surely have gone further had he not lost seven years due to the fighting in Europe. He skippered both Devon clubs, making 44 appearances for Plymouth and 137 for Exeter.

GODDEN, ANTHONY LEONARD

Goalkeeper: 38 apps
Born: Gillingham, Kent, 2 August 1955
Career: Napier Secondary Modern School (Gillingham), Leonard Star FC, Eastcourt United, Gillingham and District Schools, Medway and Kent Schools, Gillingham (amateur, August 1969), Ashford Town (August 1971), Wolverhampton Wanderers (trial, June–July 1975), West Bromwich Albion (August 1975), Preston North End (loan, September 1976), Happy Valley FC/Hong Kong (guest, 1978), Luton Town (loan, March–April 1983), Walsall (loan, October–December 1983), CHELSEA (loan, March 1986; signed for £40,000, August 1986), Birmingham City (£35,000, July 1987), Bury (loan, December 1988), Sheffield Wednesday (loan, March–April 1989), Peterborough United (July 1989), Wivenhoe Town (July 1990), Colchester United (non-contract, March–May 1991), Warboys Town (season 1991–92), Torquay United (season 1992–93); March Town (manager, July 1993); King's Lynn (coach, December 1993; manager, February 1994); Bury Town (manager/coach, May 1996); also Northampton Town (part-time coach, 1996–97); later associated with Rushden and Diamonds, Lincoln City, Peterborough United, Leicester City, Derby County, Notts County, and Derby County again in 2003–04, all as a goalkeeping coach, while also having a spell as manager of Wisbech Town
In October 1981, goalkeeper Tony Godden set a record for West Bromwich Albion that will take some beating – he appeared in his 228th consecutive first-team match and in doing so eclipsed defender Ally Robertson's previous total of successive outings by a considerable margin. He spent over ten years at The Hawthorns, during which time he amassed almost 330 senior appearances, played in the FA Cup semi-final and also in the UEFA Cup. Generally a safe handler of the ball, he was a fine shot-stopper but was perhaps vulnerable at times on high crosses. He was signed initially on loan by Chelsea boss John Hollins to solve a crisis following an injury to Eddie Niedzwiecki and with Steve Francis out of form. He remained at Stamford Bridge for just over a season before returning to the Midlands to sign for Birmingham City. Godden once scored a goal from 90 yards when clearing his lines playing for Peterborough United reserves against Northampton Town in 1989–90. He later helped the Cobblers reach the Third Division play-offs. Godden's professional career realised more than 450 senior appearances.

GOLDBAEK, BJARNE
Midfield: 21+20 apps, 5 goals
Born: Nykoping Falster, Denmark, 6 October 1968
Career: Naested/Denmark (professional, October 1986), FC Schalke 04/Germany (August 1990), 1 FC Kaiserslautern/Germany (May 1991), Tennis Borussia/Germany (February 1994), 1 FC Köln/Germany (August 1994), FC Copenhagen/Denmark (July 1996), CHELSEA (£350,000, November 1998), Fulham (£500,000, January 2000; retired June 2003)

Bjarne Goldbaek was a dependable right-sided midfield player who could also fill in at right-back. Physically strong with a powerful right-foot shot, he was already an established Danish international and had made over 200 senior appearances at club level before moving to Stamford Bridge in 1998. He did a good job with Chelsea before moving down the Thames to Craven Cottage where he became a firm favourite with the Fulham supporters. He helped the Cottagers win the First Division championship in 2001 and made over 100 appearances for the club before retiring in the summer of 2003.

Goldbaek gained 28 full, 1 'B', 4 Under-21 and 5 youth caps for Denmark.

GOODWIN, JOSEPH
Outside-left: 2 apps
Born: London, *circa* 1883
Career: CHELSEA (amateur, season 1905–06)

A relatively unknown amateur winger, Joe Goodwin spent one season at Stamford Bridge (Chelsea's first) and appeared in two preliminary rounds of the FA Cup, against Southend United and Crystal Palace when he deputised for John Kirwan.

GOULDEN, LEONARD ARTHUR
Inside-forward: 111 apps, 19 goals
Born: Hackney, London, 16 July 1912 – *Died*: Cornwall, 14 February 1995
Career: Holborn Street School (West Ham, London), Dagenham (briefly), West Ham United (amateur, July 1931), Chelmsford (amateur, December 1931), Leyton (amateur, July 1932), West Ham United (professional, April 1933), CHELSEA (£5,000, August 1945; retired May 1950 when appointed coach), Watford (manager, November 1952–July 1956; acted as general manager, October 1955–February 1956); coached in Libya (two years); Watford (coach, July 1959–May 1962), Banbury United (secretary–manager, October 1965–March 1967), Oxford United (trainer/coach, January 1969–February 1970); also worked as a sub-postmaster (1956–59) and was later employed at a United States Air Force base in Northamptonshire

Quick-witted dexterity carried inside-left Len Goulden past many a lunging defender. Regarded as the best English-born player in his position during the two seasons leading up to WW2, he gained 14 full caps (scoring 4 goals) and would have collected many more had not Hitler and his army decided to attack when they did. However, he still appeared in six wartime internationals and twice represented the Football League.

He had played for his country as a schoolboy v. Wales and Scotland in 1926 and made 255 senior appearances for West Ham (55 goals) plus another 152 during the war (57 goals), gaining a Regional Cup winner's medal in 1940. As a guest player, he helped Chelsea win the Football League South Cup in 1945 – and these surprisingly were his only two honours at club level.

A brainy footballer, he could change the point of attack with one flash of brilliance, sweeping out a pass fully 40 yards, and he could also hold the ball up when under pressure. He made his senior debut at Chelsea (following his move from Upton Park) in a 3rd round FA Cup draw with Leicester City in January 1946, scoring his first goal in the replay five days later. His best season as manager came with Watford in 1953–54 when the Hornets finished fourth in Division Three (S). He later took Banbury from the West Midlands League in to the Southern League. His son Roy was also an England schoolboy international who played for Arsenal and Southend United.

GRAHAM, GEORGE
Inside-forward: 102 apps, 46 goals
Born: Bargeddle, Lanark, 30 November 1944
Career: Coatbridge Schools, Swinton FC (West Scotland), Coatbridge Boys, Aston Villa (groundstaff, December 1959; professional, December 1961), CHELSEA (£5,950, July 1964), Arsenal (£50,000, plus Tommy Baldwin, September 1966), Manchester United (£120,000, December 1972), Portsmouth (November 1974), Crystal Palace (November 1976), California Surf/NASL (loan, March–July 1978; retired as a player May 1980), Crystal Palace (youth-team coach/assistant manager, June 1980); Queens Park Rangers (coach, 1981), Millwall (manager, December 1982–May 1986), Arsenal (manager, May 1986–May 1995), Leeds United (manager, September 1996–September 1998), Tottenham Hotspur (manager, October 1998–March 2001); later worked on TV as a match summariser/pundit

George 'Stroller' Graham never established himself at Villa Park although he did play in the 1963 League Cup final against Birmingham City. After leaving the club he went on to greater things, both as a player and manager. He formed a terrific striking partnership at Chelsea with Barry Bridges, netting almost a goal every two games and collecting a League Cup winner's medal in 1965. As a Gunner, he starred in 296 matches and hit 77 goals, won League championship and FA Cup winner's medals in 1971, a Fairs Cup winner's medal (1970) and runner's-up awards in the FA Cup (1972) and League Cup (1968 and 1969). The first player ex-Chelsea boss Tommy Docherty signed when he took over at Manchester United, Graham captained a struggling Reds side in 1973 and again the following year when they were relegated from the First Division. He made 44 appearances for United and followed up with over 60 for Pompey as they dropped into Division Three before ending his playing days with 51 outings for Palace, helping the Eagles win promotion to the Second Division in 1977. During his League career, Graham scored 105 goals in 455 appearances, his best set of figures coming with the Gunners. Capped by Scotland as a schoolboy and youth team player, he also represented his country twice at Under-23 level and starred in 12 full internationals. Moving into management with Millwall, his first success was to lead the Lions to victory in the final of the Football League Trophy in 1983, also guiding the Londoners to promotion from Division Three two years later. As boss of Arsenal, Graham won two League titles in 1989 and 1991, the League Cup in 1987, finished runners-up in the same competition in 1988 and celebrated the Double in 1993. Graham also guided Leeds into Europe in 1998 before taking charge of Spurs, his last club.

GRANT, ANTHONY

Full-back/midfield: 0+1 app.
Born: Lambeth, London, 4 June 1987
Career: CHELSEA (apprentice, June 2003)
After some very promising displays in the reserve and youth teams, England Youth international Tony Grant was handed his Premiership debut as a late substitute in front of almost 68,000 fans at Old Trafford as Chelsea completed a seasonal double over Manchester United in May 2005. Nicknamed 'Judge', he first signed for the Blues as a nine year old.

GRANVILLE, DANIEL PATRICK

Defender: 19+7 apps, 1 goal
Born: Islington, London, 19 January 1975
Career: Cambridge United (apprentice, April 1991; professional, May 1993), CHELSEA (£300,000, March 1997), Leeds United (£1.6 million, July 1998), Manchester City (£1 million, August 1999), Norwich City (loan, October–November 2000), Crystal Palace (£500,000, December 2001)
Danny Granville made 114 appearances for Cambridge United but struggled to adapt to life at a higher level with Chelsea, spending barely five months at Stamford Bridge yet during that time he gained both League Cup and ECWC winning medals (1998). When he moved to Elland Road, the Blues made £1.3 million profit from the deal. An England Under-21 international (capped three times), he failed to bed down at Leeds but then made 80 appearances for Manchester City whom he helped, as he did Palace, gain promotion to the Premiership in 2002 and 2004 respectively.

GRAY, WILLIAM PATRICK

Outside-right/inside-forward/left-back: 172 apps, 15 goals
Born: Dinnington, County Durham, 24 May 1927
Career: Dinnington Colliery FC, Wolverhampton Wanderers (amateur, season 1943–44), Gateshead (amateur, 1945), Leyton Orient (professional, May

1947), CHELSEA (March 1949), Burnley (£16,000, August 1953), Nottingham Forest (June 1957), Millwall (player–manager, November 1963–May 1966), Brentford (manager, July 1966–September 1967), Notts County (manager, September 1967–September 1968), Fulham (coach, January 1969), Nottingham Forest (groundsman, seasons 1970–75)

After just 20 games for Orient, Billy Gray quickly settled in at Stamford Bridge and was capped by England 'B' v. Switzerland in 1949. He developed into a fast and clever left-winger and was a regular throughout his stay with Chelsea during which time the team twice reached the FA Cup semi-final. After 130 games and 32 goals for Burnley he moved to Nottingham Forest and in 1959 gained an FA Cup winner's medal. In a distinguished career Gray amassed over 500 League appearances and then, as a manager, he guided Millwall to runner's-up spot in both the Fourth and Third Divisions in the successive seasons of 1965 and 1966.

GREAVES, JAMES

Inside-forward: 169 apps, 132 goals
Born: East Ham, London, 20 February 1940
Career: Lakeside Manor Boys Club, Dagenham Schools, London Schools, Essex Boys, CHELSEA (amateur, April 1955; professional, May 1957), AC Milan/Italy (£80,000, June 1961), Tottenham Hotspur (£99,999, December 1961 – Spurs' manager Bill Nicholson was reluctant to make him a £100,000 footballer), West Ham United (£200,000, March 1970 in a package deal involving Martin Peters, valued at £146,000 and Greaves at £54,000), Barnet (May 1971); later with Chelmsford City, Brentwood Town and Woodford Town (retired 1976); became a TV pundit (with Ian St John)

There has seldom been an opportunist to equal Jimmy Greaves! For many a season he caused chaos to opposing defences, scoring goals at will with his unerring ability as a striker. He was certainly a star performer, although at times he would seem innocuous, even anonymous as he hovered around in centre-field. Then suddenly, like a shark, he would strike when least expected. He would suddenly appear from nowhere to score a brilliant individual goal, sweep forward, again unnoticed, for a close range tap-in. He would rise to drill home a powerful or sometimes delicate header or simply get on the end of a pin-point cross from either flank to spear the ball past the keeper. He scored goals from seemingly impossible angles and opposing defenders everywhere simply hated him! Besides his splendid haul for Chelsea, he netted 9 times in Italian football; claimed a staggering 267 goals in 380 appearances for Spurs (hitting 360 in 420 first-team games all told) and weighed in with 13 in 40 outings for the Hammers. Add to that his England record of 44 goals in 57 full internationals, played between 1959 and 1967, another 13 goals in his 12 Under-23 matches; 3 more for an England XI; 5 in 10 Inter-League games, 1 for the Rest of the World and 6 in 2 youth internationals. In a wonderfully successful career, hot-shot 'Greavesie' scored 554 goals (in 750 games) at club and international level,

357 of which came in the English First Division alone. He actually netted his 100th League goal at the age of 20. He secured 40 hat-tricks (in all games) and actually scored against 36 of the 38 clubs he opposed in the Football League, only failing to find the net against Crystal Palace and Huddersfield Town. Prior to signing as a pro he netted 114 goals in intermediate football for Chelsea. He made his scoring League debut against his future club, Spurs, in August 1957 and he also netted on his debuts for Spurs, AC Milan and West Ham, as well as for England (v. Peru in May 1959). Without doubt he accumulated a tremendous set of statistics.

Surprisingly, for all his efforts on the field, he collected only three medals at club level – helping Spurs twice lift the FA Cup in 1962 and 1967 and succeed in the European Cup-Winners' Cup in 1963. He sadly missed out when England won the World Cup in 1966. He started the competition, playing against Uruguay, Mexico and France but was then struck down by hepatitis and replaced in attack by the man who scored a hat-trick in the final, Geoff Hurst. Greaves and Hurst then played alongside each other in the West Ham forward line at the end of the 1969–70 season and throughout 1970–71.

One of only 4 players to score 5 goals in a League game, Greaves actually achieved this feat on 3 occasions – for Chelsea against Wolves (won 6–2, home, August 1958), Preston North End (won 5–4, away, December 1959) and West Bromwich Albion (won 7–1, home, December 1960). In fact, in the home game with Preston in August 1959, Greaves scored a hat-trick in a 4–4 draw – thus netting 8 against the Lillywhites in 2 matches. He top-scored for the Blues in the 1960–61 season with 41 goals (still a club record) and now lies in fourth place (behind Bobby Tambling, Roy Bentley and Peter Osgood) in Chelsea's all-time scoring list. Greaves also scored in five successive England games in 1960-61, netting twice v. Northern Ireland, grabbing a hat-trick v. Luxembourg, striking once v. Spain, securing a brace v. Wales and notching a second treble against Scotland. Unfortunately in later life, Greaves fell victim to a creeping illness – serious alcoholism – which he graphically explains in his book: *This One's On Me*. Thankfully, he overcame the problem and built a new career for himself as Ian St John's witty companion on ITV's Saturday lunchtime soccer programme. A crowd of 45,799 attended Greaves' testimonial match in October 1972 when Spurs played the Dutch side Feyenoord at White Hart Lane.

GREENWOOD, RONALD, CBE

Defender: 66 apps

Born: Burnley, 11 November 1921

Career: CHELSEA (amateur guest, September 1940; signed October 1943), Belfast Celtic (guest, WW2), Bradford Park Avenue (December 1945), Brentford (March 1949), CHELSEA (October 1952), Fulham (February 1955), Walthamstow Avenue (July 1955–May 1957); also Oxford University (coach for three years, mid-1950s); Eastbourne United (manager, August 1957–June 1958), Arsenal (assistant manager, August 1958), then England

Youth and Under-23 manager; West Ham United (manager, April 1961–August 1974; then general manager until December 1977); England (manager December 1977–July 1982), Brighton and Hove Albion (director, November 1983–85); also acted as technical adviser to FIFA for the 1966 and 1970 World Cup finals)

Ron Greenwood was 24 years old when released by Chelsea but he returned to Stamford Bridge at the age of 31 a much more mature footballer and in 1955 gained a League championship medal. He made his debut for the Blues against Crystal Palace as an amateur in a wartime fixture in December 1940 before 940 hardy spectators at the Bridge. He moved to Bradford in 1945 after being told that he was not guaranteed first-team football with Chelsea. He made 59 League appearances in three seasons at Park Avenue before joining second Division Brentford for whom he made over 150 senior appearances, gaining an England 'B' cap in 1949 and also representing the London FA, the London Combination and the FA whilst at Griffin Park. By now a stylish, unflappable centre-half, he returned to Stamford Bridge in 1952 and had 21 outings when the title was won in 1954–55. Part of an unsure defence at Fulham, he gained an FA coaching badge as a player and held part-time coaching positions at Oxford University and Walthamstow Avenue during the 1950s, taking his first steps into club management in 1957 with non-League side Eastbourne.

Greenwood was a close friend of England boss Walter Winterbottom who engaged him as the country's Under-23 and youth-team coach. He then served as assistant to manager George Swindon at Arsenal before taking charge of West Ham whom he led to FA Cup and ECWC glory in 1964 and 1965 and to the runner's-up spot in the 1966 League Cup final. It was Greenwood who developed England's World Cup winning trio of Bobby Moore, Martin Peters and Geoff Hurst and he also nurtured Johnny Byrne. Greenwood, whom Alf Ramsey said was 'ten years ahead of his time' in terms of soccer management, upset the Hammers' supporters by exchanging Peters for Jimmy Greaves; Peters went from strength to strength but Greaves was a flop at Upton Park. Greenwood was awarded the CBE in 1981 for services to football.

GREGG, ROBERT EDMOND

Inside-forward: 51 apps, 6 goals
Born: Ferryhill, County Durham, 19 February 1904 – *Died*: Durham, 1991
Career: Ferryhill Athletic (1918), Consford Juniors (1919) Winlaton Juniors (1920), Spennymoor United (1921), Shilton Colliery (1922), Durham City (May 1924), Ferryhill Athletic (July 1926), Darlington (professional, September 1926), Sheffield Wednesday (£2,000, May 1928), Birmingham (£2,200, January 1931), CHELSEA (£1,500, September 1933), Boston United (free transfer, June 1938), Sligo Rovers (free, September 1940; retired May 1944)

Bob Gregg was an extremely useful inside-forward who played a significant part in helping Sheffield Wednesday win the First Division championship in 1929 before moving to Birmingham for whom he lined up in the 1931 FA Cup final defeat by West Bromwich Albion. In fact, Gregg had a first-half goal disallowed in the final with the score-sheet blank. He linked up with Chelsea at the age of 29 with perhaps his best years behind him. He failed to settle at Stamford Bridge, having his best season in 1933–34 when he netted 3 times in 30 senior outings. He scored 7 goals in 37 outings for the Owls and 15 in 75 for Birmingham.

GRIFFITHS, ROBERT

Half-back: 45 apps
Born: Chapleton, Scotland, 9 November 1903 – *Died*: Scotland, 1970
Career: Pollock Juniors (Glasgow), CHELSEA (July 1931; retired May 1941)
Bob Griffiths, despite his height of 5 ft 8 in., was a very useful defender who spent ten years at Stamford Bridge. A loyal servant, he acted as reserve to Peter O'Dowd, Allan Craig and Bob Salmond before establishing himself in the first team in 1937–38 when he made 36 appearances as team captain. He joined the Wartime Police Reserve in September 1939 but remained a registered player with the Blues until his retirement.

GRODAS, FRODE

Goalkeeper: 26+1 apps
Born: Songdal, Norway, 24 October 1964
Career: Lillestrom SK/Norway, CHELSEA (loan, September–October 1996; signed on a free transfer, November 1996), Lillestrom SK/Norway (May 1997)
Norwegian international goalkeeper Frode Grodas turned down an offer from Sturm Graz to sign for Ruud Gullit's Chelsea as experienced cover for Kevin Hitchcock following Dimitri Kharine's serious knee injury and Nick Colgan's broken arm – long-term injuries that ruled them both out of first-team contention. Well built, strong and agile, Grodas stood 6 ft 2 in. tall and weighed 14 st. 7 lb, and did very well in his only season of Premiership football, lining up behind his fellow countryman Erland Johnsen on several occasions to help the Blues finish sixth in the table. Chelsea signed giant Dutchman Ed De Goey in July 1997 and with Kharine expected to regain full fitness, Grodas became surplus to requirements and returned to Lillestrom. He won over 30 full caps for his country.

GRONKJAER, JESPER

Winger: 77+42 apps, 11 goals
Born: Nuuk, Denmark, 12 August 1977
Career: Aalborg BK/Holland (April 1994; professional, August 1995), Ajax Amsterdam/Holland (July 1999), CHELSEA (£7.8 million, December 2000), Birmingham City (£2.2 million, July 2004), Atletico Bilbao/Spain (£1.4 million, December 2004)
Jesper Gronkjaer had scored 21 goals in 142 League games in Dutch League

football when Chelsea signed him for a huge fee just before Christmas 2000. A fast-raiding winger with a lot of skill and able to occupy both flanks, he tended to overdo the clever stuff at times and his crosses were not always well received! He lost his place at Stamford Bridge for a short time but was always in the frame for a recall as manager Claudio Ranieri was a firm believer in wingers. When new boss José Mourinho moved into Stamford Bridge, Gronkjaer quickly moved out, joining his former team-mates Mario Melchiot and Mikael Forssell at Birmingham City. Now capped at senior level more than 50 times, Gronkjaer also played for Denmark in 13 Under-21 internationals and he actually turned down an approach from the Spanish club Sevilla to join Birmingham but finally did move to Spain with Bilbao after failing to settle at St Andrew's.

GUDJOHNSEN, EIDUR SMARI

Striker: 152+74 apps, 75 goals
Born: Reykjavik, Iceland, 15 September 1978
Career: FC Valur/Iceland (amateur, September 1994; professional, September 1995), PSV Eindhoven/Holland (March 1996), KR Reykjavik/Iceland (1998), Bolton Wanderers (free transfer, August 1998), CHELSEA (£4 million, July 2000)

Blond striker, full of grim determination, with loads of pace and an eye for goal, Eidur Gudjohnsen formed a terrific partnership in Chelsea's front line with Jimmy-Floyd Hasselbaink and after the latter had left, he continued to do the business up front, scoring some cracking goals. Indeed, in his first four seasons at the Bridge, Gudjohnsen netted 59 times for the Blues while Hasselbaink weighed in with 87. Hernan Crespo, the disgraced Romanian Adrian Mutu and others all played alongside Gudjohnsen at various times.

Bolton certainly took a huge gamble when signing him from his home-town club, but he adapted well to English conditions and netted 26 goals in 73 games for the Lancashire club before his transfer to Stamford Bridge. He celebrated his debut for Chelsea by helping them win the 2000 FA Charity Shield. Honoured by Iceland at youth-team level, he then gained 11 Under-21 caps before going on to appear in more than 30 full internationals. Gudjohnsen is known as the 'Iceman'. He gained both League Cup and Premiership winner's medals in 2005.

GULLIT, RUUD

Forward/midfield/sweeper: 50+14 apps, 7 goals
Born: Parmaribo, Surinam, 1 September 1962
Career: Meerboys FC/Holland (September 1977), DWS/Holland (August 1978), FC Haarlem/Holland (professional, July 1979), Feyenoord/Holland (April 1981), PSV Eindhoven/Holland (August 1983), AC Milan/Italy (£6.5 million, August 1987), Sampdoria/Italy (free transfer, June 1994), AC Milan (January 1995), CHELSEA (free, July 1995; appointed player–manager,

1996; sacked February 1998), Newcastle United (manager, August 1998–August 1999); worked in the media and also acted as adviser and coach to the Dutch FA; later appointed manager of Feyenoord (2004)

Football intelligence was the hallmark of Ruud Gullit's career. From his early days when playing as a sweeper for Barry Hughes' Haarlem he progressed to Feyenoord, PSV, to his leadership of the AC Milan revival in the late 1980s and then into management in England with first Chelsea and then Newcastle. Along the way he also demonstrated that players can look beyond the narrow confines of the game with his vehement support for the release of black South African leader Nelson Mandela. And he would surely have won the coveted European Footballer of the Year award more than once had it not been for a niggling knee problem which severely interrupted his career. Milan paid a world record fee for his services in 1987 and were rewarded with the Italian championship in his first season and the European Champions Cup in his second and third. Amazingly he helped Milan win their second Champions trophy against Benfica in 1990, despite having played in only two League games that season.

Injury worries and an overflow of foreigners at the San Siro resulted in Milan coach Fabio Capello releasing Gullit on a free transfer in 1994. He soon returned to Milan, however, and continued to perform his skills before switching his allegiance to Chelsea. He played very well for the Blues and became a huge favourite with the Stamford Bridge faithful. He replaced Glenn Hoddle as manager but unfortunately things didn't quite work out according to plan, although Chelsea did win the FA Cup in 1997. His idiosyncratic style of management got under the skin of both directors and players and he was dismissed in 1998, replaced by Gianluca Vialli. The charismatic Gullit then took over the reins from Kenny Dalglish as manager at Newcastle before he, himself, was followed into the St James' Park hot seat by Bobby Robson.

Away from club football where he made over 400 appearances, Gullit had a topsy-turvy international career with Holland. He scored 17 goals in 64 outings and skippered his country to European Championship success in 1988, but midway through the 1994 World Cup campaign he quit – a decision that stunned Dutch football. A year later, however, he made a sensational comeback only to pack in for a second time on the eve of the finals.

HALES, KEVIN PETER
Defender/midfield: 25+2 apps, 2 goals
Born: Dartford, Kent, 13 January 1961
Career: Kent Schools, CHELSEA (apprentice, May 1977; professional, January 1979), Leyton Orient (July 1983–May 1993)

Kevin Hales suffered with a series of niggling injuries during his time at Stamford Bridge and as a result failed to establish himself as a regular member of the first team. In the end he was certainly a player who 'got away' – as he developed into a tenacious, lively midfielder who made well over 350 senior appearances for Orient (exactly 300 in the Football League) during his ten years at Brisbane Road. He also played cricket as a schoolboy for Kent.

HALL, GARETH DAVID
Full-back/midfield: 148+21 apps, 5 goals
Born: Croydon, Surrey, 12 March 1969
Career: CHELSEA (apprentice, August 1984; professional, April 1986), Sunderland (loan, December 1995; signed for £300,000, January 1996), Brentford (loan, March 1997), Swindon Town ('Bosman' free transfer, May 1998), Havant and Waterlooville (July 2001)

During his ten years at Stamford Bridge, Gareth Hall helped Chelsea win the Second Division title in 1989 and the Full Members' Cup in 1990 and gained one Under-21 and four full caps for Wales (v. Yugoslavia, Holland, Finland and Israel) between 1987 and 1989. He later added five more full caps to his tally – having represented England as a schoolboy (qualifying to play for Wales later because his mother was born in Caerphilly).

After transferring to Sunderland (signed by Peter Reid) he collected a First Division championship medal in 1996. A versatile player, able to occupy a number of positions, he graduated through Chelsea's intermediate and reserve teams and was voted the club's Young Player of the Year in 1985. Well built, positive in his actions, he had a terrific engine and was never found wanting. He made his League debut for the Blues in a 2–1 defeat at Wimbledon in May 1987 as a substitute. Hall became the target of the boo-boys at Sunderland and this affected his game. He left the Wearsiders in 1998 having appeared in 53 first-class games in two and a half years. He then made almost 100 senior appearances for Swindon prior to entering non-League football in 2001.

HALSE, HAROLD JAMES
Centre-forward: 111 apps, 25 goals
Born: Stratford, London, 1 January 1886 – *Died*: Essex County Hospital, Colchester, 25 March 1949
Career: Park Road School (Wanstead), Newportians (Leyton), Wanstead, Barking Town (1904), Clapton Orient (amateur, August 1905), Southend United (June 1906), Manchester United (£350, March 1908), Aston Villa (£1,200, July 1912), CHELSEA (May 1913); guest for Clapton Orient (WW1); Charlton Athletic (July 1921; retired May 1923; scout until 1925); later ran a tobacconist shop at Walton-on-Naze

Harold Halse, who scored an aggregate of 204 goals while playing for Newportians and Wanstead and followed up with 91 for Southend in 1906–07, netted just 45 seconds into his debut for Manchester United – the first of 50 goals in 124 appearances for the club – and when United beat Swindon 8–4 in the 1911 FA Charity Shield, Halse hit 6 goals. He gained an FA Cup winner's medal with both United and Aston Villa and collected a runner's-up medal in the same competition with Chelsea in 1915, a feat later equalled by Ernie Taylor who did it with Newcastle United, Blackpool and Manchester United in the 1950s. Not a player to catch the eye, Halse was, nevertheless, one of the finest marksmen of his day. Small, rather slight in build, he had the knack of snapping up the half-chance – a real top-class opportunist. He served Chelsea superbly well during the last two pre-WW1 campaigns and the first of peacetime football in 1919–20. One of the most respected footballers of his day, he was capped once by England, played twice for the Football League XI (1913 and 1914) and won both First Division championship and runner's-up medals with United and Villa respectively in 1912 and 1913. Halse's goals-per-games record during his first-class career was exceptional and it would certainly have been a lot better had not his career been savaged badly by WW1 which cost him four potentially vintage seasons. He captained Charlton in their first season in the Football League (1921–22).

HAMILTON, IAN MICHAEL
Midfield: 3+2 apps, 2 goals
Born: Streatham, London, 31 October 1950
Career: Streatham and London Schools, CHELSEA (juniors, October 1965; professional, January 1968), Southend United (£5,000, September 1968), Aston Villa (£40,000, June 1969), Sheffield United (July 1976), Minnesota Kicks/NASL (three summers: 1978, 1979 and 1980); San Jose Earthquakes/NASL (May–August 1982); Rotherham United (football in the community officer, mid- to late '80s); later worked for the Nike organisation, coaching soccer while also being engaged as a play-scheme organiser at Sheffield University, arranging soccer classes for youngsters at the local Ritz Super Sports centre

England Youth international 'Chico' Hamilton had a terrific left foot and did some sterling work for each of his four English clubs. He netted 65 goals in a total of 308 League games, played in two League Cup finals for Villa (1971 and 1975) and was the youngest player ever to appear in a First Division game for Chelsea, aged 16 years, 4 months, 18 days v. Spurs in March 1967. Unfortunately there were far too many players of similar style and, indeed, vying for the same position during his time at Stamford Bridge.

HAMPSHIRE, STEVEN GREGOR
Midfield: 0+1 app.
Born: Edinburgh, 17 October 1979
Career: CHELSEA (apprentice, April 1996; professional, April–July 1997), Dunfermline Athletic (January 2000)

A reserve at Stamford Bridge, Steve Hampshire's only senior game for Chelsea was as a second-half substitute for Ruud Gullit in a League Cup clash with Blackburn Rovers in October 1997.

HAMPTON, COLIN MICHAEL KENNETH
Goalkeeper: 82 apps
Born: Brechin, Scotland, 1 September 1890 – deceased by 1980
Career: Brechin City, Motherwell, CHELSEA (April 1914–May 1924), Brechin City (August 1924), Crystal Palace (April 1925–May 1926)
A Scottish League XI representative during his Motherwell days, goalkeeper Colin Hampton understudied the likes of Jim Molyneux and Howard Baker for the last two and first three seasons either side of WW1. Indeed, he made only 32 appearances in those 5 campaigns before having decent runs in the first team in 1922–23 and 1923–24. Sound and reliable and able to kick long and straight, Hampton was a machine-gunner in Mesopotamia during WW1. Whilst out on patrol, his car was shattered by enemy bombs and after being taken prisoner he started to walk to Constantinople but before he and his fellow prisoners arrived, the armistice was declared. He was subsequently awarded the Military Medal for gallantry.

HANSON, ADOLPH JONATHAN
Outside-left: 45 apps, 9 goals
Born: Bootle, Merseyside, 27 February 1912 – deceased at 1990
Career: Bootle JOC, Everton (trial in 'A' team, 1930), Liverpool (professional, November 1931), CHELSEA (£7,500, July 1938); guest for Bolton Wanderers, Chester, Crewe Alexandra, Liverpool, Manchester City, New Brighton, Rochdale, Southport, Tranmere Rovers and Wrexham during WW2; South Liverpool (player–manager, August 1946), Shelbourne United/Ireland (player–manager, July 1948), Ellesmere Port Town (player–manager, February 1949–50)
An England wartime international against Scotland in February 1941, 'Alf' Hanson was a no-nonsense footballer, quick and direct, whose aggregate career figures were impressive: 220 League and FA Cup appearances for Liverpool and Chelsea, 61 goals scored. Unfortunately he lost seven years due to the hostilities yet still managed to play regularly, guesting for ten different clubs. Ironically, he made his debut for Chelsea against his former club Liverpool (away) on the opening day of the 1938–39 season.

A plumber by trade, Hanson was the brother of the Bolton Wanderers goalkeeper Stan Hanson.

HARDING, AUGUSTUS WILSON
Full-back: 5 apps
Born: Chesham, Buckinghamshire, 1886 – *Died*: France, 1916
Career: Tottenham Hotspur (amateur, 1905), CHELSEA (amateur, December 1906; professional, June 1907), Exeter City (September 1913)
A reserve full-back at Stamford Bridge for almost seven years, Gus Harding made his League debut in December 1907 against Preston North End (won 4–2) when he stood in for Tommy Miller. A very sporting character, on and off

the field, his loyalty was rewarded with a benefit match in February 1913. Harding, who made seven appearances for Exeter, was sadly killed in action during WW1.

HARFORD, MICHAEL GORDON
Striker: 33+1 apps, 11 goals
Born: Sunderland, 12 February 1959
Career: Lambton Star Boys' Club (Sunderland), trials with Newcastle United and Sunderland; Lincoln City (professional, July 1977), Newcastle United (£216,000, December 1980), Bristol City (£160,000, August 1981), Birmingham City (£100,000, March 1982), Luton Town (£250,000, December 1984), Derby County (£450,000, January 1990), Luton Town (again, £325,000, September 1991), CHELSEA (£300,000, August 1992), Sunderland (£250,000, March 1993), Coventry City (£200,000, July 1993); Wimbledon (£75,000, August 1994, player–coach May 1997; then coach and assistant manager to May 2001), Luton Town (coach, May 2001–May 2003, then director of football; later senior coach, August 2004), Nottingham Forest (assistant manager/coach, November 2004; caretaker-manager, December 2004), Swindon Town (assistant manager/coach, January 2005), Nottingham Forest (assistant manager, February 2005), Rotherham United (manager, April 2005)

Striker Mick Harford drew up a magnificent record as a professional footballer, scoring over 230 goals in more than 700 senior appearances for no fewer than 10 different clubs over a 20-year period. His transfer fees totalled £2.25 million.

With Luton, Harford won the League Cup in 1988 and the following year collected runner's-up medals in both the Simod Cup and League Cup, scoring at Wembley against Nottingham Forest in the latter final. He was also capped twice by England at senior level, lining up against Israel and Denmark in 1988–89, and starred in one game for his country's 'B' team. He took over from Frank Worthington at Birmingham and scored an average of a goal every three games at St Andrew's. He drew up his best set of figures with Luton (217 appearances, 94 goals) and during his time at Stamford Bridge he also netted a goal every three games.

Harford's move from Newcastle to Bristol City in 1981 was somewhat controversial. At the time of the deal the Ashton Gate club was on the verge of bankruptcy and could not meet the agreed instalments on his transfer fee. Newcastle appealed to the Football League who ordered Bristol City to return Harford to St James' Park on a free transfer. Rather than doing this, City immediately sold him to the Blues, with the £100,000 fee involved going to Newcastle, leaving City with a balance of £60,000. Harford had his first taste of senior management with Nottingham Forest late in 2004, following the resignation of Joe Kinnear.

HARLEY, JONATHAN
Left–back/midfield: 30+12 apps, 2 goals
Born: Maidstone, Kent, 26 September 1979
Career: CHELSEA (apprentice, April 1996; professional, March 1997), Wimbledon (loan, October–November, 2000), Fulham (£3.5 million, August 2001), Sheffield United (loan, October–December 2003), West Ham United (loan, January–March 2004), Sheffield United (free transfer, July 2004)

Capped by England at youth and Under-21 levels, playing in three matches in the latter category, Jon Harley won the FA Cup with Chelsea in 2000. He had to battle hard and long to earn a place in the first XI at Stamford Bridge (owing to the excellent form shown by Celestine Babayaro) and made only 42 appearances in 5 years. Enthusiastic and hard-working, he has scored some stunning goals during his career including his first for Chelsea against Watford in the Premiership in February 2000, a goal which proved to be the match-winner.

HARMER, THOMAS CHARLES
Midfield: 9 apps, 1 goal
Born: Hackney, London, 2 February 1928
Career: Tottenham Juniors, Tottenham Hotspur (amateur, August 1945), Finchley (1946), Tottenham Hotspur (professional, August 1948), Watford (£6,000, October 1960), CHELSEA (£3,500, September 1962; retired as a player, April 1963, continued as youth-team coach until June 1967)

Little Tommy Harmer, with his cunning technique and smart dribbling skills, was aptly nicknamed the 'Charmer'. Despite his small frame (he was only 5 ft 6 in. tall and weighed just 8 st. 9 lb), he teased and tormented defenders all over the country, often easing past opponents almost twice his size. He scored 51 goals in 222 first-class games for Spurs before having a decent spell with Watford. He then gave Chelsea excellent service as a coach after making only a few first-team appearances during the 1962–63 Second Division promotion-winning season. In fact, it was Harmer who scored the winning goal against Sunderland in the penultimate League game that finally clinched a place in the top flight. He continued to make the odd appearance at reserve team level when engaged as a coach at Stamford Bridge. Later Harmer worked as a warehouseman in Hatton Garden and then as a messenger for an Israeli bank based in London's West End.

HARRIS, ALLAN JOHN
Left–back: 98+4 apps, 1 goal
Born: Hackney, London, 28 December 1942
Career: CHELSEA (juniors, April 1956; professional, June 1960), Coventry City (£35,000, November 1964), CHELSEA (£45,000, May 1966), Queens Park Rangers (£30,000, July 1967), Plymouth Argyle (March 1971), Cambridge United (July 1973–April 1974); later assistant manager to boss

Terry Venables at Queens Park Rangers (October 1980), CF Barcelona/Spain (May 1984), Tottenham Hotspur (December 1988–June 1991); coached in the Middle East, then Malaysia (national team coach, 2001–04); now a football agent

An England schoolboy and youth international and elder brother of Ron Harris (q.v.), Allan Harris was a fringe player at Stamford Bridge during each of his two spells, initially competing for a full-back spot with the Sillett brothers, Eddie McCreadie, Ken Shellito and also Marvin Hinton. He made his League debut in October 1960 and went on to make over 300 appearances in that competition until retiring in 1974. In 1967, along with Cliff Jones (Spurs), Harris was the first substitute named for an FA Cup final (he did not come off the bench). The Harris brothers, Allan and Ron, played together in Chelsea's senior side for the first time in December 1962 in a home League game against Plymouth Argyle. Promotion to the First Division was achieved that season.

HARRIS, CHARLES

Full-back/centre-half: 2 apps
Born: Wanstead, London, 1 December 1885 – *Died*: London, *circa* 1967
Career: CHELSEA (September 1905–April 1909), Swansea Town (July 1909), CHELSEA (trainer, seasons 1910–40)

Reserve defender Charlie Harris spent four seasons as a player at Stamford Bridge. In that time he made just two senior appearances, lining up at centre-half against Stockport County (away) in Chelsea's first-ever League game in September 1905 and then at right-back in an FA Cup tie against Crystal Palace two months later. After returning to the Bridge, Harris gave the club 30 years' service on the training staff.

HARRIS, JOHN

Full-back/centre-half: 364 apps, 14 goals
Born: Glasgow, 30 June 1917 – *Died*: Yorkshire, 24 July 1988
Career: Swindon Town (amateur, 1932), Swansea Town (professional, August 1934), Tottenham Hotspur (February 1939), Wolverhampton Wanderers (May 1939); guest for Southampton, CHELSEA during WW2; CHELSEA (signed for £8,000, August 1945), Chester (player–manager, July 1956–April 1959), Sheffield United (manager, April 1959–July 1968; then general manager to August 1969; manager, again to December 1973; then chief scout to 1976), Sheffield Wednesday (coach, late 1970s)

Like his father Neil (of Newcastle United) John Harris became a manager at the end of a distinguished playing career – and they were one of the very few father-and-son combinations to become managers. Harris junior made over 400 senior appearances at club level, plus several more during WW2 when he was capped by Scotland against England in April 1945. Further international caps would have surely come his way had he been a fraction taller. Initially an inside-forward, he failed to make the grade at Swindon but broke into football bigtime at Swansea where his father was manager. Unfortunately he did not get a chance at White Hart Lane or at Molineux (the latter owing to the war) but after that he went on to give Chelsea supreme service as a defender for 11 years. In that time he made 364 first-class appearances and over 100 during WW2, 70 coming as a guest prior to signing permanently in 1945.

He played in the 1944 and 1945 finals of the Football League Cup (South), gaining a winner's medal in the latter v. Millwall at Wembley. Harris, who was converted into a centre-half by Blues' boss Ted Drake, was without doubt a dominant figure on the field of play. In 1950, he was described as being 'a clean and studious player, exceptionally good with his head and strong in the tackle'. In 1954–55, as skipper, he celebrated with a winner's medal as Chelsea won the League championship for the first time in the club's history. As a manager, he guided Sheffield United to the FA Cup semi-finals and Second Division title in 1961 and ten years later again lifted the Blades into the top flight as champions.

HARRIS, RONALD EDWARD
Defender: 784+11 apps, 14 goals
Born: Hackney, London, 13 November 1944
Career: CHELSEA (apprentice, August 1960; professional, November 1962), Brentford (player–coach, May 1980–November 1983), Aldershot (manager, November 1984–May 1985); bought the Bramhill golf course in Wiltshire for £400,000 and reputed to have sold same for £2 million in 1989 to golf pro Roger Mace and ex-Doncaster Rovers goalkeeper Glen Johnson; now runs a holiday chalet and fishing complex in Warminster, Wiltshire

Ron Harris holds two Chelsea records – most senior appearances for the club (795) and most League appearances (655) – and he was an ever-present in the side in four seasons: 1964–65, 1966–67, 1972–73 and 1974–75. Nicknamed 'Chopper', he was a terrific defender who played for England at both schoolboy and youth team levels before earning four Under-23 caps. He developed through the junior and intermediate ranks at Stamford Bridge to make his League debut for the Blues against Sheffield Wednesday (won 1–0) in February 1962 and established himself in the side in 1963, retaining his place (injuries and suspensions apart) until 1980 when he moved to Griffin Park. No one can, in fact, equal the service given to Chelsea football club by the seemingly evergreen Ron Harris who was a pillar of strength in the Blues' defence whether occupying a full-back, wing-half or even centre-half position. An amazingly fit athlete, strong on the ground and in the air, he used to play with his sleeves rolled up above the elbows even in the coldest weather. Harris, an FA Youth Cup winner, played in four major Cup finals for Chelsea – gaining a runner's-up medal in the 1967 FA Cup and 1972 League Cup finals while collecting winner's prizes in the 1970 FA Cup and 1971 European Cup-Winners' Cup finals. A Chelsea legend, Harris's two appearance records will, I feel, stand forever. A truly great player who even starred in more than 65 games for Brentford, thus taking his tally of career appearances past the 850 mark.

HARRISON, MICHAEL JOHN

Outside-left: 64 apps, 9 goals

Born: Ilford, Essex, 16 April 1940

Career: CHELSEA (juniors, May 1955; professional, April 1957), Blackburn Rovers (£18,000, September 1962), Plymouth Argyle (£2,000, September 1967), Luton Town (£1,500, June 1968; retired, injured, May 1970); later resident in Devon

An England schoolboy international who went on to gain three Under-23 caps, Mike Harrison was a product of the Stamford Bridge nursery. A tall, well-built player, extremely quick, he made his League debut in April 1957 at Blackpool but remained virtually a reserve for the next six years, appearing only spasmodically in the first XI. He had his best spell in the senior side in 1961–62 when he scored 3 times in 22 Second Division matches. After leaving the Bridge he netted 43 goals in 182 League and Cup appearances for Blackburn, had only one part-season with Plymouth and joined Luton soon after the Hatters had won promotion to the Third Division.

HARROW, JACK HENRY

Full-back: 333 apps, 5 goals

Born: Beddington, Surrey, 8 October 1888 – *Died*: London, 19 July 1958

Career: Mitcham FC (1906), Mill Green Rovers (August 1907), Croydon Common (June 1908), CHELSEA (£50, March 1911; retired, June 1926; retained on club's training staff until 1938); then worked for Mitcham Council until 1956

Jack Harrow began as a centre-forward and once scored eight goals in a game for Croydon Common. He was then converted into a wing-half before settling down at full-back, the position he enjoyed most. He appeared to look far too casual out on the pitch and often waited until the last second to get in a tackle, which was usually timed to perfection. He made his League debut for Chelsea in December 1911 against Hull City and gained a regular place in the side in 1913. He played in the 1915 FA Cup final but then lost practically four years to WW1 before returning to action on demob from the Army, helping the Blues win the London Victory Cup in 1919. He continued to serve the club superbly well for a further seven years and in all was associated with Chelsea for more than a quarter of a century. An England international, Harrow was capped twice, against Ireland in 1922 and Sweden the following year. He also played for the Football League v. the Southern League in 1914.

HARWOOD, JOHN ARTHUR

Centre-half: 4 apps

Born: Somerstown, West Sussex, 1 February 1889 – *Died*: London, 1966

Career: Tooting Town (March 1908), Southend United (April 1910), CHELSEA (May 1912), Portsmouth (March 1913), Swansea Town (free transfer, May 1922), Aberdare Athletic (seasons 1924–27), Barrow (season 1927–28), Fulham (trainer, 1930s); Royal Naval Volunteer Reserve (1939–41)

Reserve defender Jack Harwood (who could play as a wing-half or pivot) deputised in four games for the injured Sam Downing during his ten-month stay at Stamford Bridge. He went on to appear in 41 League games for Pompey, 45 for Swansea and 103 for Aberdare.

HASSELBAINK, JERREL (JIMMY-FLOYD)

Striker: 156+35 apps, 87 goals
Born: Paramaribo, Surinam, 27 March 1972
Career: SC Paramaribo (1991), Campomaiorense/Portugal (May 1995), Boavista/Portugal (August 1996), Leeds United (£2 million, July 1997), Atletico Madrid/Spain (£12 million, August 1999), CHELSEA (£15 million, July 2000), Middlesbrough (free transfer, July 2004)

Jimmy-Floyd Hasselbaink gave Chelsea four wonderful years of all-action, hard-shooting forward-play. He averaged 22 goals in 43 games per season but did not receive a single club medal to show for his efforts. Prior to moving to Stamford Bridge, he had already scored 90 goals in 154 League games playing in Portugal and Spain, and had also become an established international with Holland for whom he would gain a total of 23 caps and score 9 goals (up to 2004). Powerful, with a terrific right-foot shot, he loved to have a crack at goal from any distance and was often on target. He formed a superb partnership up front for the Blues with Eidur Gudjohnsen and in the four seasons they played together at the Bridge, they amassed a total of 146 goals, Hasselbaink claiming 87. In his first season with Middlesbrough, he struck home another 16 goals to take his career tally past the 200 mark.

HATELEY, ANTHONY

Striker: 32+1 apps, 9 goals
Born: Derby, 13 June 1941
Career: Derby schoolboy football, Normanton Sports Club, Derby County (schoolboy forms, July 1955), Notts County (amateur, May 1956; professional, June 1958), Aston Villa (£20,000, August 1963), CHELSEA (£100,000, October 1966), Liverpool (£100,000, July 1967), Coventry City (£80,000, September 1968), Birmingham City (£72,000, August 1969), Notts County (£20,000, November 1970), Oldham Athletic (£5,000, July 1972), Bromsgrove Rovers (May 1974), Prescot Town (July 1975), Keyworth United (December 1978; retired August 1979); employed in Everton's lottery office, then by Thwaites Brewery, Nottinghamshire, and later worked for a local soft drinks company

Tony Hateley was a soccer nomad whose career realised 211 goals in 434 club appearances. An out-and-out striker, he was tall, muscular and exceptionally strong in the air. He helped Notts County win the Third and Fourth Division championships in 1960 and 1971 and was an FA Cup finalist with Chelsea in 1967, beaten 2–1 by Spurs.

Aston Villa's top marksman three seasons running (1963–66), he is one of only two players to score four goals in a League Cup game for that club, doing so in a 7–1 home win over Bradford City in 1964. When he moved to Chelsea in 1966, Hateley was only the second £100,000 footballer in Britain at that time (following Alan Ball). He was bought, in effect, to replace broken-leg victim Peter Osgood and to partner another new recruit, Tommy Baldwin, up front. He netted 9 times in 33 appearances in his only season at Stamford Bridge, making his debut in the London derby with Spurs. His son, Mark Hateley, played for Coventry City, QPR, Leeds United, Hull City, Portsmouth, Glasgow Rangers and England (32 caps). He scored 50 goals in the Football League and 115 in 222 games during his 2 spells at Ibrox Park.

HAY, DAVID

Defender/midfield: 118+2 apps, 3 goals
Born: Paisley, Scotland, 29 January 1948
Career: St Mirren Boys' Club, St Mirren Boys' Guild, Celtic (professional, February 1965), CHELSEA (£225,000, August 1974; retired, injured, September 1979); Motherwell (assistant manager, November 1979; manager, September 1981–May 1982); coached in the USA; later manager of Livingston (briefly); Celtic (manager, May 1983–June 1987; later chief scout at Parkhead for three years in the mid-1990s); Dunfermline Athletic (manager, 2004)

David Hay, one of the most adaptable class talents ever, was without doubt an outstanding footballer north of the border. He joined Chelsea at the age of 26, having accumulated almost 200 first-class appearances for Celtic with whom he won medals galore – five League championships, two Scottish Cups and one League Cup, plus runner's-up prizes in the latter two competitions, plus another after defeat in the 1970 European Cup final. He also gained three Under-23 and 27 full caps for his country and represented the Scottish League on four occasions. He was superb in the 1974 World Cup finals prior to his transfer to Chelsea.

He made his senior debut for the Blues on the opening day of the 1974–75 League season against Carlisle United (lost 2–0) and quickly settled down in centre-field with his fellow countryman Charlie Cooke and John Hollins. During his last two seasons at Stamford Bridge, Hay was badly affected by a tedious knee injury and an eye problem. He underwent five operations including two on his eyes and made only 16 appearances in that time. Hit in the eye by an arrow as a lad, he wore contact lenses from the age of eight and as a young Celtic player told nobody about his plight. Prior to 1972, however, he certainly produced some excellent displays as an aggressive, ball-winning yet dominating midfielder or as a totally reliable and confident defender who occupied every position along the back line. As manager of Celtic, Hay guided the Bhoys to the runner's-up spot in both the League championship and League Cup in 1984. He then led them to victory in the Scottish Cup and to second spot in the League the following season. He won the Premier Division title in 1986 and claimed the runner's-up prize again in both the League and League Cup in 1987 before Billy McNeill returned for a second spell in the hot seat at Parkhead.

HAYWOOD, JOHNSON WILLIAM

Half-back/inside-forward: 23 apps, 2 goals

Born: Eckington, Derbyshire, 1899 – *Died*: 1972

Career: Eckington FC, CHELSEA (professional, March 1921), Halifax Town (May 1924), Yeovil and Petters United (March 1925), Portsmouth (December 1925), Barrow (March 1926), Scunthorpe and Lindsey United (seasons 1927–30)

After a bright enough start to his League career – he scored on his debut against Aston Villa in front of almost 60,000 fans at Stamford Bridge in March 1922 after a year in the reserves – Bill Haywood lost his way and was eventually replaced in the side by Buchanan Sharp. He netted only one more goal in ten League games during the remainder of his career.

HAZARD, MICHAEL

Midfield: 42+7 apps, 10 goals

Born: Sunderland, 5 February 1960

Career: Sunderland Boys, Durham Schools, Tottenham Hotspur (apprentice, July 1976; professional, February 1978), CHELSEA (£310,000, September 1985), Portsmouth (£100,000, January 1990), Swindon Town (£130,000, September 1990), Tottenham Hotspur (£50,000, November 1993; released June 1995), Hitchin Town (seasons 1995–97)

An exceptionally talented midfielder, a grafter with good technique although a tad suspect on stamina at times, Mickey Hazard linked up with Glenn Hoddle at White Hart Lane and developed the knack of scoring vital goals. Indeed, he netted 23 times in 138 first-class games for Spurs, appearing in the 1982 League Cup final defeat by Liverpool, winning the FA Cup (v. QPR) that same year and then gaining a UEFA Cup winner's prize in 1984. He then lost his place and chose to transfer to Stamford Bridge in the hope of regular first-team football. However, due to injuries and illness and disputes with the management, he failed to find his best form with the Blues and subsequently moved to Fratton Park before linking up with his former Spurs' colleagues Ossie Ardiles and Glenn Hoddle at Swindon. He returned to Spurs in 1993 (with Ardiles as manager). On retiring from top-class football in 1999, Hazard had amassed over 440 senior appearances and scored 59 goals at club level.

HENDERSON, GEORGE HUNTER
Half-back: 64 apps, 1 goal
Born: Ladthorpe, Selkirk, Scotland, 2 May 1880 – *Died*: Scotland, 1957
Career: Queen's Park (amateur, April 1900), Dundee (January 1902), Glasgow
  Rangers (November 1902), Middlesbrough (July 1905), CHELSEA (April
  1905), Glossop (May 1909–April 1910)

A Scottish international, capped against Ireland in 1904, George Henderson
also represented Glasgow against Sheffield in the annual inter-city fixture. A
stylish and talented half-back, he possessed a crisp, timely tackle and a feature
of his overall play was his superb volleying. A Scottish Cup winner in 1903 and
a finalist in 1904 and 1905, he appeared in 43 games for Rangers before
transferring to Middlesbrough.

HEWITT, THOMAS JOHN
Full-back: 8 apps
Born: Connah's Quay, Wales, 26 April 1889 – *Died*: Cardiff, 12 December 1980
Career: Sandycroft FC (April 1906), Connah's Quay United (August 1907),
  Saltney (professional, July 1908), Wrexham (May 1910), CHELSEA (£350,
  March 1911), South Liverpool (August 1913), Swansea Town (June 1914;
  retired April 1920), Aberaman (manager, June 1920–May 1922); later
  worked as a commercial traveller

Tom Hewitt, an engineer by trade, spent just two seasons at Stamford Bridge
where he had to fight for first-team football along with Walter Bettridge and
John Cameron. He did have injury problems from time to time and played in
only eight League games, making his debut in December 1911 against Glossop
when he replaced Bettridge at right-back. He won eight full caps for Wales –
three with Wrexham, three with Chelsea and two with South Liverpool – and
during an uneasy career, suffered a badly twisted knee, severely damaged ankle,
broken arm, dislocated collar bone and concussion. He helped Sandycroft and
Connah's Quay win the Chester and District League title in 1907 and 1908
respectively and was a Welsh Cup finalist with Swansea in 1915. Hewitt was
aged 90 when he died.

HIGGS, FRANK JARY
Goalkeeper: 2 apps
Born: Willington-on-Tyne, Northumberland, September 1910 – *Died*: 1956
Career: Bedlington United (1926), Seaton Delaval (1927), CHELSEA
  (professional, October 1928), Linfield (May 1930), Barnsley (May 1931),
  Manchester City (June 1932), Aldershot (June 1933), Walsall (July 1934),
  Carlisle United (March 1935), Southend United (April 1937), Barrow
  (August 1938); did not figure after WW2

Signed as cover for Sam Millington, Frank Higgs played in just two League
games for Chelsea during his time at Stamford Bridge – lining up against
Tottenham Hotspur in front of 60,000 fans for his debut in September 1929 and

against West Bromwich Albion at The Hawthorns a week later. He accumulated just 99 League appearances in 11 years (49 for Carlisle).

HILSDON, GEORGE RICHARD

Inside-left/centre-forward: 164 apps, 107 goals
Born: Bow, London, 10 August 1885 – *Died*: London, 7 September 1941
Career: East Ham Schools, South West Ham, Clapton Orient, Luton Town (May 1902), West Ham United (August 1903), CHELSEA (May 1906), West Ham United (June 1912), Chatham (June 1919), Gillingham (May 1921; retired November 1921)

The first player to score 100 competitive goals for Chelsea, 'Gattling Gun' George Hilsdon was a marksman to savour. He could unleash bullet shots with either foot and is one of only four players to net five goals in a League game for the Blues, doing so on his debut against Glossop North End in September 1906. He also netted a sixtimer for the club, in a 9–1 1st round FA Cup win over Worksop Town in January 1908. With his powerful shooting (from any reasonable distance) he was instrumental in helping the Blues win promotion to the First Division in 1907 with a tally of 27 goals. He was on top of his game for five years or so before his form dipped alarmingly in 1911–12 (only one goal in ten outings). One reporter stated: 'He had become too sociable, too careless with his strength and vitality.' In the summer of 1912 he returned to Upton Park, serving the Hammers well until the outbreak of WW1. He hit 35 goals in 92 games for West Ham. Severely affected by mustard gas poisoning during the hostilities, he recovered and went on to assist Chatham and Gillingham before hanging up his boots at the age of 38. Thereafter he was a regular supporter at Stamford Bridge. One of the club's all-time greats, he won eight caps for England (1907–09), played in one international trial (South v. North) and also represented the Football League, scoring a hat-trick v. the Irish League in 1906. For many years, a statuette of a footballer – modelled on Hilsdon – decorated a weathervane on the roof of the stand at the north end of Stamford Bridge.

HINSHELWOOD, WALTER ALEXANDER ALAN

Outside-right: 14 apps, 1 goal
Born: Chapelhall, London, 27 October 1929
Career: Sutton United (May 1945), Fulham (professional, October 1946), CHELSEA (part-exchange deal involving Jim Bowie, January 1951), Fulham (£3,000, May 1951), Reading (£2,500, December 1952), Bristol City (February 1956), Millwall (£1,000, June 1960), Toronto/Canada (May–October 1961), Newport County (November–December 1961); later with Deal Town (season 1963–64)

Wally Hinshelwood spent just 15 weeks at Stamford Bridge before returning to Craven Cottage. He made his debut v. Stoke City in February 1951 at a time when the outside-right position was causing some concern. Hinshelwood, who developed into a very fine winger, one of the best in the lower divisions, went on to amass a career total of 336 League appearances, scoring 50 goals, and without doubt played his best football with Reading and Bristol City. He skippered the latter club and as a 'Robin' represented the League South v. League North. Later in life he worked as a caretaker for Croydon Corporation. His son Martin, was appointed Chelsea's combination team coach in 1985, having retired after making 82 senior appearances for Crystal Palace (1970–78). Another son, Paul, an England Under-21 international, made 319 appearances for Palace (1973–83) and also played for Oxford United, Millwall and Colchester United.

HINTON, MARVIN

Defender: 328+16 apps, 4 goals
Born: Croydon, Surrey, 2 February 1940
Career: Norwood and District Boys, Croydon Schools, UGB Pantiles FC, Charlton Athletic (amateur, August 1955; professional, April 1957), CHELSEA (£30,000, August 1963), Barnet (June 1976), Crawley Town (August 1978), Horsham (season 1981–82); started his own removal business but was involved in a head-on car crash and is now unable to work; he lives in Crawley, Sussex

Marvin Hinton was a cultured centre-half who was also very effective as a full-back. He had performed as an inside-forward in Charlton's second XI and scored a hat-trick against Arsenal reserves before making his League debut for the 'Addicks' against West Ham in 1957. He remained at The Valley for 8 years, making 145 senior appearances and gaining 3 England Under-23 caps (v. Scotland, Turkey and Belgium in 1962) before moving to Chelsea. He settled in nicely at Stamford Bridge and in 1966 was in Alf Ramsey's initial 40-man squad for the World Cup finals. Nicknamed 'Lou', he was a fine positional player with a smart tackle, a fine reader of the game, and collected FA Cup final runner's-up and winner's medals with the Blues in 1967 and 1970 respectively, having won the League Cup in 1965. He missed out in the 1972 League Cup final, when manager Dave Sexton elected to stay with John Dempsey and David Webb as his central defensive partnership and prefer Paddy Mulligan at right-back. After 13 excellent years at Stamford Bridge, Hinton joined Barnet where he linked up with another former Chelsea star, Jimmy Greaves. Marvin's son, Darren, joined Chelsea as a junior in 1988 but did not make the grade.

HITCHCOCK, KEVIN JOSEPH

Goalkeeper: 131+4 apps
Born: Canning Town, London, 5 October 1962
Career: Barking (April 1981), Nottingham Forest (£15,000, August 1983), Mansfield Town (£14,000, February 1984), CHELSEA (£250,000, March 1988), Northampton Town (loan, December 1990–February 1991); returned to CHELSEA (retired, May 1999)

Goalkeeper Kevin Hitchcock spent over 11 years at Stamford Bridge and was rewarded with a testimonial for his bold efforts. He had to compete for the number one position with no fewer than five internationals but was always there when called into action, producing several quality performances both at home and away. He was the club's longest-serving player when he came off the subs' bench for his first taste of Premiership football for two years, as a second-half replacement for the injured Ed De Goey against Charlton Athletic on Easter Saturday 1999. This was to be the last of his 135 outings for the Blues – his first having come in March 1988 in a 4–4 draw at Oxford United. During a fine career Hitchcock, who was one of the most popular players at the Bridge, amassed 377 League and Cup appearances – 224 for Mansfield with whom he won the FRT in 1987. Ten years later he lifted the FA Cup with Chelsea and then earned winner's medals in both the League Cup and ECWC in 1998.

HODDINOTT, FRANCIS THOMAS

Inside-forward: 32 apps, 4 goals

Born: Brecon, Wales, 27 November 1894 – *Died*: Southend, Essex, 12 November 1980

Career: Brecon Lads' Club, Aberdare Athletic (June 1913), Army football (1914–19), Watford (August 1920), CHELSEA (£3,500, June 1921), Crystal Palace (£1,000, May 1923), Rhyl (July 1926), New Brighton (£500, May 1927), Newark Town (player–manager, August 1928), Grantham Town (free transfer, June 1931; retired April 1932), Chelmsford City (trainer, 1932–35); later worked on pleasure boats at Southend until outbreak of WW2

When he joined Chelsea as a 26 year old, Frank Hoddinott was already the owner of two Welsh caps, gained against England and Scotland the previous season. Choosing football ahead of boxing, he still fought in the ring as an amateur when on Watford's books but was quickly told to toss away his gloves and concentrate on his feet. He did well and went on to have a useful career, making over 220 senior appearances. He went straight into the Chelsea side, making his debut against Blackburn Rovers in August 1921 and retained his place in the forward line until January 1922 when Jack Cock returned from injury. He had one decent eight-match run in the senior side the following season before moving across London to Selhurst Park. Described as being 'crafty, with rare cunning', he scored a 19-minute hat-trick for Crystal Palace against Stoke in November 1923.

HODDLE, GLENN

Midfield: 22+17 apps, 1 goal

Born: Hayes, Middlesex, 27 October 1957

Career: Spinney Dynamoes, Harlow and District Schools, Essex Schools, Tottenham Hotspur (apprentice, April 1974; professional, April 1975). AS Monaco/France (£800,000, July 1987–December 1990), CHELSEA (non-contract, January 1991), Swindon Town (free transfer as player–manager, March 1991), CHELSEA (£75,000, player–manager, June 1993; retired as a player, May 1994; resigned as manager, June 1996); appointed England head coach (July 1996; resigned August 1998); Southampton (manager, January 2000–April 2001), Tottenham Hotspur (manager, April 2001–July 2003); TV match summariser; Wolverhampton Wanderers (manager, December 2004)

After recovering from a serious knee injury as a teenager, Glenn Hoddle went on to score 132 goals in 590 appearances for Spurs. After a three-year spell in French football, he returned to England with another knee injury in December 1990. A month later he signed for Chelsea but only appeared in the second team. He then bossed Swindon Town, taking over from another ex-Spurs star, Ossie Ardiles. In June 1993, he returned to Stamford Bridge as manager, a position he held for three years before quitting to take over as head coach of England. After failing miserably in the 1998 World Cup finals in France he resigned and early in 2000 he returned to club management with Southampton. Then in April 2001 he completed the full circle by taking over as boss of Spurs. He stayed at White Hart Lane for just over two years and later turned down the vacant manager's job at West Bromwich Albion (November 2004) before taking over the hot seat of Baggies' arch-rivals Wolves the following month.

Honoured by England at youth and 'B' team levels, Hoddle was a superb midfield player with great on-the-ball skills, vision, perfect timing, balance and stunning right-foot shot (he scored some spectacular goals, many from distance). Recipient of 12 Under-21 and 53 senior caps, his first in 1979 against Bulgaria, Hoddle helped Spurs win promotion from the Second Division in 1978 and was twice an FA Cup winner in 1981 and 1982, netting the decisive penalty in the replay of the latter final v. QPR. A loser in the 1982 League Cup and 1987 FA Cup finals, in between times he gained a UEFA Cup winner's medal in 1984 and later won the French League title with Monaco. He was also voted Young Footballer of the Year in 1980. Chelsea finished 11th, 14th, 11th and 11th again in the Premiership, lost in the 1994 FA Cup final and played in Europe during the four years he was in charge at Stamford Bridge. He was obviously well past his best when he turned out for the Blues, but nevertheless he still had something to offer. Hoddle made more than 850 club and international appearances during his 20-year career.

HOGH, JESS
Defender: 11+6 apps
Born: Aalborg, Denmark, 7 May 1966
Career: AAB Aalborg/Denmark (June 1985), Fenerbahce/Turkey (August 1995), CHELSEA (£300,000, July 1999; retired, injured, February 2001)

Jess Hogh, 6 ft 1 in. tall and weighing almost 12 st., was signed by Chelsea in the summer of 1999 at a time when wholesale changes were being made within the club. An able deputy to the French trio of Marcel Desailly, Frank Leboeuf and Mario Melchiot, he managed only 11 starts (6 in the Premiership) during his first season before being struck down with a serious ankle injury which subsequently led to an early retirement. Already an established Danish international when he transferred from Turkey, the experienced 33 year old took his tally of senior caps to 57 during his stay at Stamford Bridge. He gained League championship medals in both Denmark and Turkey and made well over 100 appearances in 4 seasons with Fenerbahce, having previously spent 10 years with Aalborg.

HOLDEN, ARTHUR

Outside-left: 20 apps, 1 goal
Born: Billingshurst, near Crawley, Sussex, 23 September 1882 – *Died*: 1950
Career: Cadmore Hill, Fareham, Portsmouth (August 1900), Southend United (April 1905), Plymouth Argyle (August 1907), CHELSEA (April 1908), Plymouth Argyle (August 1910), Aberdeen (November 1911; also acted caretaker-manager when Jimmy Phillip was absent; left club March 1915); did not figure after WW1

A fast-raiding winger who tended to overdo the clever stuff at times, Archie Holden was initially a reserve at Stamford Bridge before appearing in 16 League games during the 1909–10 season. He lost his place in the side to Marshall McEwan. Holden scored 7 goals in 80 appearances in his two spells with Plymouth.

HOLLINS, JOHN WILLIAM, MBE

Wing-half: 592 apps, 64 goals
Born: Guildford, Surrey, 16 July 1946
Career: Guildford Schoolboys, CHELSEA (junior, July 1961; professional, July 1963), Queens Park Rangers (£80,000 June 1975), Arsenal, CHELSEA (June 1983 as player–coach; retired as a player, May 1984; continued as a coach/assistant manager to John Neal; appointed manager, June 1985, remaining in office until March 1988); then worked as a financial adviser; Queens Park Rangers (reserve team coach, February 1995); later Swansea City (manager, July 1998–May 2001)

John Hollins stands third in Chelsea's all-time appearance list (behind Ron 'Chopper' Harris and Peter Bonetti) and shares the record with Harris of being an ever-present in four seasons: 1969–70, 1971–72, 1972–73 and 1973–74. He also holds the record for most consecutive appearances – total 167 – amassed between 14 August 1971 and 25 September 1974, and of these, 135 came in the Football League, 10 in the FA Cup, 18 in the League Cup and 4 in the European Cup-Winners' Cup. Voted Chelsea's Player of the Year twice (in 1970 and 1971), he was awarded the MBE for services to football in 1982. An all-time Chelsea great, Hollins made his senior debut for the Blues in a League Cup tie v. Swindon Town and, in fact, he made only three appearances in his first season as a professional (1963–64) but the following term missed only one game as he went from strength to strength, developing into a superb attacking wing-half.

Energetic, strong, deliberate, a fine passer of the ball with a powerful right-foot shot, he was confident in everything he did and was a key member of the side during a period when the club was on a high, reaching five major finals in seven years. Hollins triumphed in three – the League Cup in 1965, the FA Cup in 1970 and the European Cup-Winners' Cup in 1971 – and collected a runner's-up prize in the FA Cup and League Cup finals of 1967 and 1972 respectively. An England youth-team player, he played in two Under-23 internationals for his country before earning his only full cap against Spain in May 1967. He also represented the Football League on three occasions (1967–71). It was a sad day when he left Stamford Bridge for QPR in 1975, but nine years later he returned for one more season and helped the Blues win the Second Division title before losing his job after the team had gone four months without a win. He then concentrated on the coaching side of the game. During his time with Arsenal, for whom he made 173 senior appearances, he won the European Cup-Winners' Cup (again) in 1980 and also the FA Charity Shield, and was voted Gunners' Player of the Year in 1982. His father Bill played for Stoke City and Wolves and his brother Dave Hollins was a goalkeeper with Brighton and Hove Albion, Newcastle United, Mansfield Town, Nottingham Forest and Aldershot and won 11 caps for Wales.

HOLTON, PATRICK CARR

Full-back: 1 app.
Born: Hamilton, Lanarkshire, 23 December 1935
Career: Motherwell (1955), CHELSEA (£6,000, March 1959), Southend United (August 1960–March 1961)
Pat Holton failed to make an impact in English football and after just one League game for Chelsea (a 4–0 defeat at Leeds in March 1959 when he deputised for Richard Whittaker) and 11 for Southend, he returned to Scotland.

HOPE, JAMES PRENTICE

Wing-half: 1 app.
Born: East Wemyss, near Kirkcaldy, Fife, August 1905 – *Died*: Scotland, 1977
Career: East Fife (1922), South Shields (1926), Gateshead (May 1928), CHELSEA (November 1930–May 1932), Dysart FC (briefly); later lived and worked in Dunfermline
Unable to gain a place in the first team at Stamford Bridge, owing to the presence and form of Sid Bishop, Willie Ferguson and Sam Irving, Jim Hope was nevertheless a reliable reserve who served in Chelsea's second XI for 18 months. His only senior game was against Blackburn Rovers (home) in October 1931 when he deputised for Ferguson at left-half.

HOPKIN, DAVID

Midfield: 24+22 apps, 1 goal

Born: Greenock, Scotland, 21 August 1970

Career: Port Glasgow Boys' Club, Morton (professional, October 1989), CHELSEA (£300,000, September 1992), Crystal Palace (£850,000, July 1995), Leeds United (£3.25 million, July 1997), Bradford City (£2.5 million, July 2000), Crystal Palace (£1.5 million, March 2001), Morton (August 2002)

Red-haired wide midfielder with a terrific engine, David Hopkin made his debut for Morton in March 1990 and went on to appear in over 50 games for the Scottish club before joining Chelsea for whom he had to work hard and long without really establishing himself in the first XI. In his first season at Selhurst Park, Palace lost in the play-off final at Wembley to Leicester City. He took his tally of League and Cup appearances in English soccer to over 280 before returning to Morton in 2002.

Hopkin gained one 'B' and seven full caps for Scotland after leaving Stamford Bridge.

HORN, GEORGE

Inside-left/half-back: 2 apps

Born: West Ham, London, 1887 – *Died*: circa 1965

Career: Tunbridge Wells Rangers (1907), West Ham United (briefly during season 1908–09), CHELSEA (May 1909), Peterborough and Fletton United (June 1913–May 1915); did not play after WW1

A reliable reserve, George Horn helped Chelsea's second XI win the South-East League championship during his four years at Stamford Bridge. He made his debut for the Blues at inside-left in a 4–1 defeat at Bradford City in April 1910. In his second game, as a right-half a week later, Sheffield Wednesday were defeated 4–1 at Stamford Bridge.

HORTON, JOHN WILLIAM

Outside-left: 66 apps, 15 goals

Born: Fairburn, Castleford, Yorkshire, 14 July 1905 – *Died*: 1992

Career: Kippax Athletic, Freystone Colliery, Castleford Town (1924), Bury (trial, 1925), Charlton Athletic (free transfer, May 1926), CHELSEA (March 1933), Crystal Palace (June 1937; retired, injured, May 1939)

Jack Horton, well built and strong in his actions, spent just over four seasons at Stamford Bridge but was only a regular in the side during the 1933–34 campaign when he netted 8 goals in 35 League and Cup appearances. He moved on following the arrival of Bill Barraclough. He scored 56 goals in 272 games for Charlton while serving under four different managers.

HOUSEMAN, PETER

Winger: 325+18 apps, 39 goals

Born: Battersea, London, 24 December 1945 – *Died*: Oxford, 19 March 1977

Career: CHELSEA (junior, April 1961; professional, December 1962), Oxford
United (£30,000, May 1975, until his death in 1977)

An orthodox left-winger, Peter Houseman found it difficult to win the admiration of the Chelsea supporters at first, but some brilliant displays eventually made him a firm favourite with the 'The Shed' faithful. After signing professional forms for the Blues, he made his League debut against Sheffield United just before Christmas 1963, but it was another four years before he finally established himself in the side. He often played second fiddle to some of the big signings, but in the end it was he who kept the transfer men out. He appeared in all 54 of Chelsea's first-team matches in 1969–70, but scored only 3 goals in his 42 League outings and 1 in the League Cup, yet netted 6 times in 8 FA Cup ties, helping the Blues win the trophy after a replay against Leeds United. Houseman, aged only 32, was tragically killed in a car crash in 1977 just hours after playing in a League game for Oxford.

HOUSTON, STEWART MACKIE

Full-back/defender: 10+4 apps

Born: Dunoon, Argyll, Scotland, 20 August 1949

Career: Port Glasgow Rangers (1965), CHELSEA (professional, August 1967), Brentford (£17,000, March 1972), Manchester United (£55,000, December 1973), Sheffield United (free transfer, July 1980; later player–coach), Colchester United (player–coach, August 1983–April 1986), Plymouth Argyle (coach, briefly), Arsenal (coach, 1986; appointed caretaker-manager twice following the sackings of George Graham and Bruce Rioch; resigned September 1996), Queens Park Rangers (manager, September 1996–May 1997), Tottenham Hotspur (assistant manager/coach to Graham, October 1998–April 2001), Walsall (assistant manager/coach, August–September 2002), Queens Park Rangers (scout, 2003)

Signed by Tommy Docherty, Stewart Houston spent most of his time with Chelsea on the injured list. He played in only 14 first-class games during his 5 years at Stamford Bridge, but after leaving the Blues he developed into a quality left-back, gaining one Under-23 and one full cap for Scotland and appearing in more than another 500 senior games, including 250 for Manchester United. He helped the Reds win the Second Division title in 1975 and collected a runner's-up medal after the 1976 FA Cup final defeat by Southampton, yet missed the 1977 final v. Liverpool when he tore ankle ligaments a fortnight before the big day. He followed up in 1982 by winning the Fourth Division title with Sheffield United where he became player–coach under Martin Peters. Houston's father was a professional footballer with St Mirren.

HOWARD, TERRY

Defender: 6 apps

Born: Hornchurch, Essex, 26 February 1966

Career: CHELSEA (apprentice, April 1982; professional, February 1984), Crystal Palace (loan, January–February 1986), Chester (loan, January 1987), Leyton Orient (March 1987), Wycombe Wanderers (February 1995–May 1996)

A tall and resilient defender, able to occupy several positions, England Youth international Terry Howard was the backbone of Chelsea's reserve team for three seasons during which time he deputised in the League team for Joey Jones and Darren Wood at right-back. He went on to appear in 407 first-class games for Orient and 66 for Wycombe.

HUDSON, ALAN ANTHONY

Midfield: 188+1 apps, 14 goals

Born: Chelsea, London, 21 June 1951

Career: London Schools, CHELSEA (schoolboy forms, 1965; apprentice, April 1966; professional, June 1968), Stoke City (£240,000, January 1974), Arsenal (December 1976), Seattle Sounders/NASL (£120,000, October 1978), Hercules FC/Spain (1980), CHELSEA (£23,500, August 1983), Stoke City (January 1984; retired May 1985); later opened a nightclub in Stoke-on-Trent and penned a column in the *Sporting Life* as well as working for the media in general; recovered from a serious illness and now lives in east London

Alan Hudson's progress as a teenager was severely hampered by a bone infection that caused him to miss a lot of football. He signed for Chelsea as a 14 year old and after serving his apprenticeship, turned pro in 1968, making his League debut in February 1969 when the Blues crashed to an embarrassing 5–0 defeat at Southampton. The following season he gained a regular place in the side and literally shot to stardom overnight, gaining the first of his ten England Under-23 caps in March 1970. Unfortunately injury ruled him out of that season's FA Cup final win over Leeds United, but he returned to full fitness and was a key member of Chelsea's victorious European Cup-Winners' Cup team (v. Real Madrid) the following year. Then, in 1972, he was a losing finalist in the League Cup final against his future club Stoke City, and in 1978 he was a loser with Arsenal in the FA Cup final v. Ipswich Town. Rewarded with two full England caps (v. West Germany and Cyprus in 1975), Hudson was at times quite masterful on the ball, swaying and weaving his way past defenders to create scoring opportunities for his colleagues. During his career he made over 350 senior appearances. Hudson was awarded a goal that never was, playing for Chelsea against Ipswich Town in a League game at Stamford Bridge in September 1970. His shot struck the outside netting and angle woodwork but referee Roy Capey signalled a goal. Despite the protests of the Ipswich players and officials, the goal stood and Chelsea went on to win 2–1.

HUGHES, HARRY JAMES
Centre-half: 1 app.
Born: Nuneaton, Warwickshire, 8 October 1929
Career: Symington FC (1945), Southport (professional, August 1950), Army
football, CHELSEA (February 1951), Bournemouth (£1,500, June 1952),
Gillingham (free transfer, July 1958; retired May 1962); later ran the Spurs
club shop for 11 years before becoming self-employed, living in Guildford,
Surrey

Tall and well-built, defender Harry Hughes made only one senior appearance
for Chelsea, deputising for John Saunders against Liverpool (home) in August
1951. He made 281 League appearances after leaving Stamford Bridge (204 for
the Gills).

HUGHES, JOHN PAUL
Utility: 15+8 apps, 2 goals
Born: Hammersmith, London, 19 April 1976
Career: CHELSEA (apprentice, May 1992; professional, July 1994), Stockport
County (loan, December 1998–January 1999), Norwich City (loan, March–
April 1999), Southampton (free transfer, March 2000), Burnley (trial, July
2001), Luton Town (August 2001–May 2004)

An England schoolboy international, John Hughes developed through the ranks
at Stamford Bridge and made his League debut for Chelsea against Derby
County in January 1997. Unable to gain a regular first-team place, he had loan
spells at Edgeley Park and Carrow Road before moving to Southampton. He
later made 87 appearances for Luton.

HUGHES, LESLIE MARK, MBE, OBE
Striker/midfield: 109+14 apps, 39 goals
Born: Wrexham, 1 November 1963
Career: Ysgol Rhiwabon, Rhos Aelwyd Boys (Under-16s), Wrexham
Schoolboys, Manchester United (apprentice, June 1980; professional,
November 1980), Barcelona/Spain (£2.5 million, August 1986), Bayern
Munich/Germany (on loan, 1987), Manchester United (£1.5 million, July
1988), CHELSEA (£1.5 million, July 1995), Southampton (£650,000,
1998), Everton (free transfer, March 2000), Blackburn Rovers (free, October
2000); Welsh national team manager (November 1999–October 2004),
Blackburn Rovers (manager, September 2004); stayed on briefly as manager
of Wales after his appointment as Blackburn boss

In his two spells at Old Trafford, striker Mark Hughes scored 162 goals in 473
appearances. He also helped the Reds win the FA Cup on three occasions (1985,
1990 and 1994), the European Cup-Winners' Cup (1991), the Football League
Cup (1992), two Premier League championships (in 1993 and 1994), the
European Super Cup (1991) and the FA Charity Shield (1993 and 1994). After
leaving Old Trafford he added another FA Cup winner's medal to his collection

with Chelsea (1997) and also helped the Blues win both the European Cup-Winners' Cup and League Cup in 1998. His winning of four FA Cup medals is a competition record. Capped 72 times by Wales, whom he also represented at schoolboy, youth and Under-21 levels (gaining five caps in the last category), in his prime Hughes was one of the best 'leaders of the attack' in the professional game. Able to hold the ball up and then lay it off to a colleague, he had strength, skill, could head a ball with great power and direction and possessed a powerful right-foot shot.

Nicknamed 'Sparky', he won the PFA Player of the Year award on two occasions (1989 and 1991) and is one of only a handful of players to have scored in the FA Cup, League Cup and European Cup-Winners' Cup finals, his two goals seeing off Barcelona in the last competition in 1991. He helped Blackburn regain their Premiership status in 2001, the same year he took his career appearance tally (in all major competitions, for clubs and country) past the 750 mark (230 goals scored). In February 2002, at the age of 38, Hughes returned home to Wales and helped Blackburn beat Spurs 2–1 to win the League Cup at the Millennium Stadium, Cardiff. He then did very well in rebuilding the Welsh national team before entering into Football League management with his former club Blackburn early in the 2004–05 season after Graeme Souness had moved to Newcastle. He was awarded the OBE in 2004 for services to football.

HUGHES, THOMAS ALEXANDER
Goalkeeper: 11 apps
Born: Dalmuir, Scotland, 11 July 1947
Career: Clydebank (juniors, 1963), CHELSEA (July 1965), Aston Villa (£12,500, June 1971), Brighton and Hove Albion (loan, February–March 1973), Hereford United (£15,000, August 1973; retired October 1982; then manager at Edgar Street to March 1983)

Tommy Hughes was the unfortunate understudy to Peter Bonetti at Chelsea and made only 11 appearances for the London club despite winning two Scottish Under-23 caps. After breaking a leg he was subsequently replaced by Villa's John Phillips and then ironically after recovering from that setback, he was transferred to Villa Park! He struggled to hold down a first-team place and after a loan spell at Brighton moved to Hereford. He went on to amass more than 250 appearances for the Bulls, helping them win the Third Division title in 1976. However, after suffering relegation, Hughes by now the manager, then saw his team successfully gain re-election to the Football League at the end of the 1979–80 season. But things didn't improve all that much on the pitch and he found himself out of a job when the curtain came down on the 1982–83 campaign.

J. T. Robertson H. A. Keare (*Director*) F. W. Parker (*Hon. Fin. Sec.*)   Jas. Miller and Harry Ransom (*Trainers*) W. Lewis (*Secretary*)
(*Manager*)   Byrne   M'Roberts   Foulke (*Capt.*) Copeland Mackie   M'Ewan   Craigie   Jack White (*Assist. Trainer*)
                        Moran   Donaghy   T. Miller Jas. Robertson   O'Hara   Windridge   Key   Kirwan
                              M'Dowland   Seaton   Wolfe   Watson

CHELSEA F.C.
Photo: Baker & Dixon

Chelsea FC team group 1905–06 — the club's first season in the Football League.
The Blues finished third in Division Two.

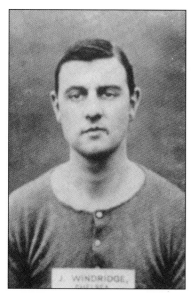

Jimmy Windridge scored 58 goals in
152 games for Chelsea, 1905–11.

Bill 'Fatty' Foulke — Chelsea's first
goalkeeper, who once weighed over
25 stone.

Vivian Woodward — an England
international at senior and amateur
levels who scored 34 goals in
116 appearances for Chelsea.

John Kirwan — an Irish international
and Chelsea's first left-winger.

Hughie Gallacher — Scottish international
centre-forward who netted 81 goals in
144 games for Chelsea during the 1930s.

LEFT: Northern Irish international wing-half Billy Mitchell made 117 senior appearances for the Blues between 1933 and 1939. MIDDLE: Jimmy Argue played for Chelsea before, during and after the Second World War. RIGHT: George Mills — an England international who in 10 years at Stamford Bridge (1929—39), made 239 appearances and scored 123 goals.

LEFT: Bob Salmond — centre-half in Chelsea's last pre-WW2 season of 1938—39.
MIDDLE (FIRST): Peter O'Dowd — England international centre-half of the 1930s.
MIDDLE (SECOND): Joe Payne scored ten goals in one League game for Luton Town before joining Chelsea. RIGHT: Dick Spence — an England international outside-right who was 39 years of age when he made his last appearance for Chelsea in 1947.

Tommy Lawton — England international centre-forward who was Britain's first £20,000 footballer in 1947.

Chelsea goalkeeper Harry Medhurst clears his lines during Chelsea's FA Cup semi-final clash with Arsenal at White Hart Lane in 1950.

Chelsea goalkeeper Chick Thomson went on to win the FA Cup with Nottingham Forest in 1959.

Defender Stan Wicks made 21 League appearances in the 1954—55 championship-winning side.

Derek Saunders made
223 appearances in 6 years with
Chelsea (1953–59).

England full-back Peter Sillett made 288
appearances for Chelsea (1953–62).

Stan Willemse partnered Sillett at full-back
for three seasons in the mid-1950s.

Outside-right Eric Parsons was an
ever-present in Chelsea's League
championship-winning side of
1954–55.

Frank Blunstone played on the
opposite flank to Parsons in the
1950s and made 347 appearances
for the Blues.

Goalkeeper Mike Pinner, an England
amateur international, made one
appearance for Chelsea in 1962.

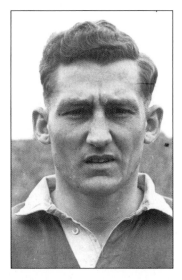

Roy Bentley — Chelsea and England
centre-forward and League
championship-winner in 1955.

After acting as reserve to Harry Medhurst, goalkeeper Bill Robertson went on to appear in 215 games for Chelsea, gaining a League championship medal in 1955.

Goalkeeper Vic Woodley was first choice at Stamford Bridge for six out of eight seasons, making 272 appearances in total.

Goalkeeper Reg Matthews represented England as a Third Division player with Coventry City before joining Chelsea.

Billy Gray also played for Leyton Orient, Burnley and Nottingham Forest, and was an FA Cup winner in 1959.

England international winger Peter Brabrook also played for West Ham United and Leyton Orient.

Ron Greenwood, former Chelsea centre-half who won a League championship medal in 1955, was England manager from 1977 to 1982.

HUGHES, WILLIAM MARSHALL

Left-back/centre-half: 105 apps

Born: Carmarthen, Wales, 6 March 1918 – *Died*: Birmingham, 16 June 1981

Career: Llanelli Boys' and Swansea Grammar Schools, Archer Corinthians, Llanelli FC, Watchers Celtic FC, Llanelli Town (August 1934), Swansea Town (loan, March–April 1935), Birmingham (£5, professional, May 1935); guest for Arsenal, Heart of Midlothian, Queens Park Rangers, Tottenham Hotspur and West Ham United during WW2; Luton Town (£11,000, July 1947), CHELSEA (£12,000, March 1948), Hereford United (August 1951), Flint Town (January 1954; retired May 1955); later scout for Chester and landlord of the Bluebell Inn at Halkyn; then steward of the Wolesley Car Social Club (Birmingham)

After a brief flirtation with rugby as a schoolboy, Billy Hughes (who was a teenage car mechanic) quickly took up soccer and matured into an extremely skilful full-back (who also played at centre-half). An effective ball-winner with an educated left foot, he always tried to be constructive in his play, passing the ball to a colleague rather than thumping it aimlessly downfield in hope rather than judgement. He appeared in 170 games for Birmingham (110 in peacetime football) before joining Luton in 1947. He never quite settled in at Kenilworth Road but following his move to Chelsea he regained his form and gave the Blues excellent service for more than four years. He played in only four games when Birmingham won the Football League (S) title in 1946 and was a Welsh Cup winner with Flint Town in 1954. On the international front, Hughes won 10 full and 14 wartime and Victory international caps for Wales, skippering his country on several occasions, and represented Great Britain against the Rest of the World in 1947. He made his League debut for Birmingham as a 17 year old against Manchester City in 1936 and was 29 when he played his first game for Chelsea against Charlton in 1948. During the 1936–37 season, Hughes and Cyril Trigg set up a new record for being the youngest pair of full-backs in League football, aged 17, when they faced Aston Villa in a First Division game. He made a total of 243 League appearances during his career.

HUMPHREYS, PERCY

Inside-forward: 46 apps, 13 goals

Born: Cambridge, 3 December 1880 – *Died*: Stepney, London, 13 April 1959

Career: Cambridge St Mary's, Cambridgeshire County, Queens Park Rangers (July 1900), Notts County (July 1901), Leicester Fosse (June 1907), CHELSEA (£350, February 1908), Tottenham Hotspur (December 1909), Leicester Fosse (October 1911), West Hartlepool (player–manager, June 1913), FC Basle/Switzerland (coach, July 1914), Norwich City (November 1914–April 1915); did not play after WW1

Percy Humphreys established himself as an enthusiastic, smart young striker at QPR, finishing as top scorer with 12 goals in his only season with the club. He then developed his game further with Notts County (for whom he claimed 66 goals), representing the Football League against the Scottish League in March 1903 before gaining a full cap for England v. Scotland a month later when he partnered future Chelsea star Vivian Woodward in attack. After moving to Leicester, he became a huge favourite with the Filbert Street fans and netted 25 goals in 44 games before transferring to Chelsea in 1908. Retaining his scoring form with the Blues (13 goals in just under 50 starts), he then proceeded to do likewise with Spurs (netting 29 times in 50 League and Cup games). He didn't figure at all when he returned for a second spell with Leicester. Humphreys initially signed a three-year contract with Basle in Switzerland but with war imminent, he returned to England after just four months. He was asked to go back to his coaching job in Switzerland after the hostilities, but declined. Humphreys was nicknamed 'Headless Humphreys' because he always kept the ball at his feet – he was a master dribbler.

HUNTER, GEORGE CHARLES
Wing-half. 32 apps, 2 goals
Born: Peshawar, India, 16 August 1886 – *Died*: London, February 1934
Career: Peshawar junior football/the Army, Maidstone (1906), Croydon Common (August 1907), Aston Villa (February 1908), Oldham Athletic (£1,200, January 1912), CHELSEA (£1,000, March 1913), Manchester United (£1,300, March 1914–May 1915); guest for Belfast Celtic, Croydon Common, Birmingham, Sunderland and Brentford during WW1; Portsmouth (August 1919; retired May 1922)

Well built, powerful and noted for his tough and vigorous tackling, George 'Cocky' Hunter – the comedian in the camp – was rather reckless at times and often conceded free kicks in dangerous positions while also giving away his fair share of penalties! However, his fiery temperament could be an advantage and he was always a useful member of the team. He made almost 100 appearances for Villa with whom he won a League Championship medal in 1910 and twice represented the Football League in 1911, also playing for Birmingham County FA v. London in 1909. He made 32 appearances for Chelsea before being released – his manager and colleagues being unable to control him! He went on to skipper Manchester United and played behind the great Billy Meredith during his time at Old Trafford. He was in trouble with United's directorate in January 1915 and was suspended *sine die* for failing to comply with training regulations and as the club captain it was thought he should have set a better example. Hailing from a military background (born ten miles from the Khyber Pass), Hunter saw active service in France and Gallipoli during WW1 when he served as a company sergeant-major. In August 1930, Hunter was sentenced to three months' hard labour for deserting his wife and children.

HUTCHESON, JOHN HUGHIE McGEAVY
Wing-half: 22 apps, 1 goal
Born: Larbert, Scotland, 31 March 1909 – *Died:* Scotland 1980
Career: Larbert Thistle, Falkirk (1929), CHELSEA (March 1934), Ipswich
   Town (August 1938), Crittall Athletic (June 1939); did not play after WW2
A former miner in Scotland, Jock Hutcheson was the stalwart of Chelsea's
second XI for three seasons, and when called up for first-team duty, he
continued to perform admirably as deputy to internationals Billy Mitchell and
Harry Miller. A cartilage injury effectively ended his League career.

HUTCHINGS, CHRISTOPHER
Full-back/midfield: 97+4 apps, 3 goals
Born: Winchester, Hampshire, 5 July 1957
Career: Southend United (apprentice, July 1973), Southall (April 1975), Harrow
   Borough (May 1977), CHELSEA (£5,000, July 1980) Brighton and Hove
   Albion (November 1983), Huddersfield Town (£28,000, December 1987),
   Walsall (August 1990), Rotherham United (July 1991–May 1993); various
   coaching appointments (1993–2000); Bradford City (manager,
   August–November 2000), Wigan Athletic (assistant manager/coach from
   June 2001)
Chris Hutchings spent three and a third seasons at Stamford Bridge during
which time he produced some fine performances, his all-action play when
driving forward from the back or midfield giving opponents plenty to think
about. He started out with Southend, but surprisingly drifted into non-League
football with Southall and Harrow Borough before returning to the League
scene with Chelsea in 1980, signed by manager Geoff Hurst. After leaving the
Blues he played in 175 senior games for Brighton and 131 for Huddersfield and
accumulated a total of 468 League appearances for his five clubs. He lost his job
at Bradford after just 12 matches in charge. Transferred from Stamford Bridge
to Hove in 1983, Hutchings had been fined £250 three months earlier for using
insulting words to a policeman at the end of a League match between Brighton
and Chelsea.

HUTCHINSON, IAN
Forward: 137+7 apps, 58 goals
Born: Derby, 4 August 1948 – *Died:* London, 19 September 2002
Career: Burton Albion, Cambridge United, CHELSEA (£2,500, July 1968;
   retired, injured, July 1976); later ran a pub in Windsor with Peter Osgood,
   whom he also doubled up with in an after-dinner-speaking duo
Said to be one of Chelsea's biggest bargains of all time, Ian Hutchinson
developed one of the longest throws in the game – once heaving the ball 60
yards across the penalty area. It was from one of these mighty throw-ins that
defender David Webb headed the winning goal v. Leeds United in the 1970 FA
Cup final replay at Old Trafford. One of the stars of the Chelsea team in the

1970s, he won two England Under-23 caps (v. Wales and Scotland in 1970–71). Unfortunately he suffered his fair share of injuries during his career including a broken leg, dislocated knee and severely damaged ankle, but he always bounced back until announcing his retirement in 1976. He was only 53 when he died.

HUTH, ROBERT
Defender: 21+20 apps, 2 goals
Born: Berlin, Germany, 18 August 1984
Career: CHELSEA (apprentice, April 2000; professional, August 2001)
Standing 6 ft 2 in. tall and weighing almost 13 st., Robert Huth looks and is a commanding figure at the heart of the defence. He was the fifth youngster blooded into the Premiership by Chelsea during the 2001–02 season but owing to the form of many other quality footballers in the same position, he has since found it difficult to establish himself in the senior side. Blues youth-team coach Steve Clarke predicted a very fine future for the likeable German, who has already represented his country at senior level. He gained a Premiership winner's medal in 2005 after making 15 appearances.

HUXFORD, CLIFFORD GEORGE
Half-back: 7 apps
Born: Stroud, Gloucestershire, 8 June 1937
Career: CHELSEA (junior, July 1952; professional, February 1955), Southampton (player-exchange deal involving Charlie Livesey, May 1959), Exeter City (May 1967), Worcester City (July 1968), Basingstoke Town (player–coach, May 1969), Aldershot (player–coach, May 1971), Basingstoke Town (player–coach, February 1974), AC Delco FC/Hampshire (September 1976), Bashley (coach, season 1988–89), Trotton FC (coach, July 1989), Fareham (manager, November 1989–April 1994), later Brockenhurst FC (manager); became a self-employed painter and decorator near Southampton
A well-built half-back, rugged and hard-tackling, Cliff Huxford was unable to win a first-team place at Stamford Bridge despite some impressive displays in the reserves. As a forceful, indomitable captain, he went on to make 316 appearances for Southampton whom he helped gain promotion into the top flight for the first time in the club's history in 1966. Huxford was capped by England at youth-team level. His son played under him at Fareham and his brother had one game for Swindon Town.

ILES, ROBERT JOHN
Goalkeeper: 14 apps
Born: Leicester, 23 June 1955
Career: AFC Bournemouth (apprentice, June 1971; professional, February 1973), Poole Town (1974), Weymouth (1975), CHELSEA (£10,000, June 1979), Wealdstone (June 1983–85)
Bob Iles acted as deputy to four different goalkeepers during his five years with

Chelsea – Peter Bonetti, Petar Borota, Steve Francis and John Phillips. He had his best season in terms of first-team appearances in 1978–79 when he played in seven League games.

IRVING, SAMUEL JOHNSTONE
Wing-half: 97 apps, 5 goals
Born: Belfast, 28 August 1894 – *Died*: Dundee, December 1968
Career: Shildon Athletic (1910), Newcastle United (trial, 1911), Galashiels United (August 1911), Esh Winning FC (1912), Bristol City (November 1913), Dundee (March 1915), Blyth Spartans (1919), Shildon Athletic (1921), Dundee (1922), Partick Thistle (1923), New York Centrals/USA (1925), Cardiff City (in exchange for Joe Cassidy, July 1926), CHELSEA (March 1928), Bristol Rovers (May 1932; retired May 1933); later managed a billiard saloon in Dundee

A sharp-tackling fetch-and-carry player, Sammy Irving played a big part in Chelsea's promotion campaign from the Second Division in 1930. He had earlier won the FA Cup with Cardiff City (1927 v. Arsenal) and gained 18 full caps for Northern Ireland (2 with the Blues) between 1923 and 1931. During his nomadic career he appeared in more than 200 League games north and south of the border.

ISAAC, ROBERT CHARLES
Defender: 13 apps
Born: Hackney, London, 30 November 1965
Career: CHELSEA (apprentice, April 1982; professional, December 1983), Brighton and Hove Albion (£35,000, February 1987)

An England Youth international, Bob Isaac could occupy any of the three half-back positions and also played at full-back. A reliable reserve at Stamford Bridge, he made his League debut in a 3–1 win at Watford in March 1985 when he deputised for Colin Pates.

JACKSON, ALEXANDER SKINNER
Outside-right: 77 apps, 29 goals
Born: Renton, Dumbartonshire, May 1905 – *Died*: Egypt, 15 November 1946
Career: Renton School, Dumbarton Academy (1918), Renton Victoria (August 1919), Dumbarton (July 1922), Aberdeen (£100, March 1923), Bethlehem Star in Pennsylvania/USA (August 1923), Aberdeen (August 1924), Huddersfield Town (£5,000, May 1925), CHELSEA (£8,500, September 1930), Ashton National (August 1932), Margate (February–April 1933), Nice/France (season 1933–34, retired aged 29)

In his heyday during the 1920s, Alex Jackson's performances on the right-wing impelled the more flowery sports writers to dub him the 'Flying Scotsman', the 'Gay Cavalier' and the 'Wing Wizard'. A superlative footballer, he was certainly one of the greatest outside-rights of his era. A wanderer, liable to pop up and score goals from any position, he was fast and brainy with an immaculate command over the ball. Capped 17 times by Scotland between 1925 and 1930, he was a League championship winner with Huddersfield in 1925 and also played in two losing FA Cup finals with the Terriers in 1928 and 1930. He scored 8 goals in 40 appearances for Aberdeen and 89 in 203 League and Cup games for Huddersfield. He died in a car crash whilst serving in the Army in Egypt.

JACKSON, JOHN

Goalkeeper: 51 apps
Born: Glasgow, 29 November 1906 – *Died*: Nova Scotia, Canada, 12 May 1965
Career: Kirkintilloch Rob Roy, Partick Thistle (1928), CHELSEA (June 1933; retired May 1942); guest for Brentford in WW2; later emigrated to Canada where he became a golf professional (having played in the 1950 British Open)

Agile and alert, as brave as a lion, marvellously secure, John 'Jakey' Jackson was listed in the top ten best goalkeepers of the 1930s. He served Chelsea splendidly for nine years, although his appearance record certainly doesn't do him justice, simply because he had another excellent keeper to battle with for first-team football in Vic Woodley. Indeed, he replaced Woodley in the side at the start of the 1933–34 season, but in the fifth game at Huddersfield he suffered a nasty injury that kept him out for three weeks. Woodley returned and Jackson had to fight to regain his place. He got back into the side in November 1934 but lost out to Woodley again before WW2. He made a further 74 appearances for the Blues during the hostilities. Very much on the small side (like England's Harry Hibbs), he won eight full caps for Scotland (four with Chelsea) between 1931 and 1936 and also represented the Scottish League on four occasions. He was a Scottish Cup finalist with Partick in 1930.

JACKSON, WILLIAM

Outside-left: 26 apps, 5 goals
Born: Farnworth, Lancashire, 15 July 1902 – *Died*: 1974
Career: Leyland (1919), Altrincham (1920), Darwen (1922), Sunderland (May 1924), Leeds United (September 1925), West Ham United (May 1927), CHELSEA (February 1928), Leicester City (May 1931), Ashford Town (briefly), Bristol Rovers (May 1932), Cardiff City (May 1934), Watford (January 1935), Chorley (March 1937–August 1939); did not play after WW2

A useful left-winger, two-footed Billy Jackson was regarded as a reserve-team player during his three years at Stamford Bridge. He had his best run in the first team during the second half of the 1928–29 campaign when he deputised for George Pearson. He scored 23 goals in 123 League appearances during his much travelled career.

JAROSIK, JIRI
Midfield: 6+14 apps
Born: Czechosolvakia, 27 October 1977
Career: Sparta Prague/Czech Republic (amateur, 1994; professional, October 1995), Slovan Liberec/Czech Republic (on loan, two separate spells), CSKA Moscow/Russia (May 2003), CHELSEA (£3.7 million, January 2005)

Jiri Jarosik made his debut for Chelsea as a second-half substitute in the home 3rd round FA Cup tie against Scunthorpe United in January 2005, doing well in a hard-earned 3–1 victory. He then followed up with a gritty performance in the Premiership win at Tottenham a few days later. Before his move to Stamford Bridge, the Czech Republic international (capped over 40 times at senior level) had scored against the Blues in a 2004 Champions League encounter for CSKA and quickly settled into José Mourinho's astute system, despite being used mainly as a substitute. The tallest outfield player at Stamford Bridge (at 6 ft 4 in.) he is fast and clever, has a superb first touch, spots an opening quickly and certainly adds a new dimension to Chelsea's ever-efficient midfield engine room. He won two League championships with Sparta Prague (2000 and 2001 with current Blues' goalkeeper Petr Cech) and one with CSKA (2003), also gaining a runner's-up medal with Sparta (2002) and with CSKA (2004). In 2005, he was the recipient of League Cup and Premiership winner's medals with Chelsea.

JASPER, DALE WILLIAM
Defender/midfield: 13+2 apps
Born: Croydon, Surrey, 14 January 1964
Career: CHELSEA (apprentice, April 1980; professional, January 1982), Brighton and Hove Albion (free transfer, May 1986), Crewe Alexandra (free, July 1988–May 1991)

Unfortunately Dale Jasper's career with Chelsea was severely interrupted by injury and misfortune. A classy player on his day, he skippered the reserve side to the Combination title in 1985 before going on to make 49 League appearances for Brighton and 111 for Crewe.

JENKINS, RICHARD GEORGE CHRISTOPHER
Outside-right: 4 apps
Born: Westminster, London, 1880 – Deceased by 1974
Career: London University (amateur), London Polytechnic (amateur), Corinthians (amateur), CHELSEA (amateur, August–October 1924, and January–April 1925), Corinthians (February 1925)

An England amateur international with ten caps to his name, Richard Jenkins was one of the famous Corinthian footballers who assisted Chelsea (when available) during the 1924–25 season.

JENKINS, THOMAS FREDERICK
Inside-forward: 5 apps
Born: Stockton-on-Tees, 5 December 1925
Career: Queen of the South (August 1945), CHELSEA (£8,000, July 1949), Barry Town (June 1951), Kettering Town (1953), Leicester City (July 1954), Kettering Town (January 1955–May 1956)

Perhaps a shade too small and light to make his mark in League football, Tommy Jenkins moved to Chelsea with a big reputation but never really settled down at Stamford Bridge, spending most of his time in the second team. He failed to get a game with Leicester.

JOHNSEN, ERLAND
Defender: 170+14 apps, 1 goal
Born: Fredrikstad, Norway, 5 April 1967
Career: Fredrikstad/Norway, Bayern Munich/Germany (1987), CHELSEA (£306,000, November 1989); returned to Norway (June 1997)

Norwegian defender Erland Johnsen, who gained 24 full international caps for his country, was Chelsea's Player of the Year in 1996. A hard-tackler, strong and resourceful, he went off injured on his debut for the Blues in the London derby with QPR a month after moving from the German Bundesliga. He recovered full fitness and went on to give good value for money for eight years before returning to his homeland.

JOHNSON, GARY JACK
Forward: 18+4 apps, 9 goals
Born: Peckham, London, 14 September 1959
Career: CHELSEA (apprentice, April 1976; professional, September 1977), Crystal Palace (loan, during season 1978–79), Brentford (December 1980), Pietersburg Rangers/South Africa (May 1982), Aldershot (August 1985–May 1987)

Despite an excellent goals-per-games ratio, Gary Johnson, keen and aggressive, never looked like establishing himself in Chelsea's first XI. He later did well in South Africa and also for Aldershot, for whom he scored 19 goals in 61 games.

JOHNSON, GEOFFREY HENRY
Full-back: 5 apps
Born: Putney, London, 1885 – *Died*: South Wales, 1930
Career: Southend United (1903), Clapton Orient (December 1908), CHELSEA (March 1911), Portsmouth (August 1913), Bristol Rovers (briefly 1914), Merthyr Town (1915); did not play after WW1

Reserve to Walter Bettridge and Jock Cameron, Geoff Johnson made only five League appearances in two seasons at Stamford Bridge, moving to Pompey following the arrival of another full-back, Jimmy Sharp. He made 84 senior appearances for Orient.

JOHNSON, GLEN McLEOD

Right-back: 51+10 apps, 4 goals

Born: East Ham, London, 23 August 1984

Career: West Ham United (apprentice, April 2000; professional, August 2001), Millwall (loan, October–November 2002), CHELSEA (£6 million, July 2003)

Capped by England at youth and at Under-21 level (seven times), attacking right wing-back Glen Johnson appeared in his first full international against Denmark in November 2003 and is still adding to his tally of senior caps. He had appeared in only 24 club games before becoming the first signing made under the new Abramovich regime. Strong, comfortable on the ball, he covers the ground well and defends resolutely when required. A star of the future, he gained winner's medals for League Cup final and Premiership triumphs in 2005.

JOHNSTONE, DEREK JOSEPH

Utility: 1+3 apps

Born: Dundee, 4 November 1953

Career: St Columba's FC (Dundee), Dundee Schools, Glasgow Rangers (schoolboy forms, December 1968; professional, July 1970), CHELSEA (£30,000, September 1983), Dundee United (loan, 1984), Glasgow Rangers (£25,000, January 1985), Partick Thistle (June 1986-87); later worked for *Sportscene* (BBC Scotland's equivalent of *Match of the Day*) and also covered sport for Radio Clyde

Derek Johnstone occupied eight different positions during two spells with Glasgow Rangers for whom he amassed an excellent record of 210 goals in 546 appearances. He starred in three Scottish League championship-winning sides (1975, 1976, 1978), in five Cup final-winning teams (1973, 1976, 1978, 1979, 1981), was a League Cup winner on four occasions (1971, 1978, 1979 and 1981) and won the European Cup-Winners' Cup in 1972. He also received three Scottish Cup runner's-up medals. Twice voted Scotland's Player of the Year in 1978 and 1983, Johnstone was rewarded with 14 full caps by his country (2 goals scored), won 6 more at Under-23 level and also represented the Scottish League once and played in schoolboy, youth and amateur internationals.

A burly six-footer and demonstrably a utility man (he would play anywhere just to get a game), he was superb in the air, efficient with both feet on the ground and lethal in front of goal. He was almost 30 when he moved to Chelsea and never really settled in at Stamford Bridge, playing in only four games before returning to Scotland. Johnstone holds the record for being the youngest player ever to appear in a major British Cup final – aged 16 years, 354 days when, on 24 October 1970, he scored for Rangers against Celtic in the League Cup. It was only his third senior game for the Gers. He is listed in Rangers' 50 all-time greats.

JOKANOVIC, SLAVISA

Midfield: 28+25 apps
Born: Novi Sad, Yugoslavia, 16 August 1968
Career: Vojvodina Novi Sad/Yugoslavia (1986), Partizan Belgrade/Yugoslavia (April 1990), Real Oviedo/Spain (July 1993), Tenerife/Spain (August 1995), Deportivo la Coruña/Spain (June 1999), CHELSEA (£1.7 million, October 2000; retired, June 2002)

Yugoslavian international central midfielder Slavisa Jokanovic was capped 64 times at senior level, 6 with Chelsea. He scored 21 goals in 68 League games for Partizan and 31 in 208 games for his 3 Spanish League clubs before moving to Chelsea, being manager Claudio Ranieri's first signing following Roberto Di Matteo's injury. A League winner with three different clubs – Vojvodina in 1989, Partizan in 1993 and Deportivo in 2000 – and a domestic cup-winner with Partizan in 1992, he was hard-working and aggressive, a ball-winner who was always an aerial threat at set pieces.

JONES, EVAN

Forward: 21 apps, 4 goals
Born: Trehafod, near Pontypridd, South Wales, 20 October 1888 – *Died*: Bedwelty, Wales, August 1972
Career: Trehafod FC (1905), Aberdare (April 1907), CHELSEA (£300, September 1909), Oldham Athletic (£400, February 1911), Bolton Wanderers (£750, May 1912); guest for Newport County (season 1918–19); Swansea Town (August 1919), Pontypridd (July 1920), Llanbradach (March 1921), Porth (August 1921; retired April 1922); went to work down the Trefor pit at Lewis Merthyr Colliery, Trehafod; continued as a collier through the 1931 strike and despite suffering a compound fracture of the right leg in a mining accident he remained in employment until 1938; after the war he worked at the Maritime Washery, Maesycoed, Pontypridd, before taking his final job with the Western Welsh Bus Company in Caerwent

Signed as cover for George Hilsdon, Evan Jones was a powerful, fearless striker, strong in the air, who scored a hat-trick on his London League debut for Chelsea before making his initial start in the First Division against Aston Villa shortly afterwards (September 1909). He found it hard going at Stamford Bridge, although he did win two Welsh caps in 1910 v. Scotland and Ireland (later gaining five more). He was snapped up by Oldham boss David Ashworth and became a star performer for the Latics, scoring 25 goals in 50 League games, following up with 24 in 90 outings for Bolton before WW1 intervened. When Jones' nephew was born, he persuaded his sister to name him Vivian, after his great pal at Chelsea, Vivian Woodward.

JONES, JOSEPH PATRICK

Full-back/centre-half: 89+2 apps, 2 goals

Born: Llandudno, North Wales, 4 March 1955

Career: Mostyn Secondary School, Llandudno Estates FC, Llandudno Swifts, Clywd and Conwy Under-15s, Caernarfonshire Under-15s, Wrexham (apprentice, April 1971; professional, January 1973), Liverpool (£110,000, July 1975), Wrexham (£220,000, October 1978), CHELSEA (£34,500, October 1982), Huddersfield Town (£35,000, October 1985), Wrexham (£7,000, August 1987; player–coach November 1989; senior coach, 1992)

Having already amassed more than 300 League appearances for his two previous clubs, Joey Jones joined Chelsea at a time when morale was at rather a low ebb at Stamford Bridge. However, with his vast experience and lively attitude, he quickly got into the swing of things, his dressing-room banter helping restore some confidence in the team. A resilient defender, able to play at centre-half as well as full-back, he produced some determined performances out on the field. A Welsh international, capped 70 times at senior level (1976–86) and on four occasions by the Under-23s, Jones helped Liverpool win successive League championships in 1976 and 1977, the European Cup in the latter year, two Charity Shields and was an FA Cup runner-up, also in 1977. He helped Chelsea clinch the Second Division title in 1984. After three years with the Blues he moved to Huddersfield and then returned to Wrexham for a third spell in 1987, eventually retiring as a player in 1992 with more than 700 League and Cup appearances under his belt (35 goals). In March 1986, Jones broke Ivor Allchurch's long-standing record of 69 caps when he played in his 70th senior international against the Republic of Ireland in Dublin.

JONES, KEITH AUBREY

Midfield: 57+12 apps, 10 goals

Born: Dulwich, London, 14 October 1965

Career: CHELSEA (apprentice, April 1982; professional, August 1983), Brentford (£40,000, September 1987), Southend United (£175,000, October 1991), Charlton Athletic (£150,000, September 1994), Reading (free transfer, July 2000; retired June 2002)

Capped by England at schoolboy and youth-team levels, Keith Jones was a hard-tackling, competitive right-sided midfielder who progressed through the junior and intermediate ranks at Stamford Bridge to make his League debut as an apprentice against Barnsley in March 1983. He became a regular squad member the following season and made almost 70 senior appearances before moving to nearby Brentford in 1987. When he retired from competitive football, Jones had amassed over 620 senior appearances for his 5 major clubs (50 goals).

JONES, THOMAS BENJAMIN

Outside-left: 62 apps, 13 goals

Born: Frodsham, Cheshire, 23 March 1920 – *Died*: December 1972

Career: Ellesmere Port (August 1937), Tranmere Rovers (September 1941), CHELSEA (October 1947), Accrington Stanley (July 1953), Dartford (July 1954; retired 1956)

A very popular player at Stamford Bridge, Benny Jones had his best season with Chelsea in 1948–49 when he appeared in 31 senior games. A determined, hard-running player with a powerful shot, he lost seven years of his career to WW2 and ended his playing days with 123 League appearances to his credit.

JONES, VINCENT PETER

Midfield: 52 apps, 7 goals

Born: Watford, 5 January 1965

Career: Wealdstone (April 1983), Wimbledon (£10,000, November 1986), Leeds United (£650,000, June 1989), Sheffield United (£700,000, September 1990), CHELSEA (£575,000, August 1991), Wimbledon (£700,000, September 1992), Queens Park Rangers (£500,000, March 1998; player–assistant manager, August 1998; retired March 1999); he had already become a film star (when employed by QPR), making his debut in *Lock, Stock and Two Smoking Barrels*; he negotiated a settlement with QPR on the remainder of his initial three-year contract

One of football's tough guys, strong in every department, Vinny Jones was a powerful, aggressive midfielder who certainly had his fair share of problems with referees – he was once booked after just four seconds of a League game against Manchester City and was sent off 13 times during his career. In his first spell with Wimbledon, Jones appeared in more than 100 games and gained an FA Cup winner's medal in 1988. In his second spell he made a further 221 appearances. He was a Second Division championship winner with Leeds United in 1990 and went on to play in nine full internationals for Wales. He retired in 1999, having played in a total of 486 senior games at club and international levels.

KEENAN, JOSEPH JOHN

Midfield: 0+3 apps

Born: Southampton, 14 August 1982

Career: CHELSEA (apprentice, August 1998; professional, October 1999), FC Westerlo/Belgium (season loan, August 2004–May 2005)

Injuries, including a broken leg, severely disrupted Joe Keenan's career with Chelsea and after six years at Stamford Bridge he was loaned out for a season to the Belgian club FC Westerlo having played in just three senior games for the Blues, all as a substitute.

KELL, LEONARD WILLIAM
Inside-forward: 3 apps
Born: Billingham, County Durham, 27 May 1932
Career: CHELSEA (amateur, June 1948; professional, March 1952), Norwich
City (June 1954)
Because there were so many other good players of a similar style and who could
also occupy the inside-forward positions, Len Kell was a regular member of
Chelsea's reserve team during his time at Stamford Bridge. He made his League
debut in the London derby with Arsenal in September 1953 when over 55,000
fans saw the Blues win 2–1 at Highbury.

KEMBER, STEPHEN DENNIS
Midfield: 144+6 apps, 15 goals
Born: Croydon, Surrey, 8 December 1948
Career: Surrey and Croydon Schools, Crystal Palace (apprentice, July 1964;
professional, December 1965), CHELSEA (£170,000, September 1971),
Leicester City (£80,000, July 1975), Vancouver Whitecaps/NASL (loan,
April–July 1978), Crystal Palace (£50,000, October 1978), Vancouver
Whitecaps/NASL (March 1980–July 1980); Crystal Palace (youth-team
coach; then manager, November 1981–June 1982); managed Whyteleafe
FC/Diadora League (mid-1980s to early '90s); Crystal Palace (manager,
briefly in 2003); also ran a wine bar in Croydon
An England Youth international, Steve Kember was Chelsea's most expensive
footballer when he moved from Selhurst Park in 1971. An England Under-23
international (capped three times) he had gradually matured through the ranks
with Palace and quickly developed into a classy midfield player. An ever-present
when the Eagles won promotion to the First Division in 1969, he became
skipper of Palace and produced some outstanding performances before his
transfer to Stamford Bridge – at a time when Palace needed extra money. He
made his debut for Chelsea a week after joining (v. Sheffield United, away) and
went on to appear in 150 senior games for the club, partnering the likes of
Charlie Cooke, John Hollins, Alan Hudson, Ian Britton and Ray Wilkins in the
engine room before moving to Filbert Street, following relegation in 1975. He
later helped Palace gain promotion from the Second Division (with Terry
Venables in charge) in 1979. He returned to take charge of Palace for a second
time almost 40 years after first joining the club as a teenager.

KENNEDY, GEORGE
Half-back: 12 apps
Born: Dumfries, 1885 – *Died*: Passchendaele, December 1917
Career: Maxwelltown Volunteers, Lincoln City (May 1906), CHELSEA (May
1908), Brentford (June 1910–May 1913)
Versatile half-back George Kennedy, tall and well built, followed manager
David Calderhead to Chelsea. He spent only one season at Stamford Bridge

before moving to nearby Brentford for whom he made 73 appearances in the Southern League. He was killed in action during WW1.

KEVAN, DEREK TENNYSON
Centre-forward: 7 apps, 1 goal
Born: Ripon, Yorkshire, 6 March 1935
Career: Ripon Secondary Modern School, Harrogate and District Schools, Ripon City, Ripon YMCA, Sheffield United (trialist, April–May 1951), Bradford Park Avenue (amateur, July 1951; professional, October 1952), West Bromwich Albion (£3,000, July 1953), CHELSEA (£50,000, March 1963), Manchester City (£35,000, August 1963), Crystal Palace (July 1965), Peterborough United (March 1966), Luton Town (December 1966), Stockport County (March 1967), Macclesfield Town (August 1968), Stourbridge (August 1969), Ansells FC (December 1969–June 1975); WBA All Stars (seasons 1972–85; later manager 1985–93); also West Bromwich Albion Lottery Agent (1983–84); now retired and living in Castle Vale, Birmingham, having previously worked in a pub, a brewery, as a delivery driver and also as a drier for a sign-making company

Derek Kevan's brief stay at Stamford Bridge came just as Chelsea were set to clinch promotion from the Second Division. However, he and manager Tommy Docherty had disagreements and he quickly moved on. Previously a West Bromwich Albion great, he was certainly a big fella, standing 6 ft tall and weighing almost 13 st. Powerful in every aspect of forward play, he had a big heart, heaps of stamina and a lust for goals. He could head a ball as hard as some players could kick one and packed a fierce shot in his right foot and a fair one in his left! He won 14 full caps for England (8 goals scored); played 4 times for the Under-23 team and also represented the Football League. He spent almost 10 years at The Hawthorns, scoring 157 goals, including 5 in a League match v. Everton in 1960. Five years earlier he had scored twice on his debut for Albion in a 2–0 home win over the Merseysiders. He set a new post-war scoring record for Manchester City with 30 League goals in 1963–64 and in 1967 gained a Fourth Division championship medal with Stockport. During his League career, 1952–68, 'The Tank' (as he was so often called) netted 235 goals in 440 matches, topping the First Division scoring charts in 1961–2 with 33. Admittedly he was a shade clumsy at times, especially when he first joined Albion, but he developed into one of the greatest strikers The Hawthorns' fans have ever seen. It was a pity, but he joined Chelsea five years too late!

KEY, GEORGE BROWN
Wing-half: 56 apps, 2 goals
Born: Dennistoun, Glasgow, 11 February 1882 – *Died*: Glasgow, Scotland, November 1958
Career: Parkhead Juniors (Glasgow), Heart of Midlothian (July 1899),

CHELSEA (August 1905–May 1909); later with Ballieston Rangers (Glasgow)

'Geordie' Key was a crowd-pleaser, a midfield general with a nippy style, a tireless and attack-minded footballer who spent four years at Stamford Bridge, having his best season in 1905–06 when he made 35 of his 56 senior appearances. Chelsea's first right-half, he was replaced in the side by George Henderson. A Scottish Cup winner with Hearts in 1901 and a finalist two years later, he was capped by Scotland against Ireland in 1902. At 5 ft 4 in., he is one of the smallest players ever to assist Chelsea.

KEZMAN, MATEJA

Striker: 14+27 apps, 7 goals

Born: Belgrade, Yugoslavia, 12 April 1979

Career: Partizan Belgrade/Yugoslavia (professional, May 1998), PSV Eindhoven/Holland (£7 million, July 2000), CHELSEA (£5.2 million, July 2004), Atletico Madrid/Spain (£5.3 million, June 2005)

Mateja Kezman scored 140 goals in 4 seasons for PSV, including 105 in only 122 Dutch League games and top scoring in 3 out of 4 campaigns with totals of 24, 35 and 31 respectively – a better set of statistics than Marco Van Basten or Ruud van Nistelrooy before him. As a consequence, he arrived at Chelsea with the reputation as one of Europe's deadliest strikers. The Serbian international actually turned down both Charlton Athletic and West Bromwich Albion in favour of a career at Stamford Bridge and although not a regular in the side, when called into action by manager José Mourinho he certainly gives a good account of himself. His strike record in the Premiership has so far let him down – but as one reporter said: 'You write him off at your peril.'

He made his debut in the Premiership against Manchester United at Stamford Bridge on the opening day of the 2004–05 season and scored his first Premiership goal (to the delight of himself, his manager and the fans) in the last minute from the penalty spot in the 4–0 home win over Newcastle United in December. He went on to gain winner's medals in both the League Cup and the Premiership that season, scoring in the victory over Liverpool in the former. In October 2003, a kidnap threat was made against Kezman. He was placed under 24-hour police protection after British and Dutch officers uncovered a plot by criminals from his native Serbia to hold him, his wife Emilia and son Lazar to ransom.

KHARINE, DMITRI VICTORVITCH

Goalkeeper: 146 apps

Born: Moscow, 16 August 1968

Career: CSKA Moscow/USSR (professional, 1988), CHELSEA (£200,000, December 1992), Celtic (September 1999–May 2002)

Standing 6 ft 2 in. tall and weighing 13 st. 9 lb, Dmitri Kharine was precisely the right height and build for a goalkeeper and he certainly performed well between the posts during the first five years of his stay at Stamford Bridge. He lost his place to Ed De Goey when Blues' boss Gianluca Vialli abandoned his ploy of rotating his goalkeepers. A serious knee injury then sidelined him for quite a while and after regaining full fitness he moved to Parkhead where he stayed for four years, acting mainly as cover for Jonathan Gould and Rab Douglas. Capped 38 times by Russia, he successfully applied for English citizenship in 1998.

KIRKUP, JOSEPH ROBERT

Full-back: 62+7 apps, 2 goals
Born: Hexham, Northumberland, 17 December 1939
Career: Hickley Juniors (Northumberland), Northumberland County Schools, West Ham United (amateur, September 1956; professional, May 1957), CHELSEA (£27,000, March 1966), Southampton (exchange deal involving David Webb, February 1968), Durban City/South Africa (player–coach, February 1974); returned to England in 1976 to run a pub in Alton, Hampshire; also owned a sports shop in Cranleigh near Guildford before running his own newsagent's business in Ewell, Surrey

Capped by England as a youth-team player and on three occasions at Under-23 level, constructive, unflappable and resourceful full-back 'Gentleman Joe' Kirkup won the European Cup-Winners' Cup with West Ham in 1965 and was substitute for Chelsea (v. Spurs) in the 1967 FA Cup final. He brought a sense of maturity to the Blues' defence and was an important member of the senior squad for two years before moving to The Dell.

KIRWAN, JOHN HENRY

Outside-left: 76 apps, 18 goals
Born: County Wicklow, Ireland, 1878 – *Died*: 9 January 1959
Career: Southport, Everton (July 1898), Tottenham Hotspur (July 1899), CHELSEA (August 1905), Clyde (May 1908), Leyton (June 1909), coach in Holland (September 1910), Livorne FC/Switzerland (coach, 1923)

John Kirwan occupied the left-wing position with pride and commitment during Chelsea's first two seasons of League football. Fast, direct and a splendid crosser of the ball, he was always a thorn in opposing defences and scored his fair share of goals while creating several opportunities for his colleagues. He helped Spurs win the Southern League championship in 1900 and the FA Cup a year later and formed a wonderfully exciting left-wing partnership with David Copeland at White Hart Lane and Jimmy Windridge at Stamford Bridge. He scored 97 goals in 343 first-team matches for Spurs and won 4 of his 17 Irish caps as a Chelsea player. Kirwan grabbed hold of the ball after Spurs had won the FA Cup in 1901 and kept it in his possession until his death.

KITAMIRIKE, JOEL DERICK

Defender: 1 app.

Born: Kampala, Uganda, 5 April 1984

Career: CHELSEA (apprentice, May 2000; professional, April 2001), Brentford (loan, September 2003–May 2004), Aldershot Town (free transfer, August 2004), Dundee (free, January 2005)

An England Youth international central defender, powerfully built, Joel Kitamirike's only senior outing for Chelsea came as John Terry's partner against Hapoel Tel Aviv in the UEFA Cup in 2001. He made 25 appearances for Brentford before dropping into non-League football, but signed for Dundee FC in January 2005.

KITCHENER, RAYMOND ALAN

Outside-left: 1 app.

Born: Letchworth, Hertfordshire, 31 October 1930

Career: Letchworth Town (amateur, 1947), Hitchin Town (semi-professional, August 1949), CHELSEA (professional, July 1954), Norwich City (September 1956), Biggleswade FC (May 1957), Amesbury Rovers (1959; retired 1965); returned to his trade as an electrician and resides in Letchworth

Reserve to England international Frank Blunstone and also Jim Lewis at Stamford Bridge, unselfish left-winger Ray Kitchener made just one League appearance for Chelsea, in the 2–2 draw with Manchester City at Maine Road in February 1956. He had 19 senior outings for Norwich.

KJELDBJERG, JAKOB

Defender: 65+1 apps, 2 goals

Born: Denmark, 21 October 1969

Career: FC Silkeborg/Denmark, CHELSEA (£400,000, August 1993; released May 1995); returned to Denmark

After settling down as partner to Erland Johnsen, unfortunately a spate of niggling and tedious injuries forced 6 ft 2 in. Danish international central defender Jakob Kjeldbjerg to miss most of the 1994–95 season and as a result was released by the club. Glenn Hoddle's first signing for Chelsea, he was good in the air and sound enough on the ground and in fact did very well initially before struggling to keep himself fit.

KNIGHT, LEON LEROY

Striker: 0+1 app.

Born: Hackney, London, 16 September 1982

Career: CHELSEA (apprentice, April 1998; professional, September 1999), Queens Park Rangers (loan, March–May 2001), Huddersfield Town (loan, October 2001–May 2002), Sheffield Wednesday (loan, July 2002–April 2003), Brighton and Hove Albion (£100,000, July 2003)

An England Youth and Under-20 international, Leon Knight remained a registered player with Chelsea for five years before leaving Stamford Bridge after failing to establish himself in the first XI. He did very well when on loan to Huddersfield (17 goals in 37 games) and was top scorer for Brighton in his first season with 27 goals in 53 appearances.

KNOX, THOMAS

Outside-left: 21 apps
Born: Glasgow, 5 April 1939
Career: East Stirling (professional, September 1957), CHELSEA (£5,000, June 1962), Newcastle United (£10,000, February 1965), Mansfield Town (£5,000, March 1967), Northampton Town (£5,000, December 1967), St Mirren (August 1969), Tonbridge (June 1972)

Tricky winger Tommy Knox had been Eddie McCreadie's team-mate at East Stirling and he followed his fellow Scot to Stamford Bridge four months later. He had struggled hard to get into the Scottish club's first XI – and it was much the same at Newcastle and indeed at Stamford Bridge – but he did a little better with Mansfield (60 games) and Northampton (32) in the lower divisions.

LAKE, GEORGE

Wing-half: 1 app.
Born: Manchester, March 1896 – *Died*: France, October 1918
Career: Manchester City (amateur 1912; professional, April 1913), CHELSEA (trial, August–September 1913, signed permanently, October 1913; still registered with the club at time of his death)

A well-built wing-half, George Lake had very little time to show his worth at Stamford Bridge owing to the outbreak of WW1. In fact, he was one of the last British soldiers to be killed in action during the hostilities. His only League outing for the Blues was away to West Bromwich Albion in April 1914.

LAMBOURDE, BERNARD

Utility: 43+17 apps, 3 goals
Born: Guadeloupe, West Indies, 7 May 1971
Career: Cannes/France (1991), Bordeaux/France (1995), CHELSEA (£1.6 million, July 1997), Portsmouth (loan, September–October 2000), SC Bastia/France (June 2001)

Able and confident enough to play at right-back, centre-half or in midfield, Bernard Lambourde was a valuable asset to the Chelsea squad. A calm, resourceful footballer, good on the ball with an eye for goal. Faced with fierce competition, he was allowed to leave by manager Claudio Ranieri at the end of the 2000–01 season. He won the League Cup and Charity Shield with Chelsea in 1998 and 2000 respectively.

LAMPARD, FRANK JAMES
Midfield: 204+13 apps, 49 goals
Born: Romford, Essex, 20 June 1978
Career: West Ham United (apprentice, June 1994; professional, July 1995), Swansea City (loan, October–November 1995), CHELSEA (£11 million, July 2001)

Son of the former West Ham United and England full-back of the same name, Frank Lampard, like his father, went on to gain full international honours for his country and in 2005 had earned almost 30 full, 1 'B' and 19 Under-21 caps to go with those he had collected at youth-team level. Now rated as one of the best attacking midfielders in world football, he missed only one of Chelsea's 59 competitive games in 2003–04 when he also passed the milestone of 100 consecutive Premiership appearances. The following season he was once again a key member of the side, producing some powerful and outstanding performances in the centre of the park alongside Claude Makelele, Joe Cole and Geremi, playing in all 59 first-class matches. Now an established figure in the England team, Lampard signed a new five-year contract with Chelsea in 2004. Voted FWA Player of the Year in 2005, he was also the top scorer from midfield with a total of 19 goals, leading from the front as the League Cup and Premiership trophies came to Stamford Bridge.

LANGLEY, THOMAS WILLIAM
Forward: 139+13 apps, 43 goals
Born: Lambeth, London, 8 February 1958
Career: CHELSEA (associated schoolboy forms, 1970; apprentice, May 1973; professional, April 1975), Queens Park Rangers (August 1980), Crystal Palace (March 1981), AEK Athens/Greece, Coventry City (March 1984), Wolverhampton Wanderers (July 1984), Aldershot (loan, March 1985), South China FC/Hong Kong (July 1985), Aldershot (August 1986), Exeter City (July 1988), Billericay Town (May 1989), Slough Town (1991–92)

During an adventurous career, Tommy Langley scored 87 goals in 368 Football League games and gained one England Under-23 cap plus others at schoolboy and youth-team levels. He was only 16 years, 9 months old when he made his league debut for Chelsea against Leicester City in November 1974 before establishing himself in the first XI in 1977–78. An enthusiastic and totally committed player, he actually scored 39 of his 43 goals in the 128 games he played in during his last three seasons with the Blues – despite a lot of unfair criticism.

LANGTON, JOSEPH
Wing-half: 3 apps
Born: Crook, County Durham, 1898 – *Died*: Durham, 1965
Career: CHELSEA (professional, October 1919; free transfer, April 1922); later with Shildon

Owing to the form of Tommy Meehan, Tom Wilding and David Cameron, Joe

Langton had to fight hard and long for first-team football during his three years at Stamford Bridge and was handed just three senior games, the first against Blackburn Rovers in May 1921.

LAUDRUP, BRIAN
Forward: 8+3 apps, 1 goal
Born: Vienna, Austria, 22 February 1969
Career: IF Brondby/Denmark (professional, March 1987), Bayer Uerlingen/Germany (May 1989), Bayern Munich/Germany (August 1990), Fiorentina/Italy (March 1993), AC Milan/Italy (February 1994), Glasgow Rangers (June 1994), CHELSEA (free transfer, June 1998), FC Copenhagen/Denmark (briefly, November 1998), Ajax Amsterdam/Holland (December 1998–2000)

Brian Laudrup won a total of 82 full caps for Denmark, despite being born in Austria. Unfortunately he was a huge disappointment at Chelsea – this, after starring in the 1998 World Cup finals. Nicknamed the 'Great Dane' he won the Danish Cup with Brondby in 1989, lifted the European Championship with Denmark three years later, helped Fiorentina gain promotion to Serie 'A' in Italy in 1994 and scored 45 goals in 151 games for Rangers. He helped the Gers win the Scottish League title, was Scotland's Footballer of the Year in his first season at Ibrox Park (1994–95) and went on to win two more League titles north of the border before joining Chelsea. Laudrup was also voted Denmark's Footballer of the Year three times – in 1989, 1992 and 1995. His father, Finn Laudrup, was a Danish international while his elder brother, Michael, played for KB Copenhagen, IF Brondby, SC Lazio, Juventus, CF Barcelona, Real Madrid and Ajax Amsterdam, among others, and won over 100 caps for Denmark.

LAVERICK, ROBERT
Outside-left: 7 apps
Born: Castle Eden, Trimdon, County Durham, 11 June 1938
Career: CHELSEA (amateur June 1953; professional, June 1955), Everton (February 1959), Brighton and Hove Albion (June 1960), Coventry City (July 1962–April 1963), Corby Town (August 1963); later King's Lynn

After entering League football with Chelsea in a 4–2 defeat at West Bromwich Albion in February 1957, England Youth international left-winger Bobby Laverick, powerfully built with a good turn of foot, enhanced his career with Everton for whom he also made his debut against WBA. He later scored 20 goals in 63 League outings for Brighton. He had found it tough going to get a game in the first XI at Stamford Bridge owing to the presence of Frank Blunstone, Mike Block and Jim Lewis.

LAW, THOMAS

Full-back: 319 apps, 19 goals
Born: Glasgow, 1 April 1908 – *Died*: London, 17 February 1976
Career: Bridgton Waverley/Glasgow (December 1924), CHELSEA (£10, May 1925; retired May 1939)

The rock of Chelsea's defence for ten full seasons, Tommy Law was a first-time tackler, quality kicker, strong in the air and marshalled his colleagues admirably. Not blessed with great pace, he simply held his position perfectly and was never really given a roasting by an opposing winger. Nimbleness of thought compensated for a lack of yards per seconds and he demonstrated the extent to which a footballer's head can save his legs. Law's rise to soccer eminence, like his performances on the field, was made in the shortest time possible. He appeared in only five junior games in Scotland before moving to Chelsea and he quickly found Stamford Bridge to be home from home. When he made his debut for the Blues against Portsmouth in September 1926, there were seven other Scots in the team. He won two full caps for his country, both against England – the first in that wonderful 5–1 victory in 1928 when the Scots were dubbed the 'Wembley Wizards'. Despite lucrative offers from abroad, Law spent his entire professional career – all 14 years – at Stamford Bridge. He was, without doubt, a wonderful servant to Chelsea Football Club and remained an avid supporter of the Blues until his death at the age of 67. He was present at both the 1967 and 1970 FA Cup finals and the 1972 League Cup final. Law turned down a move to the French club Nîmes in 1933.

LAWTON, THOMAS

Centre-forward: 95 apps, 70 goals
Born: Bolton, 6 October 1919 – *Died*: Nottingham, 6 November 1996
Career: Tonge Moor Council, Castle Hill and Foulds Road schools (Bolton), Bolton and Lancashire Boys, Bolton Wanderers (amateur, September 1933), Sheffield Wednesday (amateur, August 1934), Hayes Athletic (amateur, January 1935), Rossendale United (amateur, March 1935), Burnley (amateur, May 1935; professional, October 1936), Everton (£6,500, December 1936), CHELSEA (£11,000, November 1945), Notts County (£20,000, November 1947), Brentford (March 1952), Arsenal (£10,000 plus James Robertson, September 1953), Kettering Town (£1,000, player–manager, February 1956), Notts County (manager, May 1957–July 1958), Kettering Town (manager, November 1963–April 1964; then director from 1965), Notts County (coach and chief scout, October 1968–April 1970); later a publican in Lowdham, Notts; lived in Nottingham until his death

After netting 570 goals in 3 seasons playing schoolboy football in Burnley, Tommy Lawton became the youngest-ever player to score a League hat-trick when, at the age of 17 years, 4 days, he netted 3 times for Burnley against Spurs in October 1936. This was only his fifth game for the Clarets. As an Everton player, he was 17 years, 130 days old (the youngest prior to Wayne Rooney) when he made his debut in a 7–2 away defeat at Wolves in February 1937. Then, 232 days later, he hit the target against Liverpool in October 1937 and to this day remains the youngest scorer in a Merseyside derby. The following season (1938–39) and still a teenager, he finished as the Blues' top marksman with 34 goals in 38 games when the League title was won. In fact, his first five senior goals were scored when he was nineteen years old.

Ideally built for a centre-forward, Lawton was a master in the air, brilliant on the ground, a constant threat to defenders, and was universally regarded (by players, managers and coaches alike) as one of the greatest of his era – despite suffering from flat feet. He moved to Chelsea just in time to play against Moscow Dynamo, when 82,905 fans packed into Stamford Bridge, and scored 20 goals in 26 Regional League and FA Cup games that season (1945–46), bagging 30 in 39 outings the following campaign. He was then surprisingly transferred to Notts County for £20,000 – a record fee at that time.

Lawton's extraordinary promise as a youngster was completely realised as he went on to score 232 goals in 390 League games up to 1956. He went on to register a magnificent record for the Merseysiders of 222 goals in 209 first-team matches, including 152 in 114 WW2 fixtures. He also claimed 22 goals in 23 outings for England, with two fourtimers against Holland and Portugal in 1946 and 1947 respectively, and he netted 24 goals in 23 wartime internationals. He represented the Football League on two occasions (once as a Chelsea player in 1947) and was a Third Division (S) winner with Notts County in 1950. Lawton had a testimonial match at Goodison Park in November 1972.

LEADBETTER, JAMES HUNTER
Inside-forward: 3 apps
Born: Edinburgh, 15 July 1928
Career: Edinburgh Thistle, CHELSEA (July 1949), Brighton and Hove Albion (August 1952), Ipswich Town (June 1955), Sudbury Town (June 1965); after retiring worked in various jobs in and around Ipswich before returning to Edinburgh

A slim-lined Scottish ball-playing inside-forward, Jimmy Leadbetter battled hard and long without success at Stamford Bridge but after leaving Chelsea he went on to greater things with Brighton (120 appearances, 33 goals) and Ipswich Town (375 games, 49 goals). After being switched to the left-wing by Alf Ramsey he became a star performer for Ipswich as they rose from the Third Division (S) to take the Football League championship in double-quick time. Leadbetter, like his colleagues, gained medals for triumphs in three different divisions – in the Third South in 1957, the Second in 1961 and the First in 1962.

LEBOEUF, FRANK

Defender: 200+4 apps, 24 goals
Born: Marseilles, France, 22 January 1968
Career: Hyeres/France (professional, March 1986), Meaux/France (December 1986), Laval/France (August 1988), Strasbourg/France (January 1991), CHELSEA (£2.5 million, July 1996), Olympique Marseilles/France (July 2001); played in Qatar (from June 2003; retired June 2005)

Frank Leboeuf scored 63 goals in 311 League appearances in French football before joining Chelsea and he continued to produce the goods at Stamford Bridge, giving the Blues excellent service for five years before returning to his home-town club.

Strong in every aspect of defensive play, he was certainly a rugged performer, totally committed, and adored by the fans who gave him cult-like status. He won six trophies with Chelsea: the FA Cup in 1997 and 2000, the League Cup, European Cup-Winners' Cup and Super Cup all in 1998, and the Charity Shield in 2000. He also gained over 40 full caps for France, helping his country win the World Cup in 1998 and the European Championship two years later.

LEE, COLIN

Centre-forward/full-back: 200+23 apps, 41 goals
Born: Plymouth, Devon, 12 June 1956
Career: Bristol City (apprentice, June 1972; professional, June 1974), Hereford United (loan, November–December 1974), Torquay United (£8,000, January 1977), Tottenham Hotspur (£60,000, October 1977), CHELSEA (£200,000, January 1980), Brentford (£17,500, July 1987; retired 1989; then Youth Development Officer), Watford (youth team manager, July 1989; manager, March–November 1990; then assistant manager/coach), Reading (Youth Development Officer, July 1991; later assistant manager/coach), Leicester City (assistant manager/coach, July 1994), Wolverhampton Wanderers (assistant manager/coach, December 1995; manager, November 1998–January 2001), Torquay United (caretaker-manager, March–May 2001), Walsall (manager, January 2002–May 2004)

Initially Colin Lee was an exciting marksman with a sound technique. Indeed, after failing to find the net for Bristol City or Hereford, he scored 15 goals for Torquay and 21 for Spurs, making a sensational start to his career at White Hart Lane by notching four times in a 9–0 home League win over Bristol Rovers. At the end of that season promotion was gained to the First Division. His debut for Chelsea was against Cardiff City (home) in March 1980 and for the next five years he was a regular in the side, helping the Blues win the Second Division championship in 1984 and the Full Members' Cup two years later. He scored a brilliant hat-trick in a 6–0 home League win over Newcastle three years after netting his fourtimer for Spurs – and both games were shown on TV. When David Speedie and Kerry Dixon started to produce the goods up front in the mid-1980s, Lee was successfully switched to full-back where he performed admirably. He retired as a player in 1989 having scored 78 goals in 370 senior appearances. Unfortunately, he did not have much success as a manager, although he did keep Torquay United in the Football League in 2001.

LEE, DAVID JOHN

Defender: 148+45 apps, 13 goals

Born: Kingswood, Bristol, 26 November 1969

Career: CHELSEA (apprentice, April 1986; professional, July 1988), Reading (loan, January–February 1992), Plymouth Argyle (loan, March–May 1992), Portsmouth (loan, August–September 1994), Sheffield United (loan, December 1997–January 1998), Bristol Rovers (free transfer, December 1998–May 1999), Crystal Palace (free, October 1999), Colchester United (free, January 2000), Exeter City (free, February 2000; retired March 2000)

Capped by England as a youth-team player, David Lee went on to appear in ten Under-21 internationals during his time with Chelsea, gaining a Second Division championship medal in 1989 and a League Cup winner's medal in 1998. A versatile defender, with two good feet and a footballing brain, he was able to play as a full-back, centre-half or sweeper, was also confident in midfield and at times appeared up front where he was more than useful, his strength serving him well against tough opponents. He lost his place in the first team at Stamford Bridge in the early 1990s but was always ready and willing when called into action, despite being loaned out to four different clubs. Lee had the ill-luck to get himself sent off after just 12 minutes when making his debut for his last club Exeter City v. York City in February 2000. Surprisingly he ended his 14-year career with fewer than 250 senior appearances to his name (190 in the Football League).

LEE, JOHN

Outside-left: 7 apps, 1 goal

Born: Sheffield, April 1890 – *Died*: Hull, 10 August 1955

Career: Bird In Hand FC (Sheffield), Hull City (June 1913), CHELSEA (£1,500, February 1920), Watford (March 1923), Rotherham United (June 1925–May 1927); later returned to Hull to live and work

Quite tall and weighty for a winger, Jack Lee scored 51 goals in 163 first-team games for Hull (including WW1 action) before joining Chelsea for a substantial fee in 1920. Unfortunately he failed to adapt to the rigours of First Division football and languished in the reserves for most of his three years at Stamford Bridge.

LE SAUX, GRAEME PIERRE

Full-back/midfield: 280+32 apps, 20 goals

Born: Jersey, 17 October 1968

Career: St Paul's FC (Jersey), CHELSEA (professional, September 1986), Blackburn Rovers (£750,000, March 1993), CHELSEA (£5 million, August

1997), Southampton (£500,000 plus Wayne Bridge, July 2003; reitred May 2005)

An attacking left-back or left-sided midfielder, Graeme Le Saux served Chelsea superbly well in 2 spells covering a total of 13 years. In that time he appeared in more than 300 senior matches, gained a League Cup winner's medal in 1998 and won the Charity Shield in 2000. He also collected 16 England caps to add to his tally of 20 he won with Blackburn, for whom he starred in their Premiership triumph in 1995. As well as his senior outings for his country he also played in one 'B' and four Under-21 internationals. Strong and powerful, he enjoyed a challenge and on several occasions found himself in the referee's notebook. But his commitment out on the pitch was second to none and, although battling against niggling injuries, in 2004 he reached the personal milestone of 500 competitive appearances for clubs and country.

LEWINGTON, RAYMOND
Midfield: 87+5 apps, 4 goals
Born: Lambeth, London, 7 September 1956
Career: CHELSEA (schoolboy forms, 1971; apprentice, May 1972; professional, February 1974), Vancouver Whitecaps/NASL (£40,000, February 1979), Wimbledon (loan, September–December 1979), Fulham (£50,000, March 1980), Sheffield United (July 1985), Fulham (£20,000, player–manager, July 1986–June 1990; appointed chief scout July 1990; then caretaker-manager, November–December 1991; assistant manager, 1991–94), Crystal Palace (coach, seasons 1994–96), Brentford (manager, briefly in 2001), Watford (manager, July 2002; sacked March 2005)

A useful ball-winning midfielder who perhaps lacked that bit of extra skill required to become a top-line player in the First Division. An ever-present in 1976–77 when he helped Chelsea gain promotion to the top flight, Ray Lewington made over 400 League and Cup appearances during his professional career. He moved into management at Fulham at the age of 29.

LEWIS, FREDERICK ARTHUR
Full-back: 26 apps
Born: Broughton Gifford, Wiltshire, 27 July 1923
Career: Aylesbury (August 1938), Royal Navy (WW2), CHELSEA (professional, March 1946), Colchester United (June 1953–May 1955)

Fred Lewis, neat and compact with a good technique, was a reserve-team player for most of his seven years with Chelsea, having his best season at senior level in 1947–48 when he played in 12 First Division games, deputising in the main for Danny Winter at right-back. He made his League debut for the Blues in front of 61,000 fans at Stamford Bridge v. Bolton Wanderers in August 1946 and later appeared in more than 90 senior games in two seasons for Colchester.

LEWIS, JAMES LEONARD

Centre-/inside-forward/winger: 95 apps, 40 goals
Born: Hackney, London, 26 June 1927
Career: Walthamstow Avenue (1944), Leyton Orient (November 1950), Walthamstow Avenue (April 1951), CHELSEA (September 1952), Walthamstow Avenue (May 1958; retired April 1962)

Jim Lewis, who remained an amateur throughout his career, was one of the most famous non-professional footballers of the 1940s and '50s, gaining 49 caps at amateur level. He helped Chelsea win the Football League title in 1955 when he scored six goals in 17 games. Four years later he was presented with an illuminated address for his six years' dedicated service at Stamford Bridge. A strong runner, direct, and possessing a powerful shot in both feet, he shared the outside-left position with Frank Blunstone and eventually moved back into non-League football when Mick Block took over on the left flank. Lewis's father, Jack, was also an England amateur international between the two world wars.

LINFOOT, FREDERICK

Outside-right: 41 apps, 1 goal
Born: Whitley Bay, Northumberland, 12 March 1901 – *Died*: 1979
Career: Smith's Dock FC (Newcastle), Leeds City (March 1919), Lincoln City (£250, October 1919), CHELSEA (July 1920), Fulham (March 1924–April 1926)

Signed by manager David Calderhead (ex-Lincoln), Fred Linfoot averaged ten games a season during his Chelsea career – down to the fact that there were other players of similar style registered with the club at the same time. A sprightly winger with good ball control, he joined Lincoln from Leeds City in 1919 at an auction following the folding up of the Yorkshire club by the Football League due to illegal payments to players.

LIVESEY, CHARLES EDWARD

Forward: 42 apps, 18 goals
Born: West Ham, London, 6 February 1935
Career: Shipham Road School (West Ham), West Ham Boys, Bata Club (East Ham), Wolverhampton Wanderers (trial, 1954), Custom House FC (1955), Southampton (trial, March 1956; professional, April 1956), CHELSEA (£20,000, plus Cliff Huxford, May 1959), Gillingham (£2,000, August 1961), Watford (£2,500, October 1962), Northampton Town (£1,500, August 1964), Brighton and Hove Albion (free transfer, September 1965), Crawley Town (June 1969; retired 1971)

Charlie Livesey developed through the ranks at The Dell and scored 15 goals in 28 games for the Saints before transferring to Chelsea with Cliff Huxford moving in the opposite direction. Well built, with a strong right-foot shot, he did well at Stamford Bridge but never quite had the quality to make him a real top-class player. After leaving the Blues he drew up a fine scoring record in the lower sectors and when he moved into non-League football in 1969, he had netted over 120 goals in more than 350 competitive games, including 28 in 126 Third Division games for Brighton.

LIVINGSTONE, STEPHEN CARL
Centre-forward/-half: 0+1 app.
Born: Middlesbrough, 8 September 1968
Career: Coventry City (apprentice, August 1984; professional, July 1986), Blackburn Rovers (£450,000, January 1991), CHELSEA (£350,000, March 1993), Port Vale (loan, September 1993), Grimsby Town (£140,000, October 1993), Carlisle United (free transfer, August 2003; contract cancelled, May 2004)

Steve Livingstone's stay at Stamford Bridge lasted just six months during which time he appeared once for the Blues (as a second-half substitute against Manchester United at Old Trafford in April 1993); he also had a loan spell with Port Vale. However, with Grimsby he performed superbly well for a decade and accumulated a fine record of 333 senior appearances and 51 goals, helping the Mariners win the Auto-Windscreen Shield in 1998. Steve's father, Joe Livingstone, played for Carlisle United, Middlesbrough and Hartlepool United during the 1960s.

LIVINGSTONE, WILLIAM RENNISON
Centre-half: 22 apps
Born: Greenock, Scotland, 8 February 1929
Career: Ardeer Recreationalists (1946), Reading (professional, April 1949), CHELSEA (June 1956), Brentford (July 1959–April 1960)

Strong in arm, body and leg, Bill Livingstone was a real 'stopper' centre-half, a robust player who feared no one. He never shirked a challenge, enjoyed a battle and gave nothing less than 100 per cent out on the field. He deputised for Stan Wicks during his Chelsea days and moved on when John Mortimore emerged on the scene. He played in 49 League games for Reading and 19 for Brentford.

LLOYD, BARRY DAVID
Midfield: 8+2 apps
Born: Hillingdon, 18 February 1949
Career: Middlesex Boys, South East of England Schools XI, Hillingdon (season 1963–64), CHELSEA (apprentice, June 1964; professional, February 1966), Fulham (£30,000 plus John Dempsey, December 1968), Hereford United (October 1976), Brentford (June 1977), Houston Hurricane/NASL (June–August 1978), Yeovil Town (manager, September 1978–July 1981), Worthing (manager, August 1981–May 1986), Brighton and Hove Albion (assistant manager, July 1986; manager, January 1987–May 1993), Worthing (consultant, mid- to late 1990s)

There were far too many players of similar style and able to man midfield when

England Youth international midfielder Barry Lloyd was with Chelsea. As a result his senior appearances were restricted to just eight – his first coming against West Bromwich Albion in April 1967. After leaving Stamford Bridge he became captain of Fulham for whom he starred in 289 games and scored 30 goals, helping the Cottagers gain promotion in 1971 as Third Division champions. He was on the subs' bench for the 1975 FA Cup final when Fulham lost to West Ham – having played in all the previous rounds. Lloyd succeeded Alan Mullery as Brighton manager in 1986, and guided Brighton to the runner's-up spot in Division Three in 1988, having led Worthing to the Isthmian Second and First Division titles in 1982 and 1983 respectively and then to the Premier League twice, in 1984 and 1985. He was replaced in the hot seat at Hove by Liam Brady.

LOCKE, GARY ROBERT
Defender: 315+2 apps, 4 goals
Born: Willesden, London, 12 July 1954
Career: CHELSEA (apprentice, July 1969; professional, July 1971), Crystal Palace (January 1983–March 1986); later played in Sweden
An England Youth international, Gary 'Mr Dependable' Locke graduated through the junior, intermediate and reserve teams at Stamford Bridge to become a pillar of strength at the heart of the Chelsea defence. He gained a regular place in the first team in 1973 and spent almost 14 years with the club before moving to Crystal Palace. Locke did not gain the credit he deserved. He produced some superb performances out on the pitch and he wasn't just a defender. He would often surge upfield, through the middle or down the flanks, to set up a scoring opportunity for a colleague. He was an ever-present when the Blues won promotion from the Second Division in 1976–77. 'Lockey' made exactly 100 senior appearances for Palace.

LOGAN, THOMAS
Centre-half: 117 apps, 8 goals
Born: Barrhead, Renfrewshire, 17 August 1888 – *Died*: Scotland, 1960
Career: Arthurlie (1906), Falkirk (1910), CHELSEA (£2,500, May 1913; retired, injured, May 1921); returned to Scotland
Having helped Falkirk win the Scottish Cup in 1913 and Scotland beat Ireland 2–1 in Dublin in his only full international outing that same year, centre-half Tom Logan became a record signing by Chelsea. Two years later he gained an FA Cup runner's-up medal when the Blues lost to Sheffield United. Universally popular because of his unassuming, quiet demeanour, he was not a flashy player but one who did the simple things out on the field. An excellent reader of the game, his judgement was first-class and he cleared his lines with great efficiency. His two brothers, Alex (Falkirk) and Jimmy (Glasgow Rangers), were both professional footballers who represented the Scottish League.

LUKE, GEORGE

Wing-half: 1 app.

Born: Hetton-le-Hole, County Durham, 9 November 1948

Career: Newcastle United, CHELSEA (March 1967), Durham City (August 1968–May 1969); later emigrated to South Africa

An England schoolboy international and failing to make an appearance for Newcastle, George Luke's only League appearance for Chelsea was at right-half against Leicester City (away) in May 1967 – a fortnight before the FA Cup final. He was only 20 when he chose to quit football for a life in South Africa. His relative, George Thomas Luke, played for Newcastle United, Hartlepool United and Darlington between 1950 and 1964.

LYON, FRANK

Full-back: 6 apps

Born: Crewe, Cheshire, 23 September 1879 – *Died*: Crewe, 1955

Career: Stockport County (briefly, 1897), Crewe Alexandra (April 1898), Watford (July 1901), Queens Park Rangers (October 1903), CHELSEA (March 1907), Crewe Alexandra (May 1908; retired, injured, May 1909); later ran his own business in Crewe

After spending the last few weeks of the 1906–07 season in the reserves, Frank Lyon made his League debut for Chelsea against Newcastle United (away) in the second game of the following campaign and did well until ousted by new signing Jock Cameron. A knee injury ended his career.

MACAULAY, JAMES AUSTIN RUSSELL

Full-back: 94 apps, 5 goals

Born: Edinburgh, 19 October 1922

Career: Edinburgh Thistle, CHELSEA (junior, 1940; part-time professional, November 1946), Aldershot (August 1951–May 1952)

'Wee Jimmy' Macaulay was a customs officer before joining Chelsea. A hard-tackling, resilient full-back, he played his first game in the blue of Chelsea during the 1940–41 wartime season and was 24 years of age before he eventually was signed officially (on demobilisation from the RAF). Owing to the fact that he worked as a civil servant in London, Macaulay signed as a part-time professional. He was a strong, hard-tackling full-back who after three useful seasons eventually lost his place in the side to Frank Mitchell. He scored 3 goals in 31 League appearances for Aldershot.

MacFARLANE, IAN

Full-back: 43 apps

Born: Lanark, Scotland, 26 January 1933

Career: Aberdeen (August 1953; professional, January 1955), CHELSEA (August 1956), Leicester City (£9,000, May 1958), Bath City (free transfer, July 1959); Middlesbrough (assistant manager/coach, 1964), Manchester

City (assistant manager/coach, 1966), Carlisle United (manager, January 1970–July 1972), Sunderland (assistant manager/coach, July 1972; caretaker-manager October–November 1976), Leicester City (assistant manager/coach, 1977–May 1982; acted as caretaker-manager April–June 1978); later Leeds United (chief scout to 1992)

A tough, hefty full-back, Ian MacFarlane (known as 'Big Man') was a reserve at Aberdeen before joining Chelsea at the age of 23. He was a regular in the side during his first season but a loss of form led to his transfer to Leicester. He later teamed up with Tony Book at Bath City in 1959 and after retiring returned to Filbert Street where he was assistant to managers Frank McLintock and Jock Wallace. As a coach, it is fair to say that on the whole he tended to be associated with highly motivated yet essentially dour sides.

MACHIN, ALEX HAROLD
Inside-forward/wing-half: 61 apps, 9 goals
Born: Shepherd's Bush, London, 6 July 1920
Career: Royal Hampshire Regiment (WW2), CHELSEA (amateur, April 1944; professional, on demobilisation, October 1945), Plymouth Argyle (June 1948), St Austell/Cornwall (June 1952; retired May 1954)

Spotted playing Army football, lightweight wing-half Alex Machin made up for a lack of strength with some ferocious tackling, not always to the liking of the referee. He held his place in Chelsea's line-up for a season and a half before being replaced by Ken Armstrong who moved into the half-back line after a spell at centre-forward. After breaking his right leg playing for Plymouth against Coventry City in 1949, he never regained full fitness and quit competitive League football in 1952.

MacINTOSH, STANLEY WILSON
Goalkeeper: 1 app.
Born: Brighton, 26 November 1905 – *Died*: London, 1976
Career: Patcham Rangers, London Caledonians (1924), CHELSEA (May 1930; retired, June 1936)

A competent goalkeeper, Stan MacIntosh was reserve to internationals Vic Woodley and/or Johnny Jackson for six years, making only one League appearance in that time – a 6–2 defeat at Derby in December 1930.

MACKIE, ROBERT
Full-back: 48 apps, 1 goal
Born: Dalry, Ayrshire, August 1882 – *Died*: Airdrie, Lanarkshire, 1943
Career: Bannockburn FC, Stenhousemuir (1902), Heart of Midlothian (May 1904), CHELSEA (August 1905), Leicester Fosse (November 1907), Airdrieonians (July 1909; retired May 1914)

Ungainly but obstinate, Bob Mackie was Chelsea's first right-back. Quick over the ground with great stamina, he was popular with the supporters and it was unfortunate that injury cost him his place in the side. The arrival of Joe Walton led to his departure to Leicester for whom he made 36 appearances before spending 6 years with Airdrie, who rewarded him with a benefit match v. Albion Rovers in 1914.

MAIR, THOMAS
Outside-left: 9 apps, 1 goal
Born: Kilmarnock, 1883 – *Died*: Scotland, *circa* 1955
Career: Galston FC/Scotland, Ayr United (1902), Leyton (1905), CHELSEA (January 1909; released May 1910); later with Stewarton FC/Scotland; did not play after WW1

One of several players who competed for the left-wing position, Tom Mair spent just the one season with Chelsea, making his Football League debut in a 2–1 win at Manchester City on Christmas Day 1908.

MAKELELE, CLAUDE
Midfield: 91+5 apps, 1 goal
Born: Kinshasa, DR Congo, 18 February 1973
Career: Brest Amorique/France (professional, March 1990), Nantes/France (June 1992), Olympique Marseilles/France (August 1997), Celta Vigo/Spain (July 1998), Real Madrid/Spain (August 2000), CHELSEA (£16.6 million, September 2003)

French international midfielder Claude Makelele made 169 League appearances for Nantes, 33 for Marseilles, 70 for Celta Vigo and 94 for Real Madrid before moving into the English Premiership with Chelsea. With his current Chelsea team-mate Geremi (q.v.), he won the Spanish League title in 2001, and the following year gained a European Champions Cup winner's medal but finished on the losing side in the Spanish Cup final.

The battery that made Real Madrid tick, he was a snip-of-a-signing by manager Claudio Ranieri and immediately slotted into his accustomed position in front of the back four. Making the game look easy, he is such an effective player who gets hold of the ball and then delivers the perfect pass to a colleague. With his athleticism, anticipation and intelligent positioning, he is the perfect cog between defence and attack. Makelele has now won almost 40 senior caps having earlier played in four 'B' internationals and three Under-21 games, and was a key figure in Chelsea's League Cup and Premiership winning sides of 2005.

MALCOLM, ANDREW
Wing-half: 28 apps, 1 goal
Born: East Ham, London, 4 May 1933
Career: Romford Boys, Essex County FA, West Ham United (groundstaff, June 1948; professional, July 1950), CHELSEA (£12,000 exchange deal involving Ron Tindall, November 1961), Queens Park Rangers (£12,000, October

1962–May 1965); played briefly in South Africa; later a licensee in Maldon, Essex

Signed after a long and distinguished career at Upton Park (he made 306 senior appearances for the Hammers), Andy Malcolm added experience to a relatively young Chelsea side and had one good season at Stamford Bridge before switching his allegiance to QPR. His place in the Blues' line-up went to a young Terry Venables. Malcolm, who played for England at schoolboy and youth-team levels and represented the Football League, gained a Second Division championship medal in 1958 as an ever-present in the Hammers' team.

MARSH, WILSON
Goalkeeper: 12 apps
Born: Hunslet, Yorkshire, March 1894 – *Died*: Scotland, 1989
Career: Woodhouse Lads' Club (Sheffield), Eckington Works FC (Sheffield), CHELSEA (December 1921), Dundee (July 1924), Kilmarnock (1927–28); became a champion golfer on the Scottish circuit

Wilson Marsh acted as reserve to three quality goalkeepers (including the famous Corinthian, Howard Baker) during his Chelsea career and therefore was restricted to just 12 senior appearances, 11 coming in 1923–24. He was 95 when he died in 1989. An elder brother, William Marsh, born in Brodsworth, played for Halifax Town in 1931.

MARSHALL, OWEN THOMAS
Full-back: 36 apps
Born: Nottingham, 17 September 1892 – *Died*: Kent, 1963
Career: Ilkeston United, CHELSEA (March 1913), Gillingham (November 1920–May 1922), Maidstone United (trial)

A capable deputy for either Walter Berridge or Jack Harrow, Owen Marshall's career at Stamford Bridge was severely hindered by WW1 during which he played only one season (1915–16). He made 39 League appearances for Gillingham.

MATTHEW, DAMIEN
Midfield: 19+8 apps
Born: Islington, London, 23 September 1970
Career: CHELSEA (trainee, April 1987; professional, June 1989), Luton Town (loan, September–October 1992), Crystal Palace (£150,000, February 1994), Bristol Rovers (loan, January 1996), Burnley (£65,000, July 1996), Northampton Town (July 1998; retired, injured, December 1998)

A creative midfielder, Damien Matthew had a tough task on his hands to capture a place in Chelsea's first team. He made only 27 appearances during his 7 years at Stamford Bridge before becoming manager Alan Smith's first signing for London rivals Crystal Palace. He was advised to quit football in 1998 following a back injury suffered playing for Northampton against Brighton in a

League Cup tie. Capped nine times by England at Under-21 level, he won a First Division championship medal with Palace in 1994.

MATTHEWS, REGINALD DERRICK

Goalkeeper: 148 apps
Born: Coventry, 20 December 1932 – *Died*: Coventry, 7 October 2001
Career: Barkers Butt School (Coventry), Modern Machines Tools FC (Coventry), Coventry City (groundstaff, December 1947; professional, May 1950), CHELSEA (£22,500, November 1956), Derby County (£12,000, December 1961), Rugby Town (player–manager, August 1968–May 1969); later worked for Massey Ferguson (Coventry) for 20 years, retiring through ill health in 1990

Reg Matthews became the country's most expensive goalkeeper when he joined Chelsea for £15-a-week in 1956. He had already made a name for himself with some splendid displays for Coventry, prompting critics (including the Southampton manager and future Chelsea boss Ted Drake) to forecast an excellent future for the courageous and confident young keeper. Indeed, during his time at Highfield Road he made 116 first-team appearances, won 5 full and 3 'B' caps for England and represented the Football League (twice in 1955–56) as well as playing for the League North v. the League South. In fact, he became the first-ever Third Division goalkeeper to play in a senior international match for England when he won his first cap against Scotland in 1956.

After Drake had secured his transfer from Coventry, Matthews then produced the goods at Stamford Bridge, although at times he was uncomfortable behind a rather hesitant defence. He went on to gain 4 Under-23 caps as an over-aged player and made almost 150 appearances for the Blues before going on to add a further 247 to his tally with Derby, finally retiring from competitive football with 525 appearances under his belt. He captained the rugby XV at Barkers Butt School before becoming a safe handler of the ball in a different code.

MAYBANK, EDWARD GLEN

Forward: 32 apps, 6 goals
Born: Lambeth, London, 11 October 1956
Career: South London Boys, CHELSEA (apprentice, April 1973; professional, February 1974), Fulham (loan, November 1976; signed for £65,000, March 1977), Brighton and Hove Albion (£237,000, November 1977), Fulham (£150,000, December 1979), PSV Eindhoven/Holland (£250,000, August 1980; retired May 1981); later formed his own publishing company, Maybank Press, in the 1980s and printed football programmes

Teddy Maybank, tall and blond, was a talented if somewhat unpredictable striker who was replaced in the Chelsea side by Steve Finnieston and left when young Tommy Langley entered the scene. He was twice signed for Fulham by ex-Chelsea boss Bobby Campbell. A knee injury, suffered with PSV, ended his career.

MAYES, ALAN KENNETH

Forward: 71+5 apps, 24 goals
Born: Edmonton, London, 11 December 1953
Career: Queens Park Rangers (apprentice, April 1970; professional, July 1971), Watford (free transfer, November 1974), Northampton Town (loan, January–February 1976), Swindon Town (£80,000, February 1979), CHELSEA (£200,000, December 1980), Swindon Town (free, July 1983), Carlisle United (free, July 1985), Newport County (loan, February–March 1986), Blackpool (free, September 1986–May 1987)

In a nomadic career, Alan Mayes served with 8 different clubs covering a period of 17 years. In that time he scored 158 goals in 395 senior appearances (132 coming in 328 League games) and without doubt played his best football with Swindon for whom he struck 83 goals in 184 games in two spells. A neat and tidy ball-player, aggressive when required, he could turn and lose his marker in the space of one square yard and possessed a strong right-foot shot. After a very good 1981–82 campaign he found it harder the following season before becoming a victim of manager John Neal's 'sell and buy' policy as he strove to rebuild the team.

MAYES, ARNOLD JOHN

Wing-half: 13 apps
Born: Wickford, near Brentwood, Essex, 8 December 1913
Career: Barking Town (1929), Crystal Palace (March 1933), Barking Town (July 1933), CHELSEA (March 1935; retired May 1946)

Understudy to Irish international wing-half Billy Mitchell and also to Sam Weaver, Arnold Mayes spent most of his time with Chelsea playing in the second XI, but always produced a solid, workmanlike performance when called into the senior side. He was a corporal in the army during WW2.

McALLISTER, KEVIN

Winger: 97+38 apps, 13 goals
Born: Falkirk, Scotland, 8 November 1962
Career: Scottish junior football, Falkirk (professional, November 1980), CHELSEA (£34,000, May 1985), Falkirk (loan, March–April 1988); released by CHELSEA (May 1990)

Lightweight winger Kevin McAllister was in the Chelsea teams that won the Full Members' Cup (1984), the Second Division championship (1989) and the Zenith Data Systems Cup (1990). Blessed with some silky skills and good pace, he bided his time at Stamford Bridge and had to battle for a first-team place with fellow Scot Pat Nevin.

McANDREW, ANTHONY

Defender: 23 apps, 4 goals

Born: Glasgow, 11 April 1956

Career: Middlesbrough (apprentice, May 1972; professional, August 1973), Vancouver Whitecaps/NASL (loan, 1976), CHELSEA (tribunal set fee of £92,500, September 1982), Middlesbrough (deal involving Darren Wood, September 1984; retired March 1986; appointed junior coach); worked as a representative for a North-east brewery; played part-time for Willington (1987); Darlington (November 1988), Hartlepool United (March–May 1989); Darlington (youth and reserve-team manager, seasons 1989–91); then coach at Leicester City, Aston Villa and Stoke City (each time under manager Brian Little)

A Scottish youth international, a rock-solid defender and naturally aggressive player (in his own words), Tony McAndrew could also play in midfield and was brought into Stamford Bridge to add some security to the back division. He skippered the side for a while but after gaining a Second Division championship medal he returned to his former club, Middlesbrough, in a deal that saw Darren Wood move south. He went on to appear in more than 350 senior games for the Teesside club, acting as skipper on several occasions. McAndrew scored two hat-tricks in his career – both for Middlesbrough in 1976 – against Sheffield United in 1976 in the League and v. South Bank in the North Riding Senior Cup final.

McAULEY, ROBERT

Full-back: 74 apps, 1 goal

Born: Wishaw, Scotland, 28 August 1904 – *Died*: Glasgow, 1994

Career: Wishaw Lads' Club, Glasgow Rangers (junior, 1919), Carsteel FC Montreal/Canada (1920), Montreal Grenadier Guards/Canada (1922), Providence Clamdiggers/Canada (1923), Fall River Marksmen/USA (1924), Glasgow Rangers (October 1930), CHELSEA (May 1932), Cardiff City (December 1936), Sligo Rovers/Ireland (May 1937), Workington (September 1938), Raith Rovers (August 1939), Glasgow Rangers (after WW2, scout, based in north-east of Scotland and chief scout until 1979)

Able to operate effectively in both full-back positions, Bob McAuley, despite lacking in pace, was one of the strongest kickers in the game and was solid in defence. After 4 years playing in Canada and North America, he had 46 outings for Rangers, gaining a Cup winner's medal in 1932 and winning two caps for Scotland (v. Ireland and Wales). Owing to the form of Tommy Law, Les Odell and George Barber, he played only 26 games in his first 2 seasons with Chelsea before producing some excellent performances in 1934–35 when he appeared in 40. Some reference books have this player's surname spelt as Macaulay.

McCALLIOG, JAMES
Midfield: 7 apps
Born: Glasgow, 23 September 1946
Career: Glasgow and District Schools, Leeds United (amateur, May 1963), CHELSEA (professional, September 1963), Sheffield Wednesday (£37,500, October 1965), Wolverhampton Wanderers (£60,000, August 1969), Manchester United (March 1974), Southampton (February 1975), Chicago Sting/NASL (May–August 1977), Lyn Oslo/Norway (player–coach, February-April 1978), Lincoln City (player–coach, September 1978–March 1979; also briefly caretaker-manager, October–November 1978), Runcorn (player–manager, July 1979–February 1980); became a publican and combined this job with that of caretaker-manager of Halifax Town (March 1990; then manager, April 1990–October 1991); Leyton Orient (scout, 1992–93); later worked as a journalist and was also licensee of the George and Dragon at Wetherby and the County Hotel, Harrogate

Jim McCalliog played in two FA Cup finals 19 years apart – scoring for Sheffield Wednesday against Everton in 1966 when he collected a runner's-up medal and laying on Bobby Stokes' goal for Southampton v. Manchester United in 1976 when he gained a winner's prize. After gaining Scottish schoolboy international honours, he failed to make the breakthrough at Elland Road and quickly joined Chelsea. Unfortunately he never quite fitted the bill at Stamford Bridge and played in only a handful of first-team games before moving to Hillsborough where his game improved considerably, developing into an excellent midfielder with a range of passes while finding time to get forward and assist his front men. However, at times he did tend to drift out of a game. Besides his schoolboy caps, McCalliog played for his country's youth team, starred in two Under-23 and five full internationals, scoring in the famous Scottish win against England at Wembley in 1967. During his career he amassed over 450 senior appearances.

McCARTNEY, DAVID
Centre-half: 3 apps
Born: Ayrshire, July 1880 – *Died*: Scotland, 1950
Career: Dalbeattie FC and Lugar Boswell FC/Scotland, Glossop North End (April 1900), Watford (October 1902), CHELSEA (August 1906), Northampton Town (May–October 1907); returned to Scotland and worked on a farm

Kept out of Chelsea's first team by Bob McRoberts, David McCartney was a tall, well-built defender, strong in the air, whose best days were spent at Glossop for whom he made over 75 senior appearances.

McCONNELL, ENGLISH

Centre-half: 21 apps
Born: Larne, Northern Ireland, 1881 – *Died*: Belfast, 1960
Career: Cliftonville (1899), Glentoran (1904), Sunderland (October 1905), Sheffield Wednesday (May 1908), CHELSEA (£1,000, April 1910), South Shields (May 1911), Linfield (May 1912–May 1915); did not play after WW1

English McConnell, an Irish international who gained 12 caps between 1904 and 1910, had a fine career both north and south of the border and was signed by Chelsea (with others) in a desperate bid to stave off relegation, to no avail. Strong and muscular, he played in over 150 League and Cup games in Ireland and made 45 senior appearances for Sunderland and 50 for Sheffield Wednesday.

McCREADIE, EDWARD GRAHAM

Full-back: 405+5 apps, 5 goals
Born: Glasgow, 15 April 1940
Career: Drumchapel Amateurs (Glasgow), Clydebank Juniors, East Stirlingshire (professional, April 1959), CHELSEA (£6,000, April 1962; retired November 1974; appointed coach; then manager, April 1975–July 1977), Memphis Rogues/NASL (player–coach, February 1978–March 1979); still living in America, working as a painter and decorator

Only the fourth player to appear in more than 400 competitive games for Chelsea, Eddie McCreadie formed a formidable partnership with Ken Shellito and they were outstanding together when the Blues won promotion to the First Division in 1963. Adventurous, aggressive, flamboyant, McCreadie, who skippered the side several times, netted a terrific goal when Chelsea beat Leicester City in the second leg of the 1965 League Cup final to win the trophy for the first time. Two years later he collected a runner's-up medal in the FA Cup final but made up for that disappointment by gaining a winner's medal in the same competition in 1970 when Leeds United were defeated after a replay. Late on his career was marred by injuries but he was rewarded for his loyalty to the club with a coaching job at Stamford Bridge, and then as manager (having taken over from Ron Suart) he guided Chelsea back into the top flight in 1977 before moving to the States. He was capped 23 times by Scotland at senior level between 1965 and 1969.

McDERMOTT, THOMAS

Inside-forward: 32 apps, 11 goals
Born: Bridgeton, Glasgow, 12 January 1878 – *Died*: Glasgow, 1961
Career: Bridgeton Amateurs, Cambuslang Hibs (April 1896), Dundee (professional, February 1900), Celtic (September 1901), Everton (July 1903), CHELSEA (October 1905), Dundee (August 1906), Hibernian (briefly), Bradford City (February 1908), Gainsborough Trinity (November 1908),

Kilmarnock (January 1909), Bradford City (March 1909), Dundee Hibernian (August 1909), Anfield Royal (June 1910), St Helens Recreationalists (season 1911–12), Wirral Railway (August 1912), Vale of Leven (April 1913), Broxburn (season 1914–15), Shamrock (season 1915–16), Clyde (season 1917–18); did not play after WW1

After scoring 5 goals in 21 games for Celtic and 19 in 71 outings for Everton, Scottish-born Tommy McDermott, skilful and cunning with an eye for goal, fought for the inside-left position at Chelsea with Jimmy Windridge. He spent two years at Stamford Bridge before moving to Dundee. Inconsistent at times, he continued playing at a high level until he was 40 years of age.

McEWAN, MARSHALL

Outside-left: 35 apps, 3 goals
Born: Rutherglen, Scotland, February 1885 – *Died*: Scotland, 1966
Career: Blackpool (professional, March 1903), Bolton Wanderers (February 1905), CHELSEA (£1,000, March 1909), Linfield (August 1911), Fleetwood (1914); did not play after WW1

A clever, canny winger, described as being 'as slippery as an eel', Marshall McEwan on his day was certainly a threat to opposing defenders, despite his rather frail physique. He was one of a band of Scots signed by Chelsea in their failed attempt to avoid relegation in 1909. He netted once in 45 games for Blackpool and scored 15 goals in 164 outings for Bolton whom he helped win the Second Division championship in 1909.

McEWAN, ROBERT

Full-back: 20 apps
Born: Edinburgh, 1881 – *Died*: Scotland, *circa* 1954
Career: St Bernard's (Edinburgh), Bury (March 1903), Glasgow Rangers (August 1904), Heart of Midlothian (March 1905), CHELSEA (August 1905), Glossop North End (August 1906), Queens Park Rangers (December 1908–May 1909); later with Broxburn; did not play after WW1

Bob McEwan, a tough-tackling full-back, began his career at Stamford Bridge in fine form but then suffered an injury, lost his place to Tommy Miller and never regained it, moving to Glossop at the start of the following season. He made 35 League appearances for Bury and 55 for Glossop.

McFARLANE, ALEXANDER

Inside-forward: 4 apps
Born: Dundee, June 1878 – *Died*: Scotland, 1945
Career: Baillieston Juniors (1893), Airdrieonians (professional, March 1895), Arsenal (April 1896), Newcastle United (£30, October 1898), Dundee (November 1901), CHELSEA (April 1913–May 1916); Dundee (secretary–manager, March 1919–December 1924), Charlton Athletic (secretary–manager, May 1925), Dundee (manager, December 1927),

Charlton Athletic (manager, June 1928–December 1932), Blackpool (manager, July 1933–July 1935)

The outbreak of the Great War ended 'Sandy' McFarlane's playing career. Prior to that he had done exceptionally well as a sturdy, hard-working inside-forward and accumulated more than 500 senior appearances with his 5 major League clubs including 333 for Dundee (71 goals scored) and 86 for Newcastle United (17 goals). He won five caps for Scotland (1904–11), represented the Scottish League on three occasions and won the Scottish Cup with Dundee in 1910. After retiring he took to management and became a relentless perfectionist, a tactician extraordinaire, highly respected both north and south of the border. He took Dundee to the 1925 Scottish Cup final (beaten 2–1 by Celtic), guided Charlton to the Third Division (S) title in 1929 and then assembled a very useful side at Blackpool, signing the future Irish international Peter Doherty for just £1,000. Some reference books spell this player's surname as MacFarlane.

McINNES, JOHN SMITH

Outside-left: 37 apps, 7 goals
Born: Glasgow, 11 August 1927 – *Died*: Bedford, October 1973
Career: Greenock Morton (professional, August 1945), CHELSEA (May 1947), Bedford Town (June 1951; retired, injured, May 1952)

During his five-year stay at Stamford Bridge, the quick-footed John McInnes had to battle against injury and illness. A clever ball-player, fast and direct, it was unfortunate that he was never given the opportunity to show off his undoubted talent longer than he did. He was only 46 when he died.

McKENNA, PETER JOSEPH

Goalkeeper: 66 apps
Born: Toxteth Park, Liverpool, 8 December 1901 – *Died*: Liverpool, 1964
Career: Bangor (August 1919), CHELSEA (May 1924), Southend United (May 1931–May 1932)

Basically Peter McKenna understudied first Howard Baker and then Sam Millington during his seven-year stay at Stamford Bridge – although in 1925–26 he did appear in 31 games when, for most of the campaign, he was regarded as first choice between the posts. Not a tall man, he was reliable and courageous and made his debut for Chelsea in a 2–1 win at Blackpool in December 1924, having his last outing in a 4–1 defeat at West Ham in September 1930.

McKENZIE, DUNCAN

Inside-forward: 16 apps, 4 goals
Born: Grimsby, 10 June 1950
Career: Nottingham Forest (junior, July 1965; apprentice, July 1967; professional, June 1968), Mansfield Town (loan, March 1970 and February 1973), Leeds United (£240,000, August 1974), RSC Anderlecht/Belgium

(£200,000, June 1976), Everton (£200,000, December 1976), CHELSEA (£165,000, September 1978), Blackburn Rovers (£80,000, March 1981), Tulsa Roughnecks/NASL (player-exchange deal involving Viv Busby, June 1981), Chicago Sting/NASL (May 1982), Bulowa/Hong Kong (June 1983); Everton (Community Officer); later columnist for the *Today* newspaper; now an accomplished after-dinner speaker, living in Newton-le-Willows, while also running his own delicatessen business

Duncan McKenzie was the first player signed by Everton from a non-British club. During a nomadic career he served with 10 different clubs worldwide and scored over 150 goals, 112 coming in 330 League games. He made his debut for Nottingham Forest in 1969 and played in his final game in Bulowa in 1983. Blessed with heaps of natural skill, he had flair and huge reserves of energy, although often doubtful commitment. He topped the Second Division scoring charts in 1973–74 (26 goals) and sat on the England bench as a substitute for the Home Internationals that same season but never represented his country. He did well at Elland Road (27 goals in 66 League games), and after his spell in Belgium, returned 'home' to Everton. He played in both the 1977 League Cup final replays but missed the decider at Old Trafford. He also helped the Merseysiders reach that season's FA Cup semi-final. He never acclimatised to a Chelsea side of limited ability but still scored some stunning goals, like he did throughout his career.

McKENZIE, KENNETH
Right-half: 1 app.
Born: Nairn, Scotland, 1887 – *Died:* Scotland, *circa* 1954
Career: Croy Juniors, Inverness Thistle (1905), CHELSEA (£25, March 1910), Cardiff City (August 1911); did not play after WW1
Owing to a wealth of similar players at Stamford Bridge, Ken McKenzie tasted League football just once with Chelsea, making his debut in a 2–0 defeat at Bolton in April 1911.

McKENZIE, KENNETH WILSON
Centre-half: 22 apps
Born: Montrose, Scotland, 1 May 1898 – *Died:* Glasgow, 1960
Career: Queen's Park (Glasgow), CHELSEA (November 1920), Cardiff City (May 1923–January 1924); later with Dalkieth (Scotland)
Deputising at the heart of the Chelsea defence for Harry Wilding, Ken McKenzie, tall, well-built with a strong kick, had his best spell in the first team between October 1921 and January 1922. He failed to make an impression at Ninian Park.

McKNIGHT, PHILIP

Wing-half: 33 apps, 1 goal

Born: Camlachie, Scotland, 15 June 1924

Career: Alloa Athletic (1944), CHELSEA (January 1947), Leyton Orient (July 1954–May 1959; later player–coach to Orient's 'A' side), Hendon (coach, late 1960s)

A long-throw expert, Phil McKnight was an ever-reliable and totally dependable reserve during his seven and a half years at Stamford Bridge. Embarking on his League career against Portsmouth in May 1948, he made only 9 appearances in his first 4 seasons with Chelsea and 24 in his last 3 before going on to play in 160 games for Orient. He represented London v. Lausanne Sports (Switzerland) in the semi-final of the Inter-Cities Fairs Cup in 1957.

McLAUGHLIN, JOSEPH

Centre-half: 268 apps, 7 goals

Born: Greenock, Scotland, 2 June 1960

Career: Morton (amateur, 1976; professional, July 1977), CHELSEA (£95,000, May 1983), Charlton Athletic (£600,000, August 1989), Watford (£300,000, August 1990–May 1992), Falkirk (June 1995), Hibernian (February–May 1996)

Central defender Joe McLaughlin appeared in more than 160 senior games for Morton before moving to Stamford Bridge in 1983. Standing 6 ft 3 in. tall and weighing over 12 st., he immediately established himself in the Blues' first team and held his position for six years before switching to Charlton, manager Bobby Campbell bringing in Ken Monkou to partner David Lee in the back line. Capped ten times by Scotland at Under-21 level and twice a Second Division championship winner with Chelsea in 1984 and 1989, McLaughlin also helped the Blues lift the Full Members' Cup in 1986. He reached the career milestone of 500 League appearances when making his debut for Hibs against Celtic in February 1996.

McMILLAN, ERIC

Wing-half: 5 apps

Born: Beverley, Yorkshire, 2 November 1936

Career: RAF, CHELSEA (amateur, February 1958; professional, April 1958), Hull City (£2,000, June 1960), Halifax Town (July 1965), Scarborough (July 1967), Port Elizabeth/South Africa (January 1969–January 1971); returned to live and work in Hull

A mobile and competent wing-half, Eric McMillan was a shade out of his depth in the First Division but after joining Hull City his game developed considerably and he went on to appear in 177 senior games for the Tigers.

McMILLAN, PAUL ANTHONY
Wing-half: 1 app.
Born: Lennox Castle, near Glasgow, 13 July 1950
Career: CHELSEA (apprentice, July 1966; professional, July 1967; retired on medical advice, February 1968); later assisted Clydebank (early 1970s)
Sadly, Paul McMillan's career with Chelsea came to an abrupt end when he was advised by his doctor to take early retirement due to illness. His only League outing came in a 6–2 home defeat by Southampton in September 1967.

McNALLY, ERROL ALEXANDER
Goalkeeper: 9 apps
Born: Lurgan, Northern Ireland, 28 July 1943
Career: Portadown (1961), CHELSEA (£5,000, December 1961), Glenavon (August 1963–May 1966)
One of the many goalkeepers signed as cover for Peter Bonetti, Errol McNally made his League debut for Chelsea in a crushing 4–0 defeat at Everton in March 1962 – at a time when the team was heading for the Second Division.

McNAUGHT, JOHN
Defender/midfield: 11+1 apps
Born: Glasgow, 19 June 1964 – *Died:* Scotland, 1996
Career: Auchengill Boys' Club, Hamilton Academical (apprentice, May 1980; professional, July 1981), CHELSEA (£70,000, April 1986; released May 1987); returned to Scotland
Versatile John McNaught scored 20 goals in 118 appearances for Hamilton before spending just over a year at Stamford Bridge. Acting as reserve to Joe McLaughlin and Colin Pates, he made his League debut for the Blues as a substitute against Watford in May 1986. He sadly died through illness at the age of 32.

McNEIL, ROBERT WILLIAM
Winger: 307 apps, 32 goals
Born: Partick, Glasgow, 10 March 1889 – *Died:* Hamilton, Lanarkshire, *circa* 1970
Career: Springburn FC (Glasgow), Hamilton Academical (August 1906), CHELSEA (July 1914; retired May 1929); Hamilton Academical (trainer, seasons 1929–39)
A Chelsea legend of the 1920s, Bobby McNeil – the dressing-room comic – spent 15 seasons at Stamford Bridge during which time he appeared in more than 300 first-class matches – and that figure would certainly have exceeded 400 if WW1 hadn't disrupted his career. Recruited with Jimmy Croal (ex-Falkirk) to form a new left-wing partnership at the Bridge, McNeil was pretty quick over distances of 30 to 40 yards, had a clever footballing brain, was a smart dribbler and possessed a strong shot. Although not a prolific marksman, he scored his

fair share of goals while creating loads more for his colleagues. He played in Chelsea's 1915 losing FA Cup final team.

McNICHOL, JOHN

Inside-forward: 202 apps, 66 goals
Born: Kilmarnock, 20 August 1925
Career: Hurlford Juniors (1940), Newcastle United (professional, August 1946), Brighton and Hove Albion (August 1948), CHELSEA (£15,000, August 1952), Crystal Palace (£3,000, March 1958), Tonbridge Wells Rangers (player–manager, June 1963; retired May 1965); later worked in both the Brighton and Crystal Palace Commercial Departments

After scoring 37 goals in 158 Third Division (S) games for Brighton, John McNichol was manager Ted Drake's first signing for Chelsea – and what great service he gave to the club. A well-built yet extremely clever footballer, hard to knock off the ball, he missed only six League games in his first three seasons at Stamford Bridge and formed a fine partnership up front with Roy Bentley. Indeed, he became an integral part of the Blues' forward-line and netted 14 goals when the League championship was won in 1955. He went on to claim another 15 goals in 205 games for Palace whom he helped gain promotion from the Fourth Division in 1961.

McROBERTS, ROBERT

Centre-forward/-half: 106 apps, 10 goals
Born: Coatbridge, near Glasgow, 12 July 1874 – *Died*: Birkenhead, 27 February 1959
Career: Coatbridge (1892), Airdrieonians (1893), Albion Rovers (1894), Gainsborough Trinity (August 1896), Small Heath (£150, August 1898), CHELSEA (£100, August 1905; retired May 1909); Birmingham (manager, July 1910–August 1915); did not figure in the game after WW1

Initially an elegant ball-playing forward, Bob McRoberts later did exceedingly well as a centre-half. Preferring to score his goals with finesse rather than slamming the ball towards the net, he netted 82 in 187 appearances for Birmingham after assisting two Scottish clubs and having a disappointing spell with Gainsborough. He was a Second Division championship winner in 1901 before becoming Chelsea's first-ever signing, but then missed the Blues' opening League game against Stockport County in September 1905. A fine header of the ball, he was made team captain at the start of the 1907–08 season and made his 100th League appearance for Chelsea in a 1–0 win at Manchester United in November 1907. He returned to Birmingham to become the club's first full-time (and paid) team manager.

MEDHURST, HARRY EDWARD

Goalkeeper: 157 apps

Born: Chertsey, Surrey, 5 February 1916 – *Died*: April 1984

Career: Woking, West Ham United (professional, November 1936); served as a sergeant physical training instructor (Essex and RA) during WW2; CHELSEA (in exchange for Joe Payne, December 1946), Brighton and Hove Albion (November 1952; retired April 1953); CHELSEA (trainer, May 1953; head trainer/coach from 1960; physiotherapist from 1973 until April 1984); also played cricket for Surrey second XI

Harry Medhurst was over 30 when he joined Chelsea. A capable goalkeeper, he established himself in the first team immediately and gave the club sterling service for five years until moving south to Brighton. A shade on the small side (at 5 ft 9 in.) he was agile and courageous and actually started his career as a centre-forward before being asked to keep goal in an emergency. He missed only one game in 1949–50 and was eventually replaced between the posts by Bill G. Robertson.

MEEHAN, THOMAS

Wing-half: 133 apps, 4 goals

Born: Harpurhey, Manchester, August 1896 – *Died*: St George's Hospital, London, 18 August 1924

Career: Harpurhey Boys' Club (1912), Walkden Central (1915), Rochdale Town (January 1917), Manchester United (£1,500, June 1917), Atherton FC (loan, 1918), Rochdale (guest, 1918–19), CHELSEA (£3,300, December 1920 until his tragic death)

Tom Meehan sadly died of polio at the height of his career. His passing stunned the football world and 2,000 mourners attended his funeral at Wandsworth. He left a widow and four children. Standing 5 ft 5 in. tall and weighing 9 st. 9 lb, he looked more like a jockey than he did a footballer, but on the field he was a stylish yet determined, thrustful and courageous competitor who was strong in defence and highly constructive when driving forward. A non-smoker and teetotaller, he was the idol of the fans and was ever-present in Chelsea's ranks in 1922–23. Capped by England against Ireland only a month before his demise, Meehan twice represented the Football League (1922) and played for the Professionals v. the Amateurs in the 1923 FA Charity Shield match. He was a marvel for his height, and a real ornament to the game. On his death, a fund was immediately started and a benefit match (Chelsea v. a London XI) raised £1,560 for his wife and family with more money raised later.

MELCHIOT, MARIO

Right wing-back: 149+16 apps, 5 goals

Born: Amsterdam, Holland, 4 November 1976

Career: Ajax Amsterdam (professional, November 1995), CHELSEA (free transfer, July 1999), Birmingham City (free, August 2004)

A Dutch international who was recognised by his country at youth-team level before winning 13 Under-21 and 11 full caps, Mario Melchiot appeared in more than 80 senior games for Ajax prior to his transfer to Stamford Bridge. Attack-minded with good pace, he made only five Premiership appearances but still gained an FA Cup winner's medal in his first season with Chelsea before establishing himself in the side from 2000 onwards. However, when the new boss arrived (José Mourinho) he moved on to join Steve Bruce's Birmingham City where he teamed up with two more ex-Chelsea players, Jesper Gronkjaer and Mikael Forssell.

MEREDITH, JOHN

Outside-right: 23 apps, 6 goals
Born: Grimsby, 12 September 1899 – *Died*: 1970
Career: Scunthorpe and Lindsey United (August 1919), Blackpool (September 1923), CHELSEA (May 1928), Reading (October 1930; retired April 1931)
A right-winger with good pace, John Meredith was an able reserve to Jackie Crawford during his two seasons at Stamford Bridge . . . this after he had scored 30 goals in 200 League and FA Cup games for Blackpool.

MIDDELBOE, NILS

Defender: 46 apps
Born: Copenhagen, Denmark, 5 October 1887 – *Died*: Copenhagen, September 1976
Career: KB Copenhagen (1905), The Casuals/London (1910), Newcastle United (briefly, August–October 1913), CHELSEA (first registered, November 1913), The Casuals (February 1922; retired May 1925)
Nicknamed 'The Great Dane', Nils Middelboe was an amateur international who, besides representing his country at that level, also won 13 full caps for Denmark. Blessed with a long, raking stride which enabled him to tackle cleanly and cover the ground quicker than most players, he was registered with Chelsea for almost ten years. However, owing to WW1, his senior outings for the Blues were limited, yet he managed to play in 125 games during the hostilities when he lined up in every defensive position from right-back to left-half and helped the Blues win the London Victory Cup. He had his best 'peacetime' season at Stamford Bridge in terms of appearances in 1921–22 when he starred in 17 League and Cup games. His colleagues presented Middelboe with a silver cigarette box inscribed 'our captain and comrade – one of the best' when he left Chelsea in 1922.

MILLAR, JOHN

Left-back: 11 apps
Born: Coatbridge, near Glasgow, 8 December 1966
Career: Clyde Amateurs, London University (student), CHELSEA (apprentice, April 1983; professional, August 1984), Hamilton Academical (loan,

October–December 1986), Northampton Town (loan, January–February 1987), Blackburn Rovers (July 1987), Heart of Midlothian (May 1991–May 1996); also represented Scotland at cricket and played both cricket and football whilst at university

After graduating through the junior ranks and captaining Chelsea's youngsters, left-back John Millar, a Scottish youth international, who was sound rather than spectacular, made his League debut as a 19 year old in February 1986 in a 4–1 home defeat by Oxford United. He was later converted into a left-sided midfielder and appeared in almost 150 games for Blackburn, and over 100 for Hearts.

MILLER, HAROLD SYDNEY

Wing-half/inside-forward: 363 apps, 44 goals

Born: Watford, 20 May 1902 – *Died*: Watford, 24 October 1988

Career: Villa Juniors (Herts), St Albans City (amateur, September 1919), Charlton Athletic (played for reserves while still an amateur with St Albans; signed professional, December 1922), CHELSEA (£1,500, June 1923), Northampton Town (free transfer, June–September 1939); did not play after WW2

'Dusty' Miller, the son of a master sign-writer, scored 11 goals in 20 games for Charlton before moving to Stamford Bridge. He settled in immediately and went on to serve the Blues for 16 years, amassing over 360 senior appearances, and helped the team win promotion in 1930. A good, competitive footballer, he was strong in the tackle, which, coupled with his constructive approach, made him one exceptionally fine player. He was successfully moved into the forward line where he performed equally as well as he had done at half-back. Capped by England at both amateur and senior levels, he gained his only full cap against Sweden in Stockholm in May 1923, scoring in a 3–1 win. Miller played in the famous match for St Albans City against Dulwich Hamlet in November 1922 when Wilf Minter created an FA Amateur Cup record by scoring all his side's goals and still ended up on the losing side, 8–7.

MILLER, THOMAS

Full-back: 120 apps

Born: Falkirk, Scotland, *circa* 1884 – *Died*: Scotland, 1966

Career: Falkirk (professional, 1902), CHELSEA (August 1905; released May 1909), Falkirk (August 1909–May 1915)

Chelsea's first ever-present in a season (in 1906–07), full-back Tommy Miller was only a small man but nonetheless was very strong and positive in his actions. Quick over short distances, he loved to overlap and used the ball well, although at times he did over-elaborate with his passing. He gained a place in Chelsea's first team owing to an injury to Bob McEwan. He remained a regular in the side for three seasons – and after a couple of pints of beer insisted that he was the 'best back in England'. He made over 150 appearances in his two spells with Falkirk.

MILLINGTON, SIMEON
Goalkeeper: 245 apps
Born: Walsall, 7 January 1896 – *Died*: *circa* 1960
Career: Walsall Phoenix, Wellington Town (August 1919), CHELSEA (January 1926; retired, injured, June 1932)

Known as 'Sam', Millington joined Chelsea a week after his 30th birthday. A very useful goalkeeper, safe and reliable and a fine shot-stopper, he was a regular in the Chelsea side for six seasons until a back injury forced him into retirement. He took over from Peter McKenna and was subsequently replaced by Vic Woodley. Always seen wearing a flat cap, he produced some brilliant displays at times and was a key member of the side that gained promotion to the First Division in 1930, missing only 4 games and keeping 14 clean-sheets.

MILLS, GEORGE ROBERT
Centre-forward: 239 apps, 123 goals
Born: Deptford, London, 29 December 1908 – *Died*: London, July 1978
Career: Arthur Street School (Peckham), Emerald Athletic, Bromley (September 1925), CHELSEA (£10, December 1929; retired May 1943; returned to Stamford Bridge after WW2 to work as a coach)

The first player to claim 100 League goals for Chelsea, George Mills – refreshingly direct with no pretentions towards embroidery – became known as 'The Bomb' at Stamford Bridge. Snapped up after scoring consistently for Bromley, he made his Football League debut in a 5–0 home win over Preston North End four days before Christmas 1929 and when that season ended Mills had 14 goals to his credit. However, over the next ten years or so – injuries apart – he had to battle for a place in the side along with the likes of Hugh Gallacher, Joe Payne and Joe Bambrick. But when he was wearing the blue shirt, he certainly did the business out on the park in terms of scoring goals. Tall, well-built, agile, enthusiastic and courageous, he netted a hat-trick on his debut for England v. Northern Ireland in October 1937 and later added two more caps to his tally with appearances against Wales and Czechoslovakia before the end of the year. He also played for the Football League v. the Irish League in 1937.

MINTO, SCOTT CHRISTOPHER
Full-back: 70+2 apps, 5 goals
Born: Wirral, Cheshire, 6 August 1971
Career: Cudham Church of England Primary and Charles Darwin Senior schools (Biggin Hill), Bromley District and Kent Schools, Charlton Athletic (apprentice, August 1987; professional, February 1989), CHELSEA (£775,000, May 1994), Benfica/Portugal (free transfer, June 1997), West Ham United (£1 million, January 1999), Rotherham United (free, August 2003)

Scott Minto made 205 appearances for Charlton before his transfer to Stamford Bridge where he was more than useful while competing with Andy Myers and

Frank Sinclair for the left-back position. Following the arrival of Graeme Le Saux he chose pastures new, in Portugal, and had 31 outings for Benfica followed by 62 for West Ham before joining Rotherham. In 1988–89 he was capped by England at youth-team level, then played in six Under-21 internationals and won the FA Cup with Chelsea in 1997, having been an FA Youth Cup runner-up with Charlton ten years earlier. He moved with his family from the Wirral to Biggin Hill when he was four years old.

MITCHELL, DAVID STEWART

Striker: 8 apps

Born: Glasgow, 13 June 1962

Career: Glasgow junior football, 1 FC Köln/Germany (1982), Glasgow Rangers (August 1983), Feyenoord/Holland (March 1985), CHELSEA, (£200,000, January 1989), Newcastle United (loan, January 1991), Swindon Town (£30,000, July 1991), Altay Izmir/Turkey (£25,000, July 1993), Millwall (£100,000, October 1993; retired April 1995); later took coaching position in Malaysia

Standing 6 ft 1 in. tall and weighing over 12 st., slim, aggressive Australian international striker Dave Mitchell (capped via his parentage) failed to make an impact in the Bundesliga. However, he scored 14 goals in 45 games for Rangers and produced some excellent displays with Feyenoord. Unfortunately he never settled at Stamford Bridge and after a loan spell with Newcastle, two seasons with Swindon (25 goals in 80 appearances) and failure in Turkey, he was then hampered by an ankle injury at Millwall.

MITCHELL, FRANK ROLLASON

Left-half: 85 apps, 1 goal

Born: Goulburn, New South Wales, Australia, 3 June 1922 – *Died*: Lapworth, Warwickshire, 2 April 1984

Career: Coventry City (amateur, August 1937); served in Royal Navy during WW2 and was a guest for Arsenal, Birmingham City, Northampton Town and Portsmouth; Birmingham City (professional, September 1943), CHELSEA (January 1949), Watford (August 1952; retired May 1958); later coach and groundsman at Kynoch's, Birmingham

After more than 100 senior games for Birmingham City, whom he helped win the Football League (South) championship in 1946 and the Second Division title two years later, Frank Mitchell edged slowly towards the 200 appearance mark with Chelsea. He then spent 6 years at Vicarage Road and when he retired, in 1958, he had played in over 400 competitive matches – this after he had decided to take up football rather than cricket (his favourite boyhood sport). Indeed, he had joined the Warwickshire club and ground as a 15 year old and was expected to make the grade as a medium pace bowler at County level (he played in 17 matches between 1946 and 1948 and took 22 wickets). He also had trials for Kent CCC and represented Cornwall and Herefordshire as well as

Knowle and Dorridge CC's. He chose, however, to concentrate on soccer and never regretted the decision. A calm, cultured footballer and splendid passer of the ball, especially across field, Mitchell was an expert penalty-taker and missed only three during his whole career. At the start of his run up, he would hitch up his shorts and then advance forward before striking the ball towards the corner of the net. He lost his place to Bill Dickson in Chelsea's starting line-up.

MITCHELL, WILLIAM

Wing-half: 117 apps, 3 goals
Born: Lurgan, Northern Ireland, 22 November 1910 – *Died*: Belfast, 1978
Career: Cliftonville/Northern Ireland (professional, April 1928), Distillery/Northern Ireland (August 1930), CHELSEA (£2,000, June 1933), Bath City (free transfer, August 1945–May 1947)
A Northern Ireland international, capped 15 times (11 as a Chelsea player) between 1932 and 1938, Billy Mitchell was a terrier in the tackle, strong and positive despite his small frame. Occasionally in trouble with the referee, he nevertheless always gave a terrific display out on the field, a magnificent club man whose senior career ended prematurely due to WW2. He made his League debut for the Blues at left-half in a 2–2 draw at Middlesbrough in February 1934.

MOLYNEUX, JAMES

Goalkeeper: 239 apps
Born: Port Sunlight, Wirral, 1885 – *Died*: Stockport, 9 January 1950
Career: Port Sunlight Works FC, Stockport County (trial, August 1906; professional September 1906), CHELSEA (£550, August 1910); guest for Stockport County during WW1; Stockport County (January 1923–May 1925); worked for the Stockport Electricity Department for over 20 years
Signed initially as cover for Jack Whitley, Jim Molyneux became first choice between the posts straightaway and missed only one game in his first season at Stamford Bridge. During the next two campaigns he shared his duties with first Whitley and then Ron Brebner before re-establishing himself as first choice in 1914–15, playing in that season's FA Cup final defeat by Sheffield United. Despite his lack of height (he was only 5 ft 9 in. tall) 'Moly' was extremely agile and had a good sense of anticipation. He was daring when he had to be and became one of the most respected keepers in the country. He helped the Blues win the London Victory Cup v. Fulham at Highbury in 1919, then appeared in a total of 165 first-team matches for Stockport, playing his last League game for the Hatters at the age of 40. When serving in the Army in October 1917, Molyneux suffered shrapnel wounds at Ypres and was sent back to England. Within two months he was out of hospital and playing for Stockport in a wartime regional game against Preston.

MONKOU, KENNETH JOHN

Defender: 117+2 apps, 2 goals

Born: Surinam, 29 November 1964

Career: Feyenoord/Holland (professional, 1982), CHELSEA (£100,000, March 1989), Southampton (£750,000, August 1992), Huddersfield Town (free transfer, October 1999; retired, injured, March 2001)

A pillar of strength at the heart of the Chelsea defence, Ken Monkou was a big man, strong and aggressive, who regularly got his head in the way where others wouldn't! He wasn't all thump and bump, however. He often tried to feed the ball to a colleague up-field and regularly placed a tempting pass into space behind opposing defenders. Capped by Holland at Under-21 level, he won the Zenith Data Systems Cup with Chelsea in 1990 before transferring to Southampton two years later. He partnered Claus Lundekvam in Saints' back line and during his seven seasons at The Dell made 233 appearances.

MOORE, GRAHAM

Forward/midfield: 72 apps, 14 goals

Born: Cascade Village, Hengoed, Glamorgan, 7 March 1941

Career: Gilfach Primary and Hengoed Secondary Modern schools, Bargoed YMCA (1956), Cardiff City (groundstaff, 1957; professional, March 1958), CHELSEA (£35,000, December 1961), Manchester United (£35,000, November 1963), Northampton Town (£15,000, December 1965), Charlton Athletic (£6,000, May 1967), Doncaster Rovers (£4,000, September 1971; retired May 1974); thereafter was a licensee in Easingwold, near York, and Hemsworth and later managed a sub-post office in Scarborough

Graham Moore broke his right leg playing for Cardiff and later broke his right shin and had a back operation playing for Charlton. In between times he did reasonably well at Stamford Bridge, Old Trafford and the County Ground, amassing 150 senior appearances. Back in 1961, Cardiff boss Bill Jones said that Moore would be 'better than John Charles'. He never got near to matching the great man – although he was a talented footballer and had the honour of scoring on his international debut for Wales as an 18 year old in a 1–1 draw with England in 1959. He later added another 20 caps to his total and also represented his country 3 times at youth-team level and on 9 occasions for the Under-23s. He also played for the Football League v. the League of Ireland in 1961 and won the Welsh Cup with Cardiff in 1959. A rugby player at school, Moore also worked briefly down the pit before turning into a forward on the soccer pitch. A talented striker, he was relegated in his first season with Chelsea but bounced straight back into the top flight when Tommy Docherty sold him to Manchester United. He was converted into a midfield player at Northampton only to find himself in a troubled side as the Cobblers slipped from the First to the Fourth Division in double-quick time.

MORAN, MARTIN

Outside-right: 67 apps, 8 goals

Born: Bannockburn, near Stirling, April 1878 – *Died*: Scotland, *circa* 1950

Career: Benburb (August 1895), Celtic (August 1898), Hamilton Academical (December 1898), Clyde (January 1899), Sheffield United (September 1899), Middlesbrough (May 1900), Millwall Athletic (August 1902), Heart of Midlothian (May 1904), CHELSEA (July 1905), Glasgow Rangers (August 1908), Celtic (September 1908; retired May 1910)

Described as the 'Muscular Midget' at Stamford Bridge, Martin Moran was Chelsea's first outside-right. Quick and clever with a good temperament, he was already a vastly experienced professional when he arrived in London and had a wonderful first season with the Blues, scoring 6 goals in 36 games. After that he lost his form and was in and out of the side before returning to Scotland in 1908. He scored 17 goals in 99 senior appearances for Millwall – his best return with any of his 9 major clubs.

MORIAS, NUNO FILIPE

Midfield: 1+3 apps

Born: Lisbon, Portugal 21 November 1985

Career: FC Penafiel/Portugal (April 2001), CHELSEA (apprentice, May 2002; professional, June 2003)

A hard-working, conscientious midfielder with a good first touch, Filipe Morias was nurtured through the ranks at Stamford Bridge before making his senior debut against Scunthorpe United (FAC) in January 2005.

MORRIS, JODY STEVEN

Midfield: 113+50 apps, 10 goals

Born: Hammersmith, London, 22 December 1978

Career: CHELSEA (apprentice, March 1995; professional, January 1996), Leeds United (free transfer, July 2003), Rotherham United (free, March 2004), Millwall (free, July 2004)

Honoured by England at both schoolboy and youth-team levels, Jody Morris went on to gain seven Under-21 caps during his time with Chelsea. He was also in the Blues' triumphant European Cup-Winners' Cup and FA Cup winning sides of 1998 and 2000 respectively and also won the Charity Shield in the latter year. A positive footballer with neat ball control and thrustful nature, he became surplus to requirements at Stamford Bridge but made only 12 appearances for Leeds before being blighted with a series of off-field problems and was eventually released from his contract. He remained in Yorkshire with Rotherham before moving back down to London in July 2004.

MORRISON, WILLIAM
Forward: 1 app.
Born: Bo'ness, Scotland, *circa* 1900 – *Died*: Scotland, 1970
Career: Linlithgow Rovers, CHELSEA (June 1924–May 1927); later Park Royal (Glasgow)

A regular but dependable reserve-team player during his three seasons at Stamford Bridge, Billy Morrison's only first-team outing came in the 1–1 home League draw with South Shields in April 1925 when he lined up at centre-forward.

MORTIMORE, JOHN HENRY
Defender: 279 apps, 10 goals
Born: Farnborough, Hampshire, 23 September 1934
Career: Woking (September 1950), Aldershot (amateur, 1954), CHELSEA (amateur, April 1956; professional, August 1957), Queens Park Rangers (£8,000, September 1965), Sunderland (March 1966); player–coach and manager in Greece for six years (1967–73); Portsmouth (manager, May 1973–September 1974), Southampton (assistant manager, June 1979–84), Benfica/Portugal (manager, August 1984), Real Betis, Seville/Spain (manager, June 1987–February 1988), Belenenses/Portugal (manager, September 1988–February 1989); later Southampton (chief scout)

John Mortimore (known affectionately as 'Morti') seemed to win everything in the air and was pretty useful on the ground as well. A strong, committed defender, he gained amateur and youth international honours for England before establishing himself in Chelsea's defence in 1957 (after two seasons in the Combination side). He remained first choice pivot until being replaced, perhaps surprisingly, by Bobby Evans and then Mel Scott, but he fought back and was an ever-present in the side that won promotion from the Second Division in 1963 and two years later he gained a League Cup winner's medal.

As a manager he guided Benfica to three successive Portuguese League titles in the 1980s, completing the Double in 1987, before quitting to take over Real Betis in Spain. He was assistant manager at The Dell first to Ted Bates and then Lawrie McMenemy.

MULHOLLAND, JAMES
Forward: 12 apps, 3 goals
Born: Knightswood, near Glasgow, 10 April 1938
Career: East Stirling, CHELSEA (£8,000, October 1962), Greenock Morton (part-exchange for Billy Sinclair, September 1964), Barrow (August 1965), Stockport County (October 1968), Crewe Alexandra (August 1970–March 1971)

As a Chelsea player Jimmy Mulholland flattered to deceive far too often and struggled against the more experienced and rugged defenders. He did much better in the lower divisions where, as a neat and tidy footballer, he scored 47 goals in 134 League games for Barrow and 5 in 32 for Stockport.

MULLIGAN, PATRICK MARTIN
Right-back: 74+5 apps, 2 goals
Born: Dublin, 17 March 1945
Career: Dublin City Schools, Stella Maris, Home Farm, Bohemians (August 1963), Home Farm, Shamrock Rovers (seasons 1964–67), Boston Rovers (July 1967), Boston Beacons/NASL (April 1968), Shamrock Rovers (season 1968–69), CHELSEA (October 1969), Crystal Palace (September 1972), West Bromwich Albion (September 1975), Shamrock Rovers (August 1979); Panathinaikos/Greece (assistant manager, season 1980–81), Galway Rovers (manager, August 1981; retired May 1982); became an insurance agent for a company in west London and later formed his own accountancy-insurance business in Dublin

Paddy Mulligan was an attacking right-back, an expert at over-lapping, steady and thoughtful – a player with ability who never was completely dominated by a winger.

A Republic of Ireland schoolboy international (1960–61), he went on to gain 51 full caps for his country (1969–80) and also served the League of Ireland (1965–69). He won four FAI Cup winner's medals (1965–66–67–69) and was a member of Chelsea's League Cup final side of 1972 (losing to Stoke City at Wembley), having appeared as a substitute for the Blues in the 1971 European Cup-Winners' Cup final against Real Madrid in Athens. All told, in a splendid career in Ireland, England and America, Mulligan amassed more than 350 senior appearances, including 224 in the Football League with Chelsea, Palace and Albion, whom he helped win promotion from the Second Division (under fellow Irishman Johnny Giles) in 1976.

MURPHY, JERRY MICHAEL
Midfield: 37 apps, 3 goals
Born: Stepney, London, 23 September 1959
Career: Crystal Palace (apprentice, September 1975; professional, October 1976) CHELSEA (free transfer, August 1985; contract cancelled, March 1988)

Left-sided midfielder Jerry Murphy made 269 senior appearances for Crystal Palace (25 goals scored) before moving to Stamford Bridge. Unfortunately he was plagued by injuries with Chelsea and struggled after a positive start. An FA Youth Cup winner with Palace in 1978, he was capped by the Republic of Ireland 3 times at senior level (1979–80) having earlier gained an England schoolboy cap at the age of 15.

MURRAY, ALBERT GEORGE
Winger: 179+4 apps, 44 goals
Born: Shoreditch, London, 22 September 1942
Career: CHELSEA (amateur, June 1958; professional, May 1961), Birmingham City (£25,000, August 1966), Brighton and Hove Albion (February 1971),

Peterborough United (September 1973; retired May 1977); later licensee of the White Horse Inn, Market Deeping, Lincolnshire

Bert Murray had a terrific burst of speed. Initially an orthodox outside-right, he later switched to right-back where his speed was a huge advantage when he came up against quick and clever wingers. He was also a useful goalkeeper, and on several occasions deputised between the posts in League matches. Nicknamed 'Ruby' he scored 17 goals in season 1964–65 – the highest by a wingman for the Blues since Dick Spence weighed in with 19, 30 years earlier. He represented England at schoolboy and youth team levels and later gained six Under-23 caps while also helping the Blues win the League Cup in 1965. He played in two losing semi-finals for Birmingham (League Cup of 1967 and FA Cup of 1968) and during his career scored 108 goals in 595 League appearances.

MUTU, ADRIAN

Striker: 30+11 apps, 7 goals
Born: Calinesti, Romania, 8 January 1979
Career: Arges Pitesti/Romania (professional, March 1996), Dinamo Bucharest/Romania (December 1998), Inter Milan/Italy (January 2000), Verona/Italy (August 2000), Parma/Italy (July 2002), CHELSEA (£15.8 million, August 2003; sacked, October 2004); trained with Dinamo Bucharest/Romania (November–December 2004), Juventus (January 2005)

Adrian Mutu was sacked by Chelsea 12 weeks into the 2004–05 season after being found guilty of drug abuse. He was suspended from football for eight months, but both Arsenal and Juventus immediately showed interest in taking him on after the ban had ended. In the meantime a disconsolate Mutu trained in his home country with Dinamo Bucharest. A Romanian international at youth, Under-21 and senior levels, gaining 32 senior caps, he didn't quite reach top form with Chelsea and, in fact, his only full season was split into two halves. Signed as a replacement for Franco Zola to play alongside Hernan Crespo, he had an excellent first four months. Blessed with a neat touch, he was direct and scored some cracking goals but then faded badly after Christmas. Prior to joining Chelsea, Mutu had scored 67 goals in 172 League games in Romania and Italy. In 2005, he was recalled to the Romanian national squad and also helped Juventus clinch Italy's Serie 'A' title.

MYERS, ANDREW JOHN

Midfield: 89+17 apps, 2 goals
Born: Hounslow, Middlesex, 3 November 1973
Career: CHELSEA (apprentice, April 1990; professional, July 1991), Bradford City (£800,000, July 1999), Portsmouth (loan, March–April 2000), Colchester United (free transfer, July 2003), Brentford (June 2004)

An England Youth international who went on to gain four Under-21 caps, versatile left-sided midfielder Andy Myers possesses good pace, attacking ability, movement and awareness and is also reliable when assisting in defence.

He spent nine years at Stamford Bridge and although never a regular in the side – his best season was in 1995–96 – he continued to produce some excellent performances. He helped Chelsea win the FA Cup in 1997 and the European Cup-Winners' Cup a year later and made almost 100 appearances for Bradford City before suffering injury problems with Colchester.

NEVIN, PATRICK KEVIN FRANCIS MICHAEL
Winger/midfield: 236+5 apps, 46 goals
Born: Glasgow, 6 September 1963
Career: Gartcosh FC (Glasgow), Clyde (professional, May 1981), CHELSEA (£95,000, July 1983), Everton (tribunal set fee of £925,000, July 1988), Tranmere Rovers (loan, March–May 1992; signed for £300,000, August 1992; retired May 1998); chairman of the PFA; later chief executive of Motherwell; later opened his own website, also worked as a match summariser on various radio and TV channels, including BBC Scotland, Sky Sports and Channel 5 – and tried his hand at journalism

One of the most stylish, graceful and well-balanced footballers in his position during the 1980s, the mercurial Pat Nevin was somewhat unorthodox on the field, being one of the game's great enigmas! He could lie dormant for long periods during a game and then burst into life, quickly becoming a match-winner when least expected. He certainly lacked consistency (much to the chagrin of his manager and supporters) and was dropped quite a few times from the first team, but on his day he gave defenders plenty to think about with his mazy dribbling skills, smart bodyswerve and electrifying pace over 30–40 yards. He was able to excite the fans at will and at times was mentioned in the same breath as the great Stanley Matthews.

He made 91 appearances for Clyde (20 goals) with whom he gained a Scottish Second Division championship medal (1982). He then transferred to Chelsea and was an instant success at Stamford Bridge, being voted the Blues' Player of the Year in 1984 and 1987. He made over 240 appearances for Chelsea, helping them win the Second Division title in 1982 and the Full Members' Cup two years later. He moved to Goodison Park after Chelsea and Everton had failed to come to an agreement over a suitable fee (valued initially at around £500,000 – an independent tribunal said he was worth £925,000). He spent a shade under four years at Goodison Park before moving to Tranmere – shortly after Howard Kendall had returned to Everton. Capped by Scotland 28 times at senior level, he also represented his country as a youth, played in 5 Under-21 and 4 'B' internationals and took part in Euro '92, helping the Scots qualify for the finals again in 1996, although not selected for the final 22. In 1987, he played for the Football League side (with Chelsea team-mate Steve Clarke) against the Rest of the World. He amassed an exceptionally fine career record of 750 club and international appearances, scoring 130 goals of which 21 came in 156 outings for Everton and 39 in 239 games for Tranmere.

NEWTON, EDWARD JOHN IKEM

Midfield: 180+33 apps, 10 goals

Born: Hammersmith, London, 13 December 1971

Career: CHELSEA (apprentice, April 1988; professional, May 1990), Cardiff City (loan, January–March 1992), Birmingham City (free transfer, July 1999), Oxford United (free, March 2000), Barnet (August 2000); Singapore/China (from September 2000)

A strong and aggressive midfielder, Eddie Newton won two England Under-21 caps and was an FA Cup winner in 1997 before helping the Blues complete the League Cup and European Cup-Winners' Cup Double. He had his best seasons at Stamford Bridge between 1992 and 1996 when he formed a very effective partnership in the engine room with Dennis Wise, Craig Burley and even Glenn Hoddle among others.

NICHOLAS, ANTHONY WALLACE LONG

Inside-forward: 63 apps, 21 goals

Born: West Ham, London, 16 April 1938

Career: CHELSEA (amateur, June 1953; professional, May 1955), Brighton and Hove Albion (November 1960), Chelmsford City (May 1962), Leyton Orient (June 1965), Dartford (March 1966–May 1968)

Strong and quick, agile, two-footed and a nuisance in and around the penalty area, Tony Nicholas – who gained England Youth honours – never quite fulfilled his early teenage promise – perhaps because he had to battle hard and long for a place in the Chelsea side with Jimmy Greaves. He scored 22 goals in 65 League games for Brighton but failed to make much of an impact with Orient.

NICHOLAS, CHARLES BRIAN

Wing-half: 29 apps, 1 goal

Born: Aberdare, South Wales, 20 April 1933

Career: Queens Park Rangers (amateur, June 1948; professional, April 1950), CHELSEA (July 1955), Coventry City (February 1958), Rugby Town (July 1962–64); later employed as a machine operator by Massey Ferguson (Coventry) while continuing to attend matches at Highfield Road for many years

An England schoolboy international, Brian Nicholas spent five years as a professional at Loftus Road before transferring to Chelsea where he acted initially as first reserve to right-half Ken Armstrong, and when John Mortimore arrived at the club, he moved to pastures new. Strong in the tackle and defensively sound, he made 121 appearances for Coventry City before being released by manager Jimmy Hill in 1962. Instantly recognisable by his bald pate, he was only 16 years of age when he made his Football League debut for QPR in 1949.

NICHOLAS, PETER

Midfield: 92+1 apps, 2 goals

Born: Newport, South Wales, 10 November 1959

Career: Gaer Junior and Dyffryn Senior Schools (Newport), Newport and Gwent Schools, Crystal Palace (apprentice April 1975; professional, December 1976), Arsenal (£400,000, March 1981), Crystal Palace (£150,000, October 1983), Luton Town (£165,000, January 1985), Aberdeen (£350,000 August 1987), CHELSEA (£350,000, August 1988), Watford (£175,000, March 1991), later Crystal Palace (coach, mid-1990s)

Honoured by his country at schoolboy level, hard-tackling midfielder Peter Nicholas went on to win 3 Under-21 and 73 senior caps for Wales and during a fine career amassed 426 League appearances (19 goals). He twice gained Second Division championship winning medals, first with Palace in 1979 and then with Chelsea ten years later. A Scottish Cup finalist with the Dons in 1988, he also won the Zenith Data Systems Cup with the Blues in 1990. A wholehearted player, he skippered the Blues in 1989–90 and during his time at Stamford Bridge produced several outstanding performances. In 1987 Nicholas became the first player from a Scottish club to win a full cap for Wales for almost 50 years, since Freddie Warren in 1938. When he appeared in his last international against Luxembourg in 1992, he set a new record for most full caps won by a Welshman.

NICHOLLS, MARK

Midfield: 16+36 apps

Born: Hillingdon, 30 May 1977

Career: CHELSEA (apprentice, May 1993; professional, May 1995), Reading (loan, December 1999–January 2000), Grimsby Town (loan, February–March 2000), Colchester United (loan, October 2000), Partick Thistle (trial, July–August 2001), Torquay United (free transfer, September 2001), Hamilton Academical (November 2001), Clydebank (November 2001)

Attacking midfielder Mark Nicholls was a fringe player at Stamford Bridge and two-thirds of his first-team appearances were made as a substitute. He gained a League Cup winner's medal with the Blues in 1998.

NICOLAS, ALEXIS

Midfield: 2+1 apps

Born: Westminster, London, 13 February 1983

Career: Aston Villa (apprentice, May 1999; professional, April 2001), CHELSEA (free transfer, December 2001; released May 2005)

A strongly built, competitive midfield player, Alexis Nicolas failed to make the first team at Villa Park. Biding his time at Stamford Bridge, he helped Chelsea win the Asia Cup (in Malaysia) in the summer of 2003, and then made his senior debut in a 4th round FA Cup tie against Scarborough in January 2004, following up with his Premiership bow in the London derby with Charlton Athletic soon afterwards. Unfortunately, following the arrival of new boss José Mourinho, Nicolas found himself playing regularly in the second team during the 2004–05 campaign.

NIEDZWIECKI, ANDZEJ EDWARD

Goalkeeper: 159 apps
Born: Bangor, North Wales, 3 May 1959
Career: Llandudno Primary and Senior Schools, Wrexham (apprentice, May 1974; professional, July 1976), CHELSEA (£45,000, June 1983; retired, injured, June 1988; retained as youth-team manager), Reading (assistant manager, November 1989; caretaker-manager April 1991), CHELSEA (reserve-team coach, July 1991–May 1995), later Blackburn Rovers (coach); also ran his own sportswear firm, specialising in goalkeeping items (initially opened in the late 1980s)

The son of Polish parents who came to Great Britain during WW2, Eddie Niedzwiecki played his early football for the Llandudno Primary Schools XI as a central defender alongside Neville Southall, his great pal and future rival for the Wales goalkeeping spot. After gaining one schoolboy and six youth caps for his country, he understudied Dai Davies at Wrexham and when he moved to Swansea City, Niedzwiecki established himself in the first team at the Racecourse Ground. He went on to make 141 appearances and played in 2 losing Welsh Cup finals of 1979 and 1983 before moving to Chelsea, signed by his former boss John Neal. Then, under the astute guidance of Peter Bonetti, he settled in well at Stamford Bridge while pushing Southall hard for a place in the national side. Earning the nickname of 'Steady Eddie', he was courageous, alert, a clean handler of the ball and delivered an enormous goal-kick, once sending the ball one bounce into his opposite keeper's arms at the other end of the ground. He made over 150 appearances for Chelsea, collecting a Second Division championship winner's medal in his first season with the club as an ever-present. He won two senior caps for his country (v. Norway in 1985 and Denmark in 1988) before injury forced him into early retirement at the age of 29 . . . after five knee operations. Niedzwiecki was sent off three times during 1982–83 when playing for Wrexham.

NUTTON, MICHAEL WILLIAM

Defender: 81+2 apps
Born: St John's Wood, London, 3 October 1959
Career: CHELSEA (apprentice, May 1976; professional, October 1977), Millwall (March 1983–May 1986)

A competent, strong-limbed central defender who had several runs in Chelsea's first team without ever really establishing himself on a regular basis. A shade on the short side, he did play exceedingly well alongside Mickey Droy between 1979 and 1981. He made 106 senior appearances for Millwall.

OAKTON, ALBERT ERIC
Outside-right: 112 apps, 28 goals
Born: Kiveton Park, Yorkshire, 28 December 1906 – *Died*: Sheffield, 5 August 1981
Career: Kiveton Park (1921), Grimsby Town (amateur, August 1924), Rotherham United (July 1926), Worksop Town (May 1927), Sheffield United (trial, March–April 1928 and again April 1930), Scunthorpe and Lindsey United (June 1930), Bristol Rovers (May 1931), CHELSEA (May 1932), Nottingham Forest (June 1937–August 1939); did not play after WW2
A dangerous player, speedy, diminutive and an expert dribbler, Eric Oakton was a constant threat to defences when in full flow. Quick off the mark, he often took on his full-back on the outside before diverting diagonally into the penalty area. After two excellent seasons with Chelsea (1932–34) he lost his way somewhat (following the arrival of Dick Spence and then Bill Barraclough) and was called into action only spasmodically during his last three campaigns before transferring to Forest in 1937. Prior to becoming a professional footballer, Oakton had worked as an electrician, a job he returned to after retiring.

O'CONNELL, SEAMUS
Inside-forward: 17 apps, 12 goals
Born: Carlisle, Cumbria, 1 January 1930
Career: Queen's Park (Glasgow), Middlesbrough (May 1953), Bishop Auckland (registered from September 1953 to May 1956), CHELSEA (registered from August 1954 to April 1955), Crook Town (August 1956), Carlisle United (February–April 1958), Crook Town (seasons 1958–61); joined his father in the cattle-breeding business in Cumbria on retiring
An amateur throughout his career, Seamus O'Connell was a quick thinker who often caused defenders enormous problems with his exciting approach play. Capped six times by England at amateur level (1953–56), he scored a hat-trick on his League debut for Chelsea in a 6–5 home defeat by Manchester United in October 1954 and at the end of that season celebrated with his colleagues as the First Division trophy came to Stamford Bridge. He netted seven times in that 1954–55 campaign when he also gained the first of his two FA Amateur Cup winner's medals with Bishop Auckland, adding his second in 1956, having collected a loser's prize in 1954. Every final was staged at Wembley with virtually capacity crowds of around 100,000 at each one.

ODELL, LESLIE FRANK
Full-back: 103 apps, 7 goals
Born: Sandy, Bedfordshire, June 1900 – *Died*: Luton, 1975
Career: Sandy FC (1915), Biggleswade Town (1919), Luton Town (amateur, August 1923), CHELSEA (amateur, August 1924; professional, September 1924; retired, injured, May 1936)
Full-back Les Odell, who was never a regular in Chelsea's first XI, gave the club

12 years' excellent service. First choice reserve to the likes of George Smith, Jack Harrow and the Scottish international duo of Tommy Law and Bob Macaulay, he had his best two seasons (in terms of outings) in 1930–31 and 1932–33. A clean kicker of the ball, he was also a very useful penalty taker and scored four times from the spot, as well as netting twice from open play in a 3–3 draw with Aston Villa on Boxing Day 1930.

O'DOWD, PETER

Centre-half: 87 apps
Born: Halifax, Yorkshire, 22 February 1908 – *Died:* 8 May 1964
Career: St Bees Grammar School (Bradford), Apperley Bridge FC (1923), Selby Town (1925), Blackburn Rovers (amateur, August 1926; professional, December 1926), Burnley (March 1930), CHELSEA (£5,250, November 1931), Valenciennes/France (£3,000, September 1935), Torquay United (trial, March 1937; retired, injured, May 1937)

A huge fellow, strong in the air and on the ground, a beautiful stylist and natural footballer, centre-half Peter O'Dowd did things in a simple way. An unruffled professional, wholly reliant on his own skill and endurance, older supporters who saw him play will to this day say that O'Dowd was the finest centre-half Chelsea have ever had. His display for England against Scotland in 1932 was outstanding – acclaimed as being one of the finest ever witnessed at international level (by an England defender). Surprisingly he won only three full caps but did represent the Football League against the Irish League in 1932. Sadly, he broke his leg in a trial game with Torquay United in March 1937 and never played again, retiring at the age of 29.

OELOFSE, ROELOF JOHANNES GYSBERTUS

Centre-half: 8 apps
Born: Johannesburg, South Africa, 12 November 1926
Career: Berea Park FC/South Africa (1945), CHELSEA (October 1951), Watford (July 1953–May 1954); returned to South Africa

One of a number of South African footballers who came over to try their luck in English football, 'Ralph' Oelofse was a tall, strong and confident-looking centre-half, who was deputy to John Harris during his two seasons at Stamford Bridge. He made his League debut in a 1–0 win at West Bromwich Albion in March 1952.

O'HARA, FRANCIS

Inside-/centre-forward: 3 apps, 3 goals
Born: Coatbridge, near Glasgow, 1881 – *Died:* Glasgow, 1964
Career: Albion Rovers (1900), CHELSEA (August 1905; released May 1906); later with Glasgow clubs Rutherglen and Belshill FC; did not play after WW1

'Pat' O'Hara was one of the many reserve-team players registered with Chelsea during their first-ever season. Deputising for Frank Pearson, he scored twice on his senior debut in a 6–1 FA Cup win over 1st Grenadiers in October 1905 and netted his other goal in the same competition v. Crystal Palace a month later.

O'HARE, JOHN
Full-back: 108 apps
Born: Armadale, Scotland, April 1910 – Deceased at 2000
Career: Shawfield Juniors (Glasgow), CHELSEA (June 1932; retired May 1941)
A fast-moving full-back with a fearless tackle, Jock O'Hare was a first-class defender, totally reliable, who was a first-team regular with Chelsea for four seasons (1935–39) before WW2 intervened. He managed a further 35 appearances during the first two wartime campaigns before retiring.

ORD, THOMAS
Midfield: 3 apps, 1 goal
Born: London, 15 October 1952
Career: Erith and Belvedere (1969), CHELSEA (professional, October 1972), Bristol City (loan, March 1974); played in the NASL for Montreal Olympic, Rochester Lancers, New York Cosmos, Vancouver Whitecaps, Seattle Sounders, Tulsa Roughnecks and Atlanta Chiefs between July 1974 and 1978, also assisting Bexley Heath United (briefly in 1975–76)
With his smartly trimmed beard and 'feather-cut' hairstyle, Tommy Ord looked much older than he really was. Although a shade ungainly at times, he was a hard worker, a grafter to the last who scored on his First Division debut for Chelsea against Stoke City in April 1973. Although he became something of a wanderer in the States, he did very well in the North American Soccer League.

ORMISTON, ANDREW PAISLEY
Centre-half: 102 apps, 1 goal
Born: Peebles, Borders, 1 March 1884 – *Died*: Glasgow, 1952
Career: Hebburn Argyle, Lincoln City (November 1907), CHELSEA (June 1909), guest for Grimsby Town and Lincoln City during WW1; Lincoln City (July 1919–May 1920); later Peebles Rovers (manager, August 1924–26)
After helping Lincoln City win the Midland League championship in 1908, 'Alec' Ormiston was one of several players who followed manager David Calderhead to Stamford Bridge. A commanding centre-half, especially good in the air, he made 20 League appearances when Chelsea gained promotion to the First Division in 1913. Ormiston's son played for Peebles Rovers (as an amateur) and Lincoln City (1937–38).

O'ROURKE, JOHN

Forward: 1 app.

Born: Northampton, 11 February 1945

Career: Arsenal (amateur, May 1961), CHELSEA (professional, April 1962), Luton Town (December 1963), Middlesbrough (July 1966), Ipswich Town (February 1968), Coventry City (November 1969), Queens Park Rangers (October 1971), Bournemouth (January–May 1974); later ran a newsagent's shop in Boscombe, Bournemouth

One of soccer's journeymen, John O'Rourke's professional career spanned 13 years during which time he scored 165 goals in 327 League games, having his best spell with Luton (64 goals in only 84 outings). An England Youth and Under-23 international, he failed to make headway at Highbury and played only once for Chelsea, in a League Cup tie against Swindon Town in September 1963. Sharp and menacing in and around the penalty area, he helped Ipswich win the Second Division title in 1967–68, notching 12 goals in the last 15 games when the pace was hotting up.

OSGOOD, PETER LESLIE

Centre-forward/midfield: 376+4 apps, 150 goals

Born: Windsor, 20 February 1947

Career: Windsor Under-11s, Spital Boys' Club (April, 1960), Windsor and Eton (July 1962), CHELSEA (amateur, April 1964; professional, September 1964), Southampton (£275,000, March 1974), Norwich City (loan, November 1976), Philadelphia Fury/NASL (December 1977), CHELSEA (£25,000, December 1978–September 1979), Spitals and Aldwyk Bay Rowdies/Gambia; then coach in The Gambia, the Far East and at a Butlin's holiday camp; Portsmouth (youth-team coach, June 1986–June 1988); ran a pub with Ian Hutchinson in Windsor; became a sports promotions manager (1990); later employed as a matchday host by the Commercial Department at Stamford Bridge and also worked jointly with Hutchinson as an after-dinner speaker; now lives near Southampton

Peter Osgood, an ex-bricklayer, jumped from playing boys' club football to amateur junior soccer, then to full-time professional in just six months. He joined Chelsea after his uncle had written to the club recommending his young nephew. He had a trial, was successful and the rest is history. After scoring twice on his senior debut for the Blues in the home League Cup tie against Workington in October 1964, Osgood gained a regular place in the side the following season, netting 11 times in 48 outings. But at the age of 19, he broke his right leg in a League Cup encounter against Blackpool (October 1966). This prompted the arrival at Stamford Bridge of strikers Tony Hateley and Tommy Baldwin, but thankfully Osgood regained full fitness, won back his first-team place at the start of 1967–68 and never looked back again! A natural crowd-pleaser, blessed with profligate talent, he could control the ball and deliver a pin-point pass in one movement. And besides creating numerous openings for his colleagues, he scored regularly himself, with both feet and his head, including a goal against Leeds United in the 1970 FA Cup replay at Old Trafford that set Chelsea up for a famous victory.

Capped six times by England at Under-23 level and on four occasions by the seniors, he also represented his country as a youth-team player and had three outings for the Football League (1968–71). Following his FA Cup triumph, he then helped Chelsea win the European Cup-Winners' Cup the following year and was a runner-up in the 1972 League Cup final. He was, in fact, the first player to score in the FA Cup, ECWC and League Cup finals. Suspended for 8 weeks early in 1971 after a pageful of bookings, he scored 5 goals for Chelsea in their 13–2 European Cup-Winners' Cup win over the part-timers from Luxembourg Jeunesse Hautcharage in September 1971. A fortnight earlier he netted a hat-trick in the 8–0 first leg win. He top-scored that season with 31 goals.

After moving to Southampton, he won a second FA Cup medal in 1976 and went on to score 33 goals in 153 outings for Saints before returning to Stamford Bridge via Norwich (loan) and the NASL. Some of his old magic had gone by now but he was still able to perform out on the pitch and in fact netted twice to bring his tally of Chelsea goals to 150, placing him joint second with Roy Bentley in the club's all-time list of marksmen. Osgood played alongside Alan Ball in the England team and also at Southampton and it was manager Ball who then appointed 'Ossie' as coach at Fratton Park in 1986.

PANUCCI, CHRISTIAN
Right wing-back: 9+1 apps, 1 goal
Born: Savona, Italy, 12 April 1973
Career: Genoa/Italy (professional, May 1991), AC Milan/Italy (August 1993), Real Madrid/Spain (November 1996), Inter Milan/Italy (August 1999), CHELSEA (loan, August–December 2000), AS Monaco/France (loan, January–May 2001); returned to Inter Milan

With Albert Ferrer out injured and Dan Petrescu departed, Chelsea boss Gianluca Vialli recruited the experienced Italian international Christian Panucci as cover on the right-hand side of the back four. He did well initially but then, after Claudio Ranieri had taken charge of team affairs, he became the most prominent casualty in the post-Vialli fall-out and after ten outings went out on loan to the French club AS Monaco. Prior to joining Chelsea, Panucci, who was confident on the ball with a good attitude, had appeared in 73 League games for Real Madrid and 145 in Serie 'A' with his 3 Italian clubs. He also scored once in 21 full internationals for his country.

PARKER, PAUL ANDREW

Right-back: 1+3 apps

Born: West Ham, London, 4 April 1964

Career: Fulham (apprentice, May 1980; professional, April 1982), Queens Park Rangers (£300,000, June 1987), Manchester United (£2 million, August 1991), Derby County (free transfer, August 1996), Sheffield United (free, November 1996), Fulham (free, January 1997), Golden Club/Hong Kong (free, February 1997), CHELSEA (free, March 1997), Heybridge Swifts (free, October 1997), Farnborough Town (December 1997), Ashford Town (director of football, January 1998), Chelmsford City (assistant manager; 2000, manager, June 2001–May 2003)

From the moment he first appeared for Fulham just three weeks after his 17th birthday, Paul Parker caught the eye of good judges. He played a handful of games when Fulham were promoted from Division Three in 1981–82 and made eight England Under-21 appearances while at Craven Cottage. Parker went into the First Division with Queens Park Rangers, with whom he won 16 of his 19 England caps, including 5 in Italy when Bobby Robson's side reached the 1990 World Cup semi-finals. The medals came after a move to Manchester United as he starred in the 1992 League Cup triumph, two Premiership successes, in 1993 and 1994, FA Cup glory, also in 1994, and victory in the Charity Shield, 1993. At right-back, Parker was an important member of the team that established United's domination of the newly formed Premiership. He played in the 1992 League Cup final victory over Nottingham Forest. His stay at Stamford Bridge was a relatively short one and he made just 4 senior appearances for the Blues before entering non-League football with Heybridge Swifts at the age of 33.

PARKER, SCOTT MATTHEW

Midfield: 19+9 apps, 1 goal

Born: Lambeth, London, 13 October 1980

Career: Charlton Athletic (trainee, April 1996; professional, October 1997), Norwich City (loan, October–November 2000), CHELSEA (£10 million, January 2004), Newcastle United (£6.75 million, June 2005)

An England international at schoolboy and youth-team levels, Scott Parker made excellent progress and went on to win 12 Under-21 caps and has also played twice for the senior side. A positive, hard-working midfielder, with a neat touch, he reads the game well and made 145 League and Cup appearances for Charlton whom he helped gain promotion to the Premiership in 2000. In and out of the side since moving to Stamford Bridge, his cause wasn't helped when he broke his foot prior to Christmas 2004. However, when selected, he never gives less than 100 per cent out on the field. He appeared in 11 Premiership games in 2004–05. Parker left Stamford Bridge in the summer of 2005, linking up with his former teammate Celestine Babayaro.

Champion marksman Jimmy Greaves,
who netted 132 goals in only
169 appearances for Chelsea.

Alan Birchenhall, an England Under-23
international who made almost 100
appearances for Chelsea.

Keith Weller played for Spurs and
Millwall before joining Chelsea and
for Leicester City after leaving
Stamford Bridge.

Scottish international wide
midfielder Charlie Cooke made
373 appearances for Chelsea in
two spells with the club.

Centre-half John Mortimore, seen
here climbing above Doug Fraser of
West Brom, made 279 appearances
for Chelsea between 1956
and 1965.

Bobby Tambling scoring against West Brom in 1965
— one of 202 goals he netted for the Blues.

Goalkeeper Peter Bonetti, seen here in action against Birmingham City in an FA Cup tie
in 1968, made 729 senior appearances for Chelsea. The other three players are
Eddie McCreadie (3), Peter Osgood (9) and Ron Harris (6), while the player in the
white shirt is former Chelsea striker Barry Bridges.

Midfielder Ray Wilkins won 84 caps for England and made over 900 club and international appearances during his 24-year career.

Full-back Tony Dorigo holds three different passports — British, Australian and Italian.

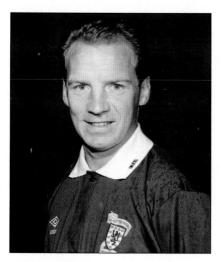

Soccer journeyman David Speedie played for 11 different League clubs and gained 10 caps for Scotland.

Vinnie Jones was an FA Cup winner with Wimbledon in 1988 — three years before joining Chelsea.

Dave Beasant played with Vinnie Jones in Wimbledon's 1988 FA Cup-winning side. He made over 150 appearances for Chelsea.

Welsh international midfielder Mickey Thomas was a soccer 'wanderer' who made well over 750 appearances during a fine career.

Dutch international Ruud Gullit played for and managed Chelsea in the 1990s.

Andy Townsend, a Republic of Ireland international, also had a varied career, assisting six different League clubs in fifteen years from 1985.

Chelsea team group from September 1986: manager John Hollins is standing on the extreme left of the second row. The team finished 14th in the First Division.

Chelsea team group from 1990–91 with manager Bobby Campbell in the centre of the front row and coach Ian Porterfield directly behind him. The team finished 11th in the First Division.

Action from the home League game against Oldham Athletic in April 1982 — Chelsea goalkeeper Steve Francis and defender Gary Locke thwart a Latics attack.

David Webb made 299 appearances for Chelsea and scored the winning goal in the 1970 FA Cup final replay.

Dave Sexton was manager of Chelsea for seven years between 1967 and 1974.

Romanian international Dan Petrescu signed from Sheffield Wednesday in 1995.

Peter Osgood, who scored for Chelsea in the finals of the 1970 FA Cup, 1971 Cup-Winners' Cup and 1972 League Cup.

Frank Lampard was voted FWA Player of the Year for 2005 — the first Chelsea player to receive this award.

Peter Houseman — a classy left-winger who played in over 300 senior games for the Blues between 1962 and 1975.

England international left-back Graeme Le Saux, who announced his retirement in May 2005.

Ex-Cannes and Bordeaux player Bernard Lambourde, who won the League Cup with Chelsea in 1998.

Italian goalkeeper Carlo Cudicini, who
gave way to Petr Cech in 2004.

One of Chelsea's all-time greats —
Italian international Gianfranco Zola
was the idol of Stamford Bridge.

Wing-half John Hollins made almost 600
appearances for Chelsea, with whom he
won FA Cup, League Cup and Second
Division championship medals.

Ed De Goey — Dutch international
goalkeeper who lost his place in the
Chelsea side to the Italian Carlo Cudicini.

PARSONS, ERIC GEORGE

Outside-right: 177 apps, 42 goals

Born: Worthing, West Sussex, 9 November 1923

Career: Worthing Boys (1938), West Ham United (junior, April 1939); Army service/British Army of the Rhine (Germany); West Ham United (professional, October 1943), CHELSEA (£23,000, November 1950), Brentford (November 1958, retired; injured, May 1961)

Eric Parsons made his League debut for West Ham against Leicester City in 1947. He went on to score 35 goals in 151 games for the Hammers before making the transition to the First Division – and more. He gained two England 'B' caps and collected a League championship winning medal in 1955 as an ever-present and scoring 11 goals as the Blues captured the Division One championship for the first time. Nicknamed 'Rabbit' and described as being the type of winger who could 'catch pigeons' or 'chase greyhounds', Parsons was pretty quick over the ground and many full-backs were given a torrid time when he was on top form. It was a pity that Tom Finney and Stan Matthews were around at the same time, because he was international class. Not unnaturally he took his fair share of punishment and despite a cartilage operation early in his career and a broken leg (with his last club Brentford) Parsons made 423 League appearances in total (89 goals). After his footballing days were over he ran his own sign-writing business for a number of years. Parsons postponed his honeymoon when he was called up at the last minute as deputy in England's continental tour in May 1949 – and was voted Man of the Match when he starred in a 4–0 'B' international win over Finland in Helsinki. He also played against Holland in the next match.

PATES, COLIN GEORGE

Defender: 345+1 apps, 9 goals

Born: Carshalton, Surrey, 10 August 1961

Career: CHELSEA (apprentice, August 1977; professional, July 1979), Charlton Athletic (£430,000, October 1988), Arsenal (£500,000, January 1990), Brighton and Hove Albion (loan, March–May 1991; signed August 1993), Crawley Town (player–manager, May–December 1995); later Arsenal (coach at club's School of Excellence)

Colin Pates made over 450 League and Cup appearances during his 18-year career. An England Youth international, capped 11 times in 1979 and 1980 when he helped his country win the 'Little World Cup', he was a Second Division championship and Full Members' Cup winner with the Blues in 1984 and 1986 respectively. Commanding a regular place in the first XI at Stamford Bridge from 1981 until his departure, he skippered the side from April 1984 and could also occupy a midfield position, but it was as a rock-solid left-sided defender that he produced his best form. Pates was the first Chelsea player to move to Charlton in 61 years ... since Reg Ticker's transfer in 1927. He teamed up with his former colleague Joe McLaughlin at The Valley.

PATON, JOHN ALOYOIUS

Outside-left: 23 apps, 3 goals

Born: Glasgow, 2 April 1923

Career: St Mungo's Academy (Glasgow), Dennistoun Waverley, Celtic (professional, August 1945), CHELSEA (£7,000, November 1946), Celtic (May 1947), Brentford (September 1949), Watford (July 1952–May 1955)

A press photographer by profession, Jock Paton was a clever winger with good pace whose stay at Stamford Bridge lasted only seven months before he returned to Parkhead.

He made his debut for Chelsea against Everton in December 1946 and during his two spells with Celtic amassed 72 senior appearances and scored 16 goals. He went on to net 14 goals in 90 League games for Brentford and 17 in 84 for Watford.

PAYNE, JOSEPH

Left-half/centre-forward: 47 apps, 23 goals

Born: Brinington Common, near Chesterfield, Derbyshire, 17 January 1914 – *Died*: Bedford, April 1975

Career: Bolsover Colliery (1929), Biggleswade Town (1932), Luton Town (July 1934), CHELSEA (£5,000, March 1938), West Ham United (part-exchange with Harry Medhurst, December 1946), Millwall (September 1947; retired, injured February 1948); made comeback with Worcester City (October 1952; retired second time, December 1952); played cricket for Bedfordshire (1937–53)

In his first-ever game as a centre-forward, for Luton Town against Bristol Rovers in a Third Division (S) game in April 1936, Joe Payne scored 10 goals in his side's emphatic 12–0 win. All his previous competitive games had been as a half-back but in an emergency he was asked to lead the Hatters' attack – and what an impact he made! He went from strength to strength after that, developing a great technique with both feet and also with his head. Strong and highly effective, he scored on his international debut for England in an 8–0 win over Finland in Helsinki in May 1937 – having just helped Luton win the Third Division (S) title. And then, as a Chelsea player, he appeared in the 1944 and 1945 South League Cup finals, gaining a winner's medal in the latter. Besides his peacetime footballing activities, Payne (who served as a sergeant in the RAF) was a prolific marksman during the hostilities, netting 107 goals (in only 116 outings) for Chelsea, including 39 in both the 1943–44 and 1944–45 campaigns. He was beset with injury problems at both Upton Park and The Den. During his entire career (before, during and after WW2) he bagged more than 220 goals in just over 250 club appearances. In one cricket match in June 1952, Payne scored 110 runs in 90 minutes. He was also a very good snooker player, with a highest break of 112.

PEACOCK, GAVIN KEITH

Forward/midfield: 119+15 apps, 27 goals

Born: Eltham, London, 18 November 1967

Career: Queens Park Rangers (apprentice, April 1983; professional, November 1984), Gillingham (loan, October 1987; signed for £40,000, December 1987), Bournemouth (£250,000, August 1989), Newcastle United (£275,000, November 1990), CHELSEA (£1.25 million, August 1993), Queens Park Rangers (£1 million, November 1996), Charlton Athletic (loan, August–September 2001); retired July 2002; later worked on BBC TV as a soccer summariser

Gavin Peacock had a wonderful career that spanned 19 years. In that time he won caps for England at both schoolboy and youth-team levels and scored 135 goals in 632 League and Cup games, including 42 in 226 in his two spells with QPR with whom he began as a midfield player. Having served with three different clubs before he was 22, he became a huge hit at St James' Park and averaged a goal every three games for the Geordies before moving to Stamford Bridge . . . after falling out with the Newcastle management. It proved to be money well spent by Chelsea as he developed into a fine striker and versatile midfielder, a tireless, willing worker with a knack of scoring goals, vital ones at that. His only major club prize was a First Division championship medal with Newcastle in 1993. His father Keith Peacock, played for Charlton Athletic and Tampa Bay Rowdies and also managed Gillingham and Maidstone United.

PEARCE, IAN ANTHONY

Defender: 0+5 apps

Born: Bury St Edmunds, Suffolk, 7 May 1974

Career: CHELSEA (apprentice, May 1990; professional, August 1991), Blackburn Rovers (£300,000, October 1993), West Ham United (£1.6 million, September 1997), Fulham (£400,000, January 2004)

Ian Pearce made his League debut for Chelsea as a substitute v. Liverpool in May 1992. Unfortunately he was never able to secure a place in the first team and as a result moved north to Ewood Park. A resourceful, determined defender, capped by England at youth and Under-21 levels, he went from strength to strength after that and in 2005 was in sight of his 300th career appearance. A Premier League championship winner with Blackburn in 1995, he was certainly a player who 'riddled out' of the Chelsea net.

PEARSON, FRANK

Centre-forward: 30 apps, 18 goals

Born: Manchester, 18 May 1884 – *Died*: Manchester, 1949

Career: Preston North End (amateur 1900; professional, May 1901), Manchester City (June 1903), CHELSEA (£250, October 1905), Hull City (October 1906), Luton Town (May 1907), Rochdale (September 1908), Eccles Borough (February 1909; retired April 1911)

Chelsea's first real centre-forward, Frank Pearson had an exceptionally good 12 months at Stamford Bridge before surprisingly leaving for Hull City (replaced by George Hilsdon). Captaining the side, he made his Blues debut against Lincoln City just after arriving from Maine Road and celebrated the occasion with two goals in a 4–1 win at Sincil Bank. He failed to make an impact with any of his three major clubs following his departure from the Bridge.

PEARSON, GEORGE WILLIAM MARCUS

Outside-right/-left: 215 apps, 35 goals

Born: West Stanley, County Durham, 21 September 1907 – *Died*: 1985

Career: Consett, Bury (professional, September 1924), CHELSEA (February 1926), Luton Town (£300, July 1933), Walsall (September 1934–April 1935); did not play after WW2

Only 5 ft 2 in. tall, George Pearson – one of the smallest players ever to appear in a senior game for Chelsea – made his debut for the club on the right-wing against Swansea Town (away) in April 1926. Succeeding Bobby McNeil, he was an automatic choice in the first XI until 1932 before losing his place to Wilf Chitty. And then with Scottish international Alex Jackson and Eric Oakton occupying the outside-right position in turn, Pearson found he had Stanley Prout and Jack Horton also vying for the left-wing spot, and as a result he moved on to Luton Town.

PERCASSI, GIANLUCA

Right-back: 0+2 apps

Born: Milan, Italy, 25 August 1980

Career: Atalanta/Italy, CHELSEA (free transfer, August 1998), Monza/Italy (October 2000)

Gianluca Percassi joined Chelsea three weeks before his 18th birthday with Sam Dalla Bona in a deal that stunned Italian football. Capped by his country at youth-team level, he found himself fourth choice at Stamford Bridge (behind Albert Ferrer, Bernard Lambourde and Mario Melchiot) and after becoming homesick, he returned to Italy after making just two substitute appearances for the Blues.

PETIT, EMMANUEL
Midfield: 71+5 apps, 3 goals
Born: Dieppe, France, 22 September 1970
Career: ES Argues/France (March 1987), AS Monaco/France (May 1988), Arsenal (£3.5 million, June 1997), CF Barcelona/Spain (£15 million, July 2000), CHELSEA (£7.5 million, July 2001; released May 2004), CF Barcelona (July–October 2004); trained with Arsenal (November–December 2004)

Hard-working, skilful and competitive in midfield, the pony-tailed 'Manu' Petit made 222 League appearances for Monaco before joining Arsenal with whom he won the Premiership, FA Cup and Charity Shield in 1998 and a second Charity Shield a year later. Capped 63 times at senior level (6 goals scored), he helped France win the World Cup and European Championship in 1998 and 2000 respectively before having three seasons with Chelsea. He had two useful campaigns initially but made only four Premiership starts in 2003–04 before becoming one of the first departures from the Bridge following the appointment of new manager José Mourinho.

PETRESCU, DANIEL VASILE
Right-back/midfield: 186+22 apps, 24 goals
Born: Bucharest, Romania, 22 December 1967
Career: Steaua Bucharest/Romania (amateur, 1984; professional, December 1985), FC Olt/Romania (loan, season 1986–87), Foggia/Italy (July 1991), Genoa/Italy (August 1993), Sheffield Wednesday (£1.25 million, August 1994), CHELSEA (£2.3 million, November 1995), Bradford City (£1 million, August 2000), Southampton (£100,000, January 2001), National Bucharest/Romania (July 2002)

'Super Dan' Petrescu had virtually five years at Stamford Bridge and in that time he produced some brilliant performances in midfield, helping the Blues win the FA Cup in 1997, and both the European Cup-Winners' Cup and League Cup in 1998. He also took his tally of full international caps for Romania to 95, having earlier represented his country at Under-21 level. A great favourite with the Stamford Bridge fans, Petrescu had the ability to ghost into an open space and punish hesitant defences. He scored some wonderful goals for the Blues (and indeed for his country) and when he returned to his native homeland in 2002 he had amassed a useful record on the English soccer scene: 231 appearances and 31 goals. Prior to moving to Hillsborough he had netted 34 times in 198 Romanian and Italian League matches.

PEYTON, GERALD JOSEPH
Goalkeeper: 0+1 app.
Born: Birmingham, 20 May 1956
Career: Atherstone Town, Burnley (professional, May 1975), Fulham (£40,000, December 1976), Southend United (loan, September–October 1983),

Bournemouth (free transfer, July 1986), Everton (£80,000, July 1991), Bolton Wanderers (loan, February 1992), Brentford (loan, September–November 1992), CHELSEA (loan, January 1993), Brentford (free, March 1993), West Ham United (free, June 1993; retired May 1994); later goalkeeping coach with several clubs including Bournemouth, Birmingham City and West Bromwich Albion

In a marvellous career, Gerry Peyton kept goal in almost 700 club matches including 393 for Fulham. A very consistent performer, he was signed on loan by Chelsea as cover for Dmitri Kharine and made his only first-team appearance as a substitute for the injured Kharine in a 2–0 defeat by Sheffield Wednesday. Capped 33 times by the Republic of Ireland, Peyton also represented his country in two Under-21 internationals and gained a Third Division championship medal with Bournemouth in 1987.

PHELAN, TERENCE MICHAEL

Left-back: 21+3 apps
Born: Manchester, 16 March 1967
Career: Leeds United (apprentice, May 1983; professional, August 1984), Swansea City (free transfer, July 1986), Wimbledon (£100,000, July 1987), Manchester City (£2.5m, August 1992), CHELSEA (£900,000, November 1995), Everton (£850,000, January 1997–May 1999)

Attack-minded, speedy and good on the overlap, Terry Phelan was already an experienced full-back by the time he joined Chelsea. He had appeared in almost 400 competitive games at club level and had been recognised on the international stage by the Republic of Ireland whom he represented at youth, Under-21, Under-23, 'B' and senior levels, winning 38 senior caps. He suffered with injuries during his brief stay at Stamford Bridge and eyebrows were raised when Everton boss Joe Royle signed him in 1997. Later plagued with calf and knee problems he was forced to quit the professional game at the age of 32. He had his best spells with Wimbledon (198 games) and Manchester City (122).

PHILLIPS, THOMAS JOHN SEYMOUR

Goalkeeper: 149 apps
Born: Shrewsbury, 7 July 1951
Career: Shropshire County Boys, Shrewsbury Town (apprentice, July 1966; professional, November 1968), Aston Villa (£35,000, October 1969), CHELSEA (£30,000, August 1970), Swansea City (loan, March 1979), Crewe Alexandra (loan, August–September 1979), Brighton and Hove Albion (£15,000, March 1980), Charlton Athletic (free transfer, July 1981), Crystal Palace (free, January 1983); to Hong Kong; then Crystal Palace (reserves 1984; retired May 1985); later ran a motor manufacturing company in Mitcham (initially set up when playing for Crystal Palace)

John Phillips was a fine, agile goalkeeper but could be rather inconsistent at times. Nevertheless, he won 4 caps at both Under-23 and senior levels for Wales and made over 50 appearances for the 'Shrews' before joining Aston Villa. Then, despite understudying Peter Bonetti at Chelsea, he still managed almost 150 outings for the Blues, helping them reach the 1971 European Cup-Winners' Cup final. He was signed by Chelsea after future Villa keeper Tommy Hughes had broken his leg and later became Alan Mullery's first capture when he took over as Charlton manager. He made a total of just nine League appearances for the last five League clubs above.

PICKERING, PETER BARLOW
Goalkeeper: 35 apps
Born: York, 24 March 1926
Career: Earswick FC (York), York City (professional, April 1944), CHELSEA (£20,000, May 1948), Kettering Town (£250, June 1951), Northampton Town (free transfer, July 1955; retired December 1957); in January 1958 emigrated to South Africa where he became a first-class cricket umpire

Well built, strong on crosses with a good punch, but a shade uncertain with ground shots, Peter Pickering spent 3 seasons at Stamford Bridge, having his best spell in the first team in his first campaign when he made 19 appearances. A record signing for a goalkeeper at that time (1948) he earned quite a reputation for stopping penalties – 7 saves from the spot in 50 games for York, 1 for Chelsea and 4 for Northampton. He appeared in 90 first-class matches for the Cobblers. As a right-hand batsman, Pickering also played in one county game for Northamptonshire v. Leicestershire in 1953, scoring 37 and 18 in his 2 innings.

PIDGELEY, LEONARD
Goalkeeper: 0+1 app.
Born: Twickenham, 7 February 1984
Career: Chelsea (apprentice, April 2000, professional July 2003), Watford (on loan, September 2003–March 2004).

Five years after joining Chelsea as an apprentice, goalkeeper Lenny Pidgeley finally got his chance in the Premiership when he came on as a late substitute (for Carlo Cudicini) in the Blues' last home game of the 2004-05 season against London rivals Charlton Athletic. He then celebrated with his team-mates afterwards as the championship trophy was presented to skipper John Terry. During his loan spell with Watford he had the unusual experience of playing against his own club, Chelsea, in a 3rd round FA Cup tie. He made 29 appearances for the Hornets while at the same time gaining honours for England at Under-20 level.

PINNER, MICHAEL JOHN, MA, LLB
Goalkeeper: 1 app.
Born: Boston, Lincolnshire, 16 February 1934
Career: Boston Grammar School, Wyberton Rangers, Notts County (junior, October 1948), Cambridge University (1950), Hendon (1951), Pegasus (1952), Aston Villa (three spells: May 1954, February 1956 and April 1957), Arsenal (October 1957), Sheffield Wednesday (December 1957), Queens Park Rangers (July 1959), Manchester United (February 1961), Middlesex Wanderers, Hendon (briefly), Chelsea Casuals, CHELSEA (October 1961), Arsenal (December 1961), CHELSEA (April 1962), Swansea Town (August 1962), Leyton Orient (October 1962; professional, October 1963), Belfast Distillery (July 1965; retired May 1967); became a prominent solicitor

Mike Pinner decided to turn professional at the age of 29, having appeared in more than 250 competitive games as an amateur and winning over 50 caps for his country at that level. He played in two Olympic Games soccer tournaments – Melbourne (1956) and Rome (1960) – and was reserve in Tokyo (1964). He represented the RAF (he was an officer in the education department) and played in four Varsity matches against Oxford University. Daring, agile and a fine shot-stopper, Pinner's only start during his two mini spells with Chelsea came in a 5–4 home League defeat by Wolverhampton Wanderers in April 1962, when both Peter Bonetti and his deputy Errol McNally were out injured. During his career he played in 32 different countries with the FA, Middlesex Wanderers, Great Britain and the England amateur side. Few players have served with so many League clubs yet achieved so little than Mike Pinner.

PLUM, SETH LEWIS
Wing-half: 27 apps, 1 goal
Born: Edmonton, North London, 15 July 1899 – *Died*: St Anne's Hospital, Tottenham, London, 29 November 1969
Career: Page Green Road School (Tottenham), Mildway Athletic (August 1912), Tottenham Park Avondale (July 1913); served in Royal Navy (WW1); Barnet (September 1919), Charlton Athletic (amateur, August 1922), CHELSEA (professional, March 1924), Southend United (May 1927); later worked as a petrol pump attendant in the Tottenham area

A tiny wing-half, purposeful with a terrific engine, Seth Plum was perhaps a surprise choice when capped by England at senior level against France in Paris in 1923, thus becoming Charlton's first-ever full international player. He had earlier represented his country as an amateur. After his switch to Stamford Bridge, his game developed considerably, especially his passing, and although never a regular in the side, he played well when called into action.

PORTER, WILLIAM ARTHUR

Outside-left: 2 apps
Born: Paddington, London, June 1884 – *Died*: London, 1945
Career: London Caledonians (amateur, August 1902), Fulham (briefly, 1903), London Caledonians (April 1904), CHELSEA (amateur, August 1905), Brighton and Hove Albion (March 1907), Luton Town (July 1907), London Caledonians (May 1908), Ilford (September 1910–April 1912); did not play after WW1

Billy Porter – who remained an amateur throughout his career – deputised for the injured Johnny Kirwan in both his League games for Chelsea for whom he was a reliable reserve.

POTRAC, ANTHONY JOSEPH

Inside-forward: 1 app.
Born: Victoria, London, 21 January 1953
Career: CHELSEA (apprentice, May 1968; professional, August 1970), Durban City/South Africa (June 1973)

With so many other players of a similar nature at Stamford Bridge, Tony Potrac was never given a chance; his only League outing was against Huddersfield Town (home) in January 1972 when he did well in a 2–2 draw.

POYET, GUSTAVO AUGUSTUS

Midfield/forward: 110+35 apps, 49 goals
Born: Montevideo, Uruguay, 15 November 1967
Career: River Plate/Uruguay (professional, December 1985), FC Grenoble/France (July 1987), Bella Vista/Brazil (August 1989), Real Zaragoza/Spain (August 1990), CHELSEA (July 1997), Tottenham Hotspur (£2.25 million, July 2001; released May 2004); playing beach football in Uruguay (2005)

A strong, powerful, attacking midfielder or striker, Gus Poyet gave Chelsea four years' excellent service, scoring some wonderful goals and creating plenty more for his colleagues. He helped Chelsea win three trophies in 1997–98 – the FA Cup, European Cup-Winners' Cup and European Super Cup, scoring the only goal in the last against Real Madrid in Monaco. Two years later he added an FA Charity Shield winner's prize to his tally. Rewarded with youth honours by his country as a teenager, Poyet went on to gain 31 full caps for Uruguay. He scored 63 goals in 239 games in Spain's La Liga (for Zaragoza) and made almost 100 appearances for Spurs (netting 23 goals).

PRIESTLEY, JOHN
Inside-forward: 204 apps, 19 goals
Born: Johnstone, Renfrewshire, 19 August 1900 – *Died*: Perth, Scotland, 9 January 1980
Career: Johnstone FC/Scotland, CHELSEA (May 1920), Grimsby Town (May 1928), St Johnstone (August 1932), Cowdenbeath (seasons 1933–35)
Originally a wing-half, Jack Priestley developed into a first-class inside-forward and after establishing himself in Chelsea's first team (1922) became a cornerstone of the side. He switched to the centre-half berth at Grimsby and helped the Mariners gain promotion to the First Division in 1929. Forceful and committed, he could pass a ball inch-perfect (given the chance) and carved out many an opening for his team-mates. Besides possessing a strong tackle, he was also a fine header of the ball.

PRIESTLEY, THOMAS JAMES MONTGOMERY
Inside-forward: 27 apps, 2 goals
Born: Belfast, March 1911 – *Died*: Belfast, December 1985
Career: Coleraine (July 1928), Linfield (August 1930), CHELSEA (£2,000, June 1933; left May 1934 but registration retained by the club; officially announced his retirement, May 1939)
Tom Priestley was one of only two players to have worn a rugby-style scrum cap in the Football League, having lost his hair through a childhood illness. Red in colour, it caused a lot of banter on the terraces, yet he never let it affect his game. A Northern Ireland international inside-forward (capped twice), he was solid yet somewhat eccentric. Joining Chelsea after fierce competition from several other leading clubs, he spent only the one season at Stamford Bridge before returning to his homeland – this after his career was halted when mud entered his eye and caused a major problem. He never again participated as a professional, although Chelsea retained his registration for several years.

PROUDFOOT, PETER
Wing-half: 12 apps
Born: Wishaw, Scotland, 25 November 1882 – *Died*: London, 4 March 1941
Career: Wishaw FC (April 1898), Wishaw United (September 1898), St Mirren (August 1900), Lincoln City (December 1900), St Mirren (July 1903), Millwall (October 1904), Clapton Orient (August 1905), CHELSEA (April 1906), Manchester United reserves (trial, April 1908), Stockport County (June 1908), Greenock Morton (August 1909), Stockport County (May 1910; retired May 1913); served in the Army during WW1; Clapton Orient (manager, three spells: April 1922–April 1929; April 1930–April 1931 and from January 1935; retired, ill health, January 1939)
A powerful footballer, tenacious in the tackle with a side-splitting shoulder-charge, Peter Proudfoot was one of the most aggressive, attacking wing-halves of his era but he was only a first-team regular with one club, Lincoln City, for

whom he scored 20 goals in 79 appearances. Famed for his unpredictable behaviour whereby he often tried to beat two, three and even four men at a time and would sometimes ignore the ball completely and fly in or lunge at the opposing goalkeeper, he was a well-known character in the footballing world. Proudfoot made his debut for Chelsea against Manchester United in April 1906 in front of 67,000 fans at Stamford Bridge. He managed Clapton Orient at three different grounds: Homerton, Lea Bridge and Brisbane Road, and in 1925–26 guided the London club to the quarter-finals of the FA Cup. When the 'Os' were relegated in 1929 he stepped down yet stayed on as an administrator whilst Arthur Grimsdell ran the team. He held a commission in the army during WW1.

PROUT, STANLEY
Outside-left: 17 apps, 3 goals
Born: Fulham, London, February 1911 – *Died*: Essex, 1980
Career: Leytonstone (amateur, August 1926), Fulham (amateur, March 1930), Park Royal (amateur, September 1930), CHELSEA (professional, August 1932), Bristol Rovers (July 1934), Chester (April 1936), Dartford (August 1937–September 1939); did not play after WW2
Stan Prout made the switch from amateur football to League soccer with apparent ease and did well during his first season at Stamford Bridge but then lost his place to Jack Horton and a year later dropped down into the Third Division.

RANDALL, ERNEST ALBERT WALTER
Centre-forward: 3 apps, 1 goal
Born: Bognor Regis, West Sussex, 13 January 1926
Career: Bognor Regis Town, CHELSEA (December 1950), Crystal Palace (June 1953), Bognor Regis Town (August 1955–May 1957)
A fast-raiding inside-forward, who made a rapid rise from non-League football into the First Division, Ernie Randall couldn't maintain his form and slowly drifted into obscurity. He made his League debut in front of almost 32,000 fans at home to West Bromwich Albion in October 1951 when he replaced the injured Bobby Smith. He scored 13 goals in 24 games for Palace.

RANKIN, JOHN PATTERSON
Inside-forward: 66 apps, 9 goals
Born: Coatbridge, near Glasgow, August 1900 – *Died*: Glasgow, 1989
Career: Hamilton Academical (August 1919), Doncaster Rovers (November 1924), Dundee (June 1925), Charlton Athletic (£250, September 1925), CHELSEA (£3,000, May 1930), Notts County (May 1934), Burton Town (April 1936–September 1939); did not appear after WW2; later ran a greengrocer's shop in Glasgow
Described in 1933 as being a 'clever ball manipulator and schemer' Jack Rankin,

a former engineer, served 6 major clubs during his career, scoring 48 goals in a total of 332 League games north and south of the border. A Scottish Cup finalist v. Celtic in 1925, he helped Charlton gain promotion from the Third Division (S) four years later but never quite settled into a set routine at Stamford Bridge despite having two decent spells in the first team during the 1931–32 and '32–33 seasons.

READ, WILLIAM HENRY
Outside-left: 4 apps
Born: Blackpool, 1885 – *Died*: Blackpool, *circa* 1955
Career: Lytham FC, Blackpool (May 1907), Colne FC (August 1909), Sunderland (February 1911), CHELSEA (May 1911), Dundee (March 1913), Swansea Town (August 1914–May 1915); did not play after WW1
Reserve to Billy Bridgeman on Chelsea's left-wing, Bill Read made his debut for the Blues against Wolves at Molineux in January 1912 when he deputised for Angus Douglas. He travelled around without ever establishing himself as a regular with any of his five clubs.

REID, ERNEST JAMES
Wing-half: 1 app.
Born: Pentrebach, near Merthyr Tydfil, South Wales, 25 March 1914 – Deceased at 2000
Career: Troedyrhiw FC, Merthyr Tydfil (briefly), Swansea Town (July 1932), CHELSEA (September 1937), Swansea Town (May 1939), Norwich City (June 1945), Bedford Town (October 1947; retired May 1949)
A tough, uncompromising defender, Ernie Reid's only senior appearance for Chelsea was against Grimsby Town at Blundell Park in November 1938 when he deputised for Sam Weaver. He played in 45 games for Norwich, 36 in the 1945–46 transitional campaign.

REILLY, EDWARD JAMES
Inside-forward: 1 app.
Born: Kensington, London, June 1886 – *Died*: London, 1960
Career: Shepherd's Bush, CHELSEA (August 1908), Fulham (July 1910–May 1911)
A Chelsea player for two seasons, Ted Reilly's only League outing came in April 1909 when he stood in for the injured Bill Bridgeman in the London derby against Woolwich Arsenal (0–0).

RHOADES-BROWN, PETER
Winger: 97+12 apps, 5 goals
Born: Hampton Court, London, 2 January 1962
Career: CHELSEA (schoolboy forms, 1976; apprentice, April 1978; professional, July 1979), Oxford United (£85,000, January 1984–May 1989),

Abingdon Town (mid-1990s); then Oxford United (commercial manager); also played for Marlow Town (1994–95)

A classy player in his own right, Peter Rhoades-Brown was nimble rather than strong, a traditional old-fashioned winger who had a wonderful bodyswerve but tended to drift out of the game for long periods, especially when the going got tough. Nevertheless, he did well for three seasons (1981–83) before Paul Canoville and Mickey Thomas started to impose themselves on the first-team squad. After leaving Stamford Bridge, Rhoades-Brown did well at Oxford, scoring 16 goals in 142 senior appearances, helping the 'U's' win the Second Division championship in 1985. Unfortunately he missed the club's 1986 League Cup final win over QPR at Wembley through injury.

RICHARDSON, FREDERICK

Centre-forward: 2 apps

Born: Middlestone Moor, County Durham, 18 August 1925

Career: Willington and Spennymoor Schools, Durham Boys, Spennymoor United Juniors, Newcastle United (trial), Spennymoor United (1944), Bishop Auckland (August 1945), CHELSEA (September 1946), Hartlepool United (October 1947), Barnsley (October 1948), West Bromwich Albion (£7,125, June 1950), Chester (£3,000, February 1952), Hartlepool United (November 1952; retired from playing June 1956); West Bromwich Albion (scout, in North-Eastern League, 1956–58); later coached locally in Hartlepool; Whickham (manager, May 1980–June 1982); now living in the North-east of England

Fred Richardson was a stocky striker, who could carve or barge his way though the tightest of defences, aided by a weighty frame. He played for Bishop Auckland in the 1946 FA Amateur Cup final, collecting a runner's-up medal. He then signed pro for Chelsea and embarked on a good career in the Football League, totting up 244 appearances and scoring 66 goals, before retiring in 1957 through injury. Kept in the reserves by Tommy Lawton, he finally made his First Division debut for the Blues in a 2–0 defeat at Everton in April 1947. During his career Richardson scored 61 goals in 244 League games, his best return coming with Hartlepool (19 in 106 outings). As a manager he guided Whickham to victory in the 1981 FA Vase Final at Wembley.

RIX, GRAHAM

Midfield: 1+3 apps

Born: Askern, Doncaster, Yorkshire, 23 October 1957

Career: Camps Mount School (Doncaster), Doncaster and Yorkshire Schools, Yorkshire Youths, Askern Juniors, Leeds United (trial), Arsenal (apprentice, June 1974; professional, June 1975), Brentford (loan, December 1987–January 1988), SM Caen/France (June 1988), Le Havre/France (free transfer, 1990), Dundee (free, July 1992), CHELSEA (non-contract player and youth-team coach, March 1994; retired as a player June 1994; appointed first-team coach to January 2001), Portsmouth (manager, February 2001–March 2002), Oxford United (manager, March 2004; appointed director of football, November 2004); released from prison in September 1999 after serving 6 months of a 12-month sentence.

Graham Rix became Chelsea's oldest debutant when he came on as a 90th-minute substitute in the European Cup-Winners' Cup clash with Viktoria Zizkov in September 1994. During his 14 years with Arsenal he scored 50 goals in 463 senior games, gained 17 full, 7 Under-21 and 3 'B' caps for England and helped the Gunners win the FA Cup in 1979. He also claimed runner's-up prizes in the 1978 and 1980 FA Cup finals and another in the ECWC final of 1980 when he missed the vital penalty in the shoot-out against Valencia. On his day, Rix was a brilliant ball-player with great vision who read the game superbly well from a wide position. He skippered Arsenal for a short time.

ROBBEN, ARJEN
Forward: 19+10 apps, 9 goals
Born: Holland, 23 January 1984
Career: FC Groningen/Holland (amateur, April 2000), PSV Eindhoven/Holland (professional, August 2001), FC Groningen (on loan during season 2001–02), CHELSEA (signed provisionally in March 2004; transfer secured for £12 million, July 2004)

Dutch international Arjen Robben scored his first Chelsea goal (the winner) in the Champions League clash away to CSKA Moscow in November 2004, having been out of action since pre-season after suffering a bad leg injury during a friendly with AS Roma. Since then he has netted many more brilliant goals and was inspirational in so many games as Chelsea surged on towards the Premiership title. Unfortunately he was injured in February (after scoring the winner at Blackburn) and missed most of the run-in to the title . . . to his huge disappointment. A wonderfully balanced player with terrific on-the-ball skills, he loves to drive forward towards the opposing goal, often cutting in from a wide position. His dribbling skills are remarkable and several defenders have been left bemused by his brilliance. He played with Mateja Kezman at PSV and rejected a move to Manchester United to sign for Chelsea. He won his first full cap in April 2003 and is now a key player in Holland's ranks, as he is at Stamford Bridge.

ROBERTS, GRAHAM PAUL
Defender/midfield: 83 apps, 22 goals
Born: Southampton, 3 July 1959
Career: Southampton (associate schoolboy), Southampton and Hampshire Schools, Scholing Sports FC (1975), Bournemouth (apprentice, August 1975), Portsmouth (apprentice, March 1976), Dorchester Town (loan, August 1976; signed permanently, October 1976), Weymouth (August 1979), Tottenham Hotspur (£35,000, May 1980), Glasgow Rangers

(£450,000, December 1986), CHELSEA (May 1988; player–coach from November 1989), West Bromwich Albion (£200,000, November 1990), Enfield (player–manager, March 1992), Chesham United (briefly), Slough Town (season 1994–95), Stevenage Borough (1995), Yeovil Town (player–manager, January 1995–February 1998), Hertford Town (manager, August 1998), Boreham Wood (manager, February 2001), Carshalton (manager, season 2002–03); soccer coach in Marbella/Spain; Clyde (manager, May 2005)

A former shop-fitter's mate, Graham Roberts started his career as a forward before developing into a rugged, no-nonsense, hard-tackling midfielder or central defender. His Football League debut came with Spurs in October 1980 v. Stoke, the first of 287 appearances for the London club (36 goals) with whom he collected two FA Cup winner's medals (1981 and 1982) as well a League Cup runner's-up medal in 1982. He won the first of his six England caps against Northern Ireland in May 1983 and twelve months later, as skipper, lifted the UEFA Cup after Spurs had beaten RSC Anderlecht in the final. Always a stern, aggressive competitor, he never gave an inch, never shirked a tackle and simply loved to be involved in a tough contest, and he took over from another hard man, Graeme Souness, also a former Spurs player, at Ibrox Park. After helping the Gers win both the Scottish Premier League and Skol Cup, he moved to Chelsea where he did superbly well, scoring a goal every four games (including a club record 13 from the penalty spot in 1988–89) and producing some exquisite performances. Quitting Stamford Bridge after an argument with chairman Ken Bates he joined West Brom but started to struggle with injuries during the latter stages of his Hawthorns career and after leaving Albion he became a fairly successful manager at non-League level. There was mayhem among the Glasgow Rangers fans when news broke that Roberts was to leave Ibrox Park. Some supporters even tried to influence the board by offering to pay his wages. Scores of Roberts' fans still exist all over Scotland to this day – for he was a very respected player north of the border, especially by the 'blue' half of Glasgow.

ROBERTSON, JAMES

Inside-forward: 31 apps, 22 goals
Born: Glasgow, 1880 – *Died*: Scotland, *circa* 1960
Career: Glasgow United, Crewe Alexandra (1901), Small Heath (£25, April 1903), CHELSEA (£50, August 1905), Glossop North End (July 1907), Leyton (August 1908), Partick Thistle (July 1909), Ayr United (May 1910), Barrow (briefly, August 1912), Leeds City (September 1912), Gateshead (May 1913; retired, injured, May 1915)

Jim Robertson, slim but nimble, played in Chelsea's first-ever League game against Stockport County in September 1905. A prolific marksman, sharp and decisive, he was third top scorer in that initial campaign despite the fact that he was never assured of his place in the starting line-up. It came as a surprise when he left Stamford Bridge at the end of the 1906–07 season. He scored 28 goals in 70 League games for Glossop.

ROBERTSON, JOHN TAIT
Wing-half: 39 apps, 4 goals
Born: Dumbarton, 25 February 1877 – *Died*: Milton, Hampshire, 24 January 1935
Career: Poinfield FC, Sinclair Swifts, Greenock Morton (1894), Everton (professional, October 1895), Southampton (May 1898), Glasgow Rangers (£300, August 1899), CHELSEA (player–manager, May 1905), Glossop North End (player–manager, January 1907), Manchester United (reserve-team manager, June 1909–May 1910); coached on continent either side of WW1; Coventry City (trainer/coach, season 1927–28)

Scorer of Chelsea's first-ever League goal, against Blackpool at Bloomfield Road in September 1905, Jackie Robertson was also the club's first player–manager, agreeing a salary of £4 a week. One of the finest footballers to move out of Scotland, he assembled a pretty useful side at Stamford Bridge and guided Chelsea to third spot in the Second Division table in 1906. It came as a shock when he chose to leave the club halfway through the next campaign for a club languishing in the lower reaches of the same division. A Scottish international, capped 16 times at senior level (1900–05), he also represented the Scottish League 6 times and played for Glasgow v. Sheffield twice in Inter-City challenge matches. A Southern League championship winner with Southampton in 1899, he then helped Rangers win three Scottish League titles in succession, 1900–02, and was a Cup winner with the Glasgow club in 1903 and runner-up in 1904 and 1905. He appeared in 130 senior games for the Gers (25 goals scored).

ROBERTSON, WILLIAM GIBB
Goalkeeper: 215 apps
Born: Glasgow, 13 November 1928 – *Died*: June 1973
Career: Arthurlie, CHELSEA (professional, July 1946), Leyton Orient (£1,000, September 1960), Dover (August 1963; retired May 1965)

Bill Robertson, a well-built, reliable and efficient goalkeeper, spent five years playing reserve-team football before getting his opportunity in Chelsea's League side – and how well he took it. Replacing Harry Medhurst towards the end of the 1950–51 campaign, at a time when the Blues were in relegation trouble, he produced some terrific displays as the last four games were all won and demotion was avoided by 0.44 of a goal. Injuries apart, he was a regular in the side for the next six seasons and collected a League championship winner's medal in 1955. After being replaced between the posts by Reg Matthews, Robertson went back into the second XI. He later appeared in 51 games for Orient.

ROBERTSON, WILLIAM HAROLD

Goalkeeper: 43 apps

Born: Crowthorne, near Reading, 25 March 1923 – *Died*: 1973

Career: Crowthorne Boys' Club, Camberley Auxillary Training Corps/Aldershot
(August 1938), RAF Lossiemouth (from 1940), CHELSEA (professional,
October 1945), Birmingham City (£2,500, November 1948), Stoke City
(£8,100, June 1952; retired May 1960); later ran a newsagent's shop in
Bucknall, Stoke-on-Trent, before moving back to his roots in Berkshire

Bill Robertson, 6 ft 1 in. tall and 14 st. in weight, was a centre-forward before
joining the forces. He top-scored for ATC when they won the Aldershot Minor
League in 1938 – his only prize as a footballer. He was persuaded to take up
goalkeeping during the war and the decision proved right, for he developed into
a quality performer, being a fine shot-stopper with good reflexes, although it
seems he was a shade hesitant at times. No relation to William Gibb, he made
his senior debut for Chelsea against Leicester City in a 3rd round FA Cup tie
in January 1946, and played 27 games in the League South that season before
sharing the number-one spot with Harry Medhurst during the next two
campaigns. Said to have had a pair of hands larger than any other goalkeeper in
the land, Robertson made just 3 appearances for Birmingham and 250 for Stoke
– a record for a Potters keeper until Peter Fox surpassed it in the 1980s. Both
Bill Robertsons were together at Stamford Bridge, 1946–48.

ROBINSON, ARTHUR CHARLES

Goalkeeper: 3 apps

Born: Coventry, 28 February 1878 – *Died*: Coventry, 15 May 1929

Career: Allesley FC, Coventry Stars, Singers FC (Coventry), Small Heath
(professional, August 1898), CHELSEA (July 1908), Coventry City (May
1910; retired April 1911 to become licensee of the Red Lion Inn, Barrass
Green, Coventry)

'Nat' Robinson made 306 appearances for Small Heath (now Birmingham
City), played in 2 England international trial matches and twice represented the
Football League before joining Chelsea in 1908 as cover for Jack Whitley. He
always donned two jerseys (whatever the weather) and it is said that he wore
only two pairs of boots throughout his entire career. He often whistled when
annoyed and named his dog 'Ninety' after the number of minutes in a game.
Described by a contemporary as all 'arms and legs' due to the way he used to
jump up and down on his line and swing his arms round in Catherine-wheel
style to put his opponents off, he was brilliant at times if somewhat eccentric,
and was one of the first keepers to dash out of his area and fly-kick the ball to
safety.

ROBSON, BRYAN STANLEY

Striker: 12+5 apps, 5 goals

Born: Sunderland, 11 November 1945

Career: Clara Vale Juniors, Newcastle United (£75, professional, November 1972), West Ham United (£120,000, February 1971), Sunderland (£145,000, June 1974), West Ham United (£80,000, October 1976), Sunderland £45,000, June 1979), Carlisle United (£10,000, player–coach, March 1981), CHELSEA (player–coach, July 1982), Carlisle United (loan, March–May 1983), Sunderland (player–coach, July 1983), Carlisle United (July 1984; later assistant manager; then manager, from August 1985), Gateshead (October 1985), Newcastle Blue Star (September 1986), Manchester United (North-east scout, season 1987–88, Old Trafford School of Excellence coach, August 1988), Hartlepool United (assistant manager/coach, October 1988), Sunderland (Community Officer, November 1988), Hartlepool United (coach, 1989), Manchester United (assistant coach, July 1991), Sunderland (assistant coach, season 1995–96)

Striker Bryan 'Pop' Robson was almost 37 years of age when he joined Chelsea. He had scored on his League debut for Newcastle v. Charlton Athletic back in September 1964 and did likewise for the Blues v. Cambridge United in August 1982. Obviously well past his best, he spent just the one season at Stamford Bridge before moving on to Sunderland where he became a successful coach. During a marvellous career, hot-shot Robson, sharp and lethal inside the penalty area, netted a total of 341 goals in 742 senior games at club level, including 265 in 674 League appearances. He gained two Under-23 caps for England and represented the Football League.

ROBSON, THOMAS HENRY

Winger: 6+1 apps

Born: Gateshead, 31 July 1944

Career: Redheugh Boys' Club (Gateshead), Northampton Town (amateur, July 1959; professional, August 1961), CHELSEA (£30,000, December 1965); Newcastle United (£13,000, December 1966), Peterborough United (£20,000, November 1968), Nuneaton Borough (May 1981), Stamford (June 1982), Northampton Town (October 1984), Chatteris FC (August 1985), Peterborough United (player–assistant coach, November 1986; retired May 1987); later worked for the Peterborough *Herald and Post* newspaper

An England Youth international, capped in 1962, Tommy Robson scored 20 goals in 74 League games for Northampton before joining Chelsea as a 21 year old. He had limited opportunities at Stamford Bridge and moved back to the North-east after 12 months, signed by Joe Harvey for Newcastle. He scored 11 goals in 50 games for the Geordies before transferring to Peterborough where he became something of an institution for the next decade and more, scoring 128 goals in 559 appearances for the Posh.

ROCASTLE, DAVID

Midfield: 37+3 apps, 2 goals

Born: Lewisham, London, 2 May 1967 – *Died*: London, 31 March 2001

Career: Roger Manwood's Boys' School, South London Schools, Arsenal (schoolboy forms, May 1982; apprentice, August 1983; professional, December 1984), Leeds United (£2 million, August 1992), Manchester City (£2 million, December 1993), CHELSEA (£1.25 million, August 1994), Norwich City (loan, January–March 1997), Hull City (loan, October–December 1997), Sabah FC/Malaysia (August 1998; retired March 1999)

David 'Rocky' Rocastle made his league debut for Arsenal v. Newcastle in September 1985 and within two seasons was a favourite with the Highbury fans, having been voted the club's Player of the Year in 1986. An attacking midfielder, strong with a powerful right-foot shot, he collected a League Cup winner's medal in 1987 and followed up with two championship winning medals in 1989 and 1991. After gaining 14 Under-21 caps, he made his full England debut under manager Bobby Robson v. Denmark in 1988 and went on to appear in 13 more senior internationals as well as appearing in 2 'B' games. After scoring 24 goals in 204 games for the Gunners he joined the reigning League champions Leeds United, but his stay at Elland Road lasted just 18 months before another £2 million transfer took him across country to Maine Road. He helped Manchester City avoid relegation from the top flight and then returned to London to sign for Chelsea. He had a productive first season at Stamford Bridge but missed most of the 1995–96 campaign with a broken toe. He got match-fit courtesy of loan spells at Carrow Road and Boothferry Park (where a close friend, Mark Hateley, was manager) but failed to get back into Chelsea's side. After a brief spell in Malaysia, Rocastle was sadly diagnosed with non-Hodgkin's lymphoma in February 2001 and he died a month later. His nine-year-old son, Ryan, was Arsenal's mascot for the 2001 FA Cup final at Cardiff's Millennium Stadium.

RODGER, GEORGE BERNARD

Centre-half: 122 apps, 2 goals

Born: Cambuslang, Glasgow, 19 December 1900 – *Died*: Glasgow, *circa* 1964

Career: Kilsyth Rangers, CHELSEA (June 1924; retired, injured, May 1931), Inverness Clachnacuddin (manager/coach, August 1931–May 1938)

Vying for a first-team place with Jack Townrow and Harry Wilding for long spells during his time at Stamford Bridge, George Rodger, well-built and strong in the air, had his best season in 1925–26 when he made 34 senior appearances. He then did well again in 1928–29 when starring in 29 matches and helping the Blues gain promotion from the Second Division. A knee injury ended his career prematurely.

ROFE, DENNIS

Full-back: 61+2 apps

Born: Epping, Essex, 1 June 1950

Career: Leyton Orient (apprentice, June 1965; professional, February 1968), Leicester City (£112,000, August 1972), CHELSEA (£80,000, February 1980), Southampton (July 1982, reserve-team coach, June 1984; first-team coach, February 1987), Bristol Rovers (coach, July 1991; assistant manager; then caretaker-manager, October 1991; manager, December 1992); later Stoke City (reserve-team manager), Leicester City (coach), Coventry City (coach), Southampton (assistant manager/coach)

An enthusiastic, wholehearted full-back with great determination, Dennis Rofe was the dressing-room comedian but out on the field he took the game seriously and produced many outstanding performances during a lengthy career. He made 189 appearances for Orient and 324 for Leicester after becoming the game's costliest full-back, a record he held for 24 hours until the Foxes sold David Nish to Derby County. He played in 54 consecutive games for Chelsea before surprisingly losing his place to Chris Hutchings and so missing out on promotion. He subsequently moved to The Dell where he remained for nine years as a player and coach. Later he teamed up with boss Gordon Strachan. Rofe was capped twice by England at Under-21 level.

ROUGVIE, DOUGLAS

Defender: 100 apps, 3 goals

Born: Ballingry, Fife, 24 May 1956

Career: Dunfermline United (August 1971), Aberdeen (apprentice, May 1972; professional, May 1973), CHELSEA (£150,000, July 1984), Brighton and Hove Albion (£50,000, June 1987), Shrewsbury Town (August 1988), Fulham (February–May 1989); later with Huntly FC/Scotland (mid-1990s)

Doug Rougvie was a no-nonsense full-back, rugged and uncompromising, who didn't care too much about his opponent, especially if he was on the timid side or indeed a shade on the small side. Once he had won the ball, he would usually thump it down field away to safety. Unfortunately, this was his weakness, for once in the air it could fall to anybody and this often upset his coaches and indeed his manager. He had to wait seven years before gaining a regular place in Aberdeen's first team. Primarily a centre-half, he switched to full-back with great effect and appeared in 308 games for the Dons, scoring 21 goals. He won two League championship medals in 1980 and 1984, three Cup-winning medals in successive seasons, 1983–84–85, collected two League Cup runner's-up prizes in 1979 and 1989, won the European Cup-Winners' Cup in 1983 and was capped once by Scotland in 1983. 'Big Doug' helped Chelsea win the Full Members' Cup at Wembley in 1986.

ROUSE, FREDERICK WILLIAM

Centre-forward: 42 apps, 11 goals

Born: Cranford, Middlesex, 28 November 1882 – *Died*: Buckinghamshire, 1953

Career: Bracknell and District Schools, Southall (1897), High Wycombe (August 1900), Wycombe Wanderers (July 1901), Shepherd's Bush FC (February 1903), Grimsby Town (professional, March 1903), Stoke (£150, April 1904), Everton (£750, November 1906), CHELSEA (£1,000, October 1907), West Bromwich Albion (£250, May 1909), Croydon Common (September 1910), Brentford (August 1911), Slough Town (February 1913; retired May 1915)

A robust player who harried and hassled defenders, Fred Rouse possessed tricky footwork and had the uncanny ability of being able to stop dead before letting fly with a strong shot. Few defenders could cope with him at his best but annoyingly he could have one good day followed by three bad ones – he was a rather inconsistent performer. He played for the Football League in 1905 and 1906 and during his League career averaged a goal every 3 games, scoring 58 times in 154 outings. He was Chelsea's first £1,000 signing when recruited from Stoke in 1907.

RUSSELL, ROBERT INGLIS

Wing-half: 4 apps

Born: Aberdour, Fife, 27 December 1919 – Deceased at 2000

Career: Airdrieonians, CHELSEA (guest player from 1943; signed permanently, December 1944), Notts County (£1,000, August 1948), Leyton Orient (free transfer, October 1948; retired, injured, April 1949)

A formidable defender, Bob Russell played in 85 WW2 games for Chelsea, appearing in both the winning League (South) Cup finals of 1944 and 1945. Unfortunately he was plagued by injury after the hostilities and managed only four senior games before moving to Meadow Lane.

RUSSELL, WILLIAM

Wing-half: 160 apps, 6 goals

Born: Muir, Hamilton, Lanarkshire, 1903 – *Died*: *circa* 1978

Career: Larkhall Juniors (1922), Blantyre Celtic (1925), CHELSEA (June 1927), Heart of Midlothian (£1,200, January 1936), Rhyl Athletic (player–manager, August 1938–September 1939); did not figure after WW2

'Jack' Russell was a thrustful wing-half who was tried as a right-winger in Chelsea's reserve side before making his mark in the first XI. Making his League debut in place of Sammy Irving in April 1928 (v. Oldham Athletic, away), he seized his opportunity the following year and remained a vital member of the squad until his departure to Tynecastle in 1936.

SALES, ARTHUR ALFRED

Centre-half: 7 apps
Born: Lewes, East Sussex, 4 March 1900 – *Died*: Dorset, 1977
Career: Redhill, CHELSEA (professional, September 1924), Queens Park
    Rangers (September 1930), Bournemouth (season 1933–34)
After doing exceedingly well as an amateur with Redhill, Archie Sales, tall and
slim, had a tough time with Chelsea, making only seven senior appearances in
six years owing to the form and presence of Messrs Rodger, Wilding and
Townrow. He had 38 outings for QPR.

SALMOND, ROBERT

Centre-half: 29 apps
Born: Kilmarnock, 22 September 1911 – *Died*: 1997
Career: Dundee North End (April 1929), Portsmouth (professional, August
    1932), CHELSEA (November 1938), Banbury Spencer (player–manager,
    August 1945–May 1947)
A tall, well-proportioned centre-half with a strong right-footed kick, Bob
Salmond made 141 senior appearances for Pompey but missed playing in the
1934 FA Cup final. He replaced Allan Craig at the heart of the Chelsea defence
and did well until WW2 intervened. He played in 62 Regional games during
the hostilities before entering non-League football with Banbury in 1945.

SAUNDERS, DEREK WILLIAM

Wing-half: 223 apps, 9 goals
Born: Ware, Hertfordshire, 6 June 1926
Career: Walthamstow Avenue, CHELSEA (June 1953; retired May 1959;
    appointed coach at Stamford Bridge); later employed as head groundsman
    and chief soccer coach at Westminster School and was also groundsman at
    Hampstead Cricket Club (London)
A busy and influential player, red-haired Derek Saunders had a tenacious
approach to the game and served Chelsea well for six years before announcing
his retirement. An England amateur international, he won the FA Amateur Cup
with Walthamstow in 1952, and then helped the Blues win the First Division
championship in 1955, appearing in all 42 League matches and scoring 1 goal,
in the 4–2 away win at West Bromwich Albion.

SAUNDERS, FRANCIS JOHN

Centre-half: 60 apps
Born: Middlesbrough, 24 August 1924
Career: Served in forces during second half of WW2; Darlington (professional,
    September 1946), CHELSEA (May 1948), Crystal Palace (August 1954),
    Chester (May 1957–May 1959)
John Saunders was mainly a squad member at Stamford Bridge, reserve to John
Harris. Standing 6 ft tall and weighing 12 st., he was rather inconsistent in his

general play and had his best season in 1952–53 when he appeared in 27 League and FA Cup games. He left Stamford Bridge when Ron Greenwood and Stan Wicks were also challenging for the centre-half spot. He made 67 League appearances for Darlington, 59 for Palace and 67 for Chester.

SAUNDERS, JAMES EDMUND
Goalkeeper: 2 apps
Born: Birmingham, 1882 – *Died*: Lincoln, *circa* 1950
Career: Glossop North End (1904), Manchester United (August 1906), Lincoln City (October 1906), CHELSEA (May 1909), Watford (£50, May 1910), Liberal Club (Lincoln) to 1915; on military service in France during WW1; Lincoln City (guest, 1918)
Understudy to Jack Whitley during his one season at Stamford Bridge, Jim Saunders made his debut for the Blues in a 2–1 defeat at Notts County on Christmas Day 1909 and two days later starred in a 2–1 home win over Newcastle United in front of more than 70,000 spectators. His manager at Lincoln and Chelsea was Dave Calderhead. He made 65 appearances for the Imps, gaining Lincolnshire Senior Cup and Midland League championship medals.

SCOTT, MELVYN DOUGLAS
Defender: 104 apps
Born: Claygate, Surrey, 26 September 1939
Career: CHELSEA (amateur, April 1955; professional, November 1956), Brentford (£10,000, March 1963–May 1967)
An effervescent character, Mel Scott was nonetheless a solid centre-half whose displays were often assured, although a distinct lack of aerial power prevented him from being a really outstanding pivot. Capped by England at youth and Under-23 levels (3 outings in the latter category), he made the first of his 104 senior starts for Chelsea in a 2–1 home defeat by Wolves in March 1958. After losing his place to John Mortimore (having made 37 appearances in his final season at Stamford Bridge) he went on to play in 157 League games for Brentford.

SHARP, BUCHANAN
Inside-forward: 72 apps, 23 goals
Born: Alexandria, Dumbarton, 2 November 1894 – *Died*: Bolton, February 1956
Career: Vale of Leven (1912), CHELSEA (November 1919), Tottenham Hotspur (March 1923), Leicester City (January 1925), Nelson (June 1926), Southport (October 1928–May 1930)
A clever ball artiste who loved to dribble his way round defenders, Buchanan Sharp also packed a powerful right-foot shot which he often delivered from distance. He took quite a while to settle down at Stamford Bridge but did play well in the 1920 FA Cup semi-final against Aston Villa. A lot of fans were

surprised when he moved to White Hart Lane in 1923. He only had 6 games for Spurs (3 goals) before scoring 21 times in his first season with Nelson.

SHARP, JAMES
Full-back: 64 apps
Born: Jordanstone, Alyth, Perthshire, 11 October 1880 – *Died*: London, 18 November 1949
Career: East Craigie (Dundee), Dundee (May 1899), Fulham (July 1904), Woolwich Arsenal (June 1905), Glasgow Rangers (£400, April 1908), Fulham (£1,000, January 1909); went over to the USA (early November 1912) but returned inside a month; CHELSEA (£1,750, late November 1912–May 1915), Fulham (trainer/coach, seasons 1920–26), Walsall (coach, seasons 1926–28), Cliftonville/Ireland (trainer/coach, season 1928–29); afterwards worked in the building trade in London

A speedy full-back, capped five times at senior level by Scotland between 1904 and 1909 and twice a Scottish League representative, Jimmy Sharp took over from Jock Cameron in Chelsea's first team. Also a fine tactical player, cultured, with a steady approach, he did very well for two seasons before losing his place to Jack Harrow. He made 116 first-class appearances for Arsenal and 126 for Fulham. Sharp was also a competent cricketer who played for Forfarshire.

SHAW, COLIN MICHAEL
Centre-forward: 1 app.
Born: St Albans, Hertfordshire, 19 June 1943
Career: CHELSEA (amateur, June 1958; professional, May 1961), Norwich City (£5,000, August 1963), Leyton Orient (March 1965), Natal/South Africa (July 1966)

Colin Shaw conjured up an impressive goal-scoring record at junior and intermediate levels (hitting a seventimer for Chelsea's teenagers in an FA Youth Cup tie v. Fulham) but he failed to carry that excellent form through to the senior side. An England Youth international, he made his only League appearance for the Blues against West Ham at home in February 1962 when he deputised for the injured Barry Bridges. He made only 11 senior appearances during the whole of his career in England.

SHEARER, DUNCAN NICHOL
Striker: 2 apps, 1 goal
Born: Fort William, Scotland, 28 August 1962
Career: Inverness Clachnaccuddin, CHELSEA (professional, November 1983), Huddersfield Town (£10,000, March 1986), Swindon Town (£250,000, June 1988), Blackburn Rovers (March–May 1992), Aberdeen (July 1992), Inverness Caledonian Thistle (August 1987–September 1999)

Flame-haired Duncan Shearer was one of the most prolific goal-scorers in League football during the five-year period from 1986 to 1991. A fine taker of chances, he lacked skill no doubt, but his work rate was second to none and his appetite for goals first-class. After failing to get a look-in with Chelsea, owing to the presence of Kerry Dixon and fellow Scot David Speedie, he quickly made up for lost ground at Huddersfield for whom he struck 48 goals in 96 competitive games before following up with a further 98 goals in 199 outings for Swindon.

SHEERIN, JOSEPH EARNAN
Striker: 0+1 app.
Born: Hammersmith, London, 1 February 1979
Career: CHELSEA (trainee, May 1996; professional, July 1997), Bournemouth (February 2000; released, October 2000)
Big and strong, Joe Sheerin was rather similar in size to 1950s star Bobby Smith, but after doing well as a junior, he failed to impress at a higher level and made just one substitute appearance for Chelsea against Wimbledon in a Premiership game in April 1997.

SHELLITO, KENNETH JOHN
Full-back: 123 apps, 2 goals
Born: East Ham, London, 18 April 1940
Career: Sutton School (Hornchurch), Hornchurch, London and Essex Schools, CHELSEA (amateur, May 1955; professional, April 1957; retired, injured, January 1969; appointed youth-team coach, June 1969; youth-team manager, December 1969; then manager July 1977–December 1978), Queens Park Rangers (assistant manager, May 1979–May 1980), Crystal Palace (coach, season 1980–81), Preston North End (assistant manager, July–December 1981), Crystal Palace (assistant manager, June 1982–November 1983), Wolverhampton Wanderers (coach, January–March 1985), Cambridge United (manager, March–December 1985), later Tonbridge Rangers (general manager, seasons 1990–92)
Ken Shellito served Chelsea as a player for 14 years. He was an aggressive yet accomplished full-back whose career was unfortunately dogged by injury and in the end was forced to retire at the early age of 28. An FA Youth Cup winner with the Blues in 1958, he made his League debut in April 1959 against FA Cup finalists Nottingham Forest in April 1959 and played his last match against SK Wiener Austria in the Inter-Cities Fairs Cup in December 1965. In between times he helped Chelsea win promotion from the Second Division in 1963, the same year he gained his only full England cap v. Czechoslovakia, having earlier represented his country at Under-23 level. He was in fine form in 1965–66 and had already been pencilled in by Alf Ramsey as a World Cup candidate before injury struck. Shellito remained at Stamford Bridge until 1978 (thus completing 23 years' service). As manager, he saw the team struggle at the wrong end of the First Division and as a result handed in his resignation. He also had a tough time as boss at Cambridge but was certainly very successful as a coach.

SHERBORNE, JOHN

Forward: 5 apps

Born: Bolton, 1 May 1916 – Deceased by 1998

Career: Chorley (August 1932), CHELSEA (professional, February 1936; retired May 1944)

Basically a reserve at Stamford Bridge, Jack Sherborne managed only 10 first-team outings for Chelsea including 5 in Regional games (3 goals) before serving in the Army in France (from 1940). He sadly received war wounds that effectively ended his playing days.

SHERWOOD, STEPHEN

Goalkeeper: 17 apps

Born: Selby, Yorkshire, 10 December 1953

Career: West Riding Schools, CHELSEA (apprentice, April 1970; professional, July 1971), Millwall (loan, October 1973), Brentford (loan, January–April 1974 and again, August 1974–May 1975), Fulham (loan, October 1976), Watford (£5,000, November 1976), Grimsby Town (July 1987), Northampton Town (August 1993), Grimsby Town (non-contract, August 1994), Lincoln City (non-contract, March–May 1995), Immingham Town (season 1995–96), Gateshead (1996–97), later Grimsby Town (youth development officer)

Standing 6 ft 4 in. tall and weighing 14 st. 7 lb in his prime, Steve Sherwood was a very capable goalkeeper whose professional career realised 586 senior appearances of which 263 were made with Watford. He gained an FA Cup runner's-up medal in 1984 when the Hornets lost 2–0 to Everton, having helped Graham Taylor's side win the Fourth Division title in 1978 and climb into the top flight in double-quick time. The son of a former Huddersfield Town keeper and brother of the Olympic hurdler John Sherwood, he started the 1975–76 as Chelsea's number one but when Peter Bonetti returned to the club he soon departed. Sherwood joined Fulham on loan 28 October 1976 and signed for Watford three days later.

SHIPPERLEY, NEIL JASON

Striker: 35+13 apps, 9 goals

Born: Chatham, Kent, 30 October 1974

Career: CHELSEA (apprentice, April 1991; professional, September 1992), Watford (loan, December 1994–January 1995), Southampton (£1.25 million, January 1995), Crystal Palace (£1 million, October 1996), Nottingham Forest (£1.5 million, September 1998), Barnsley (£700,000, July 1999), Wimbledon (£750,000, July 2001), Crystal Palace (£100,000, July 2003)

A striker from a footballing family, Neil Shipperley has a terrific engine and an eye for goal. He had to work hard to get first-team action at Stamford Bridge but when called into the side he certainly did himself proud with some enterprising displays. Capped 7 times by England at Under-21 level, he

218

travelled the country after leaving Stamford Bridge and had decent enough spells with Southampton (18 goals in 82 games), Barnsley (31 in 88), Wimbledon (36 in 95) and Palace (32 in 125). He helped Palace reach the Premiership in 2004.

SILLETT, JOHN CHARLES
Full-back: 102 apps, 1 goal
Born: Southampton, 20 July 1936
Career: Hampshire Schools, Southampton (amateur, July 1951), CHELSEA (amateur, May 1953; professional, April 1954), Coventry City (April 1962), Plymouth Argyle (July 1966), Bristol City (coach, June 1968), Hereford United (manager, July 1974–January 1978), Coventry City (three spells as coach, August 1983, 1984 and 1985; then manager, May 1987–November 1990), Hereford United (manager, May 1991–May 1992); Portsmouth (chief scout, 1992–95); then worked on Central TV (Birmingham)

Signed with his brother Peter (below), John Sillett was a strong, tenacious full-back who gave nothing away and cleared his lines with precise timing. He made his League debut for Chelsea in January 1957 against Manchester United at Old Trafford in front of 42,000 fans and gained a regular place in the side in 1958–59. A Football League representative (v. the League of Ireland in 1960), he moved to Coventry after losing his place to Ken Shellito. He and his brother appeared as full-back partners in the Blues' defence more than 80 times, having excellent spells together in seasons 1958–59 and 1959–60. He went on to appear in 109 League games for Coventry (helping them win the Third Division title in 1964) and 38 for Plymouth and as manager guided Hereford to the Fourth Division championship in 1976. Then, in 1987, after returning to Highfield Road, in company with George Curtis, he celebrated in style when the Sky Blues won the FA Cup for the first time in the club's history. In 1955, Sillett received his official call-up papers for National Service – unfortunately they came far too late, as he had already been serving in the Army for 10 months.

SILLETT, RICHARD PETER TUDOR
Full-back: 288 apps, 34 goals
Born: Southampton, 1 February 1933 – *Died*: Ashford, Kent, 14 March 1998
Career: Hampshire County Youths, Southampton (amateur, April 1948; professional, February 1950), CHELSEA (£12,000, May 1953), Guildford City (free transfer, June 1962), Ashford United (player–manager, July 1965–December 1973), Folkestone (manager, August 1974–April 1975), Ashford United (manager, January–February 1976), Hereford United (scout, seasons 1976–78), Hastings United (manager, August 1978–June 1983), Coventry City (scout, August 1983–March 1985), Ashford United (manager, April 1985–May 1987), Poole Town (appointed manager, June 1987, but unable to take up position owing to poor health), Hastings Town (manager,

seasons 1987–91); thereafter confined to his Ashford home with an arthritic knee which prevented him from working

Peter Sillett's total of 34 goals is a record for a Chelsea full-back (most of them coming from the penalty spot). Although lacking in pace, he was sound and reliable, strong in the tackle and totally committed. Much sturdier than his younger brother, he was a member of the Blues' First Division championship-winning side of 1954–55 when he played in 21 games, sharing the right-back position with John Harris. Indeed, it was his late spot-kick in front of 75,000 fans that decided the crucial end-of-season encounter against Wolves at Stamford Bridge that virtually clinched the title for Ted Drake's side. Recognised by England on three occasions at senior level (his first call-up coming against France in 1955), Sillett also gained two youth caps (pre-Chelsea days), one at 'B' team level (1956), three for the Under-23 side and played for the Football League v. the Scottish League in 1957. He was engaged as a scout at both Hereford and Coventry when his brother was manager of those two clubs. The Sillett brothers were sons of the former Southampton full-back of the 1930s, Charlie Sillett, who made 183 appearances for Saints.

SIMNER, JOSEPH
Centre-forward: 1 app.
Born: Sedgley, near Wolverhampton, 13 March 1923
Career: Penn Old Boys/Wolverhampton, Folkestone Town (August 1945), CHELSEA (professional, October 1947), Swindon Town (July 1949–May 1952)

Reserve to Roy Bentley and Hugh Billington during his two seasons at Stamford Bridge, Joe Simner's only League outing for the club was against Middlesbrough (away) in March 1948. He scored 12 goals in 30 League games for Swindon.

SINCLAIR, FRANK MOHAMMED
Defender: 211+7 apps, 13 goals
Born: Lambeth, London, 3 December 1971
Career: CHELSEA (apprentice, April 1988; professional, May 1990), West Bromwich Albion (loan, December 1991–January 1992), Leicester City (£2 million, August 1998), Burnley (free transfer, June 2004)

A right-footed wing-back or central defender with a competitive nature to his game, Frank Sinclair gave Chelsea excellent service for a decade before transferring to Leicester City in 1998. A Jamaican international, capped over 25 times, he made his League debut as a 19 year old against Luton Town in April 1991. Then, before he reluctantly left Stamford Bridge, he gained both FA Cup and League Cup winner's medals, in 1997 and 1998 respectively, and added a second League Cup winning prize to his collection with Leicester in 2000. He's now accumulated almost 450 senior appearances during his professional career. Sinclair was sent off playing for WBA at Exeter in December 1991, for pushing the referee.

SINCLAIR, WILLIAM INGLIS

Midfield: 1 app.

Born: Glasgow, 21 March 1947

Career: Greenock Morton, CHELSEA (in part-exchange for Jim Mulholland, September 1964; released March 1966), Glentoran (August 1966–May 1968)

Billy Sinclair spent two years playing junior and reserve-team football for Chelsea although he did tour Australia with the club in May–June 1965. His only League game for the Blues was in a 6–2 defeat at Burnley in April 1965.

SISSONS, JOHN LESLIE

Winger: 12+1 apps

Born: Hayes, Middlesex, 30 September 1945

Career: Middlesex Schools, West Ham United (apprentice, September 1960; professional, October 1962), Sheffield Wednesday (£60,000, August 1970), Norwich City (£30,000, December 1973), CHELSEA (£70,000, August 1974; contract cancelled May 1975), Cape Town City/South Africa (season 1975–76); later became a director of a motor and warranty company in Cape Town, South Africa

Johnny Sissons, an England schoolboy and youth international who was later capped 10 times at Under-23 level, scored as an 18 year old for West Ham in their 1964 FA Cup final triumph over Preston North End. A year later he gained a European Cup-Winners' Cup medal and collected a runner's-up prize in the League Cup final of 1966. At his peak, the 'baby-faced' winger was fast and tricky, but was well past his best when he joined Chelsea, having already amassed more than 340 League games for his 3 previous clubs. He failed to make much of an impact in a struggling side and left Stamford Bridge after 7 months.

SITTON, JOHN EDMUND

Central defender: 12+2 apps

Born: Hackney, London, 21 October 1959

Career: CHELSEA (apprentice, May 1976; professional, October 1977), Millwall (£2,000, February 1980), Gillingham (£10,000, September 1981), Leyton Orient (July 1985; then coach, May 1991–April 1995); later coached abroad

A reserve at Stamford Bridge, John Sitton had a decent run in a struggling Chelsea side towards the end of the 1978–79 season but after that did not figure in manager Geoff Hurst's plans and subsequently found a new club (Millwall). He played in 45 League games for the Lions and followed up with 107 for the Gills and 170 for Orient whom he helped gain promotion to the Third Division in 1989.

SMALE, DOUGLAS MARCUS
Outside-left: 9 apps
Born: Victoria, London, 27 February 1916 – *Died*: London, *circa* 1988
Career: Kingstonian (amateur, 1934), CHELSEA (professional, March 1937; retired, injured, May 1945); served with the RAF in India during WW2
A fringe player at Stamford Bridge before the outbreak of WW2, Doug Smale's League debut was in the London derby against Charlton Athletic at The Valley in March 1937 when almost 46,000 fans saw the home side win 1–0.

SMART, JAMES
Inside-forward: 1 app.
Born: Dundee, 9 January 1947
Career: Greenock Morton (professional, January 1964), CHELSEA (January 1965; contract cancelled, March 1966), Highlands Park FC/South Africa (seasons 1966–68)
Jimmy Smart made his only senior appearance for Chelsea in a demoralising 6–2 defeat at Burnley in April 1965. However, with so many other promising youngsters at the club, he was allowed to move on to pastures new after spending just 14 months at the Bridge.

SMERTIN, ALEXEI
Midfield: 19+6 apps, 1 goal
Born: Barnaul, USSR, 1 May 1975
Career: Dynamo Barnaul/Russia (professional, June 1992), FC Zarya/Russia (April 1994), Uralan/Russia (August 1997), Lokomotiv Moscow/Russia (February 1999), Bordeaux/France (August 2000), CHELSEA (£3.45 million, August 2003), Portsmouth (loan, August 2003–May 2004), Charlton Athletic (loan, season 2005–06)
As soon as Russian international midfielder Alexei Smertin arrived at Stamford Bridge he was immediately shipped out for a season-long loan spell with newly promoted Portsmouth, whom he helped establish themselves in the Premiership. An experienced campaigner with well over 40 senior caps to his credit, he certainly excites the crowd with his darting forward runs as well as packing a strong right-foot shot when he chooses to deliver. Very much a part of new boss José Mourinho's plans during the first third of the 2004–05 campaign, earlier in his career Smertin appeared in 42 League games for his home-town club Barnaul, 133 for Zarya (13 goals), 49 for Uralan, 39 for Lokomotiv Moscow and 84 for Bordeaux. He gained a Premiership winner's medal with Chelsea in 2005.

SMETHURST, DEREK
Striker: 18+1 apps, 5 goals
Born: Durban, South Africa, 24 October 1947
Career: Durban University, CHELSEA (as a permit player, December 1968;

professional, January 1971), Millwall (£35,000, September 1971–May 1975); later moved to Florida as a football coach (1980s)

A very useful performer and certainly an adequate deputy for both Peter Osgood and Ian Hutchinson during his three years at Stamford Bridge, Derek Smethurst joined Chelsea as a 21 year old on leaving university. He played his part in helping the Blues reach the final of the European Cup-Winners' Cup in 1971, and celebrated with a winner's medal. He scored 13 goals in 80 games for the Lions. A born-again Christian after experiencing a vision whilst watching TV in San Diego in 1978, he named his daughter Chelsea. His elder brother, Peter, played for Blackpool in 1960.

SMITH, ARTHUR JOHN

Left-back: 49 apps

Born: Aberaman, South Wales, 27 October 1911 – *Died*: Weymouth, 7 June 1975

Career: Aberaman (October 1926), Aberdare Athletic (January 1927), West Bromwich Albion (trialist, season 1927–28), Merthyr Town (April 1928), Wolverhampton Wanderers (May 1930), Bristol Rovers (August 1934), Swindon Town (May 1935), CHELSEA (£4,000, March 1938; retired March 1945); guest for West Bromwich Albion in WW2; Wolverhampton Wanderers (trainer, August 1945), West Bromwich Albion (manager, June 1948–April 1952), Reading (manager, June 1952–October 1955); later ran a pub and then a hotel in Weymouth until his death at the age of 63

A capable, wholehearted footballer, a crisp tackler and excellent passer of the ball, Jack Smith made 30 League appearances for Wolves, 4 for Bristol Rovers and 114 for Swindon before joining Chelsea. He had an excellent 1938–39 season with the Blues before his career was interrupted by the war in which he served as a flight-sergeant in the RAF. Sadly, a serious car accident in 1945 ended his playing career. Capped by Wales v. England in a WW2 international in 1940, he became West Brom's first full-time manager and guided them to promotion from Division Two in 1948–49.

SMITH, GEORGE WALTER

Full-back: 370 apps

Born: Parkhead, Glasgow, 1900 – *Died*: Glasgow, 1979

Career: Parkhead FC (1917), CHELSEA (£10, July 1921), East Fife (August 1932; retired, injured, May 1933)

A regular at full-back for Chelsea for 9 seasons (1921–30) missing only 39 League games out of a possible 378, George Smith is one of the best buys the club ever made! A forceful defender with a biting tackle, he was vigorous throughout and proved to be a terrific servant at Stamford Bridge. He made his senior debut against Blackburn Rovers at Ewood Park in August 1921 – a month after arriving from Glasgow – and played his last game just over ten years later against Sheffield Wednesday at Hillsborough in September 1931. In between times he performed superbly well alongside fellow full-backs Jack Harrow and Tommy Law and wherever he went was a huge favourite with the fans.

SMITH, JAMES HAROLD
Winger: 23 apps, 3 goals
Born: Sheffield, 6 December 1930
Career: Shildon FC, CHELSEA (professional, April 1951), Leyton Orient (May 1955; retired, injured, May 1958)

Gritty Yorkshireman Jimmy Smith was another wholehearted footballer, nippy, courageous and gutsy, his positional sense second to none. However, he never quite fulfilled his early promise and had to fight for a place in the first team at Stamford Bridge owing to the form of Frank Blunstone and Eric Parsons. He made 39 appearances for Orient before retiring.

SMITH, PHILIP
Centre-forward: 1 app.
Born: Stoke-on-Trent, *circa* 1885 – Deceased by 1975
Career: Knutton, Burslem Port Vale (August 1905), Crewe Alexandra (August 1906), CHELSEA (£250, April 1910), Burnley (September 1910–April 1911)

One of several players recruited by Chelsea towards the end of the 1909–10 season in a bid to stave off relegation. He wasn't a good signing and left Stamford Bridge after just five months. His only League outing was in the 1–0 defeat at Bristol City a week after joining. Earlier he had scored 8 goals in 26 League and Cup games for Port Vale.

SMITH, ROBERT ALFRED
Centre-forward: 86 apps, 30 goals
Born: Lingdale, near Middlesbrough, 22 February 1933
Career: Lingdale Council School, Redcar Boys' Club, Redcar United, Tudor Rose (Chelsea's nursery club, on schoolboy forms, May 1947), CHELSEA (amateur, February 1948; professional, May 1950), Tottenham Hotspur (£18,000, December 1955), Brighton and Hove Albion (£5,000, May 1964), Hastings United (October 1965), Leyton Orient (trial, March 1967), Banbury United (June 1968; retired May 1969); became a painter and decorator before a knee injury, legacy from his playing days, forced him to take early retirement; he now uses crutches

Bobby Smith developed into a bold, brave, shoulder-charging, typically 'old-fashioned' English centre-forward who scored over 250 goals at club level in a career that spanned 22 years. He was signed by Chelsea boss Billy Birrell as a 15 year old after netting goals galore playing junior football in Redcar and he continued in the same vein with the Blues, initially in the junior side, then intermediates, through the reserves and into the first team. After making his

League debut as a 17 year old in a 1–0 defeat at Bolton in September 1950, the following season proved to be his best for the Blues as he notched 16 goals in 39 games. Thereafter he spent quite a long time acting as a reserve, mainly to Roy Bentley, before his surprise transfer to relegation-threatened Spurs, Bill Nicholson signing him to replace Eddie Baily. He scored the goals that kept the team up and went on to become a household name at the club.

Without doubt, he did wonders at White Hart Lane, bagging 208 goals (including 6 hat-tricks and 5 fourtimers) in 317 games in the space of 9 years. He netted in both the 1961 and 1962 FA Cup final wins and was Spurs' top marksman in their Double-winning season of 1960–61 with 33 goals. He also netted 13 times in 15 full internationals for England (including a goal in each of his first 5 outings, all won) as he formed a terrific striking partnership at club and international level with another former Chelsea star, Jimmy Greaves. After leaving White Hart Lane he scored twice on his debut for Brighton in front of the biggest Hove crowd for three years and in 1965 helped the Seagulls win the Fourth Division title. Smith's book – *My Memories of Spurs* – was published in December 2002.

SMITH, STEPHEN
Wing-half: 23 apps, 1 goal
Born: Byker, near Newcastle, 1898 – *Died*: *circa* 1965
Career: Boldon FC (1914), CHELSEA (August 1920), Merthyr Town (June 1922–May 1924)
Steve Smith spent the first season of his Chelsea career in the reserves before making his League debut against Birmingham (home) in August 1921. He had a decent run in the side between November and April that season but was confined to the second XI after Harry Wilding was switched to the right-half position. He made over 50 appearances for Merthyr.

SORRELL, DENNIS JAMES
Wing-half: 4 apps, 1 goal
Born: Lambeth, London, 7 October 1940
Career: Leyton Orient (amateur, March 1956; professional, October 1957), CHELSEA (£10,000, March 1962), Leyton Orient (£3,000, September 1964), Romford (August 1966)
Dennis Sorrell was a well-groomed, hard-tackling wing-half who made 119 senior appearances in his two spells with Orient but failed to make an impact at Stamford Bridge.

SPACKMAN, NIGEL JAMES
Midfielder: 176+3 apps, 14 goals
Born: Romsey, Hampshire, 2 December 1960
Career: Andover FC (1976), Bournemouth (professional, May 1980), CHELSEA (£40,000, June 1983), Liverpool (£400,000, February 1987),

Queens Park Rangers (£500,000, February 1989), Glasgow Rangers (£500,000, November 1990), CHELSEA (£485,000, September 1992); Sheffield United (July 1996 as assistant manager and player–coach; later caretaker-manager August 1997–March 1998; left club in the summer of 1998); later worked as soccer summariser on Sky Sports TV

Nigel Spackman entered League football in August 1980 when he made his debut for Bournemouth in a 4–0 defeat at York. Four years later as an ever-present he helped Chelsea win the Second Division title, following up with a Full Members' Cup triumph in 1986 and then collecting a League championship medal with Liverpool in 1988. With Rangers he gained three Premier Division and both Scottish League and Scottish Cup winner's medals. Besides his impressive record with Chelsea, he made 131 appearances for Bournemouth, 63 for Liverpool, 33 for QPR, 124 for Rangers and 27 for the Blades. He netted a total of 27 goals in 557 appearances of which 430 came in the Football League.

A powerful yet lively midfielder, strong in the tackle with enormous reserves of energy, he was forever driving forward to assist his front men and then minutes later was down the other end of the field helping out his defence. The joker in the pack, he was unlucky not to win representative honours. As caretaker-manager of Sheffield United, he was given little or no money to spend on new players and was knocked back when injuries ruled out key members of his team. He also had to sell five of his star players, including Brian Deane, Jan-Aage Fjortoft and Don Hutchison, to make ends meet, and this caused friction and uneasiness within the camp and with the fans.

SPARROW, JOHN PAUL

Full-back: 68+6 apps, 2 goals
Born: Bethnal Green, London, 3 June 1957
Career: CHELSEA (apprentice, June 1972; professional, June 1974), Millwall (loan, March–April 1979), Exeter City (£10,000, January 1981; retired, injured, May 1983)

Replacing Ron Harris at left-back, John Sparrow made his League debut for Chelsea as a 16 year old in March 1974 in a 3–0 home win over Burnley. That was the first of exactly 150 club appearances he made before injury forced him into early retirement. Rewarded with both schoolboy and youth caps by England, he never quite lived up to his teenage promise.

SPECTOR, MILES DAVID ROY

Outside-left: 6 apps
Born: Hendon, 4 August 1934
Career: Hendon Grammar School, Middlesex FA, Hendon (September 1949), CHELSEA (May 1952), Hendon (June 1953), Millwall (April 1956), Hendon (October 1956–April 1959)

An amateur throughout his career, Miles Spector had three separate spells with

Hendon and in between times played three League games for Chelsea and one for Millwall. An England international at both amateur and youth-team levels, he was quick, lively and direct but was not in a position to win a regular place in the Blues' first XI owing to the presence of Frank Blunstone and Jim Lewis.

SPEEDIE, DAVID ROBERT

Striker: 197+8 apps, 64 goals

Born: Glenrothes, Scotland, 20 February 1960

Career: Adwick School, Barnsley (apprentice August 1977; professional, October 1978), Darlington (£5,000, June 1980), CHELSEA (£70,000, June 1982), Coventry City (£780,000, July 1987), Liverpool (£675,000, February 1991), Blackburn Rovers (£450,000, August 1991), Southampton (£400,000, July 1992), Birmingham City (loan, October 1992), West Bromwich Albion (loan, January–February 1993), West Ham United (loan, March–May 1993), Leicester City (free transfer, July 1993; retired, injured, January 1995); later joined coaching staff at Filbert Street, made a brief comeback with Crook Town (1996); now a football agent

In 1984 and 1986 David Speedie won the Second Division championship and Full Members' Cup with Chelsea, scoring a hat-trick in a 5–4 win over Manchester City at Wembley in the final of the latter competition. He also helped Blackburn gain a place in the Premiership in 1992 and both West Bromwich Albion and Leicester City reach the play-offs in Division Two and One respectively in 1993 and 1994 (both teams were subsequently promoted). A Scottish international (capped once at Under-21 level and on ten occasions by the seniors) he was certainly one of the game's characters. Skilful, occasionally brilliant, he was aggressive, had smart reflexes and was superb with his head (for such a small man). However, his fiery temper often got him into trouble with referees. He certainly earned his wages at Stamford Bridge where he became a firm favourite with the Blues' supporters, forming a formidable partnership with fellow striker Kerry Dixon. In all, he scored 175 goals in 611 senior games over a period of 17 years that saw him serve with 11 different League clubs, producing his best performances, by far, with Chelsea, with Coventry a close second (35 goals in 145 outings). As a player he never admitted defeat.

SPENCE, RICHARD

Outside-right: 246 apps, 65 goals

Born: Platt's Common, Barnsley, Yorkshire, 18 July 1908 – *Died*: London, March 1983

Career: Platt's Common FC, Thorpe Colliery (Barnsley), Barnsley (professional, August 1925), CHELSEA (£5,000, October 1934; retired May 1950; on club coaching staff until 1955); continued to attend matches at Stamford Bridge until shortly before his demise at the age of 74

With a total of 19 goals to his credit in 1934–35, Dick Spence holds the Chelsea record for most strikes in a season by an extreme winger. A small, dashing player with a big heart, he could turn a defender inside out at times with his trickery and pace. An instant hit with the Stamford Bridge faithful, he relished playing in front of big crowds and gave the Blues 16 years' terrific service, although WW2 disrupted his game considerably. Nevertheless, when on leave from the Police Force and the Army, he managed a further 170 unofficial first-team appearances during the hostilities, scoring an extra 50 goals. Add those figures to his peacetime statistics and his overall record for the club was splendid – 416 appearances and 115 goals. An England international, called against Austria and Belgium in 1936, he won the Third Division (N) championship with Barnsley two years earlier – his only club honour. At the age of 39 years and 57 days, Spence is the oldest player ever to appear in a first-class match for Chelsea, lining up for his last game in a blue shirt against Bolton Wanderers on 13 September 1947 (Division One).

SPENCER, JOHN

Striker: 100+37 apps, 43 goals
Born: Glasgow, 11 September 1970
Career: Glasgow Rangers (apprentice, June 1986; professional, September 1987), Morton (loan, March–April 1989), CHELSEA (£450,000, August 1992), Queens Park Rangers (£2.5 million, November 1996), Everton (loan, March–April 1998; signed for £1.5 million, May 1998), Motherwell (loan, October-December 1998; signed permanently, January 1999)

John Spencer is listed as having scored the fastest-ever goal by a Chelsea player – in 6.7 seconds from the start of a Premiership game against Leicester City in October 1994. A snip of a signing from Rangers, he was a totally committed player with a big heart, skilful, quick-thinking and decisive, especially in and around the penalty area. He made his debut for the Blues against Norwich City soon after arriving at Stamford Bridge and played his last game for the club as a second-half substitute against Wimbledon in October 1996. Scorer of the first-ever hat-trick of his career for QPR against Premiership-bound Barnsley in January 1997, he left Loftus Road for Motherwell after it was known he wouldn't be figuring in manager Gerry Francis' plans. A Scottish international at both schoolboy and youth-team levels, he went on to win 3 Under-21 and 14 senior caps.

SPOTTISWOOD, JOSEPH DOMINIC

Outside-left: 1 app.
Born: Carlisle, July 1894 – *Died*: London, *circa* 1970
Career: Carlisle United (professional, 1912), Manchester City (September 1913), Bury (March 1914), CHELSEA (August 1919), Swansea Town (January 1920), Queens Park Rangers (August 1925–April 1926)

Joe Spottiswood was unable to make headway at Stamford Bridge and left inside five months, having played in one League game, away at Manchester

United shortly before his transfer. He did very well with Swansea, scoring 10 goals in more than 160 appearances. His brother, Bob, also played for Carlisle and QPR as well as Crystal Palace, Clapton Orient and Aberdare.

STANIC, MARIO
Midfield: 54+26 apps, 10 goals
Born: Sarajevo, Yugoslavia, 10 April 1972
Career: Zeljeznicar Sarajevo/Yugoslavia (amateur, August 1988; professional, May 1989), Croatia Zagreb/Yugoslavia (July 1992), Sporting Gijon/Spain (August 1993), Benfica/Portugal (May 1994), FC Brugge/Belgium (August 1995), Parma/Italy (December 1996), CHELSEA (£5.6 million, July 2000; retired May 2004)

In a varied career Mario Stanic played League football in 6 countries for 7 different clubs over a period of 16 years. He made his debut for Zeljeznicar as a 16 year old in 1988 and scored 12 goals in 77 games before transferring to Croatia Zagreb for whom he netted 11 times in 26 outings. He then spent a season with Gijon (7 goals in 34 starts), had just over 16 months with FC Brugge (27 goals in 37 appearances) and played three and a half seasons with Parma (19 goals in 79 Serie 'A' matches) before joining Chelsea.

Unfortunately he suffered with injury problems at Stamford Bridge but always managed to give 100 per cent when called into action. A Charity Shield winner in 2000, he won a total of 49 caps for his country before quitting competitive soccer at the age of 32.

STANLEY, GARY ERNEST
Midfield: 115+5 apps, 15 goals
Born: Burton upon Trent, 4 March 1954
Career: Derbyshire Schools football, CHELSEA (apprentice, April 1970; professional, March 1971), Fort Lauderdale Strikers/NASL (loan, May–July 1979), Everton (£300,000, August 1979), Swansea City (£150,000, October 1981), Portsmouth (free transfer, January 1984), Wichita Wings/USA (June 1986), Bristol City (August–October 1988); later employed by Nynex Communications

An attacking midfielder, recommended to Chelsea by ex-player Frank Upton, Gary Stanley helped the Blues gain promotion from the Second Division in 1976–77 when he perhaps had his best season at Stamford Bridge, appearing in 38 competitive matches overall. He moved on to ease the financial situation at the club, joining Everton after a brief spell in the NASL. He always manned midfield efficiently, battling hard in whatever division he played. He quit competitive football in 1988 with more than 300 appearances under his belt (plus his games in the USA).

STARK, JAMES

Centre-half: 32 apps, 2 goals

Born: Ruchazie, Glasgow, 1880 – *Died*: Scotland, 1949

Career: Mansewood FC, Pollokshaws Eastwood, Glasgow Perthshire, Glasgow Rangers, CHELSEA (May 1907), Glasgow Rangers (October 1908), Greenock Morton (£250 plus John May, July 1910–April 1915); did not play after WW1

Capped twice by Scotland (v. England and Ireland in 1909), Jimmy Stark also represented the Scottish League on two occasions, was twice a League championship winner with Rangers (1901 and 1902), won the Scottish Cup in 1903 and gained runner's-up medals in the Cup in 1904, 1905 and 1909. A defender who made the game look easy, so economical was his style, Stark possessed fine positional sense and was a superb strategist who read the game superbly. He spent just over a season at Stamford Bridge, making his Chelsea debut in place of Bob McRoberts against Blackburn Rovers at Ewood Park in October 1907. He scored 14 goals in 203 senior games for Rangers.

STEER, WILLIAM HENRY OSCAR

Centre-forward: 4 apps, 1 goal

Born: Kingston-upon-Thames, October 1888 – *Died*: London, 1955

Career: Old Kingstonians, Kingston Town (amateur, August 1905), Queens Park Rangers (amateur, July 1909), CHELSEA (amateur, July 1912), Newry County/Northern Ireland (April 1919–May 1921)

An England amateur international, Billy Steer failed to gain a regular place in Chelsea's side despite some enterprising performances for the second XI. He made his Blues' debut in a 0–0 draw at Notts County in December 1912 and scored his only goal for the club against Everton in March 1913. He scored 37 goals in 76 games for QPR. His brother, Harold, played for QPR in 1918.

STEFFEN, WILLI

Full-back: 20 apps

Born: Switzerland, 17 March 1925

Career: Swiss junior football; Grasshopper Club (briefly), CHELSEA (amateur, November 1946–April 1947); later with FC Basel/Switzerland and Servette/Switzerland

A former pilot in the Swiss Air Force and an international at both senior (seven caps won) and non-professional levels, full-back Bill Steffen remained an amateur throughout his playing career. He spent only five months at Stamford Bridge but in that time produced some outstanding performances. Standing a fraction over 6 ft tall and extremely well built with short-cropped hair, he possessed a strong tackle and was very popular at the club with players and supporters alike. Almost 28,000 fans saw his League debut against the FA Cup holders Derby County at the Baseball Ground in November 1946.

STEIN, EARL MARK SEAN

Striker: 57+6 apps, 25 goals

Born: Cape Town, South Africa, 29 January 1966

Career: Luton Town (apprentice, April 1982; professional, January 1984), Aldershot (loan, January 1986), Queens Park Rangers (£300,000, August 1988), Oxford United (September 1989), Stoke City (£100,000, September 1991), CHELSEA (£1.45 million, October 1993), Stoke City (loan, November 1996–January 1997), Ipswich Town (loan, August–September 1997), Bournemouth (loan, March–May 1998; signed June 1998), Luton Town (free transfer, July 2000; reserve-team player–coach, May 2001), Dagenham and Redbridge (July 2001)

Scorer of 197 goals (82 for Stoke City) in 568 League and Cup games in a first-class career covering almost 20 years, Mark Stein was a lively striker with a knack of being in the right spot at the right time. Capped by England at youth-team level as a teenager, he won the League Cup with QPR in 1988 and the Freight Rover Trophy and Second Division championship with Stoke in 1992 and 1993 respectively. After a fine first season at Stamford Bridge, niggling injuries began to interrupt his game. Two of his brothers, Brian (Luton Town and Barnet) and Edward (Barnet), were also professional footballers.

STEPNEY, ALEXANDER CYRIL

Goalkeeper: 1 app.

Born: Mitcham, Surrey, 18 September 1942

Career: Surrey Schools, London Schools, Achilles FC (Surrey), Fulham (trialist), Tooting and Mitcham (Isthmian League, 1958–62), Millwall (amateur; then professional, 1963), CHELSEA (£50,000, summer 1966), Manchester United (£55,000, September 1966), Dallas Tornado (February 1979), Altrincham (player–coach, season 1979–80), Dallas Tornado (five months in 1980), later Manchester City goalkeeping coach; also worked for Stockport County and Rochdale FC Commercial Departments and acted as northern-based scout for both Exeter City and Southampton while managing a car/van rental company in Rochdale where he also worked briefly as a publican

After making just one League appearance for Chelsea (against Southampton at The Dell in September 1966) goalkeeper Alex Stepney went on to appear in 545 senior matches for Manchester United, scoring two goals, both penalties, in home League games against Leicester City and Birmingham City in September and October 1973. Before moving to the Blues, Stepney helped Millwall win promotion from the Fourth and Third Divisions in successive seasons (1965 and 1966), gained three England Under-23 caps, played for Young England against England at Stamford Bridge and twice represented the Football League. After spending barely four months with Chelsea, Matt Busby signed him to replace Dave Gaskell and Harry Gregg at Old Trafford. At the end of his first season with the Reds, Stepney – who made his debut in the local derby v. Manchester

City in front of more than 62,000 fans – collected a League championship medal. In 1968 he was the recipient of a European Cup winner's medal and also gained his only full England cap in a 3–1 win over Sweden at Wembley. In 1974–75, he missed only two games as Manchester United won the Second Division title and then appeared in successive FA Cup finals, losing to Southampton in 1976 before collecting a winner's medal v. Liverpool a year later. An unspectacular keeper, but reliable and consistent, with exceptional positional sense, Stepney sometimes made a difficult job look easy!

STONE, GEORGE

Outside-left: 25 apps, 2 goals
Born: Hertford, 27 July 1894 – *Died*: Watford, February 1940
Career: Hemel Hempstead (August 1919), CHELSEA (September 1924; released May 1928), Watford (season 1928–29)
After having a useful first season with Chelsea when he made 22 appearances, left-winger George Stone was replaced by Bobby McNeil and after that was basically a reserve-team player at Stamford Bridge.

STRIDE, DAVID ROY

Full-back: 37 apps
Born: Lymington, Hampshire, 14 March 1958
Career: CHELSEA (apprentice, April 1974; professional, January 1976), Memphis Rogues/USA (£90,000, July 1980), Millwall (January 1983), Leyton Orient (July 1984–May 1985); returned to play in the USA
Initially a left-winger, David Stride was successfully converted into a full-back in 1977, a position he enjoyed for the rest of his career. Unfortunately a hairline fracture of the skull, suffered in 1979, disrupted his progress. After leaving Stamford Bridge he appeared in 63 games for Millwall and 34 for Orient.

STUART, GRAHAM

Midfielder/forward: 89+21 apps, 18 goals
Born: Tooting, London, 24 October 1970
Career: CHELSEA (apprentice, April 1987; professional, June 1989), Everton (£850,000, August 1993), Sheffield United (£850,000, November 1997), Charlton Athletic (£1.1m, March 1999), Norwich City (on loan, January–May 2005)
An attacking midfielder, who can also play as an out-and-out forward, Graham Stuart is hard working with a goal-scoring touch who made 110 appearances for Chelsea before moving to Goodison Park. He scored on his League debut for the Blues in a 3–0 home win over Crystal Palace in April 1990 and after that his value to the club was inestimable. He represented England at both youth and Under-21 levels, gaining five caps in the latter category. He went on to play in over 160 senior games for Everton, collecting an FA Cup winner's medal in 1995. His two goals on the last day of the 1993–94 season (in a 3–2 win over

Wimbledon) kept the Merseysiders in the Premiership. In 2000 he helped Charlton reach the top flight as Division One champions and has since taken his career appearance tally close to the 500 mark.

STUBBS, LESLIE LEVI
Inside-forward: 123 apps, 35 goals
Born: Great Wakering, near Southend-on-Sea, 18 February 1929
Career: Great Wakering FC (September 1945), Southend United, CHELSEA (£10,000, November 1952), Southend United (£12,000 plus Alan Dicks, November 1958–May 1959)
Although lacking in pace, Les Stubbs was a strong, hard-working inside-left who could use both feet. He scored 5 goals in 27 League games in 1954–55 when Chelsea won the First Division championship. He netted 43 goals in a total of 105 League games for Southend.

SULLIVAN, NEIL
Goalkeeper: 7+1 apps
Born: Sutton, Surrey, 24 February 1970
Career: Wimbledon (apprentice, June 1986; professional, July 1988), Crystal Palace (loan, May 1992), Tottenham Hotspur (free transfer, June 2000), CHELSEA (free, August 2003), Leeds United (free, August 2004)
Having slipped out of favour at White Hart Lane, Neil Sullivan made an unexpected return to senior football with Chelsea following a cruciate ligament injury to reserve-team keeper Jurgen Macho. The Scottish international, capped 27 times, had not tasted first-team football for 21 months before helping the Blues defeat Reading 1–0 in a 4th round League Cup tie in December 2003. He added a further seven appearances to his tally when replacing the injured Carlo Cudicini who then suffered a broken finger while Sullivan himself also got injured, allowing Marco Ambrosio to take over between the posts. Sullivan, who made 224 appearances for the Dons and 81 for Spurs, moved on when new manager José Mourinho brought in Petr Cech.

SUTTON, CHRISTOPHER ROY
Striker: 27+12 apps, 3 goals
Born: Nottingham, 10 March 1973
Career: Norwich City (apprentice, April 1989; professional, July 1991), Blackburn Rovers (£5 million, July 1994), CHELSEA (£10 million, July 1999), Celtic (£6 million, July 2000)
After losing the services, for various reasons, of three quality strikers, namely Pierluigi Casiraghi, Mark Hughes and Gianluca Vialli, Chelsea broke the club's transfer record by recruiting 6 ft 3 in. Chris Sutton from relegated Blackburn to fill the gap. He took time to settle in at Stamford Bridge, netting only once in his first 8 Premiership matches – and it was a beauty when it arrived, a great header in a 5–0 slaughter of Manchester United in October 1999 which ended

the Reds' 29-match unbeaten run. There followed a disappointing run of 28 Premiership games without a goal and the harder Sutton tried, the more he struggled with his overall game. With Jimmy-Floyd Hasselbaink and Eidur Gudjohnsen first-choice strikers, Sutton moved to Celtic for a record fee at the end of the season. He did wonderfully well at Parkhead, helping the Bhoys win three League championships, the League Cup once and the Scottish Cup three times, including the Treble in 2001. He also played in the losing 2003 European Cup-Winners' Cup final. Sutton scored 43 goals in 127 games for Norwich, 59 in 161 for Blackburn (whom he helped win the Premiership title in 1995) and has now netted over 70 times in more than 150 appearances for Celtic. Earlier in his career he won 13 Under-21, 1 full and 2 'B' caps for England.

SWAIN, KENNETH

Full-back/winger: 127+5 apps, 29 goals

Born: Birkenhead, Wirral, 28 January 1952

Career: Liverpool, Birkenhead and Merseyside District Schools, Kirkby Boys, Bolton Wanderers (schoolboy forms, 1967), Peckham Comprehensive and Streatham Schools, Shoreditch Teachers' Training College (Surrey), South East Counties Colleges, Wycombe Wanderers (amateur, April 1973), CHELSEA (professional, August 1973), West Bromwich Albion (loan, November 1978), Aston Villa (£100,000, December 1978), Nottingham Forest (October 1982), Portsmouth (July 1985), West Bromwich Albion (loan, February–March 1988), Crewe Alexandra (August 1988–May 1989; then player–coach; assistant manager), Wigan Athletic (manager, 1993–94), Grimsby Town (reserve team coach/assistant manager, 1995; then caretaker-manager, October 1996–May 1997); FA School of Excellence technical director and coach; scouted for several clubs including Nottingham Forest and Grimsby Town; Senior FA coach (2000–01); qualified in handicrafts and PE at college

Kenny Swain was originally a left-winger before being successfully converted into a right-back after he was transferred to Villa Park, mainly for financial reasons. Blessed with neat and tidy footwork, he had the ability to cross a ball accurately on the run and proved to be a very effective player despite not being one of the quickest. He went on to gain League championship, European Cup and Super Cup winner's medals with Villa (1981 and 1982) and helped Portsmouth win promotion from Division Two in 1987 and Crewe from Division Four two years later, amassing over 750 senior appearances during a fine career. As a youngster, he played in the same Kirkby Boys side as Dennis Mortimer who was his captain when he was with Aston Villa. Indeed, Swain deputised as skipper when Morty was absent.

TAMBLING, ROBERT

Forward: 366+4 apps, 202 goals
Born: Storrington, Sussex, 18 September 1941
Career: CHELSEA (amateur, July 1957; professional, September 1958), Crystal
   Palace (£40,000 deal that also included Alan Birchenall, valued at £100,000,
   January 1970), Cork Hibernians/Ireland (October 1973); later moved to
   Havant, Hampshire, where he became a sports shop owner; then worked as
   a hod carrier before being declared bankrupt in the County Court in
   Portsmouth in 1994; a Jehovah's Witness, he now lives in Ireland

One of only four players – the other three are George Hilsdon, Jimmy Greaves
and Gordon Durie – to have scored five goals in a League game for Chelsea,
Bobby Tambling had the pleasure of registering his nap-hand away from home,
in a 6–2 win over Aston Villa in September 1966. He also claimed four
fourtimers and is the only player (so far) to have netted over 200 goals for the
Blues. Between 22 September and 22 December 1962, Tambling actually scored
in 12 out of 14 games for Chelsea, obtaining 23 goals in total. Amazingly, he
then failed to score in the League again for three months. On his day he was,
without doubt, one of the finest marksmen in the land. He grabbed a goal on
his League debut in front of 52,000 fans v. West Ham as a 17 year old in
February 1959 and went on to figure in the scoring charts in his first 11
successive seasons at Stamford Bridge. When he moved to Selhurst Park in
1970, he was presented with an illuminated address to commemorate his
wonderful scoring record as a Chelsea player.

He represented his country seven times as a schoolboy, making his debut v.
Northern Ireland in 1956 and then playing six times in 1957 v. Wales (twice),
Eire, Scotland, West Germany and Northern Ireland. Tambling then went on to
gain 3 full caps (v. France and Wales in 1963 and v. Yugoslavia in 1966) and 13
at Under-23 level while also playing for the Football League v. the Scottish
League in 1969. He helped Chelsea win promotion to the First Division in
1963, collected a League Cup winner's tankard in 1965, scoring in the final v.
Leicester City, and obtained an FA Cup runner's-up medal two years later when
he also figured on the scoresheet v. Spurs. He notched 17 goals in 76 outings for
Palace.

TAYLOR, FREDERICK

Wing-half: 171 apps, 4 goals
Born: Rotherham, 1881 – *Died*: Rotherham, *circa* 1954
Career: Rotherham Town (1904), Gainsborough Trinity (1905), CHELSEA
   (September 1906), Gainsborough Trinity (April 1907), CHELSEA
   (December 1909), Brentford (July 1920), Maidstone United (March 1921),
   Rochdale (season 1921–22)

A well-built wing-half, quick over the ground, Fred Taylor had two spells at
Stamford Bridge – the first as a squad player (no first-team appearances). When
he returned he replaced Ben Warren, finally making his debut for the club on

Christmas Day 1909, away at Notts County. A key member of the Chelsea side for four seasons (1911–15), he made a handful of appearances during WW1 before moving across London to Griffin Park. During his career, Taylor, who also occupied the outside- and inside-right positions, amassed a total of 302 League appearances (15 goals). He represented the Football League v. the Southern League in 1909.

TENNANT, ALBERT ERIC

Full-back/wing-half/inside-forward: 8 apps
Born: Ilkeston, Derbyshire, 29 October 1917 – *Died*: Surrey, 1986
Career: Ilkeston Road County School, Stanton Iron Works, CHELSEA (professional, November 1934; retired May 1953; became coach at Stamford Bridge); Guildford City (manager, June 1959)

A versatile footballer, able to occupy a number of positions, Albert Tennant produced his best form as a tough-tackling wing-half. His career, like that of so many other players, was severely disrupted by WW2, although during the hostilities he appeared in 148 Regional games for the Blues. He remained a registered player at Stamford Bridge for 19 years and then served the club for another 6 as a coach before moving into management. Although he joined Chelsea in 1934, he had to wait until January 1946 before making his senior debut at left-back in a 3rd round FA Cup tie against Leicester City.

TERRY, JOHN GEORGE

Defender: 257+18 apps, 31 goals
Born: Barking, Essex, 7 December 1980
Career: West Ham United (schoolboy forms), CHELSEA (apprentice, April 1997; professional, March 1998), Nottingham Forest (loan, March–April 2000)

A lion-hearted defender, strong in the air and on the ground, and very dangerous at set-pieces when venturing forward into the opposing penalty area, John Terry is now regarded as one of the best centre-backs in world football. He had a marvellous 2004–05 season with Chelsea, appearing in 36 Premiership matches as the League championship arrived at Stamford Bridge for only the second time in the club's history as well as winning the PFA's Player of the Year award, the first Chelsea player to do so. Known as 'JT', he has formed very effective partnerships in the Blues' back division with both William Gallas and the Portuguese international Ricardo Carvalho and prior to that played very well alongside Marcel Desailly and others. A regular member of the England side, Terry has now gained over a dozen full caps, having earlier won nine at Under-21 level. He was also an FA Cup winner with the Blues in 2000. Terry's brother, Paul, an ex-Charlton Athletic trainee, now plays for Yeovil Town.

THAIN, ALBERT EDWARD

Inside-forward: 153 apps, 50 goals

Born: Southall, Middlesex, 20 April 1900 – *Died*: 1979

Career: Metropolitan Railway Works FC, Southall (amateur, August 1919), CHELSEA (professional, April 1922), Bournemouth and Boscombe Athletic (June 1931; retired May 1932)

A long-striding inside-forward, clever on the ball, Albert Thain – signed to replace Jack Cock – was a useful scorer throughout his career, having his best spell with Chelsea in the mid-1920s when he netted 45 times in three seasons. Earlier he had scored over 40 goals for Southall. He suffered with tedious injuries early in his career and also later on and he was only 32 years of age when he retired. A very keen railway enthusiast, Thain chose to join Chelsea . . . because he could hear the sound of the underground trains passing by Stamford Bridge!

THOMAS, MICHAEL REGINALD

Midfield: 53+1 apps, 11 goals

Born: Mochdre, Powys, 7 July 1954

Career: Mochdre and Newtown Schools, Welshpool District Boys, Pentre Youth Club, Wrexham (amateur, July 1969; apprentice, July 1970; professional, April 1972), Manchester United (£300,000, November 1978), Everton (£450,000, player-exchange deal involving John Gidman, August 1981), Brighton and Hove Albion (£400,000, November 1981), Stoke City (£200,000, August 1982), CHELSEA (£75,000, January 1984), West Bromwich Albion (£100,000, September 1985), Derby County (loan, March–May 1986), Wichita Wings /NASL indoor League (£35,000, August 1986), Shrewsbury Town (August 1988), Leeds United (£10,000, June 1989), Stoke City (loan, March 1990; signed permanently, free transfer, August 1990), Wrexham (July 1991–May 1993), Conwy United (December 1994), Inter Cardiff (August 1995), Portmadoc (caretaker-manager/coach, January 1995); Inter Cardiff (briefly, August–September 1996); later manager of a soccer coaching school near Wrexham (1997–2000); also worked as a soccer summariser for Century Radio/Manchester; Rhyl (director of football, 2000–02); after leaving Wrexham in 1993, he served an 18-month jail sentence for handling counterfeit money

Mickey Thomas was a hard-working, industrious midfield dynamo who had been in League football for 13 years when he joined Chelsea, having made his debut for Wrexham in January 1972. He arrived at Stamford Bridge with over 450 senior appearances under his belt; had played on 80 different League grounds, visited 15 countries and cost more than £1.5 million in transfer deals. A Welsh international at three levels – Under-21 (2 caps), Under-23 (1 cap) and full (51 caps) – he actually gained honours with each of 7 different clubs: Wrexham, Manchester United, Everton, Brighton, Stoke, Chelsea and WBA. A member of Manchester United's FA Cup final side of 1979, he collected a First

Division runner's-up medal in 1980, having earlier won three Welsh Cup winner's medals with Wrexham (1972, 1975, 1978). He also helped the Robins win the Third Division championship (1978) and was superb in midfield when Chelsea gained promotion to the First Division in 1984. Two years later, in 1985–86, he helped Derby clinch promotion to the Second Division. He left West Brom after Baggies' manager Ron Saunders had decreed that he should live nearer to The Hawthorns than he did. Thomas refused and was subsequently placed on the transfer list.

THOME, EMERSON AUGUSTO

Defender: 20+2 apps
Born: Porto Alegre, Brazil, 30 March 1972
Career: Brazilian football, Benfica/Portugal (1994), Sheffield Wednesday (free transfer, March 1998), CHELSEA (£2.7 million, December 1999), Sunderland (£4.5 million, September 2000), Bolton Wanderers (free, August 2003; released May 2004), Wigan Athletic (June 2004)

Emerson Thome, a tall, well-built, physically strong, central defender, made 71 appearances for Sheffield Wednesday before his 10-month visit to Stamford Bridge where he had a constant battle against injury, resulting in him spending more time on the treatment table than he did on the pitch. He went on to appear in 53 games for Sunderland and 32 for Bolton.

THOMPSON, JAMES WILLIAM

Utility forward: 42 apps, 34 goals
Born: West Ham, London, 19 April 1898 – *Died*: Epsom, Surrey, August 1984
Career: Custom House (pre-WW1), Charlton Athletic (amateur, August 1919), Wimbledon (amateur, October 1921), Millwall (professional, December 1921), Coventry City (June 1923), Clapton Orient (August 1924), Luton Town (July 1925), CHELSEA (May 1927), Norwich City (May 1929), Sunderland (May 1930), Fulham (October 1930), Hull City (October 1931), Tunbridge Wells Rangers (January 1932); Dartford (manager, July 1939), CHELSEA (scout, 1940s–1957), Southampton (scout, late 1950s–early '60s)

Initially a left-winger, Jimmy Thompson was converted into a goal-scoring centre-forward at Stamford Bridge – and what a transformation it turned out to be! He struck 25 goals in only 30 games in his first season for the Blues before being dropped at the start of his second campaign in favour of Sid Elliott who had been signed from neighbours Fulham. He played only 12 games in 1928–29 yet still managed a further 9 goals before leaving to join Norwich City. Earlier in his career Thompson – a real character who insisted on being allowed to leave any club he joined on a free transfer – scored five goals on his debut for Wimbledon (October 1921). He played in only 150 League and FA Cup matches yet scored 97 goals, wearing only one pair of battered boots which had been stitched, sewn, taped and re-soled half a dozen times. It was Thompson who first spotted a young Jimmy Greaves playing Essex junior football in 1954.

THOMSON, CHARLES RICHARD
Goalkeeper: 59 apps
Born: Perth, Scotland, 2 March 1930
Career: Blairgowrie FC (1947), Clyde (professional, April 1949), CHELSEA (October 1952), Nottingham Forest (August 1957)
'Chick' Thomson was a safe and steady goalkeeper rather then being a spectacular one. Along with Bill Robertson, he shared the number one duties at Stamford Bridge for 4 seasons, helping the Blues win the League title in 1955 (16 appearances). Thomson joined Nottingham Forest in 1957 and 2 years later gained an FA Cup winner's medal and went on to make 136 appearances for the East Midlands club. His father before him had been a goalkeeper in Scottish League football.

THOMSON, JAMES
Full-back/centre-half: 40+7 apps, 1 goal
Born: Provenside, Glasgow, 1 October 1946
Career: Provenside Hibernian, CHELSEA (January 1965), Burnley (£40,000, September 1968–May 1981), Morecambe (August 1981–May 1982); worked as a representative in the brewery trade; Burnley (commercial manager, 1986–87); then sales director with Ben Shaw's Soft Drinks Company in Huddersfield; and finally back into the brewery business
A very efficient and versatile defender who had his best season with Chelsea in 1966–67 when he made 29 of his 47 first-class appearances, helping the Blues reach the FA Cup final by playing in three rounds against Huddersfield, Brighton and Sheffield Wednesday. Unable to hold down a regular place in the side, he moved to Burnley for whom he appeared in 363 games prior to his retirement in 1981. He skippered the Clarets in the Anglo-Scottish Cup final triumph over Oldham Athletic in 1979, having been an ever-present in the club's Second Division championship-winning season of 1972–73.

THOMSON, ROBERT JOHN
Centre-forward: 95 apps, 29 goals
Born: Croydon, Surrey, 29 December 1890 – *Died*: Croydon, 9 January 1971
Career: Mitcham Road School (Croydon), Croydon Common (professional, August 1910), CHELSEA (£200, September 1911), Charlton Athletic (£300, February 1922), Dartford (free transfer, August 1925; retired May 1927); thereafter worked as a local government clerical officer
Bob Thomson, who lost his left eye in a firework accident when only seven years of age, was once asked what did he do when the ball came to him on his blind side? He replied: 'I closed my eye and relied on memory.' A really aggressive, all-action centre-forward, he scored seven goals for Croydon Common in a 14–0 win over Chesham Town in 1910 and seven for Chelsea against Luton Town in a London Combination match in 1916. In between times he managed, on average, a goal every three games, including six in eight games leading up to the

1915 FA Cup final with Sheffield United when deputising for the great Vivian Woodward, who had been serving in the forces. But when Woodward was given leave to play against the Blades in the final, he turned down the opportunity, saying that Thomson had earned the right to appear in the final which Chelsea lost 3–0. Thomson, who netted 85 goals in 110 outings for the Blues during WW1, went on to secure 17 goals in 82 games for Charlton.

TIAGO, CARDOSA MENDES

Midfield: 31+20 apps, 4 goals
Born: Viani do Casteli, Portugal, 2 May 1981
Career: SC Braga/Portugal (amateur, July 1997; professional, May 1998), Benfica/Portugal (August 2000), CHELSEA (£8 million, July 2004)

Signed by new manager José Mourinho to boost the choice of midfielders at Stamford Bridge for the 2004–05 season, Tiago certainly played his part in helping bring the Premiership trophy to the club. Performing alongside Frank Lampard, Claude Makelele, Geremi and Joe Cole (among others), he scored some vital goals and battled hard and long throughout every game. A member of Portugal's Euro 2004 squad, he made his senior debut for Chelsea in the 1–0 Premiership win at Birmingham in the second game of the season and netted his first goal for the Blues three days later in a 2–0 win at Crystal Palace.

TICKRIDGE, SIDNEY

Full-back: 73 apps
Born: Stepney, London, 10 April 1923 – *Died*: London, 6 January 1997
Career: Tottenham Juniors, Tottenham Hotspur (groundstaff, August 1937), Gravesend and Northfleet (August 1938), Tottenham Hotspur (amateur, July 1939; professional, April 1946); guest for Aldershot, Dartford, Fulham and Millwall during WW2 when free from service in the Royal Navy; CHELSEA (March 1951), Brentford (July 1955; retired, injured, January 1957), Millwall (assistant trainer, 1957–60)

An England schoolboy international, Sid Tickridge was one of several players who came through the junior ranks at White Hart Lane to make a name for himself in League football. He played his first senior game in August 1941 and after appearing in more than 150 first-team games was transferred to Stamford Bridge, having been replaced by Alf Ramsey in the Spurs' line-up. He proved to be a splendid capture by Chelsea and in 1951–52 missed only one League game. Later his vast experience helped many of the younger players in the reserve team.

TINDALL, RONALD ALBERT ERNEST

Centre-forward/full-back: 174 apps, 70 goals
Born: Streatham, London, 23 September 1935
Career: Camberley Wanderers, CHELSEA (juniors, April 1951; professional, April 1953), West Ham United (£12,000, exchange deal involving Andy

Malcolm, November 1961); Reading (October 1962), Portsmouth (September 1964; retired as a player, April 1969; coach/manager, April 1970–May 1973; then general manager to May 1974; caretaker-manager September 1974); also associated with Waterlooville FC; played cricket for Surrey (1956–66); emigrated to Australia where he became director of cricket coaching in Western Australia, later state director of sport for Perth

Striking partner to the prolific Jimmy Greaves during the late 1950s, Ron Tindall was an expert at flicking the ball on rather than bringing it down and holding off an opponent. Extremely useful in the air but rather heavy on his feet at times, he scored his fair share of goals, including one on his League debut v. WBA, and created plenty of openings for his colleagues (especially Greaves). Tall and fairly quick, especially over 20–25 yards, he appeared in more than 400 career games and scored close on 100 goals, with perhaps two-thirds of them coming with his head. He represented the Football League against the League of Ireland in 1957. He played in 162 games for Surrey CCC as an all-rounder.

TOOMER, WALTER EDWARD

Forward: 1 app.

Born: Southampton, 9 February 1883 – *Died*: Southampton, 28 December 1962

Career: St John's College (Battersea), Fulham (amateur, March–April 1905), CHELSEA (amateur, September 1905), Southampton (amateur, August 1906–May 1914); served in the Royal Artillery, based in France, during WW1; employed as a schoolmaster in Southampton before taking over his father's sports outfitter's business in London Road, Southampton, which still exists today; director of Southampton FC (May 1950–52)

Born the son of a cricket-bat maker, Walter Toomer played most of his football in London where he was studying to become a teacher. An amateur throughout his career, he failed to get a game with Fulham, made just one appearance for Chelsea (in a 7–1 FA Cup defeat by Crystal Palace in November 1905) and starred in ten Southern League games for Saints.

TOWNROW, JOHN ERNEST

Centre-half: 140 apps, 3 goals

Born: Stratford, London, 28 March 1901 – *Died*: Knaresborough, Yorkshire, 1969

Career: Pelly Memorial School (West Ham), Fairburn House (1917), Clapton Orient (August 1919), CHELSEA (February 1927), Bristol Rovers (May 1932); later groundsman and coach at Fairburn House (1932–36); also worked at Becton Gasworks and later for a brewery company

An England schoolboy international v. Scotland and Wales in 1915, Jack Townrow was a centre-half noted for his coolness under pressure and self-possession. A deliberate passer of the ball (rather than one who gave it an almighty boot downfield), he was an excellent all-round defender who gave Chelsea five years' splendid service. Capped twice at senior level by England in

1925 and 1926, he also represented the Football League (v. the Army in 1926) and helped the Blues gain promotion to the First Division in 1929–30, appearing in 14 matches. His younger brother, Francis Albert Townrow, played for Arsenal, Dundee, Bristol City and Bristol Rovers between 1922 and 1933.

TOWNSEND, ANDREW DAVID
Midfield: 138 apps, 19 goals
Born: Maidstone, Kent, 23 July 1963
Career: Welling United (August 1980), Weymouth (March 1984), Southampton (£35,000, January 1985), Norwich City (£300,000, August 1988), CHELSEA (£1.2 million, July 1990), Aston Villa (£2.1 million, July 1993), Middlesbrough (£500,000, August 1997), West Bromwich Albion (£50,000, September 1999; retired as first-team player in January 2000 to take over as reserve coach at The Hawthorns, a position he held for six months before being replaced by another ex-Aston Villa player, Gary Shelton); now a TV soccer pundit

Capped 70 times by the Republic of Ireland at senior level and once by the 'B' team, midfielder Andy Townsend had an excellent career in top-class football. On his day he was an effective, hard-working performer, on a par with most of the leading professionals occupying the same position. Before joining Albion he had already made over 100 appearances for Saints, 88 for the Canaries, 138 for Chelsea, 176 for Villa and 88 for Middlesbrough. He gained two League Cup winner's medals with Villa (1994 and 1996), skippering the side in the latter final. He helped Middlesbrough regain their Premiership status at the end of his first season on Teesside. He made his debut for Chelsea in a 2–1 home League win over Derby on the opening day of the 1990–91 season and scored in his last game, a 4–2 defeat at Sheffield United in May 1993. Townsend's father, Don, was a full-back with Charlton Athletic and Crystal Palace.

TUCK, PETER GEORGE
Inside-forward: 3 apps, 1 goal
Born: Plaistow, London, 14 May 1932
Career: CHELSEA (junior, May 1948; professional, May 1951; retired, injured, June 1954)

Peter Tuck's promising career came to an abrupt end when he broke his leg, having appeared in just three League games for Chelsea in the 1951–52 season. He lined up against Newcastle United for his debut in front of 54,500 fans at St James' Park, against Bolton Wanderers (home) and Stoke City (away), scoring against the latter club in a 2–1 win.

TURNBULL, JAMES McLACHLAN
Inside-/centre-forward: 22 apps, 8 goals
Born: East Plean, Stirlingshire, 23 May 1884 – *Died*: Manchester, 1945
Career: Falkirk (junior), East Stirlingshire (1899), Falkirk (1900), Dundee (July 1901), Falkirk (August 1903), Glasgow Rangers (March 1904), Preston

North End (January 1905), Leyton FC (May 1906), Manchester United (May 1907), Bradford Park Avenue (September 1910), CHELSEA (£300, June 1912), Manchester United (trial, September 1914), Hurst FC (October 1914; retired August 1915); later ran his own business in Chorlton, Manchester

The star of Scottish football in the early 1900s, Jimmy Turnbull bagged five goals for Falkirk against Aberdeen in the semi-final of the Dewar Cup in 1906 and netted 8 times in 34 games for Rangers before moving south to Deepdale. He then claimed 15 of Leyton's 38 goals in the Southern League in 1906–07 and nipped in with 42 goals in 76 first-class matches for Manchester United whom he helped win the League championship in 1908 and the FA Cup a year later. Surprisingly he failed to score for Preston. A well-built forward, aggressive with an appetite for hard work, he scored over 100 goals all told in more than 300 club games both north and south of the border (at various levels).

TURNBULL, ROBERT HAMILTON

Centre-forward: 87 apps, 58 goals
Born: Dumbarton, 22 June 1894 – *Died*: London, 1946
Career: Albion Street Council School (Paisley), Cameronians, served with the Signal Corps of the Royal Engineers, Scotland (May 1909–January 1921), Arsenal (amateur, January 1921; professional, September 1921), Charlton Athletic (£350, November 1924), CHELSEA (£300, February 1925), Clapton Orient (free transfer, February 1928), Southend United (free, October 1929), Chatham (free, July 1930), Crystal Palace (free, July 1931; retired May 1933 to become club's trainer to May 1937)

Bobby Turnbull played a dozen games as a full-back before being switched to centre-forward in a crisis by Arsenal. During a fine career he managed on average a goal every two matches. His final tally of 98 in League football alone was quite remarkable considering that he was 27 years of age when he made his debut in the competition for the Gunners against Aston Villa in October 1921. He was top scorer at Highbury in 1922–23 with 20 goals and likewise with Chelsea in 1925–26 (with 30) and again in 1926–27 (with 23). In season 1924–25, Turnbull played for three different London clubs in three different Divisions (First, Third and Second in that order).

TYE, EDWARD

Full-back: 1 app.
Born: Stanford, Middlesex, 1890 – *Died*: London, *circa* 1955
Career: Stanford FC, CHELSEA (May 1914–May 1915); did not feature after WW1

A reserve full-back at Stamford Bridge during the last season before WW1, Ted Tye's only League outing was against Burnley (home) in December 1914 when he deputised for Jimmy Sharp in a 4–1 defeat.

UPTON, FRANK

Wing-half/full-back: 86 apps, 3 goals

Born: Ainsley Hill, Warwickshire, 18 October 1934

Career: Nuneaton Borough (1950), Northampton Town (March 1953), Derby County (June 1954), CHELSEA (August 1961), Derby County (September 1965), Notts County (September 1966), Worcester City (July 1967), Workington (player–manager, January–July 1968), Northampton Town (coach, October 1969), Aston Villa (coach, January 1970), CHELSEA (assistant manager/coach, August 1977; temporary manager, December 1978), Randers Freja/Denmark (coach, February 1979–February 1980), Dundee (coach, August 1980), Al Arabi/Saudi Arabia (coach, 1981), Wolverhampton Wanderers (coach, October 1982), Bedworth United (coach, October 1984), Coventry City (assistant manager/coach, December 1984–April 1986), IBK Keflavik/Iceland (coach, May 1987), Aston Villa (chief scout/youth development, 1988), Burton Albion (caretaker-manager, January–February 1990), Northwich Victoria (Youth Development Officer, April 1990), Sabah/Malaysia (coach, May 1990), Cheltenham Town (YTS officer, November 1990), national coach, India (January 1994–June 1995), Aston Villa (chief scout, from 1998)

A Third Division championship winner with Derby County in 1956–57, Frank Upton was a bone-crunching tackler who possessed rocket-powered shots. Known as 'The Tank', he was a forceful, determined player who made 272 appearances in two spells for the Rams. He enjoyed success at Stamford Bridge, both as a wing-half and centre-forward, helping the Blues win promotion from the Second Division in 1962–63 and lift the League Cup in 1964–65. As a coach, Upton earned a huge reputation for working with young players, and was in charge of Aston Villa's teenagers when they won the FA Youth Cup. But he also had his ups and downs, being successful with an industrial tribunal claim for wrongful dismissal by Wolves before later becoming a globetrotter in search of football.

VENABLES, TERENCE FREDERICK

Midfield/inside-forward: 237 apps, 31 goals

Born: Bethnal Green, London, 6 January 1943

Career: Dagenham and Essex Schools, London and District Schools, CHELSEA (amateur, July 1958; professional, August 1960), Tottenham Hotspur (£80,000, May 1966), Queens Park Rangers (£70,000, June 1969), Crystal Palace (exchange deal involving Don Rogers, September 1974), St Patrick's Athletic/Ireland (February 1976), Crystal Palace (coach, then manager, June 1976), Queens Park Rangers (manager, October 1980), CF Barcelona/Spain (manager, May 1984), Tottenham, Hotspur (manager, December 1988–July 1991; then chief executive to May 1993; remained a director of club until August 1993), England (head coach/manager, January 1994–June 1996), Australia (national team coach, 1996–98); ITV soccer pundit; Portsmouth (director of football, 1997), Crystal Palace (head coach, 1998–99), Middlesbrough (manager, 2001–02), Leeds United (manager, 2002–03); worked on TV (again); Australian FA (advisory coach, 2004)

Terry Venables made his Football League debut for Chelsea at the age of 17 in the London derby against West Ham in February 1960 – the first of 237 senior outings for the Blues. He was a hard-working, tenacious midfielder with good vision and a tremendous amount of stamina. An FA Youth Cup winner in 1961, he helped the Blues gain promotion to the First Division in 1963 and win the League Cup two years later. In 1967 he played against his former club for Spurs in the FA Cup final, collecting a winner's medal. The first footballer to represent England at five different levels – schoolboy, amateur, youth, Under-23 (four caps) and senior (two caps) – Venables also played for the Football League v. the Irish League in 1964. He played in 141 games for Spurs and went on to amass more than 600 appearances at club and international levels, scoring almost 70 goals.

As a manager, he guided Palace out of the Third Division in 1977 and to the Second Division championship in 1979. He then quickly led QPR to the FA Cup final of 1982 (beaten by Spurs in a replay) and then took them into the top flight in 1983 before spending four years with Barcelona, whom he saw win the Primera Liga in 1985 and finish runners-up in Spain's National Cup final 12 months later. Returning to Spurs, he duly celebrated FA Cup success in 1991 (v. Nottingham Forest) and then he almost brought England its first major honour in 30 years in Euro '96, the semi-final penalty shoot-out disaster against Germany eventually ending his hopes. Venables was George Graham's best man at his wedding in September 1967. Twenty years later he was appointed manager of Spurs while Graham was already boss of Arsenal, and Graham was godfather to one of Venables' daughters. In 1971, Venables combined with Arthur Gordon Williams to produce a novel entitled *They Used to Play on Grass*; they also collaborated on the TV series *Hazel*. Venables was manager of QPR in 1981–82 when they played home games on an artificial pitch at Loftus Road. Venables has also sung on stage with the Joe Loss orchestra. In May 1993, news broke that Spurs chairman Alan Sugar had sacked Venables as chief executive at White Hart Lane. Venables appealed and was reinstated by a High Court judge. However, the following month, he lost the High Court battle on the third day of the hearing. He remained a director of the north London club until he sold his shares in August 1993.

VERON, JUAN SEBASTIAN
Midfield: 11+3 apps, 1 goal
Born: La Plata, Argentina, 5 March 1975
Career: Estudiantes de la Plata/Argentina (professional, April 1993), Boca Juniors/Argentina (£200,000, July 1995), Sampdoria/Italy (£13 million, July 1996), Parma/Italy (£20 million, June 1998), SC Lazio/Italy (£20 million, May 1999), Manchester United (£28.1 million, July 2001), CHELSEA (£15

million, August 2003), Inter Milan (season's loan, August 2004–May 2005)
Many eyebrows were raised and eyes lit up when the shaven-headed Sebastian
Veron joined Chelsea in the summer of 2003. Described by Blues manager
Claudio Ranieri as 'the best midfield player in the world', he started off like a
house on fire and scored in the first Premiership game of the season against
Liverpool to earn the team's first League victory at Anfield for 35 years.
However, after that the Argentinian international, with almost 60 caps to his
name (8 goals), was used sparingly, producing only occasionally evidence of the
undoubted talent he possesses, including a wonderful display against his former
club Lazio in the Champions League. After seriously injuring his back on a trip
to Colombia with his country, Veron required an operation and was out of action
for quite some time, recuperating in Argentina. He returned to Stamford Bridge
and made three substitute appearances after Easter before being farmed out on
loan to Inter Milan.

A class player in his own right, Veron – one of the modern-day enigmas –
was a world record signing by Manchester United in 2001. He netted 11 goals
in 82 games for the Reds, gaining a Premiership winner's medal in 2003. Prior
to his adventure at Old Trafford, he had already made over 250 appearances at
club level, scoring 23 goals. He was a silver medal winner with Argentina in the
1996 Olympic games, won Italy's Serie 'A' title, the UEFA Cup and the
European Super Cup with Parma in 1999 and followed up by winning another
Treble (Serie 'A', Italian Cup and Italian Super Cup) with Lazio in 2000. He
won his 50th cap in the 2002 World Cup finals in Japan/South Korea. Veron's
transfer fees have amounted to almost £100 million. His father, Ramon Veron,
nicknamed 'The Witch', also played for Estudiantes de la Plata and scored at
Old Trafford when they beat Manchester United in the World Club
Championship game in 1968. Sebastian was known as 'The Little Witch' and
has a tattoo of Che Guevara on his right arm.

VIALLI, GIANLUCA

Forward: 69+18 apps, 40 goals
Born: Cremona, Italy, 9 July 1964
Career: Cremonese/Italy (amateur, August 1980; professional, July 1982),
Sampdoria/Italy (1984), Juventus/Italy (£12 million, 1992), CHELSEA
(July 1996, player–manager February 1998; sacked September 2000),
Watford (manager, July 2001–July 2002); works for Italian TV, covering
Serie 'A'

The recipient of two Italian Serie 'A' championship winning medals with
Sampdoria in 1991 and Juventus in 1995, Gianluca Vialli also won the
European Cup-Winners' Cup with the former club in 1990 and both the UEFA
Cup and UEFA Champions League with Juve' in 1993 and 1996. He then
added to his collection an FA Cup winner's medal (1997), a second Cup-
Winner's Cup medal (1998) and a League Cup winner's medal (also in 1998)
with Chelsea, all won in the space of five months. Vialli, at his peak, was a

brilliant footballer and his overall goal-scoring record was second to none. He had already netted around 200 goals in Italian football (and in various European competitions) before joining Chelsea, including 23 in 105 League games for Cremonese, 85 in 223 for Sampdoria and 38 in 102 for Juventus, plus another 16 in 60 full internationals for his country (1985–92). Shaven-haired with great on-the-ball skill, he was an elusive striker, smart and precise who just simply knew where the goal posts were every time he received the ball within shooting distance of the net. When he took over as player–manager at Stamford Bridge he lured fitness coach Antonio Pintus to the club and he certainly got the players into tip-top form. But Vialli himself couldn't get his hands on the Premiership trophy – much to his annoyance and indeed, disappointment. Vialli was the first manager to lead the Blues in the Champions League. He spent £57 million on new players during his two and a half years in charge.

VILJOEN, COLIN
Midfield: 22+1 apps
Born: Johannesburg, South Africa, 20 June 1948
Career: South African football, Ipswich Town (amateur, July 1965; professional, August 1967), Manchester City (August 1978), CHELSEA (£60,000, March 1980; contract cancelled May 1982); later became the licensee of a pub near Heathrow airport

Colin Viljoen was 31 years of age when he joined Chelsea and during his time at Stamford Bridge was never a regular in the first team. Earlier in his career he had done superbly well with Ipswich Town for whom he netted 54 goals in 372 first-team appearances, helping the Portman Road club win the Second Division championship in 1968. After adopting British nationality in 1971, he went on to win two caps for England (v. Northern Ireland and Wales in 1975).

WALDRON, COLIN
Defender: 10 apps
Born: Bristol, 22 June 1948
Career: Bury (apprentice, June 1964; professional, May 1966), CHELSEA (£25,000, June 1967), Burnley (£25,000, October 1967), Manchester United (£20,000, May 1976), Sunderland (loan, February–May 1977), Tulsa Roughnecks/NASL (April 1978), Philadelphia Fury/NASL (June 1978), Atlanta Chiefs/NASL (April, 1979), Rochdale (October 1979; retired May 1980); later became a bookmaker in Nelson, Lancashire, and also worked in business in Bury with the former Manchester City and England star Colin Bell

Colin Waldron was a very capable defender who sadly failed to make his mark at Stamford Bridge. However, he did extremely well at Turf Moor, appearing in over 300 League games for Burnley, helping them win the Second Division championship in 1972–73 and reach the FA Cup semi-finals a year later. During his career the Bristolian played in well more than 400 competitive games (in England and the NASL). His younger brother, Alan, played for Blackpool, Bolton, Bury and York City.

WALKER, ANDREW MCQUEEN
Half-back: 23 apps, 2 goals
Born: Dalkieth, Midlothian, June 1892 – *Died*: USA, 1961
Career: Bonnyrigg FC, Dundee (professional, August 1910), CHELSEA (May 1913), Newport County (August 1920), Accrington Stanley (£50, June 1922–May 1923); emigrated to the USA (August 1923 where he became a soccer coach)

Walker, a recognised half-back who could play anywhere if required, was a versatile performer. He actually made his senior debut for Chelsea (in an emergency) in the centre-forward position and celebrated with a goal in a 3–2 defeat at Oldham Athletic in September 1913. Never able to hold down a regular place in the Blues' first team, he did, however, play in the 1915 FA Cup final defeat by Sheffield United when he deputised at left-half for Laurie Abrams. He went on to captain Newport County.

WALKER, CLIVE
Forward/winger: 191+33 apps, 65 goals
Born: Oxford, 26 May 1957
Career: CHELSEA (apprentice, May 1973; professional, March 1975), Sunderland (£75,000, July 1984), Queens Park Rangers (£70,000, December 1985), Fulham (free transfer, October 1987), Brighton and Hove Albion (£20,000, August 1990), Worthing FC (£1,000, August 1992); later ran an auction house in Surrey

Clive Walker was a fast-raiding winger (or central striker) who preferred the left flank. Exciting to watch, he scored some stunning goals during his 11 years at Stamford Bridge, having his best season in 1981–82 when he netted 17 times in 45 games. From 1977 to 1983 he was a valuable member of the squad and although at times he was certainly unpredictable and quite erratic in his general play, he was nonetheless a huge favourite with the Stamford Bridge faithful. After moving on, he scored 10 goals in 50 League games for Sunderland, 1 in 21 for QPR, 29 in 109 for Fulham and 8 in 106 for Brighton, ending his senior career with a total of 128 goals in 573 competitive games for his 5 major clubs. Walker was capped by England at schoolboy level.

WALKER, THOMAS, OBE
Forward: 104 apps, 24 goals
Born: Livingston, West Lothian, 26 May 1915 – *Died*: Edinburgh, 11 January 1993
Career: Berryburn Rangers (August 1928), Heart of Midlothian (schoolboy forms, June 1929), Livingston Violet (July 1930), Broxburn Rangers (August 1931), Linlithgow Rose (December 1931), Heart of Midlothian

(professional, May 1932), CHELSEA (guest, season 1944–45; signed for £6,000, September 1946), Heart of Midlothian (player-assistant manager, December 1948; manager June 1951–September 1966), Dunfermline Athletic (administration manager, November 1966–May 1967), Raith Rovers (manager, July 1967–January 1969; club secretary; then director, October 1974; vice-chairman 1979); also briefly associated with Arthurlie FC

Distinguished Scottish international inside-forward Tommy Walker, one of the game's true 'gentlemen', was honoured by his country at schoolboy level before going on to win 20 full caps between 1935–39. He also played in eleven WW2 internationals and represented the Scottish League on five occasions. Able to play at either inside-right or left and also at centre-forward, Walker was a magnificent footballer, one of Hearts' all-time greats. A superb passer of the ball, he possessed great control, had marvellous tactical awareness, was blessed with a powerful right-foot shot and was, with his sunshine smile and tremendous sportsmanship, extremely popular with the fans. Early in his career he had considered joining the church and, in fact, during his Chelsea days attached himself to a local London boys' club where he became a much-respected leader. In 1947–48, Walker established a record total of first-class League appearances in one season, 48 (39 with Chelsea and 9 with Hearts). He was awarded the OBE in 1960.

WALTON, JOSEPH
Right-back: 53 apps
Born: North Shields, Tyneside, April 1884 – *Died*: County Durham, 1945
Career: Wallsend Park Villa (1900), Sheffield Wednesday (1903), New Brompton (1904), CHELSEA (August 1906; released May 1911), Swansea Town (August 1911); did not play after WW1

Steady and astute, strong in the tackle, Joe Walton played in 35 of Chelsea's 38 League games in 1906–07 when he partnered Tommy Miller at full-back. He made his debut for the Blues in a 9–2 home win over Glossop at the start of that season but was injured in the first game of the following campaign (v. Sheffield United). When fit, he failed to regain his position, Jock Cameron taking over his role. He did return for a spell during the last three months of 1908–09 but was a reserve during his last two years at Stamford Bridge.

WARD, JOSEPH
Half-back: 16 apps
Born: County Tyrone, Northern Ireland, August 1897 – *Died*: Ireland, *circa* 1970
Career: Cookstown, Portadown (briefly), St Johnstone (August 1919), CHELSEA (May 1920), Swansea Town (July 1922–April 1923), Cliftonville (Belfast)

Originally a centre-half, Joe Ward played mainly as a wing-half for Chelsea for whom he did reasonably well in his first season. Selected to play for Ireland against Wales in April 1921, he sadly had to withdraw at the last minute through injury and never got another chance.

WARREN, BENJAMIN
Wing-half: 101 apps, 5 goals
Born: Newhall, Derbyshire, June 1879 – *Died*: Derbyshire, 15 January 1917
Career: Newhall Town, Newhall Swifts, Derby County (professional, 1899),
    CHELSEA (July 1908; retired through ill health, February 1912)
Described by contemporary writers as the 'best wing-half in the kingdom and a
player worth three men to his side', Ben Warren, although a tad slow, was a
wonderfully consistent wing-half whose control was first-rate and his tackles
strong and timed to perfection. A fitness fanatic, he covered every inch of
ground during a match and it came as a bitter blow to Chelsea when he got
injured halfway through the 1909–10 season. He came back for one game
during the second half of that campaign as the team battled in vain to avoid
relegation to the Second Division. Capped by England on 11 occasions between
1906 and 1911, he collected an FA Cup runner's-up medal with Derby in 1903
and represented the Football League on four occasions (once as a Chelsea player
v. the Scottish League in 1908). He was forced to retire through illness and sadly
was later certified insane and spent some time in a Derbyshire asylum. It was a
terrible end for a great player who died at the age of 37. Warren was awarded a
testimonial match by Chelsea in April 1914.

WARREN, ROBERT
Centre-half: 1 app.
Born: Devonport, near Plymouth, 8 January 1927
Career: Plymouth United, Plymouth Argyle (professional, February 1946),
    CHELSEA (July 1948), Torquay United (August 1951–May 1952)
Centre-half Bob Warren had only three first-class games under his belt for
Argyle before joining Chelsea for whom he made his only appearance for the
Blues, in the 1–1 draw with Manchester United at Old Trafford in April 1949
when he deputised for John Harris. A hefty defender, rather slow to turn, he
never fitted in at Stamford Bridge and moved back to Devon with Torquay
United in 1951. Warren's twin brother, Geoff, was also a player with Plymouth
Argyle in 1946–47.

WATSON, DOUGAL JAMES
Left-half/inside-forward: 14 apps
Born: Inverness, February 1883 – *Died*: 1955
Career: Sunderland (May 1903), Portsmouth (August 1904), CHELSEA
    (September 1905), Brentford (May 1906–April 1907)
Acquired from Portsmouth prior to Chelsea's first-ever season in the Football
League, Jimmy Watson played in 13 Second Division matches as deputy for
player–manager Jackie Robertson and Tommy McDermott. He failed to make
headway with any of his other three major clubs.

WATSON, IAN LIONEL

Full-back: 9 apps, 1 goal
Born: Hammersmith, London, 7 January 1944
Career: CHELSEA (apprentice, April 1960; professional, February 1962), Queens Park Rangers (£10,000, July 1965–May 1974)

A reserve for five years at Stamford Bridge, well-built full-back Ian Watson made his debut for Chelsea in January 1963 against Tranmere Rovers in a 3rd round FA Cup tie when he stood in for Ken Shellito. He went on to appear in 232 senior games for QPR.

WATT, STEVEN

Defender: 1+1 apps
Born: Aberdeen, 1 May 1985
Career: CHELSEA (apprentice, May 2001; professional, June 2003)

A tall, well-built defender, Steve Watt did very well in the reserve and intermediate sides for two seasons before making his senior debut for Chelsea against Scunthorpe United (FAC) in January 2005 with Nuno Morias (q.v.).

WEAH, GEORGE

Forward: 13+2 apps, 5 goals
Born: Monrovia, Liberia, 1 October 1966
Career: Young Survivors/Liberia (amateur, August 1981), Bongrange/Liberia (professional, October 1984), Mighty Barolle/Liberia (July 1985), Invincible Eleven/Liberia (August 1986), Tonnerre Kiarra Yaounde/Cameroon (August 1987), AS Monaco/France (May 1988), Paris St Germain/France (June 1992), AC Milan/Italy (May 1995), CHELSEA (loan, January–May 2000), Manchester City (free transfer, August 2000), Olympique Marseilles/France (free, October 2000), Al Jazira/Indonesia (August 2001), Liberia (national team manager, from June 2002)

A Liberian international with 96 caps to his name (33 goals scored), 6 ft 1 in. striker George Weah made quite an impact when he arrived at Stamford Bridge on loan from AC Milan who had stated that he was surplus to requirements at the age of 33. After travelling by plane from Milan to London, he joined up with his colleagues for the first time at the club's training ground and had to sit and wait patiently for his international clearance to be confirmed. That done, he was then named in the Chelsea squad and duly took his place on the substitute's bench for the evening Premiership clash with rivals Tottenham Hotspur – and when he was called into action in the second-half, he headed a dramatic winning goal with just three minutes remaining. And then at the end of that season he went out and helped the Blues win the FA Cup. He had chosen Chelsea ahead of AS Roma and Olympique Marseilles and Blues boss Gianluca Vialli was delighted to have him around as he went on to score another four goals.

Prior to his brief spell at Stamford Bridge, Weah – nicknamed 'The Lion

King' in some quarters – is said to have been one of the finest footballers ever to come out of Africa.

In 1995, he was voted World, European and African Footballer of the Year, having been awarded the latter prize previously in 1989 and 1994 and collecting again in 1996.

He is also credited with having scored the greatest goal ever in the history of Serie 'A' football when he ran fully 100 yards, dribbled past seven opponents, checked and then placed the ball into the net for AC Milan against Verona in 1996. He won several honours at club level including medals for winning the 1987 Liberian League title (with Invincible Eleven); the 1988 Cameroon championship (with Tonnerre); the French Cup in 1991 and 1993, the European Cup-Winners' Cup in 1992, the French League title in 1994 and the French League Cup in 1995 (all with Paris St Germain), and Italy's Serie 'A' championship with AC Milan in 1995 and 1999. After moving into European football, he scored 47 goals in 103 League games for Monaco, 32 in 96 for PSG and 46 in 114 for Milan, following up with 4 in 14 for Marseilles. Actively involved with UNICEF (the Union Nations International Children's Emergency Fund) he also kept afloat the cash-stricken Liberian national soccer team for many years by making numerous cash donations and purchasing new playing kit.

WEAVER, REGINALD WILLIAM

Outside-right/centre-forward: 20 apps, 8 goals
Born: Clutton, near Bath, 14 September 1905 – *Died*: Gloucester, 16 July 1970
Career: Midsomer Norton (junior, 1919–20), Radstock FC (August 1922), Llanhilleth United (1924), Newport County (May 1926), Wolverhampton Wanderers (£1,000, November 1927), CHELSEA (March 1929), Bradford City (June 1932), Chesterfield (March 1933), Newport County (August 1934–May 1936)

Reg Weaver, 5 ft 9 in. tall, loved to hug the touchline when performing on the wing. Fast and clever, he won the Welsh Powderhall sprint in Caerphilly in July 1931. Top scorer for Wolves in 1928–29, he netted a total of 29 goals in only 51 games for the Molineux club before switching to Stamford Bridge where he had to work hard to get into the first XI. However, when called into action he produced some useful displays. He moved on when Hughie Gallacher teamed up with George Mills. His brother, William Walter, also played for Wolves, as well as Burnley, Everton and Accrington Stanley.

WEAVER, SAMUEL

Wing-half: 125 apps, 4 goals
Born: Pilsley, Derbyshire, 8 February 1909 – *Died*: Mansfield, 15 April 1985
Career: Pilsley Red Rose, Sutton Junction (trial), Sutton Town (1926), Hull City (£50, March 1928), Newcastle United (£2,500, November 1929), CHELSEA (£4,166, August 1936); guest for Southampton (1939–40),

Fulham (1939–44), Notts County (1942–43), Derby County (1942–43), West Ham United (1943–44), Mansfield Town (1945–46) and Wrexham (1945–46); Stockport County (December 1945; retired May 1947); Leeds United (assistant trainer, July 1947), Millwall (trainer, June 1949), Oxo Sports Club/Bromley (steward and occasional player, January 1954), Mansfield Town (trainer, September 1955; manager from June 1958 to January 1960; then assistant trainer to May 1967; scout to October 1980; also acted as caretaker-manager, November–December 1971); played cricket for Derbyshire (1934) and Somerset (1939); later masseur at Derbyshire CCC (1956–72)

A polished and powerful half-back, aggressive and progressive with a biting tackle, Sam Weaver was a star performer at Newcastle for 7 years, appearing in 229 League and Cup games and scoring 43 goals. A long-throw expert, he once delivered the ball a distance of 35 yards and helped the Geordies win the FA Cup in 1932 (in the famous goal-over-the-line final at Wembley v. Arsenal). He was also capped three times by England – versus Scotland and Ireland in 1932 and Wales in 1933 – and twice represented the Football League. He did well during his time at Stamford Bridge where he became a popular character. He skippered the side on several occasions and was an automatic choice in the left-half position for three seasons up to WW2. He played as a guest for seven different clubs during the hostilities while also appearing in a few games for Chelsea. He retired in 1947 with 370 League games under his belt (50 goals).

WEBB, DAVID JAMES
Defender: 299 apps, 33 goals
Born: Stratford, London, 9 April 1946
Career: West Ham United (amateur, May 1961), Leyton Orient (professional, May 1963) Southampton (March 1966), CHELSEA (£40,000, part-exchange with Joe Kirkup, February 1968), Queens Park Rangers (£100,000, July 1974), Leicester City (September 1977), Derby County (September 1978), Bournemouth (May 1980; player–manager, December 1980–December 1982), Torquay United (manager, February 1984–August 1985; then manager/director to June 1986), Southend United (manager, June 1986–March 1987), Milford FC/Bournemouth League (briefly in 1988), Southend United (general manager, December 1988–July 1992), CHELSEA (manager, February–May 1993), Brentford (manager, May 1993–97), Yeovil Town (manager, 1998–June 2001), Southend United (manager, October 2000–October 2001)

On Boxing Day 1968, the versatile David Webb scored a hat-trick in Chelsea's 3–1 League win over Ipswich Town. Three years later, due to injuries to both Peter Bonetti and John Phillips and the late arrival at the ground of third-choice keeper Steve Sherwood, he kept goal in a 2–0 win, also against Ipswich. A strong, well-built defender, enthusiastic and totally committed, he was twice voted Chelsea's Player of the Year (1969 and 1972) and practically received the

'Freedom of Stamford Bridge' after scoring the winning goal in the 1970 FA Cup final replay against Leeds United. The following year he helped the Blues win the European Cup-Winners' Cup and in 1972 gained a League Cup runner's-up medal. He donned every shirt available as a Chelsea player whom he served superbly well for six years. In all, he amassed a total of 555 League appearances. As a manager he guided Southend to promotion from the old Fourth Division in 1990.

WEGERLE, ROY CONNON
Forward: 18+10 apps, 4 goals
Born: Pretoria, South Africa, 19 March 1964
Career: played rugby in Johannesburg (from 1977), Witts University/South Africa (April 1982), Manchester United (trial, July–August 1982), Tampa Bay Rowdies/NASL (professional, March 1983), CHELSEA (trial, August–September 1985), Tampa Bay Rowdies, CHELSEA (£100,000, July 1986), Swindon Town (loan, March–May 1988), Luton Town (£75,000, July 1988), Queens Park Rangers (£1 million, December 1989), Blackburn Rovers (£1.2 million, March 1992), Coventry City (£1 million, March 1993–May 1994); returned to USA (retired, injured, 1995); still living and working in America

Roy Wegerle played rugby at school and turned to soccer at Witts University where he was coached by Roy Bailey, the former Ipswich Town goalkeeper. After a brief flirtation with Manchester United, he went over to the States where he developed into a smart, lively striker with good pace and a strong right-foot shot. A natural athlete, he was able to play through the centre or down the flanks and did very well in the NASL before moving to Stamford Bridge after a successful trial earlier in the season. He made excellent progress after that and gained over 20 full caps for the USA while also amassing 294 League and Cup appearances and scoring 77 goals with his 6 English clubs, having his best spell with QPR (92 games, 31 goals).

WELLER, KEITH
Forward: 49+5 apps, 15 goals
Born: Islington, London, 11 June 1946 – *Died*: Seattle, USA, 12 November 2004
Career: Tottenham Hotspur (apprentice, June 1962; professional, January 1964), Millwall (June 1967), CHELSEA (£100,000, May 1970), Leicester City (£100,000, September 1971), New England Teamen/NASL (loan, January 1979; signed for £40,000, February 1979), Fort Lauderdale Strikers/NASL (December 1980), Dallas Sidekicks/NASL (coach, 1981–82); stayed in America, based in Seattle, where he became a driver for the outside broadcast unit of an American TV company and later ran a coffee shop

Initially a striker, darting through the middle, Keith Weller later became a very effective right-winger with pace, skill and excellent crossing ability. Temperamental at times, he used to drift out of a game for long periods before bursting back into action with a flourish. He gained a European Cup-Winners' Cup winning medal with Chelsea in 1971 before moving to Filbert Street where he spent a little over six and a half seasons, scoring 47 goals in 305 appearances and collecting 4 full England caps (all in 1974). He also represented the Football League. He scored 1 goal in 21 games for Spurs and netted 41 in 135 outings for Millwall. He was only 58 when he died.

WEST, COLIN
Striker/midfield: 8+8 apps, 4 goals
Born: Middlesbrough, 19 September 1967
Career: CHELSEA (apprentice, August 1983; professional, September 1985), Partick Thistle (loan, September 1986–March 1987), Swansea City (loan, March–May 1989), Dundee (August 1990), Hartlepool United (August 1993–May 1994)

An England Youth international, quick, strong and aggressive, Colin West scored on his League debut for Chelsea against Arsenal within five minutes of taking the field in March 1987 – this, after gaining valuable experience north of the border with Partick for whom he scored 13 goals in 34 appearances. Surplus to requirements at Stamford Bridge, he went on to net 6 times in 35 League outings for Dundee and 5 times in 36 for Hartlepool.

WHIFFEN, KINGSLEY
Goalkeeper: 1 app.
Born: Welshpool, Powys, 3 December 1950
Career: CHELSEA (apprentice, April 1966–May 1967), Plymouth Argyle (trial, July–August 1967); later with Caersws (Welsh League)

Goalkeeper Kingsley Whiffen was registered with Chelsea for just one season, making his only League appearance in May 1967 against Leicester City a fortnight or so before the FA Cup final, when Peter Bonetti was rested.

WHITE, ALEXANDER
Full-back: 18 apps
Born: Armadale, West Lothian, 28 January 1916 – Deceased by 2000
Career: Bonnyrigg Rose (April 1936), CHELSEA (February 1937), Swindon Town (July 1948), Southport (July 1950–April 1951)

One of several players who served Chelsea before, during and after WW2, Alex White was a well-built, hard-tackling defender who, as a sergeant-instructor, played twice for Scotland in Army internationals against England during the hostilities. He had to wait over 9 years, until he was 30, before making his League debut for the Blues, in a 3–0 home win over Leeds United in September 1946. He had 35 League outings with Swindon.

WHITEHOUSE, BENJAMIN

Inside-forward: 13 apps, 2 goals

Born: Coseley, near Wolverhampton, 1884 – *Died*: Bilston, Staffordshire, February 1959

Career: Coseley White Star, Bilston United (August 1902), CHELSEA (November 1906), Stockport County (June 1908), Bilston United (August 1911), Brierley Hill Alliance (1912–15); did not play after WW1

Scorer of the fastest goal in Chelsea's history until John Spencer beat his record – after just 13 seconds of the home Second Division game against Blackburn Rovers in December 1907 – Ben Whitehouse was a thrusting forward who was both hard-working and aggressive. He also scored on his debut for the Blues in a 1st round FA Cup tie against Lincoln City in January 1907. He netted 25 goals in 83 senior games for Stockport.

WHITING, ROBERT

Goalkeeper: 54 apps

Born: West Ham, London, 6 January 1883 – *Died*: 1917

Career: South West Ham FC, West Ham United (briefly, 1904), Tunbridge Wells Rangers (May 1905), CHELSEA (April 1906), Brighton and Hove Albion (June 1908–May 1915)

Bob 'Pom Pom' Whiting took over from giant goalkeeper Billy 'Fatty' Foulke at Stamford Bridge and, with a safe pair of hands and good positional sense, did a wonderful job for two seasons, helping the Blues gain promotion from the Second Division in his first. He joined the club at the end of the 1905–06 campaign and made the first of his 54 appearances against Bristol City (away) in the very last game. After leaving Chelsea he appeared in over 200 games in 7 years for Brighton. He lost his life during WW1.

WHITLEY, JOHN

Goalkeeper: 138 apps

Born: Seacombe, Cheshire, 20 April 1880 – *Died*: London, 1955

Career: Seacombe Swifts, Seacombe YMCA (May 1897), Liskeard YMCA (briefly, 1898), Darwen (January 1899), Aston Villa (May 1900), Everton (August 1902), Stoke (September 1904), Tottenham Hotspur (briefly, June 1905; registration cancelled, returned to Stoke), Leeds City (April 1906), Lincoln City (September 1906), CHELSEA (July 1907; retired May 1914; then trainer until May 1939); served with Royal Flying Corps during WW1

Jack Whitley was a sound and competent goalkeeper who helped Chelsea win promotion to the First Division in 1912. Reasonably experienced when he moved to Stamford Bridge, having appeared in a century of competitive games, he then made over 100 appearances in his first three seasons for the Blues. As he aged, he acted as reserve to Ron Brebner and Jim Molyneux before retiring in 1914. Thereafter, as a trainer, he was a father figure to generations of young players and his bald head and flapping coat-tails (as he raced onto the pitch) were very much part of the Chelsea scene during the inter-war years. In all he spent 32 years at the club.

WHITTAKER, RICHARD

Full-back: 51 apps

Born: Dublin, 10 October 1934

Career: St Mary's Boys' Club (Dublin), CHELSEA (amateur, April 1950; professional, May 1952), Peterborough United (July 1961), Queens Park Rangers (July 1963–April 1964)

Dick Whittaker was a steady, reliable full-back who had one decent season of first-team football with Chelsea, making 18 appearances in 1958–59. Generally regarded as a competent reserve, he spent 11 years at Stamford Bridge before moving to Peterborough for whom he played in 82 League games. Honoured by the Republic of Ireland at three different levels – schoolboy, Under-23 and senior – he gained one cap in each of the last two categories, his full one v. Czechoslovakia in 1959.

WHITTINGHAM, ROBERT

Centre-/inside-forward: 129 apps, 80 goals

Born: Goldenhill, Stoke-on-Trent, April 1884 – *Died*: Goldenhill, Stoke-on-Trent, 9 June 1926

Career: Goldenhill Villa, Goldenhill Wanderers, Stoke (amateur, September 1902), Port Vale (professional, August 1903), Crewe Alexandra (professional, May 1906), Blackpool (July 1907), Bradford City (January 1909), CHELSEA (£1,300, April 1910), South Shields (March 1914), CHELSEA (March 1919), Stoke (September 1919; retired on health grounds, April 1920), returned with Stoke United (December 1920), Macclesfield (February 1921), Scunthorpe and Lindsey United (June 1921), Wrexham (November 1922), Goldenhill Wanderers (December 1923; retired May 1924)

Bob Whittingham's tally of 30 goals for Chelsea in season 1910–11 set a new club individual scoring record that lasted longer than any other in the Football League – some 48 years until Jimmy Greaves surpassed it in 1958–59. A big, strong, bustling type of player with a cracking right-foot shot, Whittingham – the scourge of goalkeepers – loved to collect a ball 30–40 yards from goal and set off towards his target, brushing defenders aside with his powerful frame. He made his debut for the Blues away at Bristol City in April 1910 and scored on his home debut a week later v. Bury. He weighed in with 26 goals in only 32 League games when Chelsea won promotion to the First Division in 1911–12. He scored 138 goals in 235 League games spread over a period of 13 years and, taking into consideration his efforts for other clubs, his overall record was exceptional: 211 goals in fewer than 350 games. Capped by England against Scotland in a Victory international in 1919, he also represented the Football League. He died of tuberculosis, aged 42.

Whittingham's elder brother, Sam, also played for Blackpool, Port Vale and Stoke as well as Huddersfield Town.

WHITTON, WILLIAM ARMSTRONG

Centre-forward: 39 apps, 19 goals
Born: Aldershot, Hampshire, 1900 – *Died*: Aldershot, 1971
Career: Tottenham Hotspur (August 1919), CHELSEA (March 1923; contract
    cancelled, April 1926); started his own business in 1927
Having failed to make the grade with Spurs, Bill Whitton was given a chance by Chelsea and after a slow start he did well during a period when goals were hard to come by. He scored 16 times in 23 games in 1924–25 – which proved to be his last season in League football.

WICKS, STANLEY MAURICE

Defender: 81 apps, 1 goal
Born: Reading, 11 July 1928 – *Died*: Reading, February 1983
Career: Castle Street Institute (Reading), Berks and Bucks FA (1943–45),
    Reading (amateur, 1947; professional, August 1948), CHELSEA (£13,000,
    January 1954; retired, injured, April 1956); later worked in the family carpet
    business in Reading
A tall, commanding centre-half with a solid tackle and smart headwork, Stan Wicks followed his boss Ted Drake from Elm Park to Stamford Bridge in 1954 after making 168 League appearances for Reading. Recipient of a County Youth Championship medal in 1946, he was capped by England 'B' against France 'B' and also represented the FA XI against Cambridge University before moving to Chelsea. He then gained a First Division Championship medal in 1954–55 when sharing the centre-half position with Ron Greenwood and played for the Football League against the Irish League in 1956. He was 54 when he died of cancer in 1983.

WICKS, STEPHEN JOHN

Centre-half: 161+1 apps, 8 goals
Born: Reading, 3 October 1956
Career: CHELSEA (apprentice, October 1972; professional, May 1974), Derby
    County (£275,000, January 1979), Queens Park Rangers (September 1979),
    Crystal Palace (June 1981), Queens Park Rangers (March 1982),
    CHELSEA (£450,000, July 1986–May 1987), Portsmouth (assistant
    manager to August 1989); later linked up with Paul Mariner (ex-Plymouth
    Argyle, Ipswich Town, Arsenal and England striker), to run an agency
    handling players' affairs; moved back into management with Scarborough;
    later Lincoln City (head coach/chief scout, 1995–97)
Capped by England at youth and Under-21 levels, Steve Wicks, like his namesake Stan (q.v.), was a tall, dominating centre-half, strong in the air, firm and uncompromising in the tackle and resourceful throughout. He made his

League debut in March 1975 against Ipswich Town (home) and gained a regular place in the side at the age of 19 as partner to David Hay in place of John Dempsey and Mickey Droy. He remained at Stamford Bridge for a little over 6 years and then, after serving Derby County and Crystal Palace and making over 200 appearances in 2 spells with QPR with whom he won the Second Division championship (1983) and gained a League Cup runner's-up medal (1986), he returned to the Blues for a then club record fee of £450,000. He amassed in excess of 400 games during a fine career.

WILDING, HARRY THOMAS OULTON
Centre-/inside-forward/centre-half: 265 apps, 25 goals
Born: Wolverhampton, 27 June 1894 – *Died*: Earlsfield, London, 12 December 1958
Career: Grenadier Guards, CHELSEA (professional, April 1914), Tottenham Hotspur (November 1928), Bristol Rovers (July–October 1930); later employed as groundsman at Stamford Bridge

Harry Wilding was 25 years of age when he made a scoring League debut as a centre-forward for Chelsea in a 3–2 win at Everton in August 1919. Wiry, 6 ft 1 in. tall, strong and positive, he played six games as leader of the attack before being switched into the middle-line where he performed superbly well over the next five years and more. Respected by his team-mates and opponents alike, he was in and out of the side during the late 1920s before transferring to rivals Spurs after spending 14 and a half years at Stamford Bridge. An England international trialist in February 1923, Wilding scored nine goals in nine Regional games for Chelsea in March and April 1915, collecting a winner's medal after scoring against Fulham in the London Victory Cup final. He also won the Military Medal in WW1.

WILEMAN, ARTHUR HAROLD
Inside-forward: 14 apps, 5 goals
Born: Newhall, Derbyshire, February 1889 – *Died*: France, 1916
Career: Burton United (professional, March 1907), CHELSEA (May 1909), Luton Town (November 1910), Millwall (July 1911–May 1912)

Arthur Wileman, who joined Chelsea with his brother Heneage who later did well with Southend, was a useful inside-forward, but unfortunately he didn't get a fair crack of the whip at Stamford Bridge, especially after Bob Whittingham had arrived on the scene. He was killed at war.

WILKINS, GRAHAM GEORGE

Full-back: 148+1 apps, 1 goal
Born: Hillingdon, 28 June 1955
Career: CHELSEA (apprentice, June 1971; professional, July 1972), Brentford (free transfer, July 1982), Southend United (loan, March–April 1984); retired from League football, July 1984

Brother of Raymond (q.v.), Graham Wilkins was an astute full-back with a good technique but perhaps lacked the composure to make himself a top quality First Division player. Fine on the overlap when given the freedom to attack, he spent 11 years at Stamford Bridge and made almost 150 senior appearances for the Blues, having his best seasons in the late 1970s. He made his League debut against Ipswich Town (away) on Boxing Day 1972 – ten months before his brother.

WILKINS, RAYMOND COLIN, MBE

Midfield: 193+5 apps, 34 goals
Born: Hillingdon, Middlesex, 14 September 1956
Career: Middlesex Schools, London Schools, CHELSEA (apprentice, September 1971; professional, October 1973), Manchester United (£825,000, August 1979), AC Milan/Italy (£1.5 million, June 1984), Paris St Germain/France (July 1987), Glasgow Rangers (November 1987), Queens Park Rangers (November 1989), Crystal Palace (May 1994), Queens Park Rangers (non-contract player, November 1994; then player–manager, briefly), Wycombe Wanderers (non-contract, September 1996), Hibernian (free transfer, September 1996), Millwall (free, January 1997), Leyton Orient (non-contract, February 1997), CHELSEA (assistant manager, seasons 1998–2001), Watford (assistant manager, July 2001), Millwall (coach, September 2002; assistant manager, December 2003); also a TV soccer pundit

Ray Wilkins retired as a player in 1997 with more than 900 club and international appearances under his belt – 608 in the Football League alone – and he claimed more than 60 goals. The recipient of 84 full England caps, he also represented his country at four other levels: schoolboy, youth, Under-21 (once) and Under-23 (twice) and played for the Football League v. the Scottish League in 1976. He also won the FA Cup with Manchester United in 1982–83 and gained Scottish Premier Division and League Cup winner's medals with Rangers in 1988–89. However, in June 1986, he suffered the humiliation of becoming the first England player to be sent off in the World Cup, dismissed against Morocco in Monterrey.

A midfield playmaker with superb passing ability, 'Butch' Wilkins was Chelsea's youngest-ever captain at the age of 18 when appointed in April 1975. He led the Blues to promotion from the Second Division the following season when he was also voted the Blues' Player of the Year, receiving the same award 12 months later. He rejoined his former boss Dave Sexton at Old Trafford and made almost 200 appearances for the Reds in five seasons before moving to Italy. Wilkins, who was awarded the MBE in the Queen's Birthday Honours List in June 1993 for his services to the game of football, comes from a footballing family. George, his father, played for several League clubs directly after WW2, whilst brothers Graham (q.v.) and Dean also enjoyed League careers.

WILLEMSE, STANLEY BERNARD

Full-back: 221 apps, 2 goals
Born: Brighton, 23 August 1924
Career: Brighton and Hove Albion (amateur, September 1939); served as a Marine during WW2; Brighton and Hove Albion (professional, June 1946), CHELSEA (£6,500, July 1949), Leyton Orient (£4,500, June 1956; retired September 1958); later worked as a security officer with a London firm

A tough, uncompromising full-back, strong in every aspect of defensive play, Stan Willemse played in 100 games for Brighton before moving to Stamford Bridge to replace Welsh international Billy Hughes. A huge favourite with the supporters, he gained a regular place in the side in 1952 and missed only six League games when the Blues won the First Division championship in 1954–55, forming a wonderful partnership with first John Harris and then Peter Sillett. Enthusiastic to the last, totally committed, he added a further 60 senior appearances to his tally with Orient. Capped by England as a schoolboy and later by the 'B' team (v. Switzerland in 1953) he also represented the Football League v. the Scottish League in 1954.

WILLIAMS, ERNEST WALLIS

Outside-left: 8 apps, 1 goal
Born: Ryde, Isle of Wight, April 1885 – *Died*: Isle of Wight, 1961
Career: Ryde FC, Portsmouth (amateur, December 1906), CHELSEA (amateur, November 1909), Portsmouth (amateur, August 1910), Southampton (briefly, amateur, 1911)

A fast-raiding amateur left-winger, Ernie Williams joined Chelsea around the same time as Vivian Woodward and was handed his League debut against Tottenham Hotspur (home) a week before Christmas 1909, in front of 40,000 fans. He kept his place in the side for two months before Arthur Holden was recalled. A schoolmaster, he was capped by England at amateur level in 1909.

WILLIAMS, PAUL JOHN

Centre-half: 1 app.
Born: Lambeth, London, 16 November 1962
Career: CHELSEA (apprentice, July 1979; professional, July 1980), Leatherhead (free transfer, July 1983)

A regular in Chelsea's junior and reserve teams, centre-half Paul Williams made only one League appearance, taking over from Mickey Droy in a 2–2 draw at Oldham in April 1983.

WILLIAMS, REGINALD FRANCIS
Wing-half/inside-forward: 74 apps, 17 goals
Born: Watford, 28 January 1922
Career: Watford (amateur, April 1937), CHELSEA (professional, October 1945; retired, injured, October 1951)

Unfortunately Reg Williams spent several months on the injured list during his six years at Stamford Bridge. He made his debut in the FA Cup tie with Leicester City in January 1946, played only 10 games the following season and had his best spell in the first team during the 1949–50 campaign when he appeared in half of the 42 League games, scoring 5 goals. Well built, with a neat touch, he was equally adept in defence or attack and was called into the senior England squad for matches against France and Switzerland in 1946 but only sat on the bench. He was forced to retire at the age of 29.

WILLIAMS, WILLIAM DENNIS
Inside-forward: 2 apps
Born: Leytonstone, London, June 1905 – *Died*: Ilford, Essex, 1994
Career: Fairbarn House Boys' Club (London), West Ham United (amateur, August 1920; professional, June 1922), CHELSEA (June 1927; released May 1928), Dagenham (August 1928), Grays Athletic (July 1930), Ilford (May 1933; retired May 1935); later ran his own haulage business and then a tobacconist and confectioner's shop in Ilford

Bill Williams, who gained England schoolboy honours, spent only one season with Chelsea, deputising for Albert Thain in two League games against Grimsby Town and Reading in December 1927. Earlier, he had become West Ham's youngest-ever debutant and toured Australia with a selected England party in 1925, playing in five Test Matches.

WILSON, ANDREW NESBIT
Inside-/centre-forward: 253 apps, 62 goals
Born: Newmains, Lanarkshire, 14 February 1896 – *Died*: London, October 1973
Career: Cambuslang Rangers (1911), Middlesbrough (£20; professional, February 1914); served with 6th Highland Light Infantry (August 1915); then 16th Royal Scots in France; Heart of Midlothian (guest, December 1918), Dunfermline Athletic (guest, August 1919), Middlesbrough (re-signed, August 1921), CHELSEA (£6,500, November 1923), Queens Park Rangers (October 1931), Nîmes/France (May 1932–May 1934), Clacton Town (trainer/manager, August 1934), Walsall (manager, September 1934–February 1937), Gravesend and Northfleet (manager, 1938–39); later CHELSEA (coach); after WW2 was a civil servant with the Ministry of Works (Westminster)

During WW1 (in France) Andy Wilson's left hand was shattered by a shell. He recovered and played in two Victory internationals for Scotland against England and Ireland in 1919 and then proceeded to win 12 full caps, 6 with Dunfermline

Athletic for whom he played in the 'rebel' Scottish League (scoring 104 goals in 2 seasons) and 6 with Middlesbrough. He also netted 12 goals when touring North America with his country before returning to Ayresome Park in 1921. He was leading scorer for Boro in 1921–22 with 32 goals and in 1923–24 he ended up as top scorer for both Boro and Chelsea for whom he made a scoring debut v. Preston in December 1923. By common consent, regarded as the greatest centre-forward of the early 1920s, Wilson was a thinking player who specialised in low passes to his two wingers and powerful first-time shooting when the ball was at his feet in front of goal. One of the most loyal and dedicated players ever to don a Chelsea shirt, Wilson disliked his role as manager of Walsall. Besides being a wonderfully gifted footballer, he was also a fine golfer (despite his hand injury), a decent snooker player (his best break was 101) and he represented England in a bowls international. His son, Jimmy, was a registered player with Chelsea in the 1950s.

WILSON, CLIVE EUCLID AKLANA

Left-back/midfield: 85+18 apps, 5 goals
Born: Manchester, 13 November 1961
Career: Manchester City (apprentice, April 1978; professional, December 1979), Chester City (loan, September 1982–February 1983), CHELSEA (£208,000, March 1987), Manchester City (loan, March–May 1987), Queens Park Rangers (£450,000, July 1990), Tottenham Hotspur (free transfer, June 1995), Cambridge United (August 1999; retired May 2000)

An attacking left-back who also performed well in midfield, Clive Wilson played in 115 games for Manchester City and 21 for Chester before joining Chelsea for whom he made his debut against Sheffield Wednesday in August 1987. After helping the Blues win the Second Division championship two years later, and having a loan spell back at Maine Road, he went on to appear in 199 games for QPR, 86 for Spurs and 34 for Cambridge before retiring with 569 senior games under his belt.

WILSON, KEVIN JAMES

Centre-/inside-forward: 155+36 apps, 55 goals
Born: Banbury, Oxfordshire, 18 April 1961
Career: Ruscote Sports, Banbury United (April 1978), Sheffield United (trial), Stoke City (trial), Derby County (£20,000, December 1979), Ipswich Town (£150,000, January 1985), CHELSEA (£335,000, June 1987), Notts County (£225,000, March 1992), Bradford City (loan, January 1994), Walsall (free transfer, player–coach, August 1994), Northampton Town (free, player/assistant manager, July 1997; joint caretaker-manager, October 1999; manager November 1999–September 2001), Bedford Town (manager, October 2002–September 2003), Aylesbury United (manager, October 2003 for two months), Kettering Town (manager, December 2003); teacher training college, Roehampton

A positive, agile striker, Kevin Wilson was Derby's leading scorer in 1981–82. After recovering from a broken arm (suffered v. Plymouth) he joined Ipswich, the money received by the Rams being used to fund the incoming transfers. He scored 49 goals in 125 games for Ipswich and then did well at Stamford Bridge, helping the Blues win the Second Division championship in 1989 and the Zenith Data Systems Cup a year later. After spells with Notts County, Bradford, Walsall and Northampton, Wilson moved out of top-line football at the age of 41 with a career record of 772 senior appearances (at club and international level) plus 205 goals, 199 in League and Cup action. He won 42 caps for Northern Ireland between 1987 and 1995.

WINDRIDGE, JAMES EDWIN

Inside-forward: 152 apps, 58 goals

Born: Small Heath, Birmingham, 21 October 1882 – *Died*: Small Heath, 23 September 1939

Career: Small Heath Alma (amateur, August 1899; professional, July 1901), CHELSEA (£190, August 1905), Middlesbrough (£100, November 1911), Birmingham (April 1914; retired June 1916); an all-rounder, he also played seven County cricket matches for Warwickshire between 1909 and 1913 (averaging 14.64 with the bat)

Jimmy Windridge, strong and aggressive at times, was a highly effective and individualistic yet skilful forward with an eye for goal. One of the best dribblers of his day, he did well with Birmingham before joining Chelsea with his colleagues Jim Robertson and Bob McRoberts. He made his debut for the Blues in September 1905 and remained a regular in the side until 1910. He scored seven goals in eight full internationals for England in 1908 and 1909. During WW1 he organised a scratch Birmingham side to play local charity matches to raise money for the homeless. He was the cousin of Alec Leake, the Aston Villa, Birmingham and England defender.

WINTER, DANIEL THOMAS

Full-back: 155 apps

Born: Tonypandy, South Wales, 14 June 1918 – *Died*: Trealaw, South Wales, 22 March 2004

Career: Mais-y-hof FC (Wales), Bolton Wanderers (amateur June 1935; professional, June 1936), CHELSEA (guest, September 1944–November 1945; signed for £5,000, December 1945), Worcester City (June 1951; retired May 1953); was a committee member of the players' union (PFA) during his time at Chelsea and after retiring, worked in the family building business and also for British Airways (South Wales)

Like many players of his era, Danny Winter lost the best years of his career to the war. He signed as a professional for Bolton on his 18th birthday, and had just established himself in the side when WW2 broke out, and along with the entire Wanderers' squad, enlisted in the 53rd (Bolton) Field Artillery Regiment, serving as a bombardier. Evacuated from Dunkirk, he teamed up with Chelsea as a guest player and helped the Blues beat Millwall in the Football League South Cup final at Wembley in 1945. A worthy full-back, steady rather than brilliant, he was capped twice by Wales during the hostilities and made more than 150 competitive appearances for Chelsea before struggling with an ankle injury which led to him moving into non-League football with Worcester City.

WISE, DENNIS FRANK

Midfield: 434+11 apps, 75 goals
Born: Kensington, London, 15 December 1966
Career: Southampton (trainee), Wimbledon (professional, March 1985), CHELSEA (£1.6 million, July 1990), Leicester City (£1.6 million, June 2001), Millwall (free transfer, September 2002; player–manager from December 2003; resigned May 2005)

Dennis Wise has played in five FA Cup finals, gaining winner's medals with Wimbledon in 1988 and Chelsea in 1997 and 2000, while securing runner's-up prizes with the Blues in 1994 and Millwall ten years later. He also helped Chelsea win the League Cup, European Cup-Winners' Cup and European Super Cup in 1998 and the FA Charity Shield in 2000. Certainly one of the game's characters, he has been sent off on numerous occasions and has always kept the referees busy with their notepads. Yet in his prime he was a strong, determined, admittedly sometimes reckless, midfielder, totally committed, who battled it out non-stop for the whole 90 minutes of a game (and more), a real competitor who never lay down, whether winning, drawing or losing. 'Wisey' made 165 appearances for the Dons (30 goals scored) and after leaving Stamford Bridge played 19 times for Leicester before adding majestically to his tally with Millwall. In 2004 he reached the milestone of 800 appearances at club level. He has also played in 1 Under-21, 3 'B' and 21 full internationals for England, gaining his first cap with Chelsea in 1991 against Turkey. A crowd of 27,259 attended Wise's testimonial match – Chelsea v. Bologna in July 1999.

WOLFF, FRANK

Centre-half: 1 app.
Born: East Ham, London, 1883 – *Died*: London, *circa* 1945
Career: CHELSEA (professional, August 1905; released May 1906)

A reserve centre-half at Stamford Bridge during Chelsea's initial season as a football club, Frank Wolff's only appearance came in the 7–1 FA Cup defeat by Crystal Palace on the same day the recognised first XI were fulfilling a League game against Burnley (November 1905). Some reference books show the spelling of his surname as both Wolfe and Woolf. He had a brother, George, who played for Woolwich Arsenal, Swindon Town and Nottingham Forest (1900–10).

WOLLEASTON, ROBERT AINSLEY
Midfield: 0+2 apps
Born: Perivale, London, 21 December 1979
Career: CHELSEA (apprentice, April 1997; professional, June 1998), Portsmouth (loan, March–April 2001), Northampton Town (loan, July–September 2001), Bradford City (free transfer, July 2003), Oxford United (June 2004)
A skilful, attacking midfielder, Robert Wolleaston found himself out of favour at Stamford Bridge and after three loan spells (to gain experience) he moved to Bradford, having appeared just twice as a substitute for the Blues.

WOOD, DARREN TERENCE
Full-back: 165+11 apps, 4 goals
Born: Scarborough, Yorkshire, 9 June 1964
Career: Middlesbrough (apprentice, June 1979; professional, July 1981), CHELSEA (£50,000, plus Tony McAndrew, September 1984), Sheffield Wednesday (£450,000, January–May 1989)
An England schoolboy international before joining Middlesbrough, Darren Wood appeared in 115 League and Cup games for the Teesside club before transferring to Chelsea in a cash agreed-player-exchange deal arranged by Blues boss John Neal who had been his manager at Ayresome Park. Engineered to play in midfield, Wood gained a place in the first team straightaway, and it was his attacking ability from the right-back berth that made him such a valuable player at Stamford Bridge. A strong tackler and able to get good distance with his clearances, he helped Chelsea win the Full Members' Cup at Wembley in 1986. Injury ruined his association with Sheffield Wednesday.

WOODLEY, VICTOR ROBERT
Goalkeeper: 272 apps
Born: Cippenham, Buckinghamshire, 26 February 1910 – *Died*: Bradford-on-Avon, 23 October 1978
Career: Cippenham FC, Windsor and Eton (amateur), CHELSEA (professional, May 1931), Bath City (December 1945; registration retained by Chelsea), Derby County (loan, March–May 1946), Bath City (May 1947; then player–manager to December 1949)
Vic Woodley was a very keen competitor who showed great enthusiasm between the posts. He was a fixture in Chelsea's goal through most of the 1930s and was England's number one from April 1937, when he made his debut against Scotland at Hampden Park, until the outbreak of WW2. During that time, he made 19 consecutive international appearances, the best sequence by a goalkeeper until Ron Springett surpassed it in the early 1960s. He also played in two WW2 internationals and helped Chelsea win the 1944 Football League South Cup final at Wembley and represented the Football league on three occasions in 1937–38. In 1946 Derby gave Woodley an unexpected chance to

crown his distinguished career following an injury to Frank Boulton. Needing experienced cover for the FA Cup campaign, Rams boss Stuart McMillan signed Woodley who played a blinder in the two semi-final clashes with Birmingham City and then starred in the final victory over Charlton. He extended his career with 30 games in the 1946–47 League campaign before returning to Bath.

WOODWARD, VIVIAN JOHN

Forward: 116 apps, 34 goals
Born: Kennington, London, 3 June 1879 – *Died*: London, 6 February 1954
Career: Ascham College (Clacton), the Corinthians, Clacton, Harwich and Parkeston, Chelmsford City, Tottenham Hotspur (March 1901), The Pilgrims (guest, on USA tour, 1905); joined the board of directors at Tottenham (August 1908); Chelmsford City (May 1909), CHELSEA (November 1909–May 1915; appointed to the board of directors at Stamford Bridge in 1922, remaining in office until 1930); a cricketer with Spencer CC, he played tennis and for most of his life was involved in architecture while also working as a gentleman-farmer in the 1940s

Vivian Woodward was the greatest amateur marksman of his time who had the pleasure of scoring the first League goal at White Hart Lane . . . for Spurs against Wolverhampton Wanderers on 1 September 1908, netting in the sixth minute. He went on to secure exactly 100 goals in 195 appearances for the club including 45 in 105 Southern League games and 5 in 23 FA Cup encounters. The 'perfect attacker' and brilliant solo dribbler, he was equally impressive with his heading and powers of shooting. Described as 'The human chain of lightning, the footballer with magic in his boots', Woodward, between 1903 and 1911, gained a total of 23 full caps for England and scored 29 goals – a record that stood for almost 40 years, until Tom Finney beat it in 1958. A Football League representative in 1909 and 1913, each time v. Scotland, he also starred in 67 amateur internationals, skippering the side on occasion and appeared for the United Kingdom in both the 1908 and 1912 Olympic Games. In 1910, he toured South Africa with England. In the last of his six years with Chelsea, he gained special leave from the Army to play in the FA Cup final against Sheffield United but stood down at the last minute to allow Bob Thomson (who had appeared in the earlier rounds) to take his place. As a Blue, Woodward, despite being over the age of 30, played exceptionally well at times, especially during the 1912–14 seasons when he scored 15 goals.

WOOSNAM, MAXWELL

Left-half: 3 apps
Born: Liverpool, 6 September 1892 – *Died*: 14 July 1965
Career: Liverpool and District Schools, Winchester College XI (1908–11), Trinity College Cambridge (1912–14), Cambridge University (season 1912–13), the Corinthians (August 1913), CHELSEA (amateur,

March–April 1914), the Corinthians (August 1914), Manchester City (amateur, November 1919), Northwich Victoria (October 1925; retired May 1926); employed by ICI for 31 years (1923–54), attaining the position of personnel manager; won a University Blue for soccer (as captain), golf, lawn tennis, real tennis and was 12th man in the University cricket match (v. Oxford) in 1914; as a tennis star, he won the Wimbledon doubles with R. Lycett in 1921 and reached the mixed doubles final that same year; he represented Great Britain in the Davis Cup and participated in the Olympic Games of 1920 and 1924

Dubbed the 'Admirable Crichton' of his day, the moustachio'd Max Woosnam was capped by England against Wales at both amateur and senior levels in 1922, having previously played for Wales as an amateur in 1913. Classed on par with the great C.B. Fry and able to play at centre- or left-half, Woosnam was as hard as nails, as tough as they come, and loved to use the shoulder charge. He spent just six weeks with Chelsea, playing in League games against Derby County, his future club Manchester City, and Blackburn Rovers, all of which were won without a goal being conceded. Scorer of 4 goals in 93 outings for Manchester City, his stay at Hyde Road was disrupted after injuring himself on a fence surrounding the pitch. A tremendous all-round sportsman, Woosnam retained amateur status throughout his lengthy career.

WOSAHLO, ROGER FRANK

Winger: 0+1 app.
Born: Cambridge, 11 September 1947
Career: CHELSEA (apprentice, June 1963; professional, December 1964), Ipswich Town (April 1967), Peterborough United (July 1968), Ipswich Town (July 1969–May 1970), emigrated to South Africa (June 1970)

An England schoolboy international, Roger Wosahlo was leading scorer for Chelsea's junior side but was never given a chance to show off his skills in the first team, his only game coming as a substitute v. Stoke City (home) in April 1967 when players were being rested prior to the FA Cup final with Spurs. He made only 2 appearances for Ipswich and 15 for Peterborough.

YOUNG, ALLAN ROBERT

Centre-half: 26 apps, 1 goal
Born: Edmonton, London, 20 January 1941
Career: Hornsey Schools, Barnet Juniors, Arsenal (amateur, November 1956; professional, April 1959), CHELSEA (£6,000, November 1961), Torquay United (£8,000, January 1969), Wimbledon (briefly, August–October 1971)

Defender Allan Young served Chelsea for over 7 years, having his best season in the first team in 1965–66 when he made 16 appearances. Strong and steady, he was an able deputy whenever called into the side. He made 165 appearances at junior, intermediate and reserve-team levels for the Gunners but was handed only 4 outings in the senior side. He played 67 times for Torquay.

ZENDEN, BOUDEWIJN
Midfield: 30+29 apps, 4 goals
Born: Maastricht, Holland, 15 August 1976
Career: Leonadis/Holland (junior club), MVV Maastricht (seasons 1992–94), PSV Eindhoven/Holland (professional, August 1994), CF Barcelona/Spain (July 1998), CHELSEA (£7.5 million, August 2001), Middlesbrough (loan, August 2003; signed on free transfer, July 2004)

A Dutch international (with almost 60 caps under his belt, 8 goals scored) Bolo Zenden was in and out of the Chelsea side during his two seasons at Stamford Bridge. On his day, however, he was a lively, enterprising wide midfielder with a good technique and powerful shot. He helped Middlesbrough win the League Cup in 2004 – the first major trophy in the club's history. Prior to joining the Blues, Zenden scored 23 goals in 111 Dutch First Division games for PSV, collecting a League championship medal (1997) and successive Cup winner's medals (1996 and 1997). He also netted 3 times in 64 outings for Barcelona in Spain's La Liga, helping them win the title in 1999 and finish runners-up in 2000.

ZOLA, GIANFRANCO, OBE
Forward: 260+52 apps, 80 goals
Born: Oliena, Sardinia, 5 July 1966
Career: Nuorese/Italy (professional, August 1984), Torres/Italy (May 1986), Napoli/Italy (August 1989), Parma/Italy (June 1993), CHELSEA (£4.5 million, 1996), Cagliari/Italy (June 2003)

Gianfranco Zola won Italy's Serie 'A' with Napoli in 1990 and the UEFA Cup with Parma in 1995. He then came over to England and starred for Chelsea for seven years, helping the Blues twice win the FA Cup, in 1997 and 2000, lift the League Cup in 1998, capture the European Cup-Winners' Cup in 1998 (when he scored the winning goal in the final) and carry off both the European Super Cup and FA Charity Shield in 1998. He also gained 35 full caps for Italy (netting 7 goals) and was voted Football Writers' Player of the Year in 1997.

'Franco', as he was affectionately called by the Stamford Bridge fans, was a Chelsea superstar, one of the greatest players ever to wear the club's colours. A wonderful ball artiste, he could shoot and dribble, tease and torment his opponent and he could score goals – some of them real gems. Among them was an outrageous mid-air flick from a right-wing corner in an FA Cup replay against Norwich City, a delightful, yet cunning strike against Birmingham City when he played the ball against the shin of a defender standing in the wall and then drove the rebound across the keeper, and that all-important 71st-minute winner in the ECWC final against Vfb Stuttgart in Stockholm . . . which arrived just 45 seconds after he had entered the fray as a substitute. Prior to joining Chelsea, Zola scored 112 goals in 326 Serie 'A' and 'B' games in Italy. He was made an Honorary Member of the Order of the British Empire at a ceremony in Rome in November 2004.

WARTIME GUESTS

Players who guested for Chelsea during the two world wars include:

SEASONS 1915–19
John Bird (local), Charlie Buchan (Sunderland), Herbert Butterworth (Millwall Athletic), Tommy Coyle (local), Stewart Davidson (Middlesbrough), Bill Dickie (Kilmarnock), Stan Fazackerley (Sheffield United), Joe Hughes (West Ham United), David Jack (Bolton Wanderers), Jack Rawlings (local), John Rutherford (Arsenal), Joe Smith and Ted Vizard (both of Bolton Wanderers), Jackie Whitehouse (Birmingham)

PLAYERS FACTS
- Inside- or centre-forward Charlie Buchan also played for Arsenal and during a splendid career scored more than 260 goals in well over 400 senior appearances. He won six full England caps, represented the Football League and collected an FA Cup runner's-up medal in 1927.
- Stewart Davidson made 216 appearances for Middlesbrough (1913–23), played also for Aberdeen and was capped by Scotland against England in 1921. He was Chelsea's assistant manager (initially under Billy Birrell) until July 1957. He died on Boxing Day, 1960, aged 71.
- Bill Dickie joined Chelsea at the end of the war.
- Stan Fazackerley scored for Sheffield United against Chelsea in the 1915 FA Cup final. He later played for Wolves, for whom he netted 32 goals in 77 games, helping them win the Third Division (N) title in 1924 and also assisted Accrington Stanley, Hull City, Everton, Derby County and Kidderminster Harriers and toured South Africa with the FA in 1920.
- Joe Hughes scored 15 goals in 90 Southern League games for West Ham before WW1.
- David Bone Nightingale Jack scored the first goal in the initial Wembley FA Cup final, for Bolton against West Ham United in 1923. He later gained two more Cup winner's medals (1926 with Bolton, 1930 with Arsenal) and also won three League championships with the Gunners in the 1930s. As well as assisting Plymouth Argyle and Southend United, he was capped 9 times by

England and in all scored 260 goals in 490 League games between 1920 and 1936.

- John Rutherford played for Newcastle United (1902–13) and also assisted Stoke (briefly) and Clapton Orient. He scored 27 goals in 232 games for Arsenal (1913–26). He won 11 caps for England (1904–08), represented the Football League, and won three League championship medals and an FA Cup winner's medal with Newcastle between 1905 and 1910.
- Joe Smith played in three winning FA Cup final sides with Bolton – 1923, 1926 and 1929. He scored 277 goals in 492 first-class appearances during his 19 years at Burnden Park (1908–27). He also netted 61 goals in 69 League games for Stockport County and later managed Blackpool, leading the Seasiders to FA Cup final glory over his former club Bolton in 1953, having failed in two previous finals (1948 and 1951). He also toured South Africa with Fazackerley in 1920.
- Ted Vizard scored 70 goals in 512 games for Bolton between 1910 and 1931. He gained two FA Cup winner's medals (1923 and 1926) and won 22 caps for Wales (1911–26). He later managed Swindon Town, QPR and Wolves.
- Jackie Whitehouse scored 35 goals in 115 games for Birmingham and also assisted Derby County, Sheffield Wednesday and Bournemouth.

SEASONS 1939–46

Sam Abel (Queens Park Rangers), Jimmy Allen (Clapton Orient), Alf Anderson (Bolton Wanderers), Doug Anderson (Brentford), Matt Armstrong (Aston Villa), Llewellyn Ashcroft (Tranmere Rovers), Reg Attwell (West Ham United), Jimmy Bain (Gillingham), Bert Barlow (Portsmouth), George Bedford (Northampton Town), Ralph Birkett (Newcastle United), Ian Black (Aberdeen), Wilf Bott (Queens Park Rangers), Frank Boulton (Derby County), Albert Brown (Torquay United), Harry Brown (Wolverhampton Wanderers), Robert 'Sailor' Brown (Charlton Athletic), Bill Brown (Middlesbrough), Matt Busby (Liverpool), Tom Busby (Southend United), Bill Bushby (Southend United), Malcolm Butler (Blackpool), Len Butt (Blackburn Rovers), John Campbell (Lincoln City), Alf Chalkley (West Ham United), Ken Chisholm (Partick Thistle), Harry Clifton (Newcastle United), Ernie Collett (Arsenal), Leslie Compton (Arsenal), Benny Craig (Newcastle United), Walter Crook (Blackburn Rovers), Joe Crozier (Brentford), George Curtis (Arsenal), Ted Davies (Port Vale), Fred Dawes (Crystal Palace), Jackie Deverall (Reading), Johnny Devlin (Kilmarnock), Wilf Dixon (Aldershot), Bill Dodgin (Southampton), George Duke (Luton Town), Alex Dyer (Plymouth Argyle), Charlie Evans (West Bromwich Albion), John 'Taffy' Evans (Millwall), Willie Fagan (Liverpool), Alec Farmer (Queens Park Rangers), Harry Ferrier (Barnsley), Lester Finch (Barnet), Fred Fisher (Grimsby Town), Alf Fitzgerald (Queens Park Rangers), Jimmy Fullwood (Reading), John Galloway (Glasgow Rangers), Jackie Gibbons (Tottenham Hotspur), Matt Gillies (Bolton Wanderers), Harry Goslin (Bolton Wanderers), Len Goulden (West Ham

United), Mal Griffiths (Leicester City), Albert Hall (Tottenham Hotspur), Fred Hall (Blackburn Rovers), Walter Hanlon (Clyde), Eddie Hapgood (Arsenal), George Hardwick (Middlesbrough), John Harris (Wolverhampton Wanderers), Tom Hassell (Southampton), Alex Herd (Manchester City), Tommy Hinchcliffe (Derby County), Oscar Hold (Aldershot), John Humphreys (Everton), Bill Hurrell (Millwall), Arthur Jefferson (Queens Park Rangers), Eric Jones (West Bromwich Albion), Len Jones (Plymouth Argyle), Tommy Kiernan (Celtic), Fred Kurz (Grimsby Town), Frank Jackson Latimer (Brentford), Billy Liddell (Liverpool), George Little (Doncaster Rovers), Cliff Lloyd (Fulham), Harry Lowe (Queens Park Rangers), Arnold Lowes (Sheffield Wednesday), George Ludford (Tottenham Hotspur), Willie McCall (Aberdeen), Dave McCulloch (Derby County), Jack McDonald (Bournemouth), Peter McKennan (Partick Thistle), Jack Mahon (Huddersfield Town), Sammy Malpass (Fulham), Dickie March (Queens Park Rangers), Fred Marsden (Bournemouth), David Mathie (Kilmarnock), Joe Mercer (Everton), George Milligan (Everton), Charlie Mitten (Manchester United), Paddy Molloy (Bradford City), Reg Mountford (Huddersfield Town), Ernie Muttitt (Brentford), Ron Palmer (Aldershot), Harold Phipps (Charlton Athletic), Sidney Pugh (Arsenal), Rueben Purvis (North Shields), Ted Reay (Sheffield United), David Ridley (Millwall), Alf Ridyard (Queens Park Rangers), Alick Robinson (Burnley), Don Roper (Southampton), Jock Russell (Airdrieonians), Jimmy Sanders (Charlton Athletic), Dennis Saunders (Huddersfield Town), Reg Savage (Leeds United), Laurie Scott (Arsenal), Eric Seymour Sibley (Blackpool), Tommy Sinclair (Aldershot), Gavin Smith (Barnsley), Harry Smith (Middlesbrough), Leslie Smith (Brentford), Reg Smith (Schmidt) (Millwall), Hong (Frank) Soo (Stoke City), Bill Sperrin (Finchley), Billy Strauss (Aberdeen), George Swindon (Arsenal), Len Townsend (Brentford), George Tweedy (Grimsby Town), Peter Vause (Rochdale), George Wardle (Exeter City), Eric Westwood (Manchester City), Bill Whitaker (Chesterfield), Alf Whittingham (Bradford City), Bert Williams (Walsall), Cyril Williams (Bristol City), Reg Williams (Watford), Danny Winter (Bolton Wanderers), Walter Winterbottom and Billy Wrigglesworth (both of Manchester United), and Albert Young (Arsenal)

PLAYERS FACTS
- Herbert Barlow was a 1939 FA Cup winner with Portsmouth.
- Ralph Birkett, an England international, also played for Arsenal and Middlesbrough.
- Goalkeeper Ian Black moved to Southampton in 1947 and later made 277 appearances for Fulham.
- Goalkeeper Frank Boulton also played for Arsenal, Crystal Palace and Swindon Town and made over 170 League appearances.
- Centre-forward 'Sailor' Brown also played for Nottingham Forest and Aston Villa.

- Wing-half Matt Busby, a Scottish international, later became Sir Matt, managed Manchester United for more than 25 years and survived the 1958 Munich air crash.
- Bill Bushby was also associated with Wolves, Portsmouth and Southampton.
- Len Butt also played for Mansfield Town, Stockport County and York City and appeared in over 225 League games during his career.
- Ken Chisholm played for Leeds United, Leicester City, Coventry, Cardiff City, Sunderland and Workington after WW2 and accumulated 340 League appearances to 1958.
- Leslie Compton was capped by England at the age of 36 and also played cricket for Middlesex with his brother Dennis. He made 273 appearances for Arsenal.
- Ben Craig made 99 League appearances for Huddersfield and 66 for Newcastle before WW2.
- Between 1946 and 1972, Bill Dodgin managed Southampton, Brentford, Fulham, Juventus and Bristol Rovers.
- Willie Fagan also played for Celtic (1934–36) and Preston and scored 47 goals in 158 League games for Liverpool.
- Left-winger Lester Finch was an England amateur international who also played for WBA.
- Len Goulden joined Chelsea in August 1945.
- Harry Hapgood made 440 appearances for Arsenal and won 30 caps for England.
- George Hardwick took over from Hapgood as England's left-back after WW2 and won 13 full caps; he also appeared in 143 League games for Middlesbrough and 190 for Oldham.
- John Harris joined Chelsea in 1945 and later managed Chester and Sheffield United.
- Alex Herd, father of David Herd, ex-Arsenal, Manchester United and Stoke, scored 107 goals in 257 League games for Manchester City (1932–48) and 35 in 111 for Stockport County. He played in two FA Cup finals (1933 and 1934, winning in the latter), gained a WW2 cap with Scotland and in 1947 won the Second Division championship with City.
- Oscar Hold's League career spanned 16 years (1921–37). He also played for Barnsley, Norwich, Notts County, Everton and QPR.
- Scottish international left-winger Billy Liddell (28 caps) played in the 1950 FA Cup final for Liverpool v. Arsenal and scored 229 goals in 537 senior games in 14 years at Anfield (amateur, 1938; professional, April 1939; retired May 1961).
- Scottish international centre-forward Dave McCulloch, who also played for Hearts, Brentford and Leicester, scored over 100 League goals during his career.
- Left-half Joe Mercer, OBE, won the League championship with Everton in 1939 and Arsenal in 1948 and 1953. In 1950 he won the FA Cup with the

Gunners and was voted Footballer of the Year. He later managed Sheffield United, Aston Villa, Manchester City, England and Coventry.

- Charlie Mitten, an FA Cup winner with Manchester United in 1948, scored 61 goals in 161 games for the Reds including a hat-trick of penalties v. Aston Villa in 1950. After playing in Colombia, against the wishes of FIFA, he returned to manage Newcastle United.
- Defender Harry Phipps made over 200 appearances for Charlton with whom he won the FA Cup in 1946, having been a loser 12 months earlier.
- Versatile forward Don Roper scored 95 goals in 321 games for Arsenal with whom he twice won the League title. He also had two spells with Southampton.
- Goalkeeper Jimmy Sanders, who won the FA Cup with West Bromwich Albion in 1954, made well over 300 appearances for the Baggies and later played for Coventry.
- Full-back Laurie Scott made 126 appearances for Arsenal and won 17 full and 4 'B' caps for England.
- Left-winger Leslie Smith, an FA Amateur Cup finalist with Wimbledon in 1935, won 1 senior and 13 wartime and Victory caps for England, and scored 25 goals in 130 games for Aston Villa.
- Wing-half Frank Soo (of Chinese descent) also played for Leicester City and Luton Town and won wartime honours for England.
- Goalkeeper George Swindon played in 297 games for Arsenal with whom he gained an FA Cup and three League championship medals.
- Goalkeeper George Tweedy had almost 350 outings for Grimsby and won an England cap in 1937.
- Eric Westwood made 263 appearances for Manchester City and was a Wartime Cup winner with Chelsea in 1944.
- Goalkeeper Bert Williams won 24 caps for England and made 420 appearances for Wolves with whom he won the FA Cup in 1949 and League championship in 1954.
- Cyril Williams later helped West Bromwich Albion win promotion from the Second Division in 1949 and scored 20 goals in 77 outings for the Baggies.
- Danny Winter signed for Chelsea permanently in December 1945.
- Walter Winterbottom played 27 games for Manchester United and later managed England (1946–62). He received the CBE in 1963 and was knighted in 1978.
- Left-winger Billy Wrigglesworth also played for Chesterfield, Wolves, Bolton, Southampton and Reading as well as guesting for six other clubs during WW2.

CHELSEA'S LEAGUE (SOUTH) SECOND WORLD WAR CUP FINAL TEAMS:
- 15 April 1944, Charlton Athletic 3 Chelsea 1 at Wembley
  Woodley; Hardwick (Middlesbrough), Westwood (Manchester City); Russell (Airdrieonians), Harris (Wolves), Foss; Ashcroft (Tranmere Rovers),

Fagan (Liverpool), Payne, Bowie, Mitten (Manchester United)
Scorer: Payne (penalty)

- 7 April 1945, Chelsea 2 Millwall 0 at Wembley
  Black (Aberdeen); Winter (Bolton Wanderers), Hardwick (Middlesbrough); Russell, Harris (Wolves), Foss; Wardle (Exeter City), L. Smith (Brentford), Payne, Goulden (West Ham United), McDonald (Bournemouth)
  Scorers: McDonald, Wardle

MANAGERS

1905–06	John Tait Robertson*
1907–33	David Calderhead
1933–39	Leslie Knighton
1939–52	William Birrell
1952–61	Edward Joseph Drake
1962–67	Thomas Henderson Docherty*
1967–74	David Sexton
1974–75	Ronald Suart
1975–77	Edward McCreadie*
1977–78	Kenneth John Shellito*
1978–79	Robert Dennis Blanchflower
1979–81	Geoffrey Charles Hurst
1981–85	John Neal
1985–88	John William Hollins*
1988–91	Robert Campbell
1991–93	Ian John Porterfield
1993	David James Webb*
1993–96	Glenn Hoddle*
1996–98	Ruud Gullit*
1998–2000	Gianluca Vialli*
2000–04	Claudio Ranieri
2004–	José Mourinho

* See under individual player profiles

MANAGERS FACT-FILE

- Scotsman Billy Birrell played as a forward for Raith Rovers and Middlesbrough (Second Division winners in 1927) before becoming manager of the former club in November 1927. He then had spells in charge of both Bournemouth (1930–35) and QPR (from 1935) before taking over the reins at Stamford Bridge. He guided Chelsea to two WW2 Cup finals and was responsible in a big way for launching a youth scheme at the club, taking the youngsters to two FA Youth Cup finals. Born in March 1897, died in November 1968.

- 'Danny' Blanchflower, a cultured wing-half who won 56 caps for Northern Ireland, served with Glentoran, Barnsley, Aston Villa and Tottenham Hotspur. He made 382 appearances for Spurs, whom he skippered to the Double in 1961 and also to FA Cup and European Cup-Winners' Cup glory in 1962 and 1963. He also managed Northern Ireland in the 1970s. Born in February 1926, died in December 1993.

- Dave Calderhead was Chelsea's first full-time manager, holding office for 25 years, 10 months. Known as the 'Chelsea Sphinx', he played for Queen of the South Wanderers, was in Notts County's FA Cup winning side of 1894 and managed Lincoln City for seven years (1900–07). He was capped once by Scotland. Born in June 1864, died in January 1938.

- Bobby Campbell was a wing-half with Liverpool, Wigan Athletic, Portsmouth and Aldershot between 1954 and 1967. He coached at Portsmouth, QPR, Arsenal and Fulham before taking over as manager at Craven Cottage in 1976. He was then assistant boss at Aldershot, in charge of Portsmouth (1982–84), assistant manager at Arsenal and reserve-team coach at QPR before moving to Chelsea in 1988. Born in April 1937.

- Ted Drake was a dynamic centre-forward who scored 139 goals in 184 games for Arsenal between 1934 and 1945. He also played for Southampton (1931–34) and later managed Reading (1947–52). Twice a League championship winner and the recipient of an FA Cup winner's medal with the Gunners in the 1930s, he won six England caps and in 1935 scored seven goals (in eight shots) for Arsenal in an away League game at Aston Villa. Drake also played cricket for Hampshire in the 1930s. Born in August 1912, died, Raynes Park, Surrey, May 1995.

- Geoff Hurst, now Sir Geoff, was England's 1966 World Cup winning hero with a hat-trick in the final against West Germany. A superb marksman, he scored 248 goals in almost 500 games for West Ham (1959–72) before assisting Stoke City, Cape Town, West Bromwich Albion, Cork Celtic and Seattle Sounders (NASL). He managed Telford United (from 1976) prior to taking over as assistant boss at Chelsea, moving into the manager's seat in 1979. Also employed as England's assistant coach, he was capped 4 times at Under-23 level and on 49 occasions by the senior side and netted 24 international goals. He also played cricket for Essex. Born in December 1941, he's now director of a motor insurance company.

- Leslie Knighton's playing career ended prematurely through injury at the age of 19. He then went into management with Castleford Town in 1904 and was assistant secretary of Huddersfield Town and Manchester City before taking charge of Arsenal in 1919. He then bossed Bournemouth (1925–28) and Birmingham (1928–33), leading the latter club to the 1931 FA Cup final. Born in March 1884, died in May 1959.

- José Mourinho was a player with Belenensis, Rio Ave and Sesimbra (all in Portugal), and was assistant manager/coach under Bobby Robson at Barcelona in the 1990s. He then moved into management with FC Porto in

January 2002, guiding them to the Portuguese League title in 2003 and Champions League glory over AS Monaco in Gelsenkirchen, Germany, a year later. He replaced Claudio Ranieri as manager of Chelsea in June 2004. Born in Portugal in 1965, he attended Lisbon University and acted as interpreter for Robson at Barcelona, FC Porto and Sporting Lisbon.

- John Neal was a full-back with Hull City, Swindon Town, Aston Villa and Southend United before retiring in 1967. He later became coach and then manager of Wrexham (1968–77), and was then in charge of Middlesbrough until moving to Chelsea in 1981. He was later employed as a scout by Charlton Athletic and Shrewsbury Town. Born in April 1932, now living in Edinburgh.

- Ian Porterfield scored a dramatic winning goal for Sunderland against Leeds United in the 1973 FA Cup final. A midfielder, he also served with Hearts and Rangers as a junior, Raith Rovers, Reading and Sheffield Wednesday and took his first managerial job at Rotherham United in 1979, then with Sheffield United (1981–86) and thirdly at Aberdeen before becoming assistant manager at Stamford Bridge for a short while in 1989. After that he was boss of Reading before returning to Chelsea as manager in the 1990s. He was later in charge of the Zambian national team when 18 players were killed in a disastrous plane crash in 1993. On his return to the UK he became coach at Bolton Wanderers and then assisted non-League Worthing until September 1996. Born in February 1946.

- Chelsea honoured the contract of Italian Claudio Ranieri when they dismissed him as team manager at the end of the 2003–04 season – paying him off in full. He had guided the Blues to runner's-up spot in the Premiership and into the semi-finals of the Champions League. Prior to taking over from fellow countryman Gianluca Vialli at Stamford Bridge, the relatively unknown Ranieri had coached and managed at the highest level, with Napoli, Fiorentina, Valencia and Atletico Madrid among his previous employers. He was appointed manager of one his former clubs, Valencia, in July 2004, replacing Rafael Benitez who moved to Liverpool. Born in Italy in 1947.

- Inside-forward Dave Sexton played for Chelmsford City, Luton Town, West Ham United (1952–56), Leyton Orient, Brighton and Hove Albion and Crystal Palace before retiring to become Chelsea coach in February 1962. He took over as manager of Orient in 1965 and later coached at Fulham and Arsenal before returning to Stamford Bridge as manager in 1967, taking a similar job with QPR, Manchester United and Coventry City after that, while also working as assistant manager/coach of England. He has also been employed as coach by Aston Villa. He won the FA Cup and European Cup-Winners' Cup with Chelsea (1970 and 1971) and the Third Division championship as a player with Brighton (1958). Born in London, April 1930.

- Ron Suart was a defender with Blackpool and Blackburn Rovers before becoming player–manager of Wigan Athletic in 1955. In charge of

Scunthorpe United from 1956 to 1958 and then Blackpool, he became Chelsea's assistant manager in April 1967, taking over as caretaker-boss six months later and then moving into the hot seat at Stamford Bridge in 1975. Later employed by the club as a coach, he then worked as a scout for Wimbledon. Born in 1920.

SENIOR TRAINERS

1905–07	James Millar
1907–10	Harry Ransom
1910–14	Harry Wright
1919–39	John Whitley
1939–46	Arthur Stollery
1946–53	Norman Smith
1953–60	Jack Oxberry
1960–73	Harold Medhurst
1973–88	Norman Medhurst
1988–95	Robert Ward*
1995–	Michael Banks*

* Appointed as physiotherapists

CLUB CHAIRMEN

1905–35	W. Claude Kirby
1935–36	C.J. Pratt, senior
1936–40	Colonel C.D. Crisp
1940–66	John Mears
1966–68	C.J. Pratt, junior
1968–69	L.R. Withey
1969–81	J. Brian Mears
1981–82	Viscount Chelsea
1982–2003	Kenneth W. Bates
2004–	Bruce Buck

Note: Russian billionaire Roman Abramovich bought the club for £150 million on 1 July 2003 and appointed Peter Kenyon as chief executive.

DIRECTORS (1905—2005)

Listed in alphabetical order:

Areson, Frank***	2005–
Attenborough,	
Sir Richard, CBE**	1969–82
Bates, Kenneth W.	1981–2003
Bates, Robert M.	1985–89
Bennett, J.G.	1952–58
Birch, T.*+	2001–03
Boyer, H.	1905–22
Boyer, H.J.M.	1938–48
Buck, Bruce++	2004–
Budd, J.E.C.	1931–52
Chelsea, Viscount	1964–83
Crisp, Colonel C.D.	1926–40
Dimbleby, Gordon	1983–84
Dobson, Major A.	1981–82
Hutchinson, Colin*	1986–2001
Janes, A.F.	1905–26
Janes, E.H.	1905–11
Kenyon, Peter+	2003–
Kinton, H.E.	1935–40
Kinton, T.L.	1905–22
Kirby, W. Claude	1905–35
Maltby, J.H.	1905–26
Mears, David	1977–83
Mears, H.A.	1905–12
Mears, J. Brian	1955–81
Mears, L.J. senior	1946–58
Mears, L.J. junior	1958–64/1965–78
Neal, John	1985–86
Parker, F.W.	1907–15

Pratt, J.C. senior	1922–36
Pratt, J.C. junior	1935–68
Reed, Stanley G.	1981–82
Russell, M.*	1999–2003
Schomberg, G.	1905–13
Smith, Graham W.C.	1986–89
Spears, Barrie	1984–86
Spencer, Martin	1977–78/1980–83
Tenenbaum, Eugene	2004–
Thomson, G.M.	1968–82
Thomson, Norman	1981–82
Todd, Yvonne	1989–2003
Tollman, Stanley S.	1982–91
Webb, Gordon	1982–84
Withey, L.R.	1948–69
Woodward, Vivian J.	1922–30

* also managing director
** now life vice-president
*** director of football
+ also chief executive
++ also chairman

SECRETARIES

1952–71	John Battersby
1971–75	Anthony Green
1975–78	Christine Matthews
1979–88	Sheila Marson
1988–89	Janet Wayth
1989–90	Judy Nicholas*
1990–99	Keith Lacey
1999–2004	Alan Shaw**
2004–	David Barnard

* match secretary
** company secretary

NB Prior to the appointment of Ted Drake as Chelsea manager in 1952, all the previous managers of the club held the position of secretary–manager. Mr John Battersby was officially appointed as the first full-time secretary of the club in May 1952.

ASSISTANT SECRETARIES

1905–07	William Lewis
1907–35	Albert Palmer
1935–47	Harold Palmer
1947–48	Charles E. Kemp
1949–52	John Battersby

WINNING CUP FINAL TEAMS

- London Victory Cup
  16 April 1919, Chelsea 3 Fulham 0 at Highbury
  Molyneux; Bettridge, Harrow; Davidson (Middlesbrough), Dickie (Kilmarnock), Middelboe; Ford, Whitehouse (Birmingham), Wilding, Rutherford (Arsenal), Vizard (Bolton Wanderers).
  Scorers: Rutherford (2), Wilding

- Football League (South) Cup
  7 April 1945, Chelsea 2 Millwall 0 at Wembley
  Black (Aberdeen); Winter (Bolton Wanderers), Hardwick (Middlesbrough); Russell (Airdrieonians), Harris (Wolverhampton Wanderers), Foss; Wardle (Exeter City), Smith (Brentford), Payne, Goulden (West Ham United), McDonald (Bournemouth)
  Scorers: McDonald, Wardle

- Football League Cup
  15 March 1965, (1st leg) Chelsea 3 Leicester City 2 at Stamford Bridge
  Bonetti; Hinton, R. Harris; Hollins, Young, Boyle; Murray, Graham, McCreadie, Venables, Tambling
  Scorers: Tambling, Venables (penalty), McCreadie

  5 April 1965, (2nd leg) Leicester City 0 Chelsea 0 at Filbert Street (Chelsea won 3–2 on aggregate)
  Bonetti; Hinton, McCreadie; R. Harris, Mortimer, Upton; Murray, Boyle, Bridges, Venables, Tambling

- FA Cup
  11 April 1970, (1st game) Chelsea 2 Leeds United 2 (after extra-time) at Wembley
  Bonetti; Webb, McCreadie; Hollins, Dempsey, R. Harris (Hinton); Baldwin, Houseman, Osgood, Hutchinson, Cooke
  Scorers: Houseman, Hutchinson

29 April 1970, (replay) Chelsea 2 Leeds United 1 (after extra-time) at Old Trafford
Bonetti; R. Harris, McCreadie; Hollins, Dempsey, Webb; Baldwin, Cooke, Osgood (Hinton), Hutchinson, Houseman
Scorers: Osgood, Webb

- European Cup-Winners' Cup
19 May 1971, (1st game) Chelsea 1 Real Madrid 1 (after extra-time) in Athens
Bonetti; Boyle, R. Harris; Hollins (Mulligan), Dempsey, Webb; Weller, Hudson, Osgood (Baldwin), Cooke, Houseman
Scorer: Osgood

21 May 1971, (replay) Chelsea 2 Real Madrid 1 in Athens
Bonetti; Boyle, R. Harris; Cooke, Dempsey, Webb; Weller, Baldwin, Osgood (Smethurst), Hudson, Houseman
Scorers: Dempsey, Osgood

- Full Members' Cup
23 March 1986, Chelsea 5 Manchester City 4 at Wembley
Francis; Wood, Rougvie; Pates, McLaughlin, Bumstead; Nevin, Spackman, Lee, Speedie, McAllister
Scorers: Speedie (3), Lee (2)

- Zenith Data Systems Cup
25 March 1990, Chelsea 1 Middlesbrough 0 at Wembley
Beasant; Hall, Dorigo; Bumstead, Johnsen, Monkou; McAllister, Nicholas, Dixon, Durie, K. Wilson
Scorer: Dorigo

- FA Cup
17 May 1997, Chelsea 2 Middlesbrough 0 at Wembley
Grodas; Petrescu, Minto; Sinclair, Leboeuf, Clarke; Zola (Vialli), Di Matteo, Newton, M. Hughes, Wise
Scorers: Di Matteo*, Newton
* Di Matteo's goal was the fastest ever scored in a Wembley FA Cup final (43 seconds).

- Coca-Cola League Cup
29 March 1998, Chelsea 2 Middlesbrough 0 (after extra-time) at Wembley
De Goey; Petrescu (Clarke), Le Saux; Sinclair, Leboeuf, Duberry; Newton, Di Matteo, Zola, M. Hughes (Flo), Wise
Scorers: Sinclair, Di Matteo

- European Cup-Winners' Cup
13 May 1998, Chelsea 1 Vfb Stuttgart 0 in Stockholm
De Goey; Petrescu, Granville; Duberry, Leboeuf, Clarke; Poyet (Newton),
Di Matteo, Vialli, Flo (Zola), Wise
Scorer: Zola

- European Super Cup
28 August 1998, Chelsea 1 Real Madrid 0 in Monaco
De Goey; Ferrer, Le Saux; Duberry, Leboeuf, Desailly; Babayaro, Di Matteo
(Poyet), Casiraghi (Flo), Zola (Laudrup), Wise
Scorer: Poyet

- FA Cup
20 May 2000*, Chelsea 1 Aston Villa 0 at Wembley
De Goey; Melchiot, Babayaro; Deschamps, Leboeuf, Desailly; Poyet,
Di Matteo, Weah (Flo), Zola (Morris), Wise
Scorer: Di Matteo
* This was the last FA Cup final to be staged at the original Wembley Stadium.

- Coca-Cola League Cup
27 February 2005, Chelsea 3 Liverpool 1 at the Millennium Stadium, Cardiff
Cech; Ferreira, Carvalho, Terry, Gallas (Kezman); Makele, Lampard, Jarosik
(Gudjohnsen), Cole (Johnson); Duff, Drogba
Subs not used: Pidgeley, Tiago
Scorers: Gerrard (og), Drogba, Kezman

LEAGUE CHAMPIONSHIP-WINNING SQUADS

- Division One 1954–55
Players who received medals: K. Armstrong (39 apps), Bentley (41), Blunstone (23), Greenwood (21), J. Harris (31), J. Lewis (17), McNichol (40), Parsons (42), W.G. Robertson (27), D. Saunders (42), P. Sillett (21), Stubbs (28), C. Thomson (15), S.M. Wicks (21), Willemse (36)
Leading scorers: Bentley (21), McNichol (14), Parsons (11).

- Premiership 2004–05
Players who received medals: Bridge (12+3 apps), Carvalho (22+3), Cech (35), J. Cole (19+9), Drogba (18+8), Duff (28+2), Ferreira (29), Gallas (28), Geremi (6+7), Gudjohnsen (30+7), Huth (6+4), Jarosik (3+11), G.M. Johnson (13+4), Kezman (6+19), Lampard (38), Makelele (36), Robben (14+4), Smertin (11+5), Terry (36), Tiago (21+13).
Leading scorers: Lampard (13), Gudjohnsen (12), Drogba (10), Cole (8), Robben (7)

OTHER WHO'S WHO SNIPPETS

- Winston Churchill, a player of the same name as the former prime minister, played in two Hornchurch and District League games for Chelsea as an amateur in 1956–57.
- Half-back Ned Liddell spent most of his footballing career with London clubs. He served as a player with Clapton Orient and Arsenal before WW1, managed QPR and Fulham (1929–31), was assistant manager at West Ham United and later was chief scout for Chelsea, Brentford and Spurs.
- Chelsea chairman Ken Bates played as an amateur defender for Chertsey when that club was registered as Arsenal's nursery side in the 1940s. In January 2005, he took over as chairman of Leeds United.
- A tragic motorcycling accident prematurely ended the career of young Chelsea reserve Michael Charlton, who had represented England at schoolboy and youth-team levels. He later became a salesman for a cosmetics firm.
- Tim Buzaglo, who made the headlines by scoring a hat-trick for non-League Woking in a sensational FA Cup win over West Bromwich Albion in January 1991, was a cricketer with Gibraltar and an avid Chelsea supporter. He had a trial as a 15 year old at Stamford Bridge.
- Bobby Robson was employed as a scout by Chelsea's manager Dave Sexton in 1968.
- Former Prime Minister and Conservative MP John Major has been a life-long Chelsea supporter.
- Sir Richard Attenborough, actor, film director and producer, was on the board of directors at Chelsea for 13 years: 1969–82.
- David Cameron, Ken McKenzie and John Bell, all of whom were associated with the Scottish amateur club Queen's Park, and all trained and qualified as doctors, were signed together by Chelsea in 1920.
- Roman Abramovich's other club, CSKA Moscow, became the first Russian side to win a major European trophy when they beat Sporting Lisbon 3–1 in the 2005 UEFA Cup final.

BIBLIOGRAPHY

I have referred to several books to clarify certain relevant statistics, facts and figures, individual players' details and, indeed, stories and match reports from past seasons regarding Chelsea FC. There are some conflicting facts, statistics and other information in these sources and I've made judgements as to what is likely to be correct.

The list (not including any of my previous publications on the club):

Cheshire, S. and R. Hockings (1987), *Chelsea FC Players Who's Who* (Stoke-on-Trent, Scott Cheshire)

Cheshire, S. and R. Hockings (1988), *Chelsea Football Club: The Full Statistical Story: 1905–1988* (Wembley, Middlesex, R. Hockings)

Davies, G.M. and I. Garland (1991), *Welsh International Soccer Players* (Wrexham, Bridge Books)

Farror, M. and D. Lamming (1972), *A Century of English International Football: 1872–1972* (London, Robert Hale and Co.)

FA Yearbook [1951–2000, published yearly] (London, The Football Association)

Gibson, A. and W. Pickard (1905–06), *Association Football and the Men Who Made It*, 4 vols (London, Caxton Publishing Company)

Goldsworthy, M. (1969), *The Encyclopaedia of Association Football* (London, Robert Hale and Co.)

Goldsworthy, M. (1972), *We Are the Champions: A History of the Football League Champions 1888–1972* (London, Pelham Books)

Horsnell, B. and D. Lamming (1995), *Forgotten Caps* (Harefield, Middlesex, Yore Publications)

Hugman, B.J. (ed.) (1996), *PFA Footballers' Factfile 1996–97 to 2000–01* (Hertfordshire, Queen Anne Press)

Hugman, B.J. (ed.) (1996), *PFA Footballers' Factfile 2001–02* (Basildon, AFS)

Hugman, B.J. (ed.) (1996), *PFA Footballers' Factfile 2002–03 to 2004–05* (Hertfordshire, Queen Anne Press)

Hugman, B.J. (ed.) (1996), *PFA Premier and Football League Players' Records: 1946–1998* (Hertfordshire, Queen Anne Press)

Johnson, F. (1935), *Football Who's Who* (London, Associated Sporting Press)

Joyce, M. (2002), *Football League Players' Records: 1888–1939* (Nottingham, Tony Brown/SoccerData)

Lamming, D. (1982), *Who's Who of Scottish Internationalists, 4 vols. 1872–1982* (Basildon, AFS)

Lamming, D. and M. Farror (1972), *English Internationals Who's Who: 1872–1972* (London, Robert Hale and Co.)

Pringler, A. and N. Fissler (1996), *Where Are They Now?* (London, Two Heads Publishing)

Rollin, J. (1985), *Soccer At War 1939–45* (London, Willow Books Collins)

Sewell, A. (1958), *Chelsea, Champions* (London, Soccer Book Club)

Spiller, R. (ed.) (1990), *AFS Football's Who's Who: 1902–03, 1903–04, 1907–08, 1909–10* (Basildon, AFS).

Williams, T. (ed.) (1992), *Football League Directory: 1992–1995* (London, Daily Mail)

OTHER PUBLICATIONS

AFS Bulletin (various)

Rothmans Football Yearbook (1970–2004, 35 vols), vols 1–34 (various editors)

Chelsea FC official matchday programmes (1905–2005)

Chelsea FC official handbooks/magazines (1952–2005)

Charles Buchan's Football Monthly: 1951–1969

Soccer Star (weekly): 1963–67

I have also referred to many other national newspapers, club histories and various Who's Who publications on other clubs; certain autobiographies and biographies of players and managers; and quite a number of soccer reference books for confirmation of factual points.